D0238572

TRAVEL SICKNESS

Travel Sickness

The Need for a Sustainable Transport Policy for Britain

edited by

John Roberts, Johanna Cleary,
Kerry Hamilton and Judith Hanna

LAWRENCE & WISHART
LONDON

Lawrence & Wishart Ltd
144a Old South Lambeth Road
London SW8 1XX

ISBN 0 85315 748 0

First published 1992

1000576105

Text and cover design by Jan Brown Designs
Photoset in North Wales by
Derek Doyle and Associates, Mold, Clwyd
Printed and bound in Great Britain by
Billing & Sons, Worcester

CONTENTS

List of Common Abbreviations and Acronyms   vii
List of Tables and Figures   ix

John Prescott, MP
Foreword   xiii

1 John Roberts
   The Problem of British Transport   1
2 Keith Buchan
   Enhancing the Quality of Life   7
3 Claire Holman and Malcolm Fergusson
   Environmental Targets for a National Transport Policy   18
4 John Cartledge
   Consumerism and Public Transport   35
5 Hilary Torrance
   Transport For All: Equal Opportunities in Transport Policy 48
6 Kerry Hamilton and Linda Jenkins
   Women and Transport   57
7 Nicholas James and Tim Pharoah
   The Traffic Generation Game   75
8 Stephen Joseph, Nick Lester and Mick Hamer
   The Machinery of Government   88
9 Judith Hanna and Martin Mogridge
   Market Forces and Transport Choices   102
10 Stephen Potter
   Integrating Fiscal and Transport Policies   122
11 Stephen Potter and Stuart Cole
   Funding an Integrated Transport Policy   143
12 John Roberts
   Learning From the Real Europe   160

CONTENTS

13 Phil Swann
    Urban Transport Policy: A Local Responsibility   175
14 David Banister and Penny Evans
    Accessible Transport for Rural Areas in the 1990s   182
15 Keith Buchan
    Freight Policy   193
16 Reg Dawson
    Regulating Road Haulage   204
17 Johanna Cleary and Mayer Hillman
    A Prominent Role for Walking and Cycling in Future
    Transport Policy   214
18 Laurie Pickup
    Bus Policy Development: Deregulation in a Wider
    Context   243
19 Gavin Smith
    A Transport Policy for London   253
20 Paul Salveson
    Playing Trains   264
21 John Whitelegg
    Rail's Contribution to Improving Transport and the
    Environment   281
22 Robert Caves
    Aviation Policy   291
23 Moyra Logan
    The Environmental Capacity of Airports: A Method of
    Assessment   302
24 Frank Worsford and Mark Dickinson
    British Shipping: Salvation in Europe?   311
25 John G.U. Adams
    Towards a Sustainable Transport Policy   320

Reference Bibliography   334
Notes on Contributors   348
Index   354

LIST OF COMMON ABBREVIATIONS AND ACRONYMS

AEF	Airfields Environment Federation
AONB	Area of Outstanding Natural Beauty
CEC	Commission of European Communities
CILT	Centre for Independent Transport Research in London
COBA	Cost-Benefit Analysis
CTCC	Central Transport Consultative Committee
DoE	Department of the Environment
DES	Department of Education and Science
DPTAC	Disabled Passengers' Transport Advisory Committee
DTp	Department of Transport
DTI	Department of Trade and Industry
EC	European Community
EEB	European Environmental Bureau
EFL	External Financing Limit
EIA	Environmental Impact Assessment
EUROS	European Register of Shipping
GDP	Gross Domestic Product
HGV	Heavy Goods Vehicle
HMSO	Her Majesty's Stationery Office
ICAO	International Civil Aviation Organization
LA	Licensing Authority
LPG	Liquefied Petroleum Gas
LRPC	London Regional Passengers' Committee
LRT	Light Rail Transit
LSPU	London Strategic Policy Unit
MEA	Manual of Environmental Assessment
MMC	Monopolies and Mergers Commission
MTRU	Metropolitan Transport Research Unit
NATS	National Air Traffic Service(s)
NEF	New Economics Foundation
NPV	Net Present Value

NTS	National Travel Survey
OECD	Organization for Economic Co-operation and Development
OFT	Office of Fair Trading
PRP	Perceptual Road Pricing
PSI	Policy Studies Institute
PSV	Public Service Vehicle
PTE	Passenger Transport Executive
RCO	Regional Cycling Officer
RHA	Road Haulage Association
RTPI	Royal Town Planning Institute
SACTRA	Standing Advisory Committee on Trunk Road Assessment
SEA	Single European Act
SEEDS	South East Economic Development Strategy
SSSI	Site of Special Scientific Interest
TEC	Training and Enterprise Council
TEST	Transport and Environment Studies
TPP	Transport Policy and Programme
TRRL	Transport and Road Research Laboratory
TUCC	Transport Users' Consultative Committee
VED	Vehicle Excise Duty

LIST OF TABLES AND FIGURES

2-1. Quality-of-Life Objectives for Transport. 15
3-1. Provisional Emission Reduction Targets for the Principal Gaseous Pollutants Based on Environmental Protection Criteria. 28
3-2. Proposed Bubble Limits for the Principal Gaseous Pollutants for the Year 2005. 29
3-3. Car Emission Reduction Targets for the Year 2005. 30
6-1. Percentage of Journeys Made by Men and Women for Various Purposes, Broken Down by Age. 59
7-1. Car Ownership and Use in Selected Western Countries, 1988. 81
10-1. Primary Energy Requirements of Different Travel Modes in the UK. 125
10-2. Illustrative Example of a Rebate/Surcharge System for Company Car Taxation. 134
10-3. Index of Projected Increase in Passenger Kilometres and Energy Use in UK Domestic Flights, 1986-2010. 140
11-1. Motorway Schemes in Preparation at 1 January 1990. Estimated Works Cost. 146
11-2. All Purpose Trunk Road Schemes in Preparation at 1 January 1990. Estimated Works Cost. 147
11-3. Recent and Planned EFL for British Rail. 148
11-4. Proposed Light Rail and Trolley Bus Schemes and Planned Funding. 150
11-5. M1 Programme Schemes in Preparation at 1 January, 1990. Estimated Works Cost. 158
11-6. Midland Mainline Electrification Costs (£ million). 158
11-7. Motorway Widening Programme. 159
12-1. Passenger Car Stock in Various Countries, 1970 and 1987 in Thousands, and Cars and Taxis/1000 people in 1987. 162
12-2. Road and Rail Infrastructure 1987. 164
12-3. Road Passenger and Freight Volumes, bn v-km, 1970 and 1987 and Percentage Change. 165

12-4. Passenger Transport in Britain and Germany, 1966 and 1986, bn p-km. — 166

12-5. British and German Transport Investment 1986. — 167

12-6. Company Cars as a Proportion of the National Car Stock and New Cars. — 168

13-1. Allocation of Responsibilities for Urban Transport. — 176

14-1. Car Ownership Levels 1985/86. — 186

15-1. Effects of Banning Certain Weights of Goods Vehicles Within the M25. — 196

17-1. Modal Distribution With all Motorized Trips of Less Than Five Kilometres Made by Cycle. — 216

17-2. Pedestrian Fatality Rate per Kilometre and *per Capita*, by Age Group. — 220

17-3. Casualty Rates per Billion Person Kilometres by Mode of Travel, 1978 and 1988. — 220

17-4. Fatality Rate per Kilometre Travelled by Mode, Vehicle Involvement With Pedestrian Fatalities, and Traffic Volumes, 1977-87. — 221

17-5. Ratio of Fatal Accidents to Fatal and Serious Injury Road Accidents Combined, Great Britain, 1968, 1978 and 1988. — 222

17-6. Percentage of Journeys on Foot or Cycle, by Age and Sex, 1975/76 and 1985/86. — 223

17-7. Adult Access to Cars in Great Britain, 1968, 1978 and 1988. — 224

17-8. Distribution of Journeys by Mode Including and Excluding Journeys of Under One Mile, 1985/86. — 227

17-9. Percentages of Journeys by all Modes and by Walking and Cycling, Over Distances of Less Than one Mile, by Age and Sex, 1985/86. — 228

17-10. Ratio of Number of Journeys on Foot to the Number by Public Transport, by Age and Sex, 1975/76 and 1985/86. — 229

19-1. Central London – A Proposal for Tram Routes and Footstreets in the City and its Environs. — 259

19-2. Interchange Stations – A Proposed Network. — 260

21-1. Differential Impact of Road and Rail Freight Transport on a Number of Environmental Variables. — 284

21-2. Differential Impact of Road and Rail Passenger Transport on a Number of Environmental Variables. — 284

21-3. Journeys per Person per Week by Mode and Purpose. — 287

24-1. The UK Registered Merchant Fleet (of Ships Over 500grt).   312

25-1. Growth Indices GDP, Tonne-kms of Freight and Passenger-kms; 1952 = 100.   321

25-2. Travel by Britons by Cycle, Bus, Train, Car and Plane.   323

FOREWORD

JOHN PRESCOTT, MP

I welcome the publication of this important book, which comes at an appropriate moment – as the final curtain is drawn across the thirteen years of failed Tory experiments with our transport systems and with the travelling public.

A modern economy needs a modern transport system, which Britain lacks, and nowhere in the world has the free market been able to provide the necessary infrastructure to prepare for the economic challenges of the twenty-first century.

Britain is on the geographical periphery of Europe. The 1992 Single Market and the opening of trade with Eastern Europe demands that we have good quality transport and communications. The Channel Tunnel means that we are part of the wider European network, and to avoid being nothing more than a branch line to nowhere, it is vital that we have infrastructure able to compete with Europe's faster rail speeds and greater gauge standards.

→ Transport is not simply about getting from A to B – it is central to the quality of people's lives, the environment and the economic needs of the nation. It is about giving access to all sections of the community – including those without cars, women who are the main users of public transport, pensioners on low incomes, the disabled and those with young children or heavy loads. Transport should be safe, reliable, efficient, clean and comfortable, at a price that people can afford.

We must recognize that we cannot build our way out of the crisis of congestion and pollution by spending more and more on new and wider roads. Dr John Adams estimates that the current £20,000,000,000 road-building programme will only increase total road capacity by 5 per cent, yet the Department of Transport has predicted that traffic will grow by 83-142 per cent by 2025.

We must find ways to encourage people to use their car less and public transport more, as well as question some of the decisions that generate an unnecessary increase in transport movement in the first place.

The 1990s will not solve the crisis of congestion – but we can begin to manage traffic demand more effectively, and start to cope with the problem. This book offers exciting and imaginative ideas to increase the efficient use of our existing infrastructure capacity through the integration of road and rail with land use planning.

The Conservatives have been totally isolated in their dogmatic experiment with privatization, deregulation and unleashing the free market on every aspect of transport – and doesn't it show. No other government in Western Europe – right, left or centre – has dragged its country into the mire of hideous congestion costs and environmental destruction that Britain is suffering.

'Integrated transport system' is a phrase often quoted but rarely defined, due to intellectual laziness on the part of those who argue its case. It really means that the whole is greater than the sum of its parts. The parts need to be co-ordinated to work together, not against each other – and the only body that can establish the regulatory framework that makes this possible is the Government. It is absurd that the Conservative Government not only doesn't know how to do it, but is actively hostile to the idea of doing it.

That is why the CBI, the TUC, the London Tourist Board, Chambers of Commerce throughout the country, local authorities of all political persuasions, the technical press and virtually every national newspaper, the European Commission and other EC countries, even the Institute of Directors and many others are united in their disgust at the collapse of our transport system. Although many of them believe in the competitive model, they have all realized that in transport in the 1990s there is a crying need for Government action to end the spiral of decline. Only the Tory Government knows better.

A major influence on transport in the 1990s will be the European Community. Transport attitudes have already moved away from total reliance on the free market towards a regulated, integrated form of competition within the EC. For example, it is now impossible for a member state to develop separate shipping or aviation policies, as they are now so intertwined with each other's.

When Labour published *Moving Britain Into the 1990s* a couple of years ago, it was widely acclaimed as the best informed and most radical party programme for transport. It attracted much attention from academics and campaigners who had long since despaired of politicians who had not even recognized the realities of the transport crisis, never mind proposed ways to tackle the problem.

This prompted discussions with Dr John Roberts and others which led to a unique opportunity to bring together people and groups who in their own work exert great influence over policy but who had never pooled their thinking with others in related areas.

A meeting at the RMT Trade Union college at Frant in November 1990 was followed by a weekend gathering at Ruskin College Oxford in March 1991. This brought together representatives from all the transport modes, PTAs, PTEs, academics, environmentalists, transport campaigners, unions and managers of all political parties. It was a unique forum in which we submitted our policies for examination, criticism and advice, but without seeking endorsement. The purpose was to sharpen the focus and direction of the debate about the need for integration of our different transport systems.

Certainly the sparks flew, but all would agree that this exchange of views was impressive and influential. That process of discussion is clearly reflected in the written contributions brought together here.

I am pleased with the blend of contributions, some from academic theorists and others with practical day-to-day experience in industry, covering all aspects of transport policy. It will have a significant influence on new integrated transport thinking in the 1990s, whatever Government is in office.

Of course, common agreement was not always achieved on all issues at that conference or in this book. I myself cannot accept that there is no role for high speed rail as argued by Dr John Whitelegg.

I believe that high speed rail is an essential part of our connections to the new modern Europe in which trains run at 300mph on dedicated track, not the top speed of 140mph that we currently have in Britain. They can help shift people away from unnecessary journeys by car, and they can compete effectively with short-haul aircraft flights, linking in to our major airports to prevent environmental damage and cut congestion costs on overcrowded roads and at overflowing airports. High speed trains are not a mirage of expensive but pointless technology like Concorde, but a vital part of mass transit for all of our citizens, not an elite few.

This kind of integration will require new thinking at Government level. It demands that the Department of Transport itself is restructured, and acts more as a strategic authority responsible for planning our infrastructure needs with a ten to twenty-year vision.

Rather than relying solely on the need for a financial rate of return from transport infrastructure, the Government must prepare an integrated financial package to meet our investment needs, working together with private financial resources.

The decision-making process should be more open and democratically accountable. Passenger and consumer bodies should be given a more effective and powerful role to influence decisions and hold operators to account. Building on the experience of PTAs, many decisions should be taken at regional level. And it is outrageous that there is a conflict of interest over safety – the Safety Inspectorates responsible for investigating abuses of safety are currently accountable to the Department of Transport which itself takes the operating decisions affecting levels of safety.

Transport has moved to the top of the political agenda in recent years, sparking a discussion about the travel needs of a modern economy and civilized community in the twenty-first century. This book is an important contribution to that debate. I am delighted to be involved in this exciting policy area, and very much look forward to meeting the challenges that face us all.

1

THE PROBLEM OF BRITISH TRANSPORT

JOHN ROBERTS

If you give people freedom to move, more or less in whatever way they wish, and you also incorporate in that freedom a scantly punished ability to kill and maim other people, to consume earth resources in whatever way necessary to sustain this freedom, and to mutilate the environment with the roads and track and the effluents from the mechanized vehicles needed to move beyond a certain distance; if you have a small land area and a high population; if you do not intervene in the way land uses are put together or separated, and in the densities at which people live; if you have implicitly (often explicitly) different rules for the rich and the poor; if your system of government naturally follows a process of transport disintegration; if you sell off the public assets of your transport system as an act of faith in a religion of market-worship ... then you have a problem.

Britain has precisely this problem. Britain is perpetually poised on the edge of transport gridlock. The efforts of politicians contribute to, rather than diminish, the likelihood of this predicament. That we have not yet succumbed to this fate is not for their want of trying: the cut-backs and increased fares on rail services; the frequent and repeated congestion on motorways; the almost invariable delays in taking off from London's two main airports; to say nothing of the actual *encouragement* to travel. These are enough to create real diseconomies and disruptions without parallel in a supposedly unified Europe.

There is little doubt that, as a percentage of GDP, Britain's transport costs – which the consumer bears to create a profit for those who bought the service from its original owners, the taxpayers of Britain – are of a scale and character unknown in mainland Europe. In that

Europe

Europe, the private traveller manipulates the system for the best deal that can be obtained; the public traveller is assured of transport being provided as a service from the state. There, its service quality will vary from tolerable to superb, but the price required to use it will invariably be relatively low, partly because it does not have to achieve the near-impossible – i.e., provide a profit – and partly because pricing is used to try and maintain some kind of equilibrium. The state effectively intervenes in the private road travel market.

The peculiarly dogmatic fixation of recent British governments with minimal state intervention has led to one of the worst transport systems, public and private, in Europe. The economic-liberal dogma does not fulfil its promises: provincial buses, for example, were deregulated primarily, we were told, as a way of introducing competition. What in fact happened was that the large operators proceeded systematically to buy out the smaller operators: a public monopoly was exchanged for a private monopoly, and the private one frequently cost the user more and provided a vastly inferior service, if one were provided at all, on the less patronized routes.

monopoly on buses

The concept of integration was clearly inimical to *laissez-faire* strategies. The Tyne and Wear Metro, a significant contribution to public transport in Britain, was on its introduction deemed to be the primary public route into central Newcastle and a number of other towns in the area. The bus services which ran parallel routes were transformed into feeder services to the metro stations, with interchangeable tickets. When deregulation arrived, the buses reverted to competing with the metro on virtually the same routes – the independence of each service was ensured, and road congestion increased. Integration was exchanged for disintegration.

London has not yet experienced widespread deregulation of its public transport system, but it appears likely (if the Conservative Government retains power after the 1992 general election). Once again a blind adherence to misconceived principle seems set to win out over opposition from all sectors, including private bus operators, and despite a tendering system which is working well.

Some sensible ticketing policies, even if not perfected, have attracted many new users to the bus and tube networks, still intact as a public service. The growing importance of London as a financial centre, and of service industries in general, have also attracted many new users to the British Rail suburban services. While satisfaction of demand is not necessarily the ideal solution, the advantages of carrying commuters on efficient public transport systems are so manifest that there has been a powerful case here for increasing the system's capacity. One simple, cheap, and rapidly implementable way of doing this was to create continuous bus lanes on the main radial routes into London and allow the buses to operate traffic signals in their favour as they approached them. What was the political response? To price people off these crowded systems, and to reduce service frequency.

In many countries, the complaint is often heard that transport decision-makers lack the imagination necessary to solve problems. In Britain, we have yet to *address* transport problems. Transport has been regarded purely as a potential profit centre, with scant consideration of the public service dimension. British Rail discusses operational issues as if they were occurring in a City boardroom, and creates a field day for its accountants by dividing up its network and charging foreign operators (by 'foreign' I mean freight trains or what used to be called provincial services) to run on its track.

London Buses Ltd has broken up its bus fleet into many small operators and given all their buses new 'company' names – as if the user cared, as if the user gained any better service as a result. The user will only get a better service when buses are seen as part of an *integrated* transport service for the metropolis, allocated a specific role, and given routes where they are segregated from private cars (which should not be there at peak times). It would also help enormously if the bus fleet was modern and regarded as 'up-market' (as it is in Germany), and if interchangeable tickets were available between bus, tube and British Rail routes. If tickets were available from machines at stops, and in all manner of places other than on the bus, then buses could do what they are supposed to do, carry people expeditiously without delaying other road users, rather than playing at post office counters.

These comments can be extended to other transport services. Airport congestion in London, and the cost of travel by the former state-owned airline, have both increased following privatisation. These seem to me to be dubious achievements, warranting a rapid programme for restoring public ownership, rather than extended privatisation. Is it wholly unreasonable to believe that a transport system is about moving very large numbers of people and quantities of goods at reasonable prices, rather than cushioning a small number of shareholders?

With concerns like these, the group of transport researchers and workers represented in this volume felt that a new coherent transport policy needed to be worked out, and then presented to whoever might be interested of whatever political colour. In fact, it is hoped this collection will be read by a wide spectrum of people with different interests, positions and ideologies – transport policy should ride above sectarian positions. In Europe consensus has much more meaning than it does in Britain. On the continent, there is a widely held view that public transport is a social benefit, a service that politicians of every hue expect to subsidise generously by public expenditure. This view has also been reinforced by more recent concerns for environmental safeguards and future energy security. But none of these three elements is a serious component of British policy, if 'policy' is not too strong a word.

Following this brief prefatory chapter the book is divided into three main sections: the first three chapters ask what we need of transport, and are therefore concerned with objectives and targets that have to be reached to achieve a particular quality of life. This is the point where transport is seen as a means to an end (serving the criterion of access) rather than an end in itself (which leads to mobility, and the disasters that have followed its reckless pursuit). Much of this section is devoted to environmental targets, which are seen as having a direct impact on quality of life.

The second major section (chapters 4 to 16) is devoted to ways of achieving these objectives and targets. This is a complex procedure, which explains the section's length. Three initial chapters consider us as consumers: are we adequately taken into account by decision-makers and if not, why not? The concept 'we' is explored: who are 'we'? A wide range of disadvantaged people often get short shrift from transport policy-makers and, consequently, lack access to facilities that others take for granted. Another chapter considers the difficulties that many women have to face in getting around. Four chapters then look at broad questions: how does land use disposition and residential density affect the number and length of the trips we make, and the means of transport we use? What's wrong with the way governments appear to satisfy transport demand, but generally respond to a few powerful lobbies while largely ignoring other pressure groups? Should 'the market' determine what transport we use, or is the market an inadequate mechanism for the task? To what extent should the state intervene?

And then there is the major issue of integration or, rather, the lack of it. Why does one large group, the company car user, get subsidised to an extent well beyond the central government's grudging support of public transport? Why too is employer-provided car parking not taxed? Some discussion follows on lessons from mainland Europe, and a further two chapters compare urban and rural transport policies. This section is completed with two chapters considering current problems with the movement of freight.

The third section (chapters 17 to 24) examines particular means of transport, and their contribution to the achievement of the objectives. Walking and cycling are given pride of place, closely followed by buses and rail. The last two in this section consider policy on aviation, airports, and shipping – topics deserving a book of their own.

This approach, of setting up objectives and seeing in what specific ways they can be met, effectively meant only the briefest discussion of the private car in the above chapters. While the car has come to dominate most societies towards the end of the twentieth century, it nevertheless fails on many counts to satisfy a set of objectives which has been used again and again in several official studies. Because little action is taken, it is almost as if this failure is used to justify the car's continuing destruction of a way of life, threads of which have built up over two or three millenia.

The concluding chapter therefore considers these failings, forcing various difficult questions to be asked, even if they are not fully answered. The chapter has an abundance of material at its disposal. Chapter 7 argues that transport is a cost, not a benefit, when all its characteristics are weighed. Chapters 9 to 11 show the phenomenal cost of cars to society, and the inequitable distribution of these costs. A high proportion is levied on non-car owners or users, in the form of general national or local taxation. Many real costs are not even recognized: land occupied by these moving or stored vehicles, loss of public open space (valuable to the community but valueless to the road supplier), a variety of impacts on a sector of the Commons called environment, etc. On the rare occasion when a road proposal was compared, in cost-benefit terms, with rail's ability to take the projected passenger and freight movements, rail showed positive returns, the road scheme negative returns. But the road scheme was still built at great cost to the taxpayer at large.

Simply designing and implementing a system whereby motorists pay the full costs they incur could dramatically curb car use – a much more straightforward solution to a problem that has eluded a plethora of supposedly non-punitive policy instruments. Such a solution should in theory be attractive to a government motivated by profit – if its policies were consistent with its ideology.

While Europe is tending to follow its lead, the apotheosis of automania has been reached in the United States. It is instructive to visit several medium-sized non-megalopolitan US cities to see how obeisance to the car is virtually complete, the achievement of 'non-place' being almost unnoticed by anaesthetized commuters, with their suburbanized lifestyles. Downtown has become roundtown – much radial movement having been replaced by orbital movement. The 'freeways' intertwine, twist and turn, flatten whole corridors of erstwhile housing, shops and workplaces.

The automobilized journey to work dominates the minds of the traveller, the planner, the politician, as if this is what epitomizes quality of life. The journey is extensive, and lengthens almost annually, for one's suburban ranch house looking across unbroken countryside is only like that until the next ring of bungaloid development arrives. Parking lots occupy more space than buildings; some buildings squat over them, providing the most valuable perk of all to the employee, a free space which in the City of London, for example, would be worth over £3000 a year. Imagine the housing that could be located where car parks are now, and the reduction in travel which that would allow!

This book shows that none of this disfigurement of our cities and our lives is necessary. Britain could lead the world with innovative thinking and action about transport, in which the quality of life transcended the quantity of death.

2
ENHANCING THE QUALITY
OF LIFE

KEITH BUCHAN

This chapter sets out a new system for assessing transport schemes, policies and programmes based on quality of life objectives. It would be more rigorous and more democratic than current methods, particularly those in use for road schemes. The system would apply to all modes of transport. General objectives are used to set 'operational' objectives such as specific targets to reduce pollution or road accidents, to meet environmental quality standards such as a streetside noise limit, or to provide a number of facilities such as pedestrian areas or cycle routes. These lead to the development of schemes and timetabled programmes to achieve the targets.

STARTING AT THE BEGINNING

The fundamental idea behind objectives achievement is to relate the process of transport planning and evaluation to clear quality-of-life goals. Such general aims or objectives are frequently lost in the assessment techniques used by transport engineers and planners but they are the actual means by which people judge success or failure. Examples might be 'improving the environment', 'helping the economy' or 'making transport safer'.

These 'first order' objectives are often dismissed as being too vague or too removed from reality. However, an objectives-based approach translates these generalities into specific and measurable targets or standards, although in some cases the targets will need further research. Examples would be 'to reduce the total amount of carbon dioxide (CO_2) from motor vehicles by 30 per cent by 2010' or 'to reduce urban street noise to 60 dB(A) by 2020'. There are only two

7

examples of this approach in British transport policy: the Government's target to reduce carbon dioxide to 1990 levels by 2005 (in the meantime they will go up) and to reduce road casualties by a third by the year 2000.

When operational objectives have been set planners then have to go away and think of action programmes to achieve them. Value for money is measured by comparing how far alternative schemes or programmes meet the objectives with their cost. This provides a simple comprehensive replacement for the current procedures, which are technically complicated, incomplete and difficult to understand for public and politicians alike. It provides a positive motivation for planners and public authorities. This chapter argues that without a rational system which leads from quality-of-life objectives to detailed, operational objectives there will be no direction, no consistency and no balance in transport policy.

This contrasts very much with the usual transport study approach, in which a random series of problems is identified, often determined by what data are available or easy to collect. Why else is it that the journey to work by car or train has been so dominant in problem analysis? At least part of the answer is that it is difficult to collect information on off-peak bus travel (outside London), on off-peak and leisure travel generally, on walking and cycling, and on freight. In all these areas our basic data have been woefully inadequate.

The other current problem is that the different modes of transport have been treated separately from each other right at the start of the analysis. The use of objectives must start at the top, before any focusing down to individual modes or options. Their use is in fact dynamic, moving from quality-of-life objectives to options, through objectives assessment, option comparison, and back to quality-of-life. Before describing this process more fully, it is necessary to review the current methods in more detail.

THE CURRENT APPROACH TO TRANSPORT ASSESSMENTS

Finance
There are two basic reasons why people use formal assessment methods in transport planning. The first is financial, and can arise from normal business pressures, or from governmental requirements to meet certain targets or rates of return. Examples of this first, monetary

category, range from the financial appraisals undertaken by British Rail, to the cash flow, cost and revenue estimates of private bus operators, and the use of Cost-Benefit Analysis (COBA) to produce Net Present Values (NPVs) from Treasury discount rates by the Department of Transport.

Environment

The second source of pressure can loosely be described as social and environmental, and requires accurate assessments of a wider range of effects. This has always existed, but has gained in emphasis in recent years. The effects can be very local, and hard to define, such as 'community severance', covering a wider area, or extending to global significance, as in the case of CO_2 emissions. This growing awareness has resulted, among other changes, in the EC Directive (CEC, 1985) on Environmental Impact Statements (adopted in Planning and Highways Acts since 1988). For roads, the Department of Transport uses the Manual of Environmental Assessment (MEA) in conjunction with COBA. The MEA is currently being revised, for example to include separate consideration of night-time noise. The Standing Advisory Committee on Trunk Road Assessment (SACTRA) is also undertaking a study of how environmental factors can be better represented in transport appraisal, taking into account the thinking in the Pearce Report (1989), and *This Common Inheritance* (Secretaries of State *et al.*, 1990).

Current Problems

The fundamental dislocation between these two motivating forces has led to a variety of confrontational arguments, aided and abetted by the British legal and political system and the adversarial nature of Public Inquiries. There are many examples of how the technically correct application of established methods such as COBA, or similar programmes, and the MEA framework, have left practitioners completely unprepared for violent public reaction. They can be deeply shocked when people challenge the notion that an option must be popular – after all the engineers scored it so well in the environmental framework and COBA produced such a massive NPV.

The need for a new approach which could resolve this conflict and bring together financial discipline and the achievement of social and environmental demands led to various proposals, and eventually to the reviving of the Advisory Committee on Trunk Road Assessment, which had reported in 1979. This became a standing advisory committee and took on the acronym of 'SACTRA'. The Committee's report (SACTRA, 1986) is a milestone in the development of a new approach.

OBJECTIVES OR OBJECTIVITY?

Before exploring what the overall objectives might be for transport, there are two criticisms of the objectives based approach which need to be addressed.

Pious Hopes

The first is the accusation of vagueness. This arises because of a failure to understand the difference between the general objectives, which by their nature are both easy to agree and hard to measure, and a range of operational objectives, which have undergone a transformation into targets or indices of change, and in turn generate specific schemes and programmes.

One common problem with lists of objectives is that the general are mixed with the operational. For example, running 20 per cent more buses or cutting their journey times through priority schemes are not overall quality-of-life objectives. They may be part of a programme which achieves objectives such as accessibility (especially for those without a car), or safety (if people use buses instead of cars). On the other hand, the objective 'minimizing impact on the environment' is strictly non-operational.

The second-order, operational objectives are more technical in nature, and very demanding in terms of measurement science. They would include changes in travel time, as now, but be extended to cover more groups of travellers (including pedestrians). More radically, there would have to be more precise measurements of air and noise pollution, for example looking at night-time noise separately from the day, and assessing a scheme's contribution to global warming, as well as local carbon monoxide concentrations. In this sense, objectives achievement is no less technically demanding than the combination of COBA and MEA, or Financial Appraisal and Environmental Impact Assessment.

Reform or Replace?

The second issue which arises is whether this is all a fuss about nothing, that it is possible to improve the existing system to such an extent that many of the present problems and inadequacies are overcome. For example, the Manual of Environmental Appraisal, could be changed to include night-time noise, or measures of overall changes in CO_2 emissions from different options. The whole question of considering adequate alternatives to road schemes, or adequate alternatives to some of the new proposals for light rapid transit, can be added by making the study of a wide range of options a requirement.

It has to be said that a complete overhaul of the MEA, coupled with a non-monetized approach to traveller benefits, and organized so that one mode is not pursued with more enthusiasm than another (this latter change is probably the most difficult of all) might well produce a much fairer system. It is quite likely to end up favouring options that would also perform well under an objectives based appraisal regime.

On the other hand, the current methods are so fragmented, with some parts overdeveloped (COBA is an example) and some parts under-developed (as are many of the MEA techniques), and with so many quirks and controversial judgments inherent in the process, that any such change would have to be more a radical transformation than a reform. The endless arguments over traffic generation, modal transfer and trip redistribution (particularly the latter two in combination), the fixed trip matrix (still used for substantial schemes despite the SACTRA recommendations) cannot simply be resolved by adopting objectives and fitting the old techniques to a new framework. The infamous example of valuing open space in urban areas as close to zero, based on its *market* value, instead of its *replacement* value should not be a matter of controversy. It is comparable to a rather obvious bug in a piece of commercial computer software – it should have been corrected at once in the first upgrade.

In this sense the whole issue has become complicated by the acquisition and perpetuation of bad appraisal habits. This is at least part of the motivation behind the desire for a fresh start. This argues not for *less* science in appraisal, rather it suggests an absolute requirement for *better* science.

There is thus the need for more objectivity, independent of any move towards an objectives-based approach. Nevertheless, the use of an objectives framework does offer some clear additional advantages as well as making the removal of the existing deficiencies much easier. First, there is no 'separate development' of the operational, financial, social and environmental elements in the appraisal. This only occurs at a late stage in the evolution of options. Second, the interaction between transport and land use planning is far easier to incorporate. Finally, the whole process is more open, and makes judgments explicit, rather than concealing them in a 'black box' approach.

HOW WOULD IT WORK?

What's the Problem?

It is relatively straightforward to draw up some overall aims or objectives for transport which would command widespread support. On the other hand, it may appear that the present problems are so obvious that all that needs to be done is to list them out and come up with a set of solutions. There is nothing wrong with trying to solve problems, but what is needed is a very accurate analysis of what the problems really are. This is particularly true in transport because the most obvious solution to a problem may actually make it worse.

A good example of this is the problem of queues of traffic in a congested town centre. The obvious solution is to build more road capacity. In many towns and cities we now know that not only is this extremely environmentally damaging, it is one of the worst things we could do to improve traffic flow. The reason is that extra capacity can encourage more traffic (from a variety of effects) – and the end result is more people queuing in a similarly congested system. There are several well documented cases in London, for example the A40 Westway (GLC, 1985a), and elsewhere in the region there has been the experience of the opening, and immediate filling-up, of the M25 (Rendel, Palmer and Tritton, 1989). The release of 'suppressed demand' is a particularly serious problem in highly populated areas with high car ownership.

In this case the problem is defined as mobility failure in relation to road users. It is therefore not put in the context of accessibility for the whole population to different places by different modes. Nor is it put in the context of travel by other modes, or the general economic context of price affecting demand.

What Are we Trying to Achieve?

The alternative approach is based on the idea of setting overall quality-of-life objectives for transport, deriving operational objectives which can be accurately measured from them, and using these both in the assessment and the option development stages. In 1986, SACTRA set out the basic approach, strongly supporting the process of:

- setting overall objectives;
- identifying where they are not being met (problem definition);

- devising solutions (new ways of achieving the objectives).

This approach was accepted by the Government, and used by them in the London Assessment Studies, where a set of objectives was agreed between all the London Boroughs and the Department of Transport (DTp, ALA and LBA, 1987). Other studies have also tried to define these overall objectives, including the Metropolitan Transport Research (MTRU) 'West London Study, Stage 1' (1989), the 'Scenario Testing Exercise' undertaken by the MVA Consultancy (MVA 1988), the 'Birmingham Integrated Transport Study' (MVA, 1989), and most recently the MTRU work for local authorities in the South East (MTRU, 1990).

It should be noted that at this stage there is no definition of how the objectives are to be pursued, precisely what targets are to be set, or what the mix of private and public involvement will be in investment, regulation, pricing or operational control. This leads to a further advantage inherent in this approach. One key difference between Britain and other European countries is the violent short term fluctuations both in overall transport policy and in individual scheme approvals. This has been particularly damaging to transport projects which often require investment and management over long periods. One need only compare the stop-start, on-off railway electrification programme in Britain to the building of the French high speed TGV network.

Maximizing agreement about quality-of-life objectives is a constructive exercise, and certainly easier than mediating between conflicting proponents of one mode of transport as opposed to another. By starting at the beginning, instead of in the middle, of a policy-making and scheme design process, conclusions on the most appropriate roles of different transport modes, or on the mix of regulation, intervention or free market choice, become dependent on how far they achieve the objectives, not on whether they fit with an entrenched pro-road or pro-rail point of view.

Nor are these objectives merely academic abstractions which form the subject of debate at conferences or the basis of pure research projects. They are designed to be of practical help in defining problems and developing solutions. Many transport schemes miss opportunities to achieve worthwhile objectives because they are assessed on too narrow a basis. For example, highway junction improvements which forget pedestrians, cyclists or bus priority could often undergo modest changes or additions at the design stage which would improve conditions for other travellers. This is not simply an argument about whether a road or rail scheme should be built or not; it is about the type of scheme and the package of which it is a part.

Practical Application

The basic approach builds on setting quality-of-life objectives (e.g. 'to improve the environment') which are relatively easy to agree on and which bring people together (thus useful both for analysis and public participation). These are then translated into operational (second-order) objectives, such as w per cent reduction in road accidents, x per cent reduction in a certain pollutant, y square miles of pedestrian priority areas, or z per cent shift in public transport accessibility in the worst served areas, all accompanied by target dates. Threshold standards can also be used: for example, x dB(A) in residential streets by day, y dB(C) L1 at night, or minimum level of peak hour carbon monoxide (CO) levels in any populated area (shops, homes, workplaces etc.). These ideas are explored further in the following chapter (3) on environmental protection.

At the strategic level of appraisal the role of market competition can also be sorted out: how much can different transport markets contribute to objectives, how far can they be left to themselves, what regulations or constraints should apply? The role of private developers and public subsidies can also be included within the objectives-based approach.

Apart from people other than transport experts and technicians being able to understand such objectives, both general and operational, there are other advantages. First, conflicts which arise from a scheme meeting some objectives but undermining others become transparent – they are not obscured in computer modelling assumptions or invented values of time or of road accident death. This makes decision-making more difficult for senior public servants (and some politicians) but more democratic.

Second, the objectives can be used to design schemes as well as assessing their relative performance. This contrasts with the current use of COBA. Third, the use of objectives gives a structure to transport planning which makes it more accessible and better organized. The preparation of strategic policies requires such a basic structure in order to avoid either the 'lists' syndrome, or a series of unjustified and piecemeal judgments. Instead, there should be a natural progression from the general to the specific. It is critically important not to mix the two.

This is not to say that the objectives-based approach will remove all conflicts or disagreements. There will be considerable argument about how to apply them and it is extremely unlikely that schemes will always satisfy all the objectives. However, they give a structure within which the success and failure of transport policies and programmes can be accurately assessed.

RECENT TRANSPORT OBJECTIVES

Several attempts have been made in recent years to set out quality of life objectives for transport (LSPU, 1986; DTp, LBA and ALA, 1987; MVA, 1988; MTRU, 1989a; MVA, 1989). Many of these lists have much in common – always including safety, accessibility and the environmental impact, for example. There is some controversy as to whether economic improvement is a pure quality-of-life objective or just a means to an end, but this is also usually included.

Table 2-1 represents a collation of different sources to provide a comprehensive list, and offers an indication as to what each objective should include. Their adoption and pursuit would lead to a significant change in transport policy in Britain.

Table 2-1: Quality-of-Life Objectives for Transport.

Accessibility
- To encourage and provide a transport system which will give people access to workplaces, to shops and public buildings, to industry and commerce, to facilities like doctors' surgeries, to centres for recreation and entertainment, to other goods and services, and to one another;
- To co-ordinate transport planning with land use and economic development planning with the aim of minimizing the overall need to travel.

Environment
- To protect and enhance the quality of the environment as an objective in its own right and not merely to minimize the damage resulting from transport developments;
- To set quality standards which should apply throughout the country, not just in certain areas;
- To ensure that transport policies contribute towards reducing environmental damage nationally and worldwide;

- To set clear constraints which prevent the destruction of irreplaceable environmental assets.

Economic Development
- To create patterns of transport infrastructure which support sustainable economic development at the local and national level;
- To encourage research, innovation and technological progress both in manufacturing for, and in the operation of, the transport industries;
- To regulate the transport industry itself to provide reasonable pay and conditions and fulfilment at work.

Fairness and Choice
- To improve freedom of choice of destination and mode for everyone, tackling the inequalities that currently exist;
- To ensure that a major part of benefits from the design and operation of the transport system are distributed to those who are most in need of them.

Safety and Security
- To reduce the risks and fear of personal injury, assault and harassment on all modes of transport (including walking);
- To reduce the number, risk and level of severity of road traffic accidents for drivers, passengers, pedestrians and cyclists.

Energy and Efficiency
- To meet the accessibility requirements of residents, visitors, industry and commerce at the lowest resource cost;
- To minimize consumption of non-renewable sources of energy;
- To reduce congestion, and encourage transport efficiency.

Accountability
- To give people an unequivocal right to participate in the transport planning process;
- To establish mechanisms for people to exert influence through local democratic means over the decision-making process for transport schemes;
- To set up mechanisms by which users can directly influence the quality of service offered by the transport providers.

Flexibility
- To make the system responsive to changes in the external constraints operating on the transport system, and to new understanding about its impacts.

3

ENVIRONMENTAL TARGETS FOR A NATIONAL TRANSPORT POLICY

CLAIRE HOLMAN AND MALCOLM FERGUSSON

Transport is one of the most polluting of all human activities. Emissions, primarily from road vehicles, have a major impact on both human health and the environment. However, environmental damage is not restricted to the effects of vehicle exhaust. Pollution occurs throughout the life cycle of a vehicle, beginning with the extraction of the raw materials required, through its useful life, to final disposal. Maintenance and spare parts supply and disposal also have associated environmental impacts.

Further threats to the environment result from the provision of transport infrastructure. Demands for large areas of land for roads, car parks, and service stations continue to destroy not only unique wildlife habitats and areas of outstanding natural beauty, but also parts of our towns, homes, historic sites, and the more mundane landscapes and recreational areas which add to the quality of life for many people.

In the past, successive governments have marginalized the protection of the environment, in transport policy as elsewhere. If considered at all, it has typically been tacked on as an additional factor to be considered in any assessment, rather than being placed at the centre of policy formulation. This approach is not unusual; but in a few countries such as the Netherlands there has recently been a major change, and environmental protection targets have become central to national transport policy. As a result, transport policies are beginning to emerge which have the specific objective of minimizing the environmental impacts.

In the UK, there has been little coherent analysis of the impacts of transport on the environment, or on the kind of targets needed to solve the many problems which we face. Instead, a more conservative approach has been followed, characterized by concentration on technical fix policies such as the introduction of catalytic converters. By contrast, little or nothing has been done to limit the enormous growth in traffic, and in car traffic in particular.

This chapter argues the need for clear targets for environmental controls, with particular reference to atmospheric emissions, and to set out a framework for the proposed targets. The chapter concludes with a brief consideration of the range of policy options available to a future administration in order to limit the environmental impacts of road transport.

A FRAMEWORK FOR ENVIRONMENTAL PROTECTION

Introduction

The broader environmental implications of transport policy have been largely neglected in the planning and assessment of transport provision. This is partly because the problems of air quality have only in a few cases been regarded as acute in the UK; partly because the regional and global impacts of emissions have been poorly understood or largely ignored; and partly because the disposal of gases is free of charge within the current economic framework.

Looking in more detail at the principal atmospheric pollutants from road transport and the effects it seems clear that none of these circumstances can be expected to obtain indefinitely. Projections on this point (Fergusson and Holman, 1990) suggest that technical improvements to road vehicles can produce only limited reductions in emissions at best, particularly in the context of rapid growth in road transport demand.

The British Government has done relatively little to reduce the environmental impacts of transport, and the recent White Paper does not promise much more in the way of firm policies (Department of the Environment, 1990b). In particular, it seeks to place the onus for environmental improvements onto transport users as individuals. As a result of this stance, there are still no clear targets or policies to achieve an agreed level of environmental protection in UK transport policy.

By contrast, the Dutch Government, in recognizing the need to strike a balance between individual freedom, accessibility and environmental amenity, has concluded (Government of the Netherlands, 1990) that 'It is not enough to stick at the stage of expressing

19

serious concern and pious wishes', and that this 'implies setting limits on the external effects of our transport system – on air pollution, on energy consumption, on noise nuisance . . . at levels acceptable to future generations as well as our own'.

The advantage of setting environmental protection limits or targets is that the success of transport policy can then be measured against a quantified objective. It is thereby relatively straightforward first to measure whether the agreed target is being met; and second, to enter into a debate as to whether the chosen balance between mobility and environmental protection is the correct one.

The Regulatory Framework

To ensure that environmental protection measures are based on clear and agreed objectives which can be set against other economic and social goals, a regulatory framework is needed to embody both the general targets and specific regulatory measures.

To translate a general target or guideline into specific measures requires a three-tier process. That is, criteria for environmental protection must first be agreed on the basis of the current best available understanding of the degree of damage caused to human health or the environment by a given level of pollution. Following on from this, so-called bubble limits must be set at national level, and subsequently for each region or economic sector, defining the allowable total level of emissions to meet the objective. Finally, this process must be translated into some form of specific operational targets, and into fiscal or regulatory policies which will have the effect of reducing emissions to the agreed limit.

These three main stages are described in greater detail below. For a more detail discussion of the pollution control framework adopted within the European Community, see Haigh (1987).

Environmental Protection Criteria

Environmental protection criteria should be defined for each environmental impact, defining levels below which no damage to human health or the environment is believed to occur. This in itself would be a departure from current practice, which takes the current position as its starting point and then specifies a given measure of reduction in pollution, on the basis of technical, economic and political constraints. That is, the determination of specific environmental criteria would of itself be a move towards an objectives-led policy.

Examples of environmental protection criteria include:

- **Air Quality Targets** – Air quality targets are set at levels designed to protect the most sensitive groups within a population, with an added safety margin to reflect the scientific and medical uncertainties. The World Health Organization has already set extensive air quality guidelines (1987). Targets such as these should be viewed as a goal to be achieved within an agreed time frame.

- **Critical Loads** – This is a concept pioneered largely in the Scandinavian countries, but now also being considered by the UNECE in the renegotiation of the protocols to the Convention on Long Range Transboundary Air Pollution (CLRTAP), as an objective approach to the negotiation of emissions limits. Essentially it involves determining the level of pollution which can be tolerated by an ecosystem before damage occurs. Critical loads may determine that there is no safe level of exposure, in which case a substance may need to be eliminated from use. Critical loads of nitrogen oxides, ozone and sulphur are currently widely exceeded in Europe.

- **Noise Target Levels** – At present there is no limit set for the levels of noise to which the general public may be subjected, and redress for excessive noise can be sought only on the less specific grounds of nuisance. However, there are already thresholds in UK legislation above which residents qualify for grants for noise abatement measures in the event of road construction or aircraft noise. This or a similar standard could therefore be extended to form the basis for a future target below which all homes should in time be brought.

- **Land Use Targets** – A further set of targets not currently pursued in any formal fashion in Britain or at EC level would be explicit restrictions on land use, damage to natural habitats, and related criteria. By implication, certain planning constraints such as green belt designations and listings of buildings, the designation of sites of special scientific interest (SSSIs), areas of outstanding natural beauty (AONBs) and Ramsar sites could form part of such a system. At present, however, these designations do not offer absolute protection from damage, for example by road schemes, and a far more coherent and powerful system of controls is needed.

Bubble Limits
This term is applied to controls which specify a ceiling on the total quantity of a given pollutant which may be emitted by a country,

region, or economic sector. Ideally, these limits should be determined on the basis of the environmental protection criteria set out above, typically by using emissions inventories and computer models which reflect scientific knowledge on the emission, dispersion, transformation and deposition of pollutants.

The bubble limited approach has already been applied in the European Community to the control of acid emissions from power stations and other large industrial plant; but this was on the basis of reductions which could be achieved with known technology and at manageable cost, rather than being derived from environmental criteria. Equally, these restrictions were negotiated in isolation, rather than as part of a coherent programme of emissions control for all sources. Bubble limits have not yet been used for mobile pollution sources, for example, which are more difficult to quantify and monitor accurately.

Bubble limits would be most effective for carbon dioxide emissions, where the precise source of emissions is immaterial because there are no major local impacts. By definition a bubble limit does not specify where within the bubble emissions may occur; and at present this is proving to be a drawback to the limits on acid emissions from large plant, in that the bubble limit does not prevent local damage around intense pollution sources.

Operational Environmental Targets
Once bubble limits have been set, specific operational targets must be derived to set out in detail how the limits are to be achieved. These may take one or a number of the following forms:

- **Emissions Limits** – Atmospheric pollutants may be controlled by specifying the *rate* of emissions which is allowable for a given type of plant or process. This is the approach which has thus far been used in the transport sector to control the weight of each of the regulated pollutants which may be emitted over a given test cycle under tightly specified conditions.

- **Fuel Quality Specifications** – In addition, some pollutants can be controlled indirectly by setting a minimum specification for fuels, such as the cetane number for diesel fuel, and by setting maximum concentrations of certain substances such as lead which are allowable within the fuels. This approach is known as a product standard, and has been adopted with some success to limit transport emissions. The best known examples to date are the progressive reduction of lead concentrations in leaded fuel, and the increasing availability of unleaded petrol in European markets. Similarly, new and more stringent rquirements on particulate emissions from diesel vehicles will require significant reductions in the allowable levels of sulphur in diesel fuel in the 1990s.

- **Air Quality Standards** – Air quality standards already exist in the European Community for four pollutants, namely, lead, smoke and sulphur dioxide, and nitrogen dioxide. The EC has the power to act against national governments which allow these standards to be violated.

  It remains within the power of national governments to determine how these standards should feed back into policy. In the long term, for example, they are likely to pursue compliance through improved emissions standards; but emergency short-term measures such as banning car trips or suspending designated industrial processes may also be used during short-lived, acute pollution episodes.

  It is important at this stage to distinguish air quality standards from targets or guidelines, which are discussed above. Standards should have statutory force; but there is little point in setting standards which are so strict that they cannot be met in the immediate future. Therefore it has to be accepted that an interim standard can be different from the target level, as long as it is accompanied by a clear timetable for compliance with the more stringent long-term targets or guidelines.

- **Noise Limits** – There are two main types of noise limits to be distiguished: noise standards for vehicles, and those which specify the maximum level of noise to which people should be subjected. Vehicle noise standards are well developed in the UK, and have been improved progressively over time. As with other types of pollution, however, improvements in noise from individual vehicles have been counteracted by the growing numbers and use of vehicles. There is as yet no clear framework of noise standards to specify the allowable limits to which the general public may be subjected.

- **Vehicle Use Limits** – The total level of emissions of a given pollutant is a function of the rate of emissions, and of the level of vehicle use. Thus, emissions of the regulated pollutants from road transport in the UK have increased steadily through the 1980s in spite of more stringent emissions controls. This arises largely from the fact that the growth in traffic has exceeded the rate of improvement in emissions levels. The same is true to a far greater extent of carbon dioxide emissions.

A certain amount can be achieved by regulating fuel and emissions but limits to the level of vehicle usage are also needed to reduce the total level of emissions. To date national transport policy in the UK has set no limits to total vehicle mileage; and many would argue that the policies of the Department of Transport have actively contributed to the rapid growth in the use of cars and trucks.

- **Vehicle Recycling Standards** – Additional targets should cover the proportion of vehicle raw materials which should be recycled, and these should increase progressively over time. In Germany, the threat of imposition of a disposal levy on all new cars by the Federal Government has led manufacturers to develop wide-ranging plans for recycling. However, no specific recycling targets have been imposed as yet, although an EC directive on plastic recycling with specific targets for scrapped vehicles is in prospect.

- **Road Material Recycling Targets** – Targets should also be set for road material recycling, which is in its infancy in the UK (Environmental Data Services, 1991). At present, progress towards improving performance in the UK also seems painfully slow. To improve on this position, a progressive increase in the proportion of material to be recycled should be specified, with current best practice in Europe as an interim standard to be met over the next five years.

Summary of the Proposed Protection Framework
Outlined above is a three-tier regulatory framework for environmental protection. Elements of this framework have already been introduced in both national and EC legislation. However, a fundamental limitation of current approaches has been the starting point of the legislation. All legislation to date has been determined by the degree of abatement which can be achieved with known technology and at relatively modest cost. As a reflection of this approach, the principal of 'best available technology (or technique) not entailing excessive cost' (BATNEEC) is enshrined in the UK's Environmental Protection Act, as well as in earlier European Community documents such as Directive

84/360 on combatting air pollution from industrial plants.

As a result of the adoption of this principle, no legislation in the UK has as yet enshrined the need to meet defined environmental protection criteria – that is, the first tier of the proposed framework. The three-tier approach is needed if future targets are to be based firmly on environmental criteria and clear objectives, rather than the piecemeal and pragmatic approaches to pollution control which have been pursued to date. Within this framework, the chosen criteria are progressively translated into firm targets, which in turn engender the requisite policy changes.

Current Approaches to Environmental Protection in Transport

To date, policies on environmental protection in the transport sector have focused almost exclusively on limits to the rate of emissions of some air pollutants, and of noise levels from motor vehicles. To reduce the impact of heavy goods vehicles, a policy has also developed to keeping them away from centres of population through the construction of bypass roads and motorways.

It must be emphasized that emission limits to date have been determined on the basis of what could be achieved with the available technology at a given point in time, with no particular reference to the tolerance of the environment for any given rate of emissions. In this sense, transport policy making has consistently utilized only the third tier of the regulatory framework set out above.

In responding to global warming by limits on carbon dioxide emissions, however, a completely different approach is being adopted which is akin to the second tier of our framework. Thus far the UK Government has committed to stabilize our total national emission levels by the year 2005 (that is, to restore emissions to their 1990 level by that date). This puts Britain far ahead of the US, the USSR, and the many other nations which are currently opposed to limits. We are, however, towards the bottom of the league among our Scandinavian and EC neighbours, most of whom are pressing for emissions stabilization by the year 2000, and/or reductions by 2005. A few countries have committed to significant reductions, most notably Germany which is committed to a 30 per cent reduction from 1987 levels by the year 2005. It should be noted that at present even these target reductions are still based on what is considered reasonably achievable, rather than on any clear criteria for limiting global warming.

Aside from the unduly cautious approach of the UK Government on carbon dioxide emissions reductions, perhaps the main concern at present is the apparent reluctance of the administration to declare or even draw up targets for any particular area or sector of the economy. As a result, there is currently a stated national target for carbon dioxide emissions (that is, a national bubble limit), but no detailed plan as to how this should be achieved.

This situation is particularly absurd in relation to the transport sector, in which the forecast trends in traffic growth imply a massive *increase* in carbon dioxide emissions. For this to occur, and at the same time for Britain to meet its international undertakings, would necessitate an extremely severe reduction in emissions in some other sector of the economy. As we have previously pointed out, there are not likely to be any volunteers to take on this task (Fergusson and Holman, 1990); and it seems unreasonable to expect any one sector of the economy to furnish massive reductions while another is allowed to increase its fuel use at will. It is worth noting that a recent report from the House of Commons Select Committee on Energy has endorsed this view (House of Commons, 1991b):

> We are particularly disturbed by the Department of Transport's lack of any clear objectives in respect of transport sector energy use ... without any forecasts at all it is difficult to see how the Department could take the decisions needed to achieve transport's contribution towards stabilizing CO_2 emissions by 2005 ... A large increase in the transport sector's CO_2 emissions balanced by disproportionately heavy reductions in other sectors does not seem to us a rational way of achieving the emissions target.

PROPOSED ARRANGEMENTS AT NATIONAL AND LOCAL LEVEL

Introduction

It will be necessary for the UK administration, in implementing the environmental policies set out in this chapter, to determine the appropriate level of government for the pursuit of each policy area, and to establish arrangements for both the allocation of targets and the devolution of powers to local authorities where appropriate.

It must remain the task of central government to determine environmental criteria and to set national targets and limits. It will also remain a function of central government to embody the requirements of EC environment directives into national legislation and policy.

In some cases, it will be necessary to 'divide the cake' of national total emissions between the areas of local administration. This function would be performed by national government in accordance with agreed criteria, and in consultation with local authorities. It would then be the function of the local authorities to ensure that their area remained within its designated limits, and suitable incentives or penalties would be necessary to ensure compliance with national targets.

In this section the respective roles of central and local government and industry are illustrated using gaseous emissions as an example. Obviously, the detailed arrangements for each environmental impact will need to be determind separately, and the example given may not in all cases be directly applicable.

Targets at National Government Level

Environmental Protection Criteria and Bubble Limits

An early requirement for a more environmentally compatible national transport policy must be the establishment of environmental protection criteria for each of the principal environmental impacts. From these, bubble limits for each economic sector including transport, and for each region, must be agreed at national level.

Table 3-1 below gives an indication of the scale of reduction in emissions of gaseous pollutants required to protect human health and the environment. There is currently some scientific uncertainty in extrapolating from environmental protection criteria, such as critical loads, to reductions in emissions, and therefore the figures in this table are a first estimate. It is a priority to establish with greater certainty the degree of emission reduction required for environmental protection.

These emission reduction targets based on current emission levels, are those required, as a first approximation, to meet the appropriate environmental protection criteria. Greater reductions may be needed when scientific understanding improves. Note in particular that the target for nitrogen oxides is based on critical levels of ozone, whereas even more stringent reductions are likely to be needed to return all UK freshwater to a pristine quality.

The targets in Table 3-1 give no indication of timescales over which these reductions may take place, but from a purely environmental protection perspective it is desirable to reduce emissions as rapidly as possible. However, other social, political and economic factors will, in reality, influence the pace of pollution abatement.

Thus, when translating the targets in Table 3-1 into specific bubble

Table 3-1: Provisional Emission Reduction Targets for the Principal Gaseous Pollutants Based on Environmental Protection Criteria

Pollutant	Target Reduction	Notes
Carbon monoxide	45 per cent	Based on exceedances of the WHO eight hour air quality guideline as determined by monitoring data for London, assuming a linear relationship between ambient levels and a reduction in emissions. This excludes its influence on ozone formation and its role in climate change.
(VOCs) Volatile Organic Compounds	75 per cent	Level of reduction needed to reduce tropospheric ozone to near critical levels. The critical levels are based on exposure of sensitive vegetation over the growing season (Derwent, Grennfelt and Hov. 1991).
Nitrogen oxides	75 per cent	As VOCs
Carbon dioxide	75 per cent	Assumes that other measures are taken to reduce the impact of other greenhouse gases; that deforestation will end; and that reforestation is sustained over a period of decades. Critical levels are based on the maximum rate of migration of trees in a changing climate (Krause, Bach and Koomey, 1989).

limits, a wide range of factors including the best available technology are taken into account, and help determine the timetable for attainment of targets. It is likely that at least a decade will be required to reduce emissions to the levels indicated in Table 3-1 above. For carbon dioxide, where there is no abatement technology available, a considerably longer time scale will be required. Taking these factors into account, suggested initial bubble limits for the major gaseous pollutants are set out in Table 3-2 below.

Table 3-2: Proposed Bubble Limits for the Principle Gaseous Pollutants for the Year 2005.

Pollutant	Reduction Target (from 1988 levels)
Carbon monoxide	45 per cent
VOCs	75 per cent
Nitrogen oxides	75 per cent
Carbon dioxide	30 per cent

Operational Environmental Targets

From bubble limits such as those outlined above can be derived operational environmental targets. These would define how the bubble limits may be met on a practical level. Assuming that the reduction in emissions would be divided equally between the different modes of transport, emissions from the sector and its component subsectors can be modelled to determine the optimum means of reducing the total amount of a given pollutant released. For example, using the Earth Resources Research model of atmospheric emissions for the UK transport sector, Table 3-3 indicates how these targets may be met for the private car subsector using a combination of technical improvements, traffic management and traffic restraint. From this information, the necessary operational environmental targets at national and local levels can be determined.

Ensuring that the best available technology is introduced would be a matter for central government, using a range of policy options such as mandatory emission limits, fuel quality standards and fiscal incentives. On the other hand, traffic management schemes and traffic restraint measures are best devised and implemented at the local level.

Table 3-3. Car Emission Reduction Targets for the Year 2005.

	Carbon monoxide	VOCs	Nitrogen oxides	Carbon dioxide
Emissions in 1988	2880	314	599	65521
Estimated Emissions for 2005				
Current Trend	3703	404	771	84252
Technical Change	969	109	116	64009
Traffic Management	920	103	110	57513
Traffic Limits	740	83	89	46236
Reduction Target for Emissions 1988 to 2005	74%	74%	85%	29%

Source: Earth Resources Research, unpublished data

Notes: All emissions totals are in thousands of tonnes (kt)

Current trend indicates the estimated emissions on the assumption of the *low* forecast of traffic growth from the National Road Traffic Forecast;

Technical change refers to the introduction of controlled three way catalytic converters, plus adoption of the most fuel efficient new car models;

Traffic Management refers to reduced speed limits, plus better traffic controls in urban areas;

Traffic Limits refer to the result of limiting total traffic to the 1988 level.

Nationally determined mandatory air quality standards for the principal pollutants would also be necessary, to ensure that the policies derived from the environmental operational targets were being effective. These may not correspond to the targets in all cases, at least initially, and derogations may be allowed in some areas for a specific interim period.

These interim standards should be backed up by a clearly defined mechanism for progressive tightening of standards over time. The aim of this process would be to meet the agreed air quality targets in all areas within an agreed time frame.

Auditing of Policies and Target Compliance
Owing to the importance and the complexity of the range of

environmental targets required in national transport policy, it would be desirable to set up a specialist unit with responsibility for setting targets at national and local levels, and for co-ordinating the monitoring of target compliance.

A second function of such a unit would be to audit the transport implications, and hence the environmental impacts, of all major central government policies. This audit should be incorporated into automatic environmental impact assessments for all new policy initiatives. This requirement arises particularly in relation to transport and the environment, since many policies, such as a change in the pattern of health provision or in planning regulations, can have far-reaching effects on transport demand.

Targets at Regional Levels
Policies at the national level will have an impact on local performance which would be approximately uniform between regions. Beyond these policies, local authorities should be given emission reduction targets that could be met, as indicated above, using a package of traffic management, modal shift and traffic restraint measures, determined to suit the local conditions. It would be preferable to co-ordinate environmental operational targets on a regional scale through some form of strategic planning body, as this would be simpler to monitor and operate. The targets could then be delegated to the local level by the regional body.

It would be cumbersome to generate regional targets through complex modelling, for example of traffic conditions and vehicle stocks. Instead it would be preferable to establish *derived targets* from which actual emissions performance would be inferred.

For road traffic, the most obvious method of determining these targets would be to calculate at the national level the amount of traffic for each vehicle class, divided between a mix of speed bands and/or road categories, which could be catered for while meeting the national targets for all pollutants. These calculations would be derived from modelling exercises, such as that already undertaken and set out in Table 3-3, which would take into account the projected impacts of changes in national policy.

Traffic totals could then be allocated to the appropriate regional bodies on the basis of current traffic levels, while making allowance for any anticipated structural changes which would alter the balance between regions, such as projected population growth or economic restructuring. Other national policy considerations, such as the need for interregional equity, should also be incorporated into the arrangements at this level.

The contribution of motorways and trunk roads to total emissions could be problematic, in that regional bodies could argue that they have little or no control over through traffic using motorways and other major routes across their area of jurisdiction. In reality, long-distance traffic makes a relatively small contribution to the total trunk road traffic; but some allowance would have to be made for interregional traffic in each region. This through traffic would be set a separate emissions target within the national total; and it would be assumed that emissions would be controlled as necessary by policies at the national level, and by the authority responsible for the trunk road network.

INDUSTRY TARGETS

Introduction
Many aspects of an environmentally oriented transport policy would fall outside the direct control of government at any level. In particular, the standards of new vehicle fuel efficiency, as well as construction and material selection for both vehicles and roads, are likely to remain largely within the hands of private industry. It is therefore important that there is a mechanism for negotiation on these types of issues between industry and the different levels of government as well as the appropriate co-ordination between central and local government activities. The direct environmental impacts of industrial operations are not included in the discussion as they are outside the scope of this chapter.

The Role of Central Government
Following on the logic of the environmental protection framework, voluntary targets and standards may include specific targets for individual companies as well as for industrial sectors. Given the national or indeed international nature of many industrial enterprises, these need to be co-ordinated at national level.

There is a recent precedent for this approach in the UK, in the implementation of the Large Combustion Plant Directive from the EC. In this case, the total sulphur reduction requirement for the UK was divided by Her Majesty's Inspectorate of Pollution, after consultation with interested parties, between the electricity supply and other industries. Subsequently, the effective bubble limit for the electricity supply industry was further subdivided between National Power and PowerGen. In the case in question the workings of this process were far from transparent, but they usefully illustrate the basic principle involved. As far as an environmental transport policy is concerned similar industrial targets for, say, new vehicle fuel economy (as a proxy for reduced carbon dioxide emissions) could be similarly agreed by central government, the motor manufacturers and the individual companies involved.

There could be scope for negotiating different targets for different companies according to their specific circumstances, or for allowing tradeable permits between companies. However, such a process could prove unduly complex and take a long time to develop, and it may prove quicker and easier to impose uniform mandatory standards across the board.

Local Authority Activities
In cases such as those for vehicle or road material recycling, only some elements would fall within the remit of central government. Clearly it would be appropriate for local authorities to make the necessary specifications in roadbuilding and repair programmes to encourage recycling of road materials, and to facilitate collection, re-use, recycling and disposal facilities for scrapped cars.

CONCLUSIONS

In relation to environmental threats such as acid rain, urban smog, global warming, habitat destruction and waste disposal problems, the reductions in environmental impact which may be achieved through current policy approaches are unlikely to be adequate. There are currently good grounds for thinking that 'technical fix' solutions will effectively deal with only a few of the many problems outlined in this paper, particularly in the context of further escalations in traffic levels.

As a result, it will prove necessary for industrialized societies such as ours to reappraise our current approaches to transport and land use planning. As the importance of environmental factors is increasingly appreciated in our policies towards transport provision, the emphasis will necessarily shift away from the private car, and towards a more objectives-led appraisal of needs.

In this context, it seems clear that greater emphasis will be placed on accessibility rather than mobility, and on the fulfilment of local needs more through walking, cycling, and public transport, in the context of a land use planning framework which seeks to minimize the need for long distance travelling on a day-to-day basis.

At the present time there is a growing appreciation of the need for a 'cradle to grave' assessment of all industrial processes rather than a simple 'point of use' analysis; and of course this approach could and should apply to transport systems as to any other. In view of the wide range of environmental implications of road transport use in the UK, adoption of the environmental framework outlined above is essential to ensure that environmental impacts receive equal consideration alongside the economic and social objectives of transport provision.

4

CONSUMERISM AND PUBLIC TRANSPORT

JOHN CARTLEDGE

With the publication of the rival parties' Citizen's Charters, consumer issues have come to the forefront of political debate. This chapter explores the philosophical foundations underpinning the differing attitudes to consumer representation on each side of the partisan divide. It describes the existing arrangements in the public transport industry, and their shortcomings. The key roles which a reformed system should play are identified, and some principles upon which it should be constructed by a future government are outlined.

CONSUMERISM AND PUBLIC TRANSPORT

Traditionally, consumer concerns have been a minority issue in British political life. In the deafening rivalry of two dominant parties, respectively identified with the corporate interests of management and labour, the collective voice of consumers has been all but drowned. The views of leading business magnates and trade union officials are deemed worthy of extensive media coverage, while their counterparts in the consumer world languish in obscurity. Lacking recognition, funding, organization and political clout, the consumer movement has remained fragmented and ineffectual.

So the sudden eruption of consumerist themes onto the centre of the political stage in the first half of 1991 caught many consumer activists unawares. To be courted by politicians and civil servants for ideas that might form the centrepieces of future manifestos was an unprecedented and possibly unnerving experience. To find their traditional preoccupations – choice, access, information, safety, representation and redress – entering the currency of parliamentary debate was an exhilarating departure. To find Government and Opposition jockeying for position in a race to determine whose consumerist credentials were the stronger was a fascinating spectacle.

The first fruits of this conversion were the rival Citizen's Charters, published simultaneously in a blaze of publicity. From an initial reading, it appeared that both documents could well have originated from a single pen.

'Private utilities and public services must spell out ... precisely what their customers can expect, the targets they can achieve, who to contact if things go wrong, and how to obtain redress,' asserted Labour. 'The key principle will be ... publication of the standards of service that the customer can reasonably expect, and of performance against those standards [with] well-signposted avenues for complaint if the customer is not satisfied,' echoed the Tory Government. 'Choice, wherever possible between competing providers, is the best spur to quality improvement' is the Conservatives' conviction. 'You should have a right to the greatest possible choice in the provision of goods and services by private and public organizations' is the first of Labour's 'nine practical rights'. Small wonder that, with (apparently) so little of substance to distinguish their respective offerings, the argument between the parties has been principally about whose intellectual property has been filched by whom (The Prime Minister, 1991; Labour Party, 1991).

Closer examination does begin to reveal some significant differences. In relation to public transport provision, both Charters offer the setting, monitoring and publication of performance standards for punctuality, comfort, information and the like. Both refer to the creation of a new regulatory agency, to systems of redress for failure to deliver advertised services, and to a clearer definition of passengers' rights. But while Labour's concern is with public transport in all modes, irrespective of ownership, the Conservatives' proposals apply solely to British Rail (pending privatization) and to London Underground. For bus users it is assumed that deregulation and privatization have ensured – through the unseen hand of free market competition – that passengers' needs are now automatically met. The rapid decline in ridership and the perilous financial condition of the bus industry outside London, post-deregulation, had apparently given the Conservative Government no grounds for reconsidering its intention to visit the same treatment upon London's bus network.

Where Labour's Charter touches upon passenger safety and security, upon the needs of travellers with disabilities, and upon concessionary fares, the Government is silent about such matters. It has preferred to focus its concern upon performance-related pay for transport employees, wearing of name badges by front-line staff, and contracting out of ancillary services such as catering and cleaning. But perhaps it is in relation to consumer representation that the two Charters are most strikingly dissimilar. Despite an expressed desire for 'evidence that the views of those who use the service have been taken into account in setting standards', and its enthusiasm in other passages for tenants managing estates and parents running schools, the Conservatives are silent on the issue of how passengers' needs and views are to find expression, and who is to champion their cause. By contrast, Labour's belief that 'if individuals are involved in the design and delivery of services they are much more likely to be satisfied with the outcome' underlies a commitment that 'the powers and resources of national and regional transport consultative committees will be extended so that they can better promote the interests of rail and bus passengers.'

This difference of attitude towards user representation nicely illustrates that, beneath the surface gloss, the two Charters are the products of two very different strands of thought. Writing under the auspices of the radical rightwing thinktank, the Adam Smith Institute, Madsen Pirie has argued that:

> Privatization has provided a valid answer to the problem of insufficient attention to consumers, especially where it has been accompanied by enhanced competition and the creation of an independent regulatory agency to oversee practices within the industry ... The need is to create pressures in the public sector to achieve some of the consumer responsiveness which competition and the need for profits create in the private sector. The traditional method so far has been consumer representation, and it is ineffective. Users' councils have been tried in several state industries ... allowing chosen consumer representatives to express their views directly to management. Unfortunately there are no effective powers to back up this voice, nor any means of ensuring that those chosen are indeed representative and remain so ... There are no penalties for ignoring the voice of the Users' Council, and no sanctions for it to bring to bear. (Pirie, 1991)

Similar misgivings have been heard on the left of the political spectrum. In a Fabian pamphlet which fuelled the rise of consumerism to prominence in official Labour thinking, Martin Smith recorded that:

In the public sector, consumerists have been able to argue that consumer representation is a necessary proxy for lack of competition ... Direct consumer representation is required to ensure efficiency, fair dealing, reliability and value for money. The Atlee Government created a network of nationalized industries consumer councils. In general [these] have been ineffective in policy terms. They are heavily constrained by inadequate powers and insufficient funds, and are rarely consulted until after key industry decisions have been taken. (Smith, 1986)

But if the diagnoses have been similar, the recommended cures (reflected in the respective Charters) are entirely different. In Pirie's analysis:

The two methods discussed are called 'exit', where customers can take their cash and shop elsewhere, and 'voice', where their views are made known through a representative body. The contest between voice and exit is no contest ... Consumers of state services shall be equipped with rights which seek to provide substitutes for the rights which people have as customers in a competitive market.

Such rights turn out to be 'redress, either to enable them to access an alternative service, or at the very least, to compensate them when the state services let them down'. The effect of this

will be to improve the services far more surely than would any collective action at the political level ... Transactions by individuals achieve a positive effect on the service in general ... It will be no bad thing if the public services ... begin to respond as the private sector does to such forces, and to employ many of the mechanisms which it uses in its response.

Labour's riposte to such arguments has been a reaffirmation of its collectivist instincts. 'Democratic socialism is about people recognizing that we depend on each other, and acting together to meet our mutual needs. That is why Labour is naturally the party of the consumer.' But it has coupled this with a frank admission that 'The truth is that changes which really empower consumers and service users are not easy to achieve.' Each of the public utilities, including transport undertakings, 'will be required to draw up customer service contracts specifying the level of service customers can expect and the redress obtainable – including financial compensation – if standards are not met.' But 'for individuals to act as a countervailing force to big business, they must use their power with others. Consumers will need help in organizing themselves and an advocate to speak on their behalf.' Therefore, at both regional and national levels, there would be utility councils to 'provide a vehicle for consultation, act as pressure groups and take up grievances, and they would have full rights of access to the enterprises.' At local level their management committees would be elected by subscribers (i.e., customers), possibly with additional nominees from user groups and local or regional authorities.

> There would be improved appointment procedures, to include nomination by community organizations and recruitment through advertisement. Staff would be fully independent of industry and government. These councils would be allowed to consider all relevant matters, including prices, and they would be under a duty to represent consumers at the open hearings held by each Office of Regulation.

Subventions from the relevant utility would provide funding. Additionally, Labour would 'investigate ways of enfranchising consumers of utilities, however the utility itself is owned. These will include consumer rights to elect consumer interest board members.' (Labour Party, 1989b)

So, while the Conservative theoreticians' answer to the perceived inadequacy of formal consumer representative bodies in the public sector is to jettison them, the official Labour response is to seek means of enhancing their credibility and influence. In practice, however, the reality on both sides has been somewhat different. Each of the major utilities privatized in the Thatcher years has been placed under the supervision of a powerful and largely autonomous regulatory agency, with an array of controls over standards and prices. And each of these agencies (Ofgas, Oftel, Ofwat, Offer) has been given a parallel network of statutory consumer advisory committees. 'Voice', to adopt Dr Pirie's term, is apparently still needed.

On the Labour side, what Martin Smith has termed 'producerism' has in some quarters appeared to remain the dominant ideology, with the Party's constitutional commitment to securing 'the common ownership of the means of production, distribution and exchange' being regarded as an end in itself, and with markedly less interest devoted to achieving 'the best obtainable system of popular administration and control of each industry or service' (Labour Party

Constitution, Clause IV). A false assumption has been made that the interests of the suppliers and users of a given public service are necessarily the same. Thus public sector unions have wrongly assumed that the blinkered defence of narrow sectional interests would automatically entitle them to popular sympathy and support – a mistake for which Labour has paid a high political price. And some local councillors have persuaded themselves that by the fact of their elected status they constitute the embodiment of consumer virtue – an illusion likely to be sustained for long only by those whose tastes in reading do not extend to the correspondence columns of any local newspaper. In David Piachaud's words, Labour 'imbued with an elitist paternalism, or subservient to union interests, [has] sometimes shown scant regard for users'. (Piachaud, 1991)

It is an underlying assumption shared by all contributors to this book that public transport is an essential element in the economic and social infrastructure of a developed society. If ready access for all to employment, education, public services, social contact, shopping, and recreational pursuits demands the provision of a comprehensive, planned and co-ordinated network of transport facilities, then experience worldwide has shown that state intervention is necessary to secure this end. Individual elements in the system may be operated by privately owned enterprises, either autonomously or under contract to public authorities, but the overall scale and pattern of provision cannot safely be abandoned to the vagaries of the market. The external benefits of efficient and affordable public transport (such as energy conservation, fewer accidents, less pollution, wider access to employment opportunities, lower consumption of scarce land and construction materials, and the reduction of traffic congestion) accrue to the community at large, not to users of the system alone, and should be paid for from the public purse.

The interest of the state must therefore extend beyond a narrow (though proper) concern with policing standards of safety and commercial probity to the funding, planning and quality control of the system as a whole. If the provision of public transport is to be regarded as a duty of the state, then arrangements must be made to ensure that due account is taken of the needs and wishes of those who travel on it.

How is such consumer representation provided for today, and what is needed to enhance its effectiveness?

Despite their names, which derive from the era of the long-defunct multi-modal British Transport Commission, the Central Transport

Consultative Committee (CTCC) and its regional Transport Users Consultative Committees (TUCCs) are concerned almost exclusively with the services of British Rail and, in practice, only with its passenger sectors. Their members are appointed (and can be dismissed) by the Secretary of State for Trade and Industry, and vacancies are not publicly advertised. Their funding is controlled by the government, and their senior staff are usually recruited from British Rail. They meet *in camera*, their minutes are not published, and (except in the cases of the Central, Scottish and Welsh committees) they have no formal duty to publish annual reports, though in practice they now do so. Though they are required to consider and make recommendations regarding matters about which representations have been received from users, such recommendations have no binding force, and surveys have suggested that few users are aware of their existence. Of 431 InterCity passengers recently interviewed by the Consumers' Association, for example, none had approached a TUCC in connection with any of the service shortcomings identified (Consumers' Association, 1991). Fares are excluded from the committees' remit, and for rail closure proposals, their role is essentially only to conduct hearings into the likelihood of hardship arising.

In London, the equivalent body is the London Regional Passengers Committee. Its scope extends to include all London Transport services (Underground, Docklands Light Railway, and – pending deregulation – buses). Ironically, on the very day that its Citizen's Charter was published, the Conservative Government announced its intention of stripping the London Regional Passengers Committee of its current responsibilities *vis-à-vis* bus users in London. Its staff are independently recruited, it sits in public, and its minutes are widely disseminated. But in most other respects it labours under the same limitations as the TUCCs.

Elsewhere, bus and coach users have no formal voice at all. Most of the Passenger Transport Authorities in the major conurbations, together with a handful of shire county councils, have created *ad hoc* advisory committees which include an element of user representation, drawn from local voluntary organizations. But these have no independent existence, are often dominated by members of the authorities they are intended to advise, are not normally involved in considering individual complaints and suggestions, and cannot influence the commercial operations which now account for the bulk of bus services. The Consumer Congress has called for the creation of means 'by which bus passengers can make their views known more effectively to operators, local authorities, and the government', but this call has gone unheeded (Consumer Congress, 1985).

The Civil Aviation Authority sponsors the Air Transport Users Committee (AUC), which has a duty to advise it on means of furthering users' interests. The AUC can and does take up individual cases – irrespective of the ownership or even nationality of the carriers involved – but its existence is not widely advertised, it has little contact with other consumer agencies, and its influence is largely dependent upon the seriousness with which the CAA, its parent body, chooses to treat any recommendations it may make. And although informal liaison exists, it is entirely separate from the statutory Airport Consultative Committees (ACCs) which are intended, *inter alia*, to represent consumer interests 'on the ground'. The membership of these bodies also embraces representatives of airport management, airlines, local authorities and environmental interests. So their concerns are by no means exclusively focused on passengers' needs (though the larger ones have spawned separate passenger services sub-committees), and in most cases their composition is effectively determined by the airport operators who service them and to whom they report.

Privatization of Sealink and the British Transport Docks Board, with their consequent removal from the scrutiny of the CTCC, has effectively ended what little provision once existed for statutory consumer representation in the shipping industry – except in the case of CalMac's ferries in the west of Scotland, which remain in public ownership and thus have a somewhat uneasy relationship with the Scottish TUCC. Only in Northern Ireland are all modes of public passenger transport served comprehensively by a single statutory consumer representative agency, the General Consumer Council for Northern Ireland. By a supreme irony, this body is the creation of the very Government which has so steadfastly resisted all calls for a similar agency to be established elsewhere in the UK.

Consumer representation in the public transport industry is patchy, fragmented, poorly publicized, and lacking in political clout. That public transport users need more effective champions is easily demonstrated. For instance, a MORI survey of eight different public utilities found that in terms of overall *satisfaction* with service standards, buses and trains ranked respectively seventh and eighth (National Consumer Council, 1990). In the Office of Fair Trading's most recent 'annual consumer *dissatisfaction* survey', road, rail, sea or air transport (taken together) was the fourth most likely to have given cause for complaint in a list of fourteen service categories, and first in the list of those in respect of which no action had been taken (Office of Fair Trading, 1991). Over the years, proposals for reform have come from a variety of sources, ranging from the Independent Commission on Transport to the Co-operative Party and from the Select Committee on Nationalized Industries to the British Section of the International Commission of Jurists. But the Conservatives have failed to remedy the position. (For a full description of the composition and powers of the existing transport consumer agencies, and of alternative suggestions for their reform, see Cartledge, 1991.)

So, what should be the key functions of a reformed structure for transport consumer representation?

There are four principal strands to the work of these bodies. *First*, they are channels through which comments, suggestions and complaints from users of the services can be investigated and, where possible, remedial action initiated or appropriate recompense offered. In this capacity they help to resolve grievances in cases where an initial direct approach to the relevant operator has failed to achieve the desired result.

Second, they provide a forum for public debate on all aspects of transport provision which impinge directly on users. Timetables, vehicle design, fares structures, ticketing systems, waiting facilities, information provision, passenger security, route patterns, interchange arrangements – all these, and more besides, are issues on which passengers have views, and on which their representative bodies must be consulted if the operators' decision-making is to be adequately informed.

Third, they are the agencies through which the quality of service delivered can be monitored and reported. Whatever their other limitations, both parties' Citizen's Charters acknowledge the necessity for setting clear targets for key elements of service quality: punctuality, cancellations, capacity, cleanliness, telephone enquiries, speed of ticket issuing, lift/escalator availability, and the like. Once set, attainment of these targets must be measured and shortcomings in performance identified and analysed, so that remedial action can be taken. And, periodically, the targets themselves must be reviewed.

Fourth, they are a lobby which promotes the interests of public transport users in the wider political arena. When service failures are attributable to causes internal to the transport undertakings, then the consumer bodies will properly train their fire in that direction. But traffic congestion, poor enforcement of bus priority schemes, inappropriate siting of public services, vandalism of railway equipment, lack of investment in new rolling stock and infrastructure, and under-provision of air traffic control capacity, are all examples of factors outside operators' control which can impair the services they offer. So the consumer bodies have a duty to direct their criticism equally to national or local government when political decisions impinge adversely on public transport. In such circumstances consumer bodies make common cause with the operators in pursuit of common interests.

Labour's current transport policy statement (Labour Party, 1989a) devotes an entire chapter to consumer rights. It is the first such statement from any party to give more than a passing nod to users' interests *per se*, and as such it is warmly to be commended. Included within it is a proposal for an undefined extension of the power and resources of the CTCC and TUCCs to 'enable them to play a stronger role as the advocates for rail passengers', while the TUCCs would also be enabled to act on behalf of bus passengers. But included too is a full panoply of other administrative organs, all of which are apparently intended to have some role in consumer advocacy and protection. There are to be a 'National Transport Forum', 'transport committees of elected regional authorities' with co-opted transport users, a 'regulatory commission', a 'Public Interest Commissioner', a 'consumers' ombudsman' for British Rail, similar 'transport consumers' ombudsmen' established by regional and local authorities, and 'local independent user and consumer groups' – all of these without mention of shipping or aviation. Confusion of roles and duplication of effort would appear to be almost inescapable if this plethora of agencies was ever to materialize. So some refinement is needed for workable legislation. The following recommendations are made in an effort to reduce the confusion and ambiguities embodied in the statement.

• Unless it can be shown to be impracticable, *common arrangements* should be developed for all public transport modes, so that regulatory and consumer representative bodies at each level would have a multi-modal remit and perspective. This should extend both to passenger and freight services, whether domestic or international.

• The *regulator* (or public interest commissioner, or perhaps 'Oftrans') should not be purely a consumer champion, but should be concerned to investigate whether value is being obtained for public money, and whether defined policy objectives are being met. In auditing policy options, the regulator would be a proactive equivalent of the present Monopolies and Mergers Commission.

- *Complaint handling* should continue to be part of the function of the transport users' councils, so that their views on issues of policy can be rooted in a direct knowledge of users' concerns. There would then be no separate requirement for an ombudsman, helping to avoid an excessive proliferation of agencies. In any event, ombudsmen can only deal with complaints about performance ('Did the train run on time?') and cannot adjudicate on matters of policy ('Should this bus be re-scheduled?'). The councils should have power to require disclosure of evidence and attendance of witnesses, and the right to disregard frivolous or vexatious representations.

- The regulator should be responsible for *licensing operators* in all modes, and enforcing contract compliance. He or she should be appointed by the government, perhaps on the advice of the National Transport Forum (a deliberative and advisory body performing on a larger scale the type of work now done by the Transport Select Committee), and should have quasi-judicial powers inherited from the Traffic Commissioners and the CAA. The transport users' councils would bring appropriate cases before the regulator for adjudication, when agreement could not be reached. Such cases would relate to legal obligations rather than policy, since the latter would be the ultimate responsibility of the elected funding authority (whether at national or regional level).

- *Safety* issues should be the responsibility of a wholly separate Inspectorate, working under the aegis of the Health and Safety Executive. The case for amalgamating the (currently separate) safety authorities for the various transport modes, and for establishing a common procedure for major accident inquiries, should be actively pursued.

- *Fares* levels should be determined by the relevant funding authorities, as part of their total transport finance strategy, but the transport users' councils should be consulted about them, and should concern themselves closely with issues of fares structure and ticketing.

- The drafting of *passenger charters*, including service quality targets, should be undertaken by the transport users' councils in consultation with the operators, but in the event of disagreement the relevant funding authority would arbitrate, and they would be promulgated as part of the contract for financial support. Thereafter, the transport users' councils would monitor compliance as part of their wider quality auditing role, and would bring evidence of significant failures to the notice of the regulator who would have power to impose both financial penalties and restrictions on operators' licences.

- The *transport users' councils* should be constituted at both national and regional level. The majority of members of the national council should be drawn from the regional councils. The recruitment procedure should be as open as possible, making full use of advertising. Care should be taken to achieve a proper spread of ages, sexes, occupations, ethnic backgrounds, and geographical knowledge, and to provide for representation of people with special transport needs. Local authorities would be encouraged to make nominations but would have no automatic right to membership – being a councillor is, in itself, neither a qualification nor a disqualification for serving on such bodies. Appointments would be made by the consumer protection authority at each level. The councils' convenors would be salaried, and other members would be reimbursed for expenses and loss of earnings. Members would serve as individuals, not as the mandated delegates of any sponsoring organization.

- Regional transport users' councils should have a duty (and funds) to foster the development of genuine *local user groups*, from whose ranks in due course the majority of their own members could be recruited. Their outreach and enabling role should extend to convening users' forums, passenger surgeries and the like.

- The transport users' councils should be funded by the government and the elected regional authorities, as appropriate, but the case for recovering part or all of the cost of their operations from the transport operators should be further considered.

- The transport users' councils should *not* be represented by voting members on the management boards of transport undertakings, as this would inevitably create conflicts of interest for the members concerned, and could lead to difficulties with questions of commercial confidentiality. The councils should, however, have the right to seek direct discussions with the management boards on all relevant issues, and there may be a case for entitling them to send non-voting observers.

- The councils should recruit their own staff, for whom a proper career structure should be developed.

- The TUCCs' present role in relation to *passenger rail closures* should be transferred to the regulator, who would conduct public hearings and make recommendations to the appropriate funding authority, with which the final decision would rest. The users' councils would make representations at the hearings on behalf of users generally. Consideration should be given to extending this model to other modes.

No system of representation, however sophisticated, can alone ensure that users' needs are fully met and the highest possible standards of service attained. But a properly resourced public transport system, with rigorous safety standards and appropriate policy objectives, enjoying full political support, is one of the hallmarks of a civilized society. The current emergence of consumerism to the forefront of political life presents an opportunity to extend transport users' rights and to create an effective mechanism for ensuring that their voice is heard.

The assistance of Stephen Joseph, Nick Lester and Eric Midwinter in the preparation of this paper is warmly acknowledged.

5

TRANSPORT FOR ALL: EQUAL OPPORTUNITES IN TRANSPORT POLICY

HILARY TORRANCE

Many people are wholly or partly excluded from public transport. They are often those who need transport most, and are most adversely affected by others' use of the private car. Safety issues deter many people, particularly women, from travelling. Improvements needed to open up public transport to everyone for the most part constitute no more than the basic requirements of a good transport system. Equal transport provision would alleviate a great deal of isolation and dependency and its impact would be felt by the social services and health services. This chapter suggests basic minimum standards to be established at national level, with implementation and enforcement the responsibility of local authorities, answerable to central government and to the community.

UNEQUAL PROVISION

First let us slay the myth of the man on the Clapham omnibus. His views will represent very few bus users, who tend to be women anyway. He is exceptionally fortunate to have caught that bus, to have managed to get on to it, to have found a bus that goes where he wants to go. 'Omnibus' means 'for all' but this would scarcely describe the buses operating in Clapham today.

Public transport in Britain is inaccessible, difficult to understand or find out about, unsafe, expensive and unevenly distributed. Everyone is affected by this; many people avoid using it by travelling by car, thus adding to road congestion and pollution; others have to put up with its inadequacies. However, there are many who are not served by it at all and either live their lives within the limited confines that they can reach on foot, or just stay at home. These can include people with disabilities, elderly people, children and their carers, the unemployed and low-paid, those living in certain areas both urban and rural, people who are subjected to particular forms of prejudice, racist, sexist or homophobic. The reasons for their being excluded wholly or partially from the transport system relate to aspects that affect everyone, but them in particular: inaccessible design of buses, trains and stations; the distance to the bus stop or station and the unpredictably long wait for the bus or train, compounded by inadequate interchange facilities; lack of necessary facilities such as seating, shelter, toilets and telephones; lack of staffing to increase personal security and assist the passenger to use the system; poverty of information about services available; the cost of the fares; and extreme lack of services in certain areas.

Ironically, the people least well served by public transport are generally those who need it most. They also receive more than their fair share of the adverse effects of other people's car usage in terms of pedestrian accidents, communities torn apart by major roads, pollution, and disruption to existing bus services by traffic congestion: it is the less affluent areas that are subjected to the brunt of road-building.

The need for access to transport has increased with centralization of services: the closure of many sub-post offices and small local schools and libraries, the building of large 'out of town' supermarkets where shopping is cheaper and the consequent demise of small local shops, and the need to travel further for work, have all widened the gap between the transport haves and have-nots.

The 'walk or ride a bicycle' solution is not available to everyone or for all journeys. Small children and shopping limit the mobility of many women, while those with disabilities or illnesses including many elderly people require motorized transport. Moreover, choice is essential if we are to achieve equality of opportunity in transport provision.

PRACTICAL REQUIREMENTS

If we first look at the practicalities of a transport system offering equal opportunities to its passengers, we find that they largely coincide with general requirements of good transport provision:
• frequency and reliability of services;

- ease of interchange between transport modes and services;
- better design of buses, trains and termini in terms of access, safety, comfort, facilities;
- appropriately positioned bus-stops with shelter, seating, lighting and intelligible information;
- adequate and intelligible information about services;
- affordable fares;
- more services, including night and early morning and off-peak;
- alarm systems and safety devices with a human backup;
- transport provision where there is none at present, including buses going onto estates;
- sufficient well trained staff for safety and assistance;
- cleanliness and absence of offensive graffiti or advertising.

However, if equality is to be achieved these 'general requirements' need to take into consideration the special needs of individual passengers. For instance, access involves wheelchair access; information must be intelligible to those with sight and hearing disabilities, as well as to people who are illiterate or whose language is not English; night transport is needed for those who work unsocial hours including many black and ethnic minority workers for whom personal security is essential.

Minimum standards need to be drawn up for equal transport provision, and they need to be enforced. This can be achieved by a partnership between a national and a local transport authority with a remit to determine, impose and monitor standards, answerable to a watchdog body which can call on appropriate legislation to make good deficiencies.

TRANSPORT NEEDS OF PEOPLE WITH DISABILITIES

Transport is a prime consideration for people with disabilities. Because very few buses or rail services are accessible to wheelchairs, many people rely entirely on special services provided for them. These include Dial-a-Ride or Ring-and-Ride services run in London by London Transport and in other parts of the country by local Passenger Transport Executives and districts offering door-to-door transport in wheelchair accessible vehicles. Use of these is heavily restricted because of lack of resources: they have to be booked in advance but cannot be booked on a regular basis and only a limited number of journeys is permitted so they cannot be used to get to work or to college. London's Taxicard system, paid for by the individual local authorities, has been very popular but depends on the willingness and capacity of local authorities to finance it: several boroughs are now limiting the number of journeys permitted to one a week so it is no longer a means of getting to work or college. London Transport runs special wheelchair accessible 'Mobility Buses' on selected routes, generally operating each route once a week with one outward and one return journey. This clearly allows none of the freedom that able-bodied people expect in planning their schedule, nor does it help with the problem of getting to work or college. All these services are run on the basis that people with disabilities are lucky to be offered transport at all, ignoring the possibility that people with disabilities might work, study, take an active role in the community or live a full social life. As long as such services rely on the limited financial resources of individual councils, there cannot be any improvement. Central government funding is needed to ensure that people with disabilities can participate fully in everyday life.

Many more people with disabilities would be able to use mainstream public transport were it not for the design of our buses, trains and stations, as well as the state of our footways. The Department of Transport Disabled Passengers Transport Advisory Committee (DPTAC) specifications propose certain standards for buses involving handrail heights, painted lines etc. to help people with various disabilities, but these are only recommendations, and do not provide for wheelchair access. Deregulation has seriously impeded the powers of local authorities to enforce standards. Although some 70 per cent of new buses bought now conform to the DPTAC specification (or similar standards) few bus companies are financially able to purchase new vehicles, so most buses on the road remain the old, less accessible designs.

Considerable improvement is needed to our streets where the potholes that inconvenience everyone may render them unusable to someone with a disability. Dropped kerbs, textured surfaces, street furniture, length of phasing on pedestrian crossings are crucial. Local authorities should be under the same obligation to make public streets accessible as they are for public buildings. But improvements to the street environment must go further than this if truly accessible transport is to be made possible. Level access buses and trams can admit wheelchairs with minimal technological input, but depend on the level of kerbs. We need to work towards a uniformity in our footways and streets; this will demand a considerable investment into the infrastructure but will transform the potential of public transport.

In 1991, the European Community was close to legislating on a directive which would assert the right of all disabled people to have transport to work (COM(90)588). The directive allows the responsibility for providing this transport to lie with the employer and goes no way to promote the cause of accessible transport in general. Once again, people with disabilities are offered a concession which does not acknowledge their rights to participate in all aspects of living. A further 'Resolution on Access to Buses, Trains and Coaches' (CEMT/CM(90)21) is under discussion. In its present form it is specific about what is needed to make transport accessible to people with disabilities, although on the subject of wheelchair accessibility 'further research and exchange are necessary on the safe carriage of wheelchairs on buses ... [and] on coaches.' This resolution has some way to go before it is adopted and made legally enforceable. One can only hope that it is not diluted until it serves no purpose, like the directive on transport to work.

A European Community Directive might eventually force the hand of the Department of Transport. However, action is needed immediately to create the infrastructure that would enable the Directive to be enacted. This cannot be left to 'market forces'; legislation is needed to empower and compel local authorities to demand certain standards of access from the operators they license, while government money should be made available to operators to make access improvements to vehicles, stations etc. and to local authorities to provide necessary improvements to streets and footways. An accessible infrastructure will be expensive to achieve, but this should be a one-off expense which will put our streets on a level with other parts of Europe such as Sweden and Germany. However, as noted by DPTAC (1990) this investment should produce considerable savings in public health expenditure (see also chapter 9).

SPECIAL TRANSPORT PROVISION

If mainstream transport provision is brought up to the standard suggested in this chapter, little special transport provision will be necessary. In the meantime, there will still be people whose needs are not met, and so the importance of alternative systems will continue. Community Transport is an important initiative to bring transport to people who are not adequately served. Community Transport schemes, mainly funded by local authorities, vary in their operation. At their most basic they provide and service minibuses for use by community groups for outings. Their vehicles are generally wheelchair accessible and may be used to get people to further education classes, to take elderly people shopping, parents and small children to the seaside, and teenagers to facilities outside their immediate area. They are invaluable to a considerable range of people whose lives are otherwise limited by lack of transport, including black and ethnic minority people, representatives of all age groups and people with disabilities. Community Transport provision is dependent largely on the goodwill of the local authority. It needs to be presented as an essential service, as it caters for a considerable number of local residents, and should be accepted as an integral part of local transport planning and funding.

The development of Women's Safe Transport schemes in some parts of the country providing cheap door-to-door transport with a woman driver has enabled many women, including pensioners, women with disabilities, and ethnic minority women to attend educational, social and cultural functions from which they were formerly barred. The oldest of these is the Stockwell Lift Service in south London. The organization and funding of these vary, some operating as an offshoot of Community Transport, and with money from local authorities, the Department of the Environment and various forms of sponsorship. Unfortunately, the vagaries of voluntary sector funding have often rendered these schemes difficult to operate. Too often they are allowed too little time and too few resources to prove their ability to meet a need (London Women's Safe Transport Group, 1988).

The above are two examples of initiatives to meet local transport needs. Some local authorities have attempted to provide scheduled bus services which fill the gap left by mainstream provision, for instance, the Hounslow Hoppa, a wheelchair accessible shopping service sponsored by Hounslow Council and run by London United under contract to London Transport presents the rare phenomenon of a bus which everyone can use and which goes where people want to go.

SAFETY

There is considerable debate about whether or not public transport is safe to use. What few would question is that many passengers feel unsafe using it, and many are afraid to use it at all, particularly at night. These same people may be afraid to go out in the street, and this fear may be more or less justified according to where they live or where they have to go.

A high proportion of women and elderly people feel unsafe going out at night, or even in the day. The Greater London Council 'Women on the Move' survey in 1985 reported that almost a quarter of the women interviewed never go out at night, a result echoed in the 'Merseytravel' Harris Poll of 1988. Concern is also felt by black and ethnic minority people who are subject to racist assaults, and lesbians and gays who may be harassed or assaulted because of their sexuality. Some of them may need to travel outside the daytime hours as women, and black and ethnic minority people often work unsocial hours, while lesbians and gays, as well as ethnic minority people may have to go further for their social and cultural life. Thus the journeys they need to make are often at times when service frequencies are reduced and when stations are destaffed.

Journeys to work at rush hour may be unpleasant, but the journeys of night workers can be perilous. These are often women, fitting in work with childcare, and night workers are generally low-paid so they tend not to have cars nor to afford taxis. Many are from ethnic minorities. Women's Safe Transport schemes can help these workers. Otherwise, tax incentives should be offered to employers to provide works buses. On trading estates, a group of companies could combine resources.

To enhance the safety of travellers does not come cheap:

- services need to be increased to minimise walking and waiting;
- pedestrians should not be required to use subways and underpasses to cross roads, and where there is no alternative in stations, they must be properly lit and overseen;
- stations should be adequately staffed for safety at all times that they are open;
- buses and trains should be crewed by more than one staff member;
- technological safety devices (alarms, video cameras, emergency telephones) should be provided where they can contribute to security, but only with human backup so that help can be given;
- local authorities must have the responsibility of providing proper street lighting, and ensuring proper lighting at bus and rail stations.

The economics of safety are always a problem. If a higher level of staffing should lead to less frequent services, or the closure of stations, little has been achieved where safety is concerned because walking and waiting are increased. Although bus passengers in the cities may feel safer with crewed buses, one person operation is generally accepted in rural areas and service levels are more important. Need for numbers of staff at stations may be reduced by sensible design whereby one member of staff can see what is going on throughout the station, and has immediate radio contact when help is needed. Passengers should know when stations are not staffed so they have the option of avoiding them. The requirements of personal security had best be determined locally as there will be variations.

The responsibility for ensuring the provision of reasonably safe transport for all members of the community must lie with the regional or local authority who should consult representatives of those groups most concerned about personal safety. To encourage extra expenditure on schemes to promote personal security, a Department of the Environment or Health and Safety Executive agency could administer special funding to be used for schemes to enhance personal security, such as Women's Safe Transport, extra staffing at stations, and extra night bus services to estates. Transport planners should be fully conversant with these issues when looking at interchanges, lighting and facilities.

A CHANGE OF ATTITUDE

If we are to achieve equality of transport provision, we need first of all to regard it as a right for everyone to be able to go out and reach their destination in the normal course of their day-to-day affairs. We need to recognize the cost of denying this right: lack of mobility leads to loss of education, employment, recreation and self-sufficiency and consequently to poverty, depression and stress-related illness. Isolation intensifies the problems that undermine quality of life in Britain. The money that we decide not to invest in public transport will eventually be spent on trying to cope with these problems.

Private car ownership might appear to be the solution for many of those who are at present excluded to varying degrees from using public transport, as the private car provides accessibility, convenience and safety. However, for the people who could make best use of it, it is rarely an option they can afford. They must therefore suffer the impact of other people's cars, paying the cost in pedestrian accidents, disruption and contamination of the environment and dislocation of public transport services, while new luxury facilities for shopping and recreation offer inducements accessible only to car owners.

The solution could not possibly be for everyone to have a car;

increase in car ownership would be self-defeating in terms of congestion, pollution and environmental damage. If we are to reverse the trend of car dependence, we must look first at the local community and ask how people are to get to school, college, training centre, shops, work, park, swimming pool, sports centre, hospital, dentist, post office, Job Centre, Citizens Advice Bureau, cinema etc. We must consider whether the transport means available are failing sections of the community and why. We must then attend to the deficiencies. The needs of the community must be given priority over the motorway running through it. This in its turn means ensuring alternative transport for the car users. It means reassessing investment in road-building so that road developments take the form of tunnelling and cutting rather than new construction or widening. To achieve this will require a radical change in the planning policy and priorities of the Department of Transport and the Department of the Environment.

Standards of transport provision dictate whether or not people will be able to use the system and will be safe using it. Regulations imposing standards of reliability and design are a matter for legislation. To establish appropriate criteria wide-ranging consultation is required with a full range of potential travellers. A national forum would be required to agree minimum acceptable standards while a local forum would put these into the context of regional requirements. Having established the criteria, they need to be enforced through licensing procedures involving local authorities or Public Transport Authorities, who would be answerable to central government where minimum standards are not upheld.

Most important of all, future transport strategy must look at how best to serve the entire community, rather than weighing up the value of one potential passenger over another, and gearing the system to those nine-to-five working people who can contribute most in terms of cash. Imagination is required to encompass all possible journeys and remove the impediments in the way of so many people who wish, and need, to travel.

6
WOMEN AND TRANSPORT

KERRY HAMILTON AND LINDA JENKINS

Transport is an essential aspect of women's lives: it determines our access to a wide range of resources in society, including employment, childcare, education, health and the political process. Conversely, the transport world has been slow to see the relevance of women, women's needs or women's issues to the plans and decisions which they make.

Yet women have travel needs which are as significant as those of men, though radically different in many respects. As consumers of transport provision, however, women have too often been assumed to have identical needs to men's, or simply to be unworthy of note. A wider point, however, needs to be made at the outset. The concept that transport provision should be geared to people's needs – in the same way as, for instance, education and health provision – is a minority view in this country: public transport has been excluded from welfare state thinking.

GENDER DIFFERENCES IN TRAVEL PATTERNS

The major problem in attempting to analyse transport and travel in gender terms is, of course, that transport statistics are often not broken down by gender at all. Our knowledge about gender differences in travel behaviour, therefore, remains fragmentary at this stage. A partial picture has emerged from a small number of regionally based surveys, notably that carried out on behalf of the GLC in 1985. In many cases, however, there are no readily available national statistics.

In this section, we will draw on these available sources of data and supplement them with references to some local statistics relevant to our own study in West Yorkshire (see Hamilton, Jenkins and Gregory, 1991). The aim is to offer a synopsis of the main differences between travel patterns of men and women, to highlight the communalities in women's travel experience, while at the same time drawing attention to examples of differences between women and to the varying regional contexts which may affect gender divisions in transport.

In terms of total number of journeys made, available information indicates a fairly even split between men and women. For instance, the GLC/LRT Travel Diary Survey for Autumn 1984 indicated that women and men in the Greater London area made an average of 18.6 and 19.9 trips per head per week respectively. What this means is that, on average, men make just over one more trip per week each than women. These figures are congruent with those of the 1978/79 National Travel Survey, where the women in the sample accounted for 48 per cent of all journeys made.

When the travel indicator is mileage rather than trips, however, a very different pattern emerges. In every age group, men make substantially longer journeys on average than women, and this differentiation is most marked for people in the 30-59 age range (see Table 4.4b, National Travel Survey, 1978/79). A footnote, however, in the National Travel Survey discreetly reminds the reader that walks under one mile have been excluded from the analysis. Since other research has shown that women make a relatively high proportion of their journeys on foot and over relatively short distances this calls into question the validity of the comparison.

Nevertheless, journey length varies markedly by journey purpose, and here gender is an important covariant. For example, 40 per cent of shopping trips and 39 per cent of 'escort and other' trips, compared to only 17 per cent of journeys to the place of paid employment, were under a mile in length (DTp, 1986). Correspondingly, as Table 6-1, below shows, journeys to 'work' tend to account for a higher proportion of men's journeys while shopping and personal business trips and 'escort and other' trips account for a higher proportion of women's, at least in the 20-60 age range. Unfortunately, these statistics do not show up the gender-split as clearly as they might since shopping has been aggregated with 'personal business' and 'escort trips' with 'other trips'.

Employment status is very relevant to this pattern of gender differentiation. The differences in travel pattern between men and women in full-time employment are very slight, whereas those between women in full-time employment and those with full-time caring and domestic responsibilities are marked.

Table 6-1: Percentage of Journeys Made by Men and Women for Various Purposes, Broken Down by Age.

Journey purpose		Age 16-20	Age 21-29	Age 30-59	Age 60-64	Age 65 and over
Journeys to work	Men:	25	31	35	33	5
	Women:	25	19	22	10	2
Shopping/ Personal business	Men:	20	22	24	29	53
	Women:	26	35	40	55	62
Escort and other	Men:	1	3	6	4	2
	Women:	1	11	8	1	1

Source: DTp (1978/79:21)

Leaving aside for the moment the rather complex interrelationship between journey length, journey purpose, transport mode and gender, we will focus now on the very central issue of gender differences in the kinds of transport used. These need to be seen in the context of the overall modal split. Nationally, in 1985, buses and coaches accounted for 42 billion passenger kilometres, or 8 per cent of all passenger transport, while cars and taxis accounted for 426 billion passenger kilometres (82 per cent) and rail transport for only 36 billion passenger kilometres or 7 per cent of the total (see Table 1.1, DTp, 1986).

Generally speaking, women make proportionately more journeys by bus and on foot and as car passengers than men do. In the National Travel Survey 1978/79 sample, women made 63.3 per cent of all journeys by bus, 73.5 per cent of all journeys as a car passenger and 59.1 per cent of all walking journeys, but only 23.7 per cent of all journeys made by car drivers. Correspondingly, of all journeys made by women, the largest proportion, 41 per cent, were made on foot, while 22 per cent were made as car passengers and 16 per cent each were made as car drivers and bus users. (See Lester and Potter, 1983; Table 21). Information from the 1984 General Household Survey also underlines the relatively greater importance of bus travel for women (see DTp, 1986a: 102).

For men, on the other hand, journeys as car drivers account for almost half of all their journeys (49 per cent), while walking accounts for just over a quarter (27 per cent) and bus use and trips as a car passenger for only 9 per cent and 7 per cent each respectively. (See Lester and Potter, 1983: Table 21, based on National Travel Survey 1978/79 data). Motorcycles, bicycles and trains are, however, relatively little used forms of transport in this country (accounting for 1 per cent, 3 per cent and 2 per cent of all journeys and 1 per cent, 1 per cent and 7 per cent of total passenger kilometres respectively; see DTp, 1986a: 102). These national statistics are corroborated by more recent regional ones, with some variations, which indicate that there is a strong need both for more local studies, encompassing a wide range of geographical locations, and also for more research at national level.

In addition, there are differences between men and women in terms of the way in which they use public transport – for instance, the preponderance of women passengers is even greater in the off-peak period, as compared to peak-time bus services. To take an actual example, in Leeds, women comprise 60.5 per cent of peak time bus passengers and 64.4 per cent of off-peak passengers (see Leeds Bus Passenger Survey, 1985).

So far, we have talked only of gender 'differences' in travel patterns, almost as if the fundamental differences between men and women in terms of journey length and purpose, and transport mode, were a matter of choice – a case of 'separate but equal'. However, in the case of travel mode in particular, the choices clearly are not equal. The 'great divide' may be seen primarily as being between those who have and those who do not have the use of a car. The availability of a car for personal use has major effects on travel patterns. The more cars that are available within the household, the more people travel by car rather than by any other means of transport. For example, National Travel Survey data indicates that members of households in which there is one car make 54 per cent of their journeys by car, while, for members of households in which there are two or more cars, the proportion is 68 per cent. Car availability also increases the extent of travel generally: for instance, members of households in which there are no vehicles make an average of 32 journeys per week, compared to an average of 102.5 by households with three or more cars (see Lester and Potter, 1983: 9-10).

Since travel is rarely an end in itself, but almost always a means of reaching particular facilities, it follows that car ownership dramatically increases the level of access to resources. The extent of travel generally, and car travel in particular, are strongly related to income and socio-economic status. All the statistical indications are that owning and driving a car, and the ability to travel far and often, go hand in hand with wealth, status and power. Conversely, not holding a driving licence and not having the use of a car are major aspects of transport disadvantage. Transport disadvantage is not equally or randomly distributed throughout society, but follows the well established lines of structural social inequality. Gender is a major dimension of structural inequality, but there are others: working-class people, black and ethnic minority groups, those with disabilities and the very old and very young are also disadvantaged.

There are also, of course, important regional variations on a number of indicators of prosperity and advantage. And although 'women' can be abstracted as a category for analysis and be shown to be receiving a less than equal share of resources, they are far from a homogenous group. Having made these qualifying statements, the fact remains that the gender imbalance in car availability and licence holding is dramatic. Statistics based on the 'household' as a unit of analysis have done much to mask the full extent of the inequality. In 1980, 31 per cent of women and 68 per cent of men were qualified to drive (DTp, 1985). That is, over two-thirds of men and less than one-third of women held a full driving licence; but again there are regional variations. Results from the Panel Survey carried out by West Yorkshire Passenger Transport Executive immediately prior to deregulation (i.e., in September 1986) indicate that only 28 per cent of the women in the sample of 2,194 held a full driving licence.

Furthermore, the number of women having both a full driving licence and substantial access to a car is even smaller, though more difficult to assess. In the GLC Women and Transport Study, 34 per cent had a driving licence, but only two-thirds of these (i.e., 23 per cent of the whole sample) had primary access to a car (compared to 88 per cent of male licence holders) while 11 per cent had no access to a car at all.

Some West Yorkshire figures can be offered here for comparison. Firstly, the West Yorkshire Metropolitan County Council Transportation Survey of 1981 indicates that, for instance, among manual workers, only 9 per cent of women have both a driving licence and sole access to a car, whereas 47 per cent of men do. 'Economically inactive' women of working age ('housewives') are also very unlikely (11 per cent) to have the sole use of a car as a driver. Graham Read (1983) provides a more detailed analysis of the same data base. In the sample of 11,420 men and 12,113 women he found that 36.4 per cent of men had sole and unrestricted access to a car compared to only 9.2 per cent of women. Read (1983: 78) comments: 'A high proportion (64 per cent) of male licence holders in one car owning households are the sole driver, as opposed to 20.7 per cent of female licence holders ... Among shared vehicle users, males are far more likely to be priority users than females.'

This provides ample confirmation that all household members do not benefit equally from the presence of the car. Consequently, it is not surprising that even where there is a car, or cars, in the household, women are still inclined to be more dependent on public transport than men are. For instance, the General Household Survey reveals that, in 1982, among those living in one car households, the percentage of men using buses dropped markedly to 41 per cent while the percentage of women remained high at 69 per cent. Where there were two or more household cars, only 20 per cent of men used buses, compared to almost half (48 per cent) of the women. Among members of non-car owning households, however, the gender difference is almost absent; 84 per cent of men and 86 per cent of women had used buses in the last six months (see DTp, 1985: 103).

To the extent that a contracting public transport system fails to meet the needs of the population in general and women in particular, access to private transport becomes essential for access to a range of resources. Employment is a case in point: the indications are that there is a strong association between having access to a car and having access to employment. Those in employment are more likely to be able to afford a car, and those with cars have a better chance of finding a job.

For example, the GLC Women and Transport Survey found that 'for those women who are in paid full-time or part-time work, the most commonly used method of travel to work is as a car driver' (24 per cent compared to 21 per cent travelling by bus and 21 per cent walking; 8 per cent used British Rail; 13 per cent the Underground and 9 per cent as a car passenger), and this in a context where car travel accounts for a smaller proportion of the modal split than the national average.

THE POSITION OF WOMEN IN THE SOCIAL STRUCTURE

The Department of Employment's Family Expenditure Survey states that in 1985, it cost an average of £11.28 a week to maintain and run a motor vehicle, and the figure of £8.68 for the purchase of the vehicle, spares and accessories must be added to this, giving a total cost of £20.48 per week. However, this figure is well below that of around £35 or more per week which is quoted in, for instance, consumer magazines, and which includes an element for the depreciation of the vehicle. The Automobile Association currently gives a figure of 33.9 pence per mile as the running cost of a car with an engine size in the 1000 to 1500cc range. Multiplied by 10,000 miles per year (which is still below the average of 12,000 miles which is the rule of thumb in the motor trade) this gives a figure of £65.19 per week! (On this basis, even a car under 1000cc, with an estimated running cost of 28.26p per mile, would cost £53.80 per week, while one in the 1500-2000cc bracket at 40p per mile, would cost £76.92 per week.) Although income is not the only determinant of access to car travel, there is obviously a clear link between women's relative poverty and their low car ownership given this order of expense.

Even after many years of Equal Pay Legislation, women's pay lags far behind that of men. In 1984, women's gross hourly earnings, excluding overtime, were 73.5 per cent of men's. Additionally, because women's hours in paid employment are, on average, less than those of men, the disparity in weekly take-home pay is even greater than this comparison suggests. For instance, 30.7 per cent of women compared to 11.4 per cent of men in full-time employment worked less than a 36 hour week in 1984, while only 9 per cent of women, compared to 37.6 per cent of men worked more than 40 hours per week in their paid employment.

This economic inferiority has much to do with women's labour being less highly valued than men's: the wage differential cannot be explained in terms of differing levels of education or skill. Discrimination against women *per se* offers a more plausible explanation (Rubenstein, 1984). Additionally, women's jobs tend to be concentrated in the badly paid 'service sector' of the economy. Regional differences in wage levels also compound the inequality. For example, since almost 60 per cent of full-time workers in West Yorkshire earned less than the Council of Europe's 'decency threshold' of £125.60 per week in 1986, it is little wonder that car ownership is an option for so few (West Yorkshire Low Pay Unit, 1987).

The scale of inequality, however, runs much deeper than this. The dramatic increase in women, especially those with young children, in paid employment has been one of the most important structural changes in the labour market over the last twenty-five years. Women now comprise 46 per cent of employees – almost half working part-time: of the approximately 9 million female employees in Great Britain, 5 million worked full-time and 4 million worked part-time, while among men there were 11 million full-time, but only 0.7 million part-time employees (Social Trends, 1985).

Women's earnings as part-time workers tend to be low, not only because of the pro-rata reduction, but also because part-time workers generally are in a vulnerable position in the labour market. In West Yorkshire, for example, in 1985, 84 per cent of women part-time workers were low paid (WYLPU, 1986). Even these figures may represent an underestimate of the scale of the problem, since they are based on recorded figures. Much of the women's part-time employment is 'casual' and, therefore, not reflected in the official statistics.

Why are women so badly paid and why do they work part-time when the rewards are so low? Apart from the low valuation of women's labour, generally speaking, women have fewer employment options than men. Domestic responsibilities heavily restrict women's choice of employment. What is often overlooked, however, is that transport options also have a very strong bearing on whether a woman can take up a job or not. Where women live is often determined by the workplace of the male partner, who is defined, for the most part, as the main 'bread winner'. Such are the restrictions on employment opportunities for women that it is common for a woman returning to work afater a period of full-time childcare to take a less skilled and more poorly paid job than she originally had (e.g., qualified secretaries working as shop assistants or cleaners). Homeworking, mainly done by women and the lowest paid of all types of employment surveyed by the West Yorkshire Low Pay Unit, is probably the clearest and most extreme example of the way in which women's bargaining position in the labour market is reduced by transport and childcare constraints. According to the Department of Employment estimates, there were 400,000 home workers in Britain in 1983 – the great majority of whom were women. But recent research indicates that these figures are an understimate (see Allen and Wolkowitz, 1987).

Women's economic position cannot, however, be fully explained without an understanding of the institutionalization of the economic dependence of women upon men. Historically, the male dominated trades unions have played an active role in promoting wage inequality by supporting the idea of the 'family wage' – i.e., that wages paid to the male earner include an element for a non-earning wife and dependent children. Apart from the perpetuation of women's economic dependence on men, this system also penalizes the very large number of female headed households and overlooks the vital contribution of women's earnings to domestic finances (see, for example, Barrett and McIntosh, 1982; Himmelweit and Ruehl, 1983.) The still prevalent idea that women work for 'pin money' is, in fact a myth. In 1984, official government statistics estimated that one in ten households were female headed, but 15 per cent is probably now a more accurate figure. Additionally, it has been estimated that, without the earnings of married women, four times as many families would be living below the poverty line (see Martin and Roberts, 1984.)

Despite the well documented diversity of household and kinship formations in contemporary Britain, the systems of social welfare and taxation also continue to be based on inaccurate normative assumptions about the prevalence of the male breadwinner/female homemaker/dependent children ideal. In addition, there are myriads of more subtle ways in which the cultural ideal of marriage based on male bread winner/economically dependent female child carer pattern is disseminated and upheld (see, for example, Rappaport et al., 1982; Gibbons, 1985).

This ideology of the family has been shown by contemporary sociologists to form a corner-stone of the major institutions of society such as religion, law, education and, of course, it is also widely promulgated by the mass media, and forms the mainstay of soap operas and advertising alike. This is so strong and pervasive that to many it seems 'only natural' that women get married, give up paid employment to look after their children at home, and receive no direct payment (apart from child benefit) for the massive and vitally important job of reproducing the labour force. It is little wonder then that women's domestic and childcare labour has only recently, after a long battle by feminists, been defined as 'work' at all.

Despite the movement of women into the paid employment market, the sexual division of labour within the household persists. The result has been an expansion of women's roles rather than the achievement of gender role equality. Women's activities may reflect any combination of roles, as for example, paid employee: student; unpaid domestic labourer; carer of children, sick or elderly people. Women continue to be primarily responsible for housework, including shopping and child rearing. (For instance, the GLC Women and Transport study found that 96 per cent of the women in their sample said that no one else in the household besides themselves regularly did grocery shopping.)

Probably less visible is the unpaid work which women do caring for sick and elderly adults. Because of changes in the age structure of the population, there are now more dependent old people who need to be looked after, and the carers, whether paid or unpaid, are almost exclusively women. The implementation of 'community care' policies, for example, draws heavily on the labour of unpaid women carers (see Finch, 1984).

All of these types of 'invisible' work have important transport implications. Some, such as the high proportion of shopping and escort journeys made by women, are fairly obvious. Escorting elderly and infirm relatives on public transport journeys to hospitals, doctors, and sometimes also on shopping trips, as well as escorting children to nurseries, childminders, schools and a whole range of social and leisure activities, tend to be carried out by women, particularly when the escort journey is by bus or on foot. Others, such as women's greater reliance on off-peak services for both access to part-time employment and for trips related to their domestic and caring responsibilities, are less obvious. Additionally, the traditional classification of journey purposes is based on male assumptions about the nature of 'work'. Many journeys to friends and relatives which are categorized as 'social' may, in fact, include a significant amount of socially necessary caring work.

SOCIALIZATION AND PSYCHOLOGICAL GENDER DIFFERENCES

It can be argued, quite justifiably, that some aspects of women's position in the social structure are shared by other disadvantaged groups in society. For instance, economically dependent or low-paid young people, low-paid men, and black and ethnic minority groups are also economically disadvantaged, and so are likely to be more dependent on public transport than other groups in the population. Additionally, a minority of women have neither significant caring responsibilities nor multiple roles while a minority of men do, precisely because 'gender' is socially rather than biologically constructed. However, even the single, high-earning female and the childcaring, shopping-carrying, role-reversed male are constrained by their location within a deeply patriarchal society.

Men and women do not merely 'play different roles' (note this term implies a high degree of choice), they also tend to be different kinds of people. Gender differences in attitudes and behaviour at adulthood are largely the result of environmental, learning or 'socialization' factors (see, for instance, Maccoby and Jacklin, 1974; Hoyenga and Hoyenga, 1979; Block, 1984). To understand the full extent of gender inequality, we need to appreciate that socialization begins at birth and is a continuing process throughout the life span.

The interrelationships between gender, personality and travel behaviour appears to be an area which is wide open for research. For instance, women's relationship to the private motor car is in general somewhat different to that of men's. The discrepancy in incidence of licence holding cannot be accounted for solely in terms of economic inequality. Socialization antecedents of men's greater interest in things mechanically in general, and the motor car in particular, date back to the days of Dinky Toys, Meccano and train sets for Christmas.

The important point is that women's access to private motor transport is likely to be severely constrained by a variety of psychological factors such as lesser interest in and 'ego involvement' with cars, less developed mechanical confidence and ability, and a perception of roads as a hostile, threatening, perhaps even alien environment. In addition, it can be argued that women's lesser mobility, transport options and thus access to resources plays an important role in maintaining the existing imbalance of power.

Women's attempts to learn to drive are often (expensively) spread over a period of years (in some cases decades) and those negative attitudes and experiences in relation to both cars and driving persist long after the driving test is passed. Opportunities for driving practice, both as a learner and as a full licence holder, were often found to be constricted by the attitudes of male relatives, notably husbands (see Hamilton, Jenkins and Gregory, 1991). Uncovering these car-related patterns of dependence and control is an area requiring much more research.

ANATOMY IS DESTINY

While subscribing to the view that the 'biological' is itself socially defined and mediated, not to acknowledge that there are observed physical differences between men and women, whatever their origins, or to refuse to consider the ways in which these differences may be relevant to any particular issue, would evidently be absurd.

For instance, there are well documented average differences between men and women in height, weight and shape. These ought to have important implications for vehicle design, although this would appear to have seldom been the case. It seems likely that physical differences, in size at least, partly account for the legendary popularity of the Mini among women. Again, seat belt design takes no account of the shape of women, particularly in pregnancy. With regard to bus design, if women and children constitute a majority of passengers, should buses not be desiged primarily with their physical specifications in mind? This would have particular relevance for step height, seating design, positioning of push bells and grab rails, for example.

Gender differences in physical size and strength and mobility are also relevant to women's greater vulnerability to attack and harassment and thus greater concern with personal security as a transport issue. (The roots of male violence against women, however, have much to do with the relative *powerlessness* of women, rather than with size or strength). Again, women's footwear and clothing often restrict their mobility, making it more difficult to escape or fight off an attacker. For reasons more complex than might at first appear, therefore, women are more likely to feel vulnerable to, and less able to physically deal with, a variety of forms of assault. Women's perceptions of the likelihood of encountering assault, abuse of harassment while travelling by various transport modes therefore merits detailed investigation since this is likely to act as a restriction both on their own mobility and access, and on their uptake of public transport provision.

DEFINING WOMEN'S TRANSPORT NEEDS: THE IMPLICATIONS FOR TRANSPORT PLANNERS

The 'invisibility' of women's work is only one of the wider problems of the invisibility of women. The relevance for those involved in transport policy of the aspects of gender inequality outlined above may be summarized as follows: women, as a socially defined category of people, compared to men have –

- primary responsibility for childcare and domestic work;
- multiple roles – combining paid employment with the unpaid work of domestic labouring and caring;
- more constrained opportunities for paid employment and a much greater likelihood of being engaged in part-time and/or casual employment, usually local. (For instance, the GLC study found that 30 per cent of the employed women in their sample could reach their place of employment in less than 15 minutes; only 11 per cent of their journeys took longer than one hour. For a detailed discussion of the relative importance of gender role constraints and

travel costs in limiting women's employment options, see Pickup, 1984.);

- a socialization history which is quantitatively different from that of men, the transportation implications of which have yet to be studied;
- a smaller physical size.

Taken collectively, the transport implications of these major features may be outlined as follows:

- Women are less likely to be able to afford private transport and hence are more dependent on walking and public transport. Even when women can drive and there is a car in the household, only a minority have a primary access to a car for their own use. Furthermore, social-psychological as well as economic factors place limitations on the feasibility of car-driving as a transport options for many women.
- Women make around the same number of journeys as men, but a higher proportion of these are local or short distance. As Finch (1984: 12) comments: 'The small local area is essentially women's territory because while most men live significant parts of their lives away from their place of residence, most women (even if they do some paid work) live most of their lives in the area bounded by the local shops, the school and the bus stop.' The provision of short-distance local transport is, therefore, of prime importance for women.
- Because of women's role as carers, a significant proportion of women's journeys are made primarily to accompany a child or elderly or disabled adults. This has important implications for vehicle design and staffing considerations. It has been abundantly clear from our own research that such escort journeys are not well catered for by current public transport provision. Women with young children are the hardest hit in this respect. One-person operation, high step height and inadequate luggage space make buses an even less convenient option than walking in many cases. The problems of travelling with young children continue to be underestimated by transport planners (see Hamilton, Jenkins and Gregory, 1991).
- Shopping for food and other domestic needs is a major component of women's unpaid domestic labour. Shopping accounts for 25 per cent of women's journeys (GLC, 1985-86). It follows that on a

significant proportion of women's journey's they will be carrying heavy loads. Again, design and staffing considerations are apparent.

- Since many women have to combine two or more roles, a substantial proportion of their journeys will be multi-purpose. This often results in women's travel patterns being highly complex and variable. This does not make them amenable to simple categorization. It is unlikely, therefore, that conventional survey research will reveal an accurate picture either of women's travel behaviour or of their transport needs.

- Since almost half of women in paid employment work part-time hours, it follows that a substantial proportion of their employment related as well as other journeys (e.g. shopping trips) will be made outside of 'peak' travel times. This has implications for the realtive frequency of 'peak' versus 'off-peak' services.

- The division of both paid and unpaid labour along gender lines in our society has potentially far-reaching implications for gender differences in journey destinations or purpose, and so for route and service level planning. In addition to obvious consequences such as women being more often responsible for trips to shops, schools and health care facilities (i.e., accompanying or visiting others), there are also less obvious ones. For instance, women have been shown to take more responsibility for the 'emotional work' of maintaining socially supportive relationships, particularly within kinship groupings. Social visits made to ensure the psychological welfare of elderly realtives can be regarded as socially necessary in the same way as trips made to provide material support, such as house cleaning, babysitting or shopping. Particular attention therefore needs to be paid in research and planning terms to the nature of the transport needs associated with women's social visiting. Visits to hospitals and to friends and relatives – though these are particularly important to women – are seldom a priority for transport operators.

- Women's lower social status and smaller physical size render them more vulnerable to attacks and abuse of all kinds, primarily from men. Available research, indicates that the fear of harassment, abuse or assault effectively prohibits many women from moving around freely, especially, after dark. (See, for instance, Block 3 of the 1985 GLC Women and Transport Survey; and Lynch and Atkins, 1987). Women feel especially vulnerable while waiting for public transport and taxis. The frequency and reliability of bus and train services, as well as staffing considerations and the design and lighting of waiting facilities, are therefore particularly important to women.

IDENTIFYING WOMEN'S TRANSPORT INTERESTS

Responsibilities for transport are very fragmented, with district and borough authorities, central government and a variety of appointed executives and joint authority committees having separate spheres of influence. The deregulation of bus services in October 1986 further undermined the capacity of the Passenger Transport Executives for planning transport policy in a co-ordinated way. Results show that competitive tendering has not led to much innovation or improvement in service provision, while many services, particularly those in the evenings and at weekends and in areas of relatively low demand, have actually deteriorated. (For some examples of studies of the initial effects of deregulation, see Preston, 1988; Headicar *et al*, 1987; SEEDS, 1987; Guiver and Hoyle, 1987; Belcomber *et al*, 1987.) Added to this are the difficulties faced by PTEs in trying to provide co-ordinated time-table information and in persuading operators to keep fares steady, exacerbated by cuts in funding from central government. All this adds up to a great deal of uncertainty about the future of bus services as well as a deepening of previous regional variations in the quantity, quality and price of public transport. Any deterioration in the bus services will hit women harder than men, and the effects could be far-reaching.

So far we have centred our analysis on a needs-based approach: we have shown that women's transport needs are distinct from those of men and that they are poorly met by current transport policy and provision. This approach perhaps carries a suggestion that women as a social group are especially 'needy' – a suitable case for charity. The implication, then, would be that women's social needs outweigh their social contributions; that they were a deserving case but nevertheless a drain on resources. The refutation of this possible implication involves acknowledging the origins and causes of women's economic and social inequality. The first point to be re-emphasized here is that women's labour is underpaid, undervalued and often not recognized. The conventional yardsticks of social worth and contribution, notably taxation, take no account of women's unpaid labour. Second, women's relative deprivation has been reinforced by deliberately market-based policies. These effects are cumulative, and compound each other. For instance, reductions in off-peak services (which incidentally began long before deregulation) reduce women's access to part-time employment which, in turn, limits their purchasing power in the transport market.

These complications make it difficult as well as inappropriate to develop our gender analysis along traditional cost-benefit lines. However, it is possible to take a wider macro-economic approach to the evaluation of 'costs' and 'benefits' than is normally taken when COBA is applied to specific transport projects and policies.

If this wider approach is taken it becomes possible to present examples of ways in which women bear the the costs of particular transport policies or projects while receiving disproportionately few of the benefits. These indications run directly counter to any suggestion that women are subsidized by current patterns of transport investment and policy. First, the costs, both to the individual and to the nation, of private car travel (which mainly benefits men) are generally underestimated. At July 1979 prices, the cost of road accidents in 1980, in terms of strains on the emergency and health services and loss of production, has been estimated at £1,730,000,000 (Dawson, 1987: 8-9). Even the most readily visible costs of car travel are enormous, and only a fraction of these are met by (predominantly male) motorists through road taxes and taxes on petrol. The remainder is met by the population as a whole via taxation, rates and personal costs incurred through damage to self or property, for instance, women's primary role in caring for accident victims), but receive only a fraction of the benefits. Public funding of public transport and the pedestrian environment, from which women receive proportionately more benefit, is paltry by comparison.

There is also another way in which transport investment discriminates against women. In the Department of Transport's evaluations of proposed road-building schemes, construction costs are weighed against time-savings for motorists and others (time delays are also taken into account, but only in a narrow sense). In order to do this, a monetary value must be placed on people's time. Predictably, the time of train passengers and car drivers (mostly men) is taken to be worth around twice as much as that of bus passengers (mostly women) (Dawson, 1987: 10)!

Biases in the taxation system, peculiar to Britain, act as a further subsidy on car travel. Companies' expenditure on cars for their employees is eligible for tax relief. These 'company cars' account for somewhere between a half and two-thirds of the news cars bought each year, and an estimated one-fifth of commuting (see TEST, 1984). Altogether, the total value of such tax subsidies to the car owners has been estimated at around two billion pounds per year – i.e., two million times greater than the government subsidy to the passenger railway. Since the great majority of company car users are men, this subsidy represents another aspect of policy which discriminates against women. Furthermore, company cars make a significant contribution to traffic congestion, particularly in London (TEST, 1984; 1991a, 1991c), and heavy demands on parking space, both of which generate costs which are borne by women as pedestrians as well as in general.

In addition, over the last few decades there have been a number of trends in land use planning which have contributed to women's transport disadvantage. These can only be briefly summarized here. First, car use has encouraged the development of sprawling, low density suburbs. These are difficult for public transport to serve and also, by widening the physical separation of homes and paid work places, place additional constraints on women's employment options. This also tends to be a feature of the New Towns which sprang up in the 1960s.

Second, the 1970s were the era of motorway building in cities, a notable example being Leeds, the 'Motorway City of Europe' (Starkie, 1982). It seems to have gone largely unnoticed that this process of reshaping the cities to accommodate the car had adverse effects on the pedestrian environment, and thus on women (National Consumer Council, 1987). Major roads act as a barrier to movement between areas, whether these are pedestrianized or not, while the precincts which accompany such schemes themselves are often deserted at night, or frequented by gangs of youths, making them a virtual no-go area for women.

Third, car use has encouraged the development of large, out-of-town shopping centres and hypermarkets, to the detriment of existing town centres and local neighbourhood facilities. Not only does this affect public transport, but by having shops, and indeed all facilities, spread more widely, motorized travel has become necessary for more and more journey purposes. Consequently, the range of facilities available for pedestrians has shrunk significantly. Huge new retail developments in out-of-town locations are not only virtually inaccessible without a car, they are specifically aimed at car owners for marketing reasons. It follows that the majority of women must be dependent on someone else for access to them, despite the fact that they continued to be primarily responsible for shopping.

Fourth, the 1980s have seen continuing trends towards the centralization and 'rationalization' of a wide range of essential services such as schools and hospitals. How such reorganizations affect women's access to facilities, and their associated transport needs has, to the best of our knowledge, rarely been studied even after the event, let alone taken into account at the decision-making stage.

All four of the trends outlined above may be seen as conferring benefits on car users at the expense, in some way, of non-car users. All may, therefore, be seen as having a polarizing effect on existing transport facilities along age, class and ethnic, as well as gender lines.

Currently, the indications that gender inequalities in transport may be reduced are not hopeful. While relatively more, mainly younger, women are obtaining driving licences, the vast majority of car drivers are still men. Meanwhile, sales of new cars, having levelled off to some extent during the 1970s, reached a record level of 1.95 million in 1989 (*Observer*, 25 October 1987). While public transport is caught in the uncertainties of the deregulation era, the 1990s looks like being yet another 'Decade of the Car' – a cause for celebration for some, but cold comfort for many women waiting at the bus stop.

This paper originally appeared in *Gender, Transport and Employment* edited by M. Grieco, L. Pickup and R. Whipp and we are grateful for their permission to reproduce it here.

7

THE TRAFFIC GENERATION GAME

NICHOLAS JAMES AND TIM PHAROAH

There is no guarantee that greater mobility leads to greater satisfaction.
(OECD, 1977)

Present conditions seem designed to ensure that we attain higher and higher levels of motorization. While some see this as a sign of economic health, the social and environmental costs indicate that our growing car dependency is a problem that deserves urgent attention. Britain is still only half-way to car ownership saturation levels, and most towns and cities retain structures ideally suited to walking, cycling and public transport use. However, the more roads that are built, and the more out-of-centre, car-based developments that are permitted, the weaker these traditional urban structures become. The chapter argues for an urgent reassessment and integration of transport and planning policies and outlines a number of strategies that should be implemented to develop a more rational relationship between land uses and the transport that serves them.

INTRODUCTION

Why the 'traffic generation game'? The real problems of modern transport are associated with excessive use of motor vehicles. The processes by which this traffic is generated can be likened to a game in two ways. First, the rules of a game have no intrinsic merit; they are designed to make the game playable. Second, the appeal of a game lies in its detachment from real life. So it is with traffic generation. The tax breaks, subsidies, fare levels and planning rules appear to be designed to play a perpetual game of 'motorization', which in reality has little to do with solving transport-related problems. New rules are sometimes added, like 'freedom of consumer choice' and 'non-interference with market forces', but again the links with reality are tenuous. There is, for example, little freedom to choose a lifestyle that does not involve dependence on the car, whilst the market in clean air and quiet surroundings is grossly interfered with. Questions need to be asked about *whose* freedom, and *which* markets are to be protected, and these are too serious to be answered by game playing.

LAND USE PLANNING AND LOCATION CHOICE

All travel arises from the benefit of doing different things at different locations, and transport is thus a means to an end rather than an end in itself. It follows that transport is a cost and not a benefit, and that society will be more efficient if, for a given level of economic and other activity, the amount of travel can be reduced. The aim should therefore be to reduce overall transport costs, not just the private costs of travel but including the costs of supply, and the unwanted environmental and safety costs. Unfortunately, the trend is in the opposite direction. Households spend growing amounts on travel; journey distances are increasing; freight movement is increasing; and as larger proportions of journeys are made by private motor vehicle, the external costs of travel are becoming unmanageable. Much of this is assumed to be an inevitable if not wholly desirable consequence of economic growth, and the one third increase in car traffic between 1980 and 1988, for example, has been presented as an indicator of economic recovery and therefore 'a good thing'.

The unpleasant symptoms of this traffic growth, including environmental damage and congested transport facilities, arouse increasingly passionate feelings, but it is the overall value of the traffic itself that needs to be questioned. The fundamental objective of the spatial aspects of planning should therefore be to create settlement patterns which allow people to have better lives with less traffic. The extent to which people make travel and location choices that are consistent with this objective, however, depends on more than simply making such choices *possible*. Location planning therefore must be integrated with other aspects of transport, fiscal and social policy.

This definition of the integration of land use and transport planning takes us well away from earlier concepts which led in the 1960s and 1970s to seriously flawed plans for large-scale and highly destructive road-building in urban areas. Criticisms of that approach have been well documented (see, for example, RTPI, 1989), but the main problem was the obsession with meeting unrestrained demand for car use, and the almost total neglect of every other aspect of the transport problem (Thomson, 1969). The so-called 'Land Use Transportation Study' was a technique born of the North American culture, and miscarried to Britain and other parts of Europe. Whilst many of the shortcomings of such studies are now recognized, a legacy of mistrust still surrounds the term 'integrated land use-transport planning'.

The link between transport and land use at first sight may seem obvious, but there are at least three distinct levels on which the two need to be integrated, which are here termed 'physical', 'structural' and 'operational' integration.

Physical Integration

Buildings must be designed and located so that their users can come in and out, and to and from. The need for engineering and design to achieve a safe and efficient interface between individual buildings and the transport system should be self-evident.

Structural Integration

The need for motorized travel will not be reduced if related activities are located further away from each other. Distances between homes, workplaces, shops, health, education and recreation facilities must be kept short so that journeys can be made on foot or by bicycle. To the extent that not everyone can live within a walk or cycle trip of all the places they want to reach, facilities must be arranged at 'nodes' or along corridors of movement so that public transport can easily serve them. This 'structural integration' of transport and site-based activities should be aimed at achieving 'minimum travel'. Because land use change and new development occurs relatively slowly, major results cannot be achieved in the short term. But equally, a long-term satisfactory outcome requires proper decisions about incremental and piecemeal land use changes.

Perhaps more important, there is an urgent need to protect Britain's rich legacy of towns and cities that were laid out before the motor age, whose potential for supporting minimum travel lifestyles is being daily eroded by new roads and car parking and competition from car-based developments. This is an environmental threat which has not been fully acknowledged.

Operational Integration

'Physical' and 'structural' integration are valuable in themselves, but they tend to ignore the enormous variation in travel patterns that can occur without any change of land-use, or any change of transport infrastructure. People are continually changing the location of their various activities. For example, each year 10 per cent of people change their home, and many people change their place of work. Frequent day-to-day choices are also made about where to shop, recreate, socialize etc. Indeed, activity choice is expanding as basic community facilities like schools and hospitals are seen as marketable commodities in competition with each other, rather than as serving local populations. There is also, of course, a continual turnover of people at every stage of the life cycle! Within a few years, therefore, it is possible for travel patterns (mode, direction, time and length distribution of journeys) to have completely changed without any change at all having been made to transport infrastructure, buildings, or even the uses to which buildings are put. Activity change is therefore just as important as land use change.

To influence activity location it is necessary to integrate other aspects of public policy which affect people's decisions about how, when and where to travel. We refer to this as 'operational integration'. There are many strands of public policy involved, from vehicle and fuel taxes to road tolls and parking charges; and from housing allocation policy to school and hospital catchment areas.

The main problem, however, is the direct and indirect subsidies to private motor transport (both lorries and cars) whereby most external costs are borne by society at large and not by the users. People therefore, both as individuals and as representatives of corporate bodies, make their location decisions and their travel decisions on the basis of travel costs that are artificially low.

Thus while physical and structural integration can create the possibility for travel patterns that are less burdensome on society, these choices will not actually be made whilst other aspects of transport, taxation and public policy leave major distortions in the travel market.

CHANGING COURSE

Transport related problems result from a mismatch between what is desired, and what is available. The impression is often given that the only problem is congestion and a shortage of roadspace. But clean air, quiet surroundings, safety and security on the roads, freedom to walk and cycle, and access for everyone to good public transport are also in short supply, and shrinking fast. The answer to alleviating these shortages does not lie solely in the provision of more transport capacity, be it public or private, but in a balance between supply expansion and demand limitation.

By and large, people are not making more journeys, but they are making longer journeys, and they are making an ever-increasing proportion of their journeys by car. Land use decisions are being made which are increasing the level of car dependence. New large stores, leisure facilities and businesses that are located away from established centres remove people's choice of transport mode. Those with cars have no choice but to use them. For everyone else, reaching such facilities becomes a near impossibility. As Illich (1974) cogently stated, 'motorized vehicles can create new distances which they alone can shrink. They create them for all, but they can shrink them for only a few.'

Many journeys are made by car because of the poor quality or expensiveness of the alternatives. Perhaps the best example of such 'forced' car use is the journey to school (see Jones, 1977; Rigby, 1979). On the one hand, the proportion of children driven to school has risen as parents have become increasingly reluctant to let their children face the danger of crossing busy roads on foot and alone. This process is of course self-reinforcing, since as more people drive their children to school, so traffic levels around the school grow, increasing the level of danger for the rest. On the other hand, the creation of fewer, but larger schools means that for many children, walking to school is simply not an option, due to the distances involved (see also chapter 17).

The issue is therefore not how much access we need, but how much motorized mobility we can afford. A new policy framework within which location and development decisions are taken needs to be devised that will contribute to the objectives set out earlier in this book. This means setting a new course, and a reversal of the current trend towards land use patterns and location choices which depend on the car and the lorry as the main mode of travel. A series of problems need to be addressed directly by this new policy direction.

- Choices for non-car users are restricted, because they are forced either to use local facilities which are declining in number and quality, or to make long and arduous journeys by public transport, cycle or foot to the new facilities.

- The diversion of resources from established centres can result in the withdrawal of investment, planning neglect, poorer maintenance, the erosion of civic pride and the acceleration of decentralization.

- Direct competition with established areas (e.g., out-of-town retail developments with traditional centres) can cause economic and cultural decline.

- Fewer people using public transport or walking, heightens problems of personal security, and those reliant on public transport or their own two feet are often those who are most vulnerable to attack – for instance women, the elderly or members of ethnic minorities. The result is a further reduction in these people's freedom (see also chapter 5).

- Increasing use of cars and lorries results in more danger. The threat from high traffic levels means many children are not allowed to venture out alone, and elderly people are frightened to make trips on foot. Again the 'freedom' of car users erodes the freedom of those without.

- Development of a dispersed, car-based society necessarily has severe implications for the environment. Longer distances by car are obviously less energy efficient than short distances by foot, cycle or public transport. Similarly, extensive car use is producing serious air pollution problems. The catalytic convertor is no more than a palliative since reductions per vehicle will be overtaken by increases in vehicle use, and in any case it does nothing to reduce carbon dioxide. Most people in urban areas are also affected by problems of road noise and vibration. Finally, road-building and the development it encourages often impinges on the natural or semi-natural environment.

The popular notion that mobility is good in itself must be challenged if solutions are to be found. Much play is made of the evils of congestion but congestion is no more than a symptom. The assumption that a system is satisfactory simply because it is congestion-free is erroneous. Congestion-free cities are not uncommon in the USA, yet these cities have failed to solve other aspects of the transport problem, and the levels of environmental damage are increasingly seen to be unsustainable. In the European context, present and predicted car mileage means major environmental destruction, yet car mileage per capita is less than half that of the USA, as shown in Table 7-1. Much lower car ownership is partly a result of positive choice because of the quantity of public transport (most clearly seen in London). Conversely, much car ownership in rural areas is forced upon people because of the lack of alternatives.

Table 7-1: Car Ownership and Use in Selected Western Countries, 1988.

	Cars per 1000 people	Car kilometres per capita, per annum
UK	360	4865
France	394	5366
FRG	474	6152
Italy	296	4024
Netherlands	351	5270
Spain	282	1897
Sweden	416	6071
USA	629	11169

Although many of the underlying conditions are different, experience in the USA does provide a useful lesson for the UK. Unterman (1990) provides an excellent chronology of the US plunge to car dependency. Before the Second World War, suburban development was generally designed to be used by pedestrians, with growth usually focused around tram or train stops, often with small retail centres associated. However, after the war, returning GIs needed housing and employment. Munitions factories turned to car production, while the oil and construction industries boomed. The government focused this energy into suburban growth. Rising car ownership dictated the shape of these suburbs, and rarely did new streets include facilities for pedestrians or cyclists. Planning became reactive – simply providing road infrastructure to meet demand. Local centres were replaced by commercial strips where buildings were separated by extensive car parks. As Unterman suggests, in many cases it was safer to cross the road by car than on foot! The planning system unquestioningly shifted to its new role – everything about suburban development was seen as positive, and no one questioned the consequent environmental degradation, energy consumption, loss of community or pedestrian safety.

Britain is perhaps half or two-thirds of the way towards car saturation. But the choice we need is not between cars and more cars, but between cars and other less destructive means of getting about.

In seeking new solutions to transport problems, two major opportunities should be recognized and exploited. First, like the rest of Europe, but not the USA, over three-quarters of the population lives in urban areas which were substantially laid out before the mass motor age. We know, therefore, that we could (if necessary) survive without the car. Adjustments in lifestyle would undoubtedly be painful for some, but blissful for others. Retention of these older urban structures means that much unnecessary traffic can be avoided. Industrial restructuring over fifty to eighty years, however, would make it more difficult to manage without the lorry.

The second opportunity lies in the fact that car ownership is currently lower in Britain than in many other European countries. This is usually presented as an indicator of the economic backwardness of Britain, yet this is only because we orient our judgments around the fortunes of the motor industry rather than with broader visions of the quality of life.

The policies advocated below exploit these opportunities by conserving and regenerating the urban fabric, by promoting a new faith in the city, and by improving the quality of alternatives so that people actually choose less car travel.

SUGGESTED POLICIES

The final section of this chapter attempts to outline a set of policies which the authors believe are workable and capable of bringing major improvements.

- Patterns of land use and urban form which enable accessibility for all should be conserved and maintained as an important national asset. This could be achieved through strategic and local planning machinery, backed by national transport and land use policy. The Dutch 'Compact City' policy could be explored as a model. Research (e.g., Edwards, 1977: 117-26; Newman and Kenworthy, 1980; 1988; 1989) indicates that compact cities have significantly lower energy consumption. An immediate consequence would be a presumption against out-of-centre developments.

- New urban development should be based on a hierarchy of transport modes and economic functions. Thus daily needs should be able to be met within walking distance, whilst employment and more specialized services should be located within reasonable cycling distance, or at a location where bus or train routes are focused.

An example of such a system is the Dutch new town of Almere, near Amsterdam. Neighbourhoods are focused around infants schools and local shopping and health facilities, and provided with excellent pedestrian routes to allow access. Larger shopping centres, schools and employment areas are within reach of a dense network of cycle tracks, and also of a segregated system of bus routes which stop no more than 400m from any home. Finally, bus and cycle routes give access to railway stations, and thus to Amsterdam. In this example, cars are restricted to a small number of roads, and often access houses from the rear, the normal 'street' being for pedestrians and cyclists only.

In Toronto (Nowlan *et al.*, 1990), the introduction of more housing in the central area has already helped reduce commuting. In Portland, Oregon (Newman and Kenworthy, 1989), the local authority has reoriented its policies away from cars and towards public transport – replacing a proposed freeway with a light rail system. The city aims to focus urban growth within the light rail corridor, with the potential to save energy, reduce car ownership and use, and reduce environmental pollution. A similar policy has been adopted in Greater Vancouver, where high density development is now focused at stations along the city's new light rail system. Other cities (e.g., Vienna and Copenhagen) apply similar principles to expansion at the edge of existing settlements (TEST, 1988).

- Access involving minimum distances can also be achieved by sensitively increasing the density of urban development and by mixing land uses. Single use office developments are more likely to generate car trips than mixed developments which include shops, restaurants, health or leisure facilities. Large areas of housing will similarly generate more car trips than areas where employment, shopping and education are integrated. Cervero (1988: 429-46) cites a study carried out by the US Institute of Transportation Engineers which found that mixed land use developments in Denver reduced trip generation rates by as much as 25 per cent.

- Large office and commercial development and other major generators of passenger trips should be permitted only at focal points of the public transport system. Location at individual stations or bus-stops in suburban areas will not succeed in reducing the proportion of access by car. Car parking must be strictly limited if car dependency is to be avoided. This limitation will further encourage developers, and people who are moving, to favour locations with good access by 'town friendly' modes.

- Distribution depots and other land uses that generate large volumes of heavy goods traffic and relatively little passenger traffic should be located for convenient access to the major road network and, where possible, to freight rail or water depots.

- Strategic plans should identify a hierarchy of employment and service centres, together with a strategy for them to function without the car. Non-residential development outside these centres (such as out of town superstores) should not be permitted, with clear national and regional government backing for such decisions.

- Transport issues should be fully integrated within the planning system. The detachment of the planning system from transport issues is well illustrated by a recent RTPI report (1991) which states that 'development control tends to focus on highway rather than transport matters. An application tends to be assessed in terms of its effects on a local road network in the short term, rather than on the urban form in the longer term.' Transport should be neither an add-on extra, nor an end in itself.

  The scope of Development Plans should be widened to include non land use policy such as public transport fare and service levels, parking charges and controls, and road and traffic regulations. The objectives of Development Plans should include the reduction of traffic and car dependence. Traffic management and traffic calming schemes should come within the meaning of the term 'development'. This would have the twin advantage of encouraging town planners to take a more active interest in traffic and transport issues, and bringing such locally important issues into the statutory consultation machinery currently enjoyed only by land use proposals.

- An 'accessibility audit' should be undertaken of all developments involving a change in the use of land. This should pay particular attention to the needs of those with a physical handicap, women, children, the elderly and others traditionally left out of transport planning. Inaccessibility by certain groups of users should be a ground for refusal of planning consent.

- New transport and land use developments should also be the subject of an environmental audit, and refused where agreed pollution limits would be exceeded, as in Switzerland.

- Strategic planning authorities should have overall control over the pattern, quality, frequency and price of urban public transport services, and be responsible for their integration and marketing. The private sector should continue to be involved in the provision of services, but according to specified levels. The value of competition between operators should be exploited, but only off-road through the contract tendering process.

- All transport tax, investment, subsidies and transfer payments should be reviewed and amended to encourage environmentally and socially benign modes of travel, and to penalize other modes in relation to the damage they cause. The outcome of such a review would include removal of company car subsidies, including subsidized parking, and taxation of vehicles graduated according to the damage they cause. A 'Green' tax, such as discussed in other chapters, forms an alternative to legislation. Revenue from road user charges (as opposed to general motor taxes) should be used to finance public transport improvements, including fare subsidies if appropriate.

- Incentives for rail freight (e.g., tax exemption on industrial sites linked to rail) and break-bulk depots should be increased.

- Research is required into homeworking and other potential means of reducing physical travel using electronic communications. Views of the effectiveness of new technology as a means of reducing people's need to travel are, however, mixed. While being able to work from home, or from a small local base, may reduce people's need to travel to work, the freedom to live where they want means that many people may relocate to inaccessible rural locations where a significant amount of travel is required for other activities such as shopping, education or entertainment, and where public transport is relatively poor. Salamon (1985: 215-35) concluded that the net effect of telecommunications on travel would be minimal.

- There should be heavy investment in the quality of public transport, coupled with disincentives to use private transport. The priority should be the improvement of intra- rather than inter-urban public transport.

- There should be a substantial shift of expenditure priorities away from provision of road capacity to investment in alternative methods of travel, and away from inter-urban to urban transport.

- Policies to limit traffic should be aimed first of all at regular longer-distance car trips, and car commuting trips to inner and central city locations. (Removal of company car subsidies, for example, would be in line with this policy). The least damaging category of car trip might be the occasional short journey for which no reasonable alternative is possible.

- Interchanges, vehicles and other transport facilities should be developed as a means of encouraging multi-modal transport. Ensuring that all trains carry bicycles, and new park and ride facilities are examples. Combined transport should be promoted with environmental objectives for both freight and passenger journeys.

- Higher car purchase tax and/or other disincentives to multiple car ownership are required. Taxation should also be designed to discriminate against vehicles which create more danger and more environmental damage. Alternative types of access to cars that offer the potential to reduce car ownership, including short-term local car rental, should be the subject of research and experimentation.

- A major investment programme to implement traffic calming measures should be undertaken. The target should be to achieve a self-enforcing 20mph speed limit on all streets except main through routes in built-up areas by the end of the century. Consideration should be given to ways of funding traffic calming measures through contributions from owners of frontage property likely to benefit, and private sector sponsorship schemes. This is seen as a way of improving civic consciousness, as well as increasing the pace of implementation.

- The general non-urban speed limit should be reduced from 70 to 55mph, and enforced using electronic surveillance. Automatic speed governing of vehicles (now the subject of active experimentation in Germany) should also be studied as a medium to long-term possibility. The purpose is to reduce casualties, energy consumption and pollution, and to improve the competitive position of rail.

• Comprehensive controls over parking provision and enforcement are required. National parking standards should be set for both residential and private non-residential parking provision. These should be integrated with plans for public transport improvements and proposals relating to the other land use policies in order to reduce to a minimum the overall requirement. Incentives and taxation should be designed to reduce current over-provision, especially at office and commercial locations.

Finally, the policies outlined above should be accompanied, as far as possible, by targets so that the effectiveness of the policies can be monitored and evaluated. Such targets will need to be related to the specific objectives outlined in chapters 2 and 3. An equally important element will be information. The successful adoption of a green transport policy for Britain depends on there being a clear explanation of the policies and why they are being adopted and, subsequently, what their benefits have been.

8

THE MACHINERY OF GOVERNMENT

STEPHEN JOSEPH, NICK LESTER AND MICK HAMER

The Department of Transport is actively distrusted and has a low reputation. This chapter outlines ways to regenerate it, changing it from an emphasis on 'producers' (road haulage, road construction etc.) and a split by mode, to an emphasis on policy and a split by function. A land use-led Department of Planning and Transport is proposed, with task forces as appropriate. Links with other departments are examined, and proposals made for controlling and setting objectives for nationalized industries and quangos. The chapter also proposes substantial devolution of transport decision-making to regional and local level, subject to nationally set policy objectives. Stronger links to European policy are considered. Better environmental and consumer input to decision-making at all levels is proposed and the means to achieve this outlined. The role of a National Transport Forum as a watchdog and contributor to transport policy is discussed.

INTRODUCTION

Getting the machinery of government right is one of the most important tasks a government can attempt. The reputation of the Department of Transport, though, means that there is much to put right. It is actively distrusted on a wide scale and has an appallingly low standing inside and outside Whitehall. No single improvement could do so much good as a regeneration of the Department of Transport.

This paper considers this regeneration, including the relationships between the Department and other parts of national government, with local government, quangos, nationalized industries and Europe.

THE DEPARTMENT OF TRANSPORT

Although transport functions are considered by a number of departments of state, it is the Department of Transport which is the linchpin of governmental responsibility for transport issues. The Department of Transport, however, is ill-suited to this role. In its present structure, it is motivated largely by its own view of policies. In his famous memorandum promoting the concept of a rigged public inquiry into heavier lorries (Transport 2000, 1979), Joe Peeler, an official in the Department's Freight Directorate, said that it was necessary to overcome 'public and parliamentary opposition' to the 'departmental view'. There is no evidence that this clearly unacceptable approach has changed.

There can be little doubt but that there needs to be a full re-organization of the Department of Transport to bring about a cultural shift in its approach to its responsibilities. The Department's main focus needs to move from supporting departmental ideas to implementing the policies of the Government. That is, the basis of the Department's position must change from representing the vested interests of 'producers' towards identifying and safeguarding 'consumer' interests in transport. This would include balancing the needs of the citizen as traveller with the needs of the communities they pass through.

Currently, the Department has six types of role:

- policy-making, over the whole range of Britain's transport;
- financial allocation, including for local government, within a broad figure set by the Treasury and DoE;
- executive, on the trunk road network;
- regulatory, on issues such as road signs and traffic law;
- quasi-executive, in areas covered by nationalized industries where the DTp has a far bigger role than it will usually admit to;
- quasi-judicial.

These different roles operate in a confused way. Because the structure of the Department has reflected a producer or industrial base, rather than a user or functional base – despite the stated aims of the Department – the organization is divided more by transport mode than by departmental function, with different divisions responsible for:

- trunk roads;

- local transport;
- railways;
- public transport (excluding BR);
- aviation;
- shipping;
- freight.

Regional offices cover some of these issues but are largely roads based. Common services exist solely on such issues as information, statistics and research. An 'Urban and General Policy Unit' was set up in 1991 covering cross-modal issues such as environment and safety, and policy on urban traffic and public transport, but this unit is inadequately resourced and appears to have insufficient influence to provide a strategic approach for the Department. To complicate matters, the Scottish and Welsh offices undertake responsibility for some of these modes, principally for trunk roads.

The modal division of the Department continues up to permanent secretary level and is replicated in the ministerial division of responsibilities, with separate ministers responsible for public transport, roads and traffic, and aviation and shipping. Only the Secretary of State has any effective cross-modal view. There is one exception: transport in London's docklands is entirely the responsibility of the Minister for Public Transport.

It is this 'producerist' view of transport which is central to the Department's malfunctioning. Except when courted in aid of particular pet projects, the Department finds the public's view very hard to accept, and, indeed, makes few attempts even to discover what it is.

The most important task, therefore, is to re-organize the structure of the Department of Transport so that it no longer divides itself by mode, but by function. Broadly, therefore, this should result in four types of activity:

- policy, which should include the quasi-executive and financial allocation roles;
- regulatory, much of which might go to separate agencies or regional authorities;
- quasi-judicial, which needs to be entirely separate;
- executive, which perhaps should not be a direct function of the Department of Transport but devolved to 'arm's length' for all modes.

Such a division puts the emphasis onto the policy role of the Department. This subsumes a number of separate areas, which clearly need to be broken down, in turn. But the divisions should not repeat the mode based problems of the past. They should rather reflect the needs of users. They should also ensure that environmental and community needs are brought firmly into the picture and, in particular, that the links between transport and land use are cemented. At present these links are very weak. The Department of the Environment is responsible for land use planning and has poor relations with the Department of Transport.

OPTIONS FOR REFORMING THE DEPARTMENT OF TRANSPORT

Possibly one approach would be to recombine the Department of Transport within a Department of the Environment. Yet, given the DoE's wide range of other responsibilities, this may be too unwieldy to operate as a co-ordinated whole – a problem that existed between 1970 and 1976 when the same arrangement was in force.

A more manageable option would be a land use-led Department of Planning and Transport. The basis of this should be the planning and development control functions from the existing DoE leading the transport functions of the DTp; a structure which would, incidentally, mirror the pattern in many EC countries. The housing, local government and environmental protection sections of the DoE (the latter needs to be substantially increased in size and scope) would be separate.

Within this, the new Department of Planning and Transport should be split functionally according, broadly, to type of area and journey patterns. This would imply division on the following basis:

- international policy (excluding EC issues);
- European Community issues;
- national transport systems, regional policy and planning issues;
- rural transport and land use policy;
- urban transport and land use policy.

There should be also be overlapping divisions responsible for:

- policy co-ordination;
- user input;

- appraisal and economics;
- research;
- safety;
- environmental input.

For some of these overlapping divisions, the best way of operating would be to have members attached to each of the policy sections. For example, on safety, a post in each policy section specifically for safety would be under the control of the safety section. This already occurs with economics and seems to work well.

The policy co-ordination section would be responsible for ensuring that all the policy sections' work fitted with other departments' policies and into overall government policy. It would also be responsible for setting Departmental objectives as part of a general move towards objectives based planning.

An integral part of this section would be a limited number of high-powered task forces. These would concentrate on key issues, such as:

- integration between modes;
- global warming;
- reducing the need for transport;
- company assisted motoring;
- increasing rail freight;
- widening the use and scope of travelcards;
- traffic restraint.

The remit, timescale and reports of these task forces would all be made public, unlike the current arrangements for working parties within the Department. And though they would clearly need to include specialists from other parts of the Department, it is essential that they are led by 'high-fliers' from the policy co-ordination section.

The policy sections would be able to specify national objectives, particularly for the national transport systems and also for issues such as safety and environmental protection, to which the regional authorities would be obliged to adhere as appropriate.

Many of the other functional roles need not, and perhaps should not, be in the Department at all. For example, in the quasi-judicial and regulatory areas, all of the safety inspectorates should be part of the Health and Safety Executive, as is now the case with the Railway Inspectorate. The Department's own safety section should concentrate on issues such as safety aspects of policy and regulatory roles such as traffic signs and the Driving Standards Administration.

The quasi-judicial role of the Secretary of State should be transferred to the Lord Chancellor along with the Highways Inspectorate and the Planning Inspectorate. This would avoid the current, ridiculous cases where the offices responsible for promoting trunk roads are also responsible for advising the Secretary of State on his decision on the inspector's recommendations.

The Department does not need to maintain much of its executive role. In 1991, this consists of the trunk road network, operators' licensing and vehicle inspections, construction and use regulations and DVLA. Only a policy role is really needed – as part of the national transport systems division – with executive responsibility devolved either to local highway authorities or other agencies, set up as nationalized industries or quangos.

The quasi-executive role is more complicated. Clearly the policy aspects of dealing with BR and the other nationalized industries and quangos should be lodged firmly with the relevant policy sections: for example, inter-urban railways should be the responsibility of the national transport systems section. Where the outside body crosses a number of such sections, though (as is the case with BR), a separate unit would be needed to act as the interface between the Department, the organization as a whole and, usually, the quality commission and the safety inspectorates.

OTHER DEPARTMENTS' ROLES

The following other departments currently have a role in transport policy:

- Treasury – financing;
- Environment – land use and strategic planning; local government finance and structure; environmental protection;
- Home Office – policing;
- Trade and Industry – consumer bodies;
- Energy – energy mix, availability, price and consumption.

The links between the Department of Planning and Transport and these other Departments need examining. The relationship between the Department of Planning and Transport and the Treasury, however, would be governed by whatever rules the Government as a whole draws up to regulate relationships with spending ministries and so would not be considered here.

As has been said before, the links between land use and transport are too important to be split between different departments, and so it is proposed that the planning sections of the DoE should be transferred to what would become the Department of Planning and Transport. There would, however, remain the need for good links with the DoE, particularly in terms of environmental protection. The Department's own environment section would be responsible for developing environmental appraisals in conjunction with the DoE's environmental protection section and a new Environmental Protection Agency. Almost certainly there would need to be a permanent inter-departmental group on this issue, led by the DoE.

The regional authorities would probably take over much of the existing Home Office responsibility for traffic policing, with local authorities taking on parking enforcement. This would limit the role of the Home Office to quality standards for policing generally and to financing, and would ensure that enforcement is seen as a policy tool as part of an integrated package of measures.

It is an historical anomaly that the Department of Trade and Industry is responsible for appointing consumer bodies and a change in this responsibility seems appropriate. However, as there would need to be a much enhanced role for consumer input, this issue is considered in more detail below.

A further key link that needs to be developed is between the new Department of Planning and Transport and the Department of Energy. As transport consumes such as large proportion of national energy requirements it is essential that this features in a national energy plan, particularly since this should be looking for sustainable energy options.

NATIONALIZED INDUSTRIES AND QUANGOS

Despite the activities of the Conservative government since 1979, there remain in the transport sector both nationalized industries and a large range of quangos. The nationalized industries include British Rail, while the full list of quangos has not yet been assembled. Attention needs to be given to the purpose of all these bodies, to their objectives, and to the appointments to them. Initially, the Department of Planning and Transport should review all the existing quangos with a particular view to establishing the purpose of each, clearly and briefly. If this is not possible, the existence of that particular quango must come under close scrutiny.

Second, all of these bodies must be given straightforward objectives on an annual basis. This particularly applies to nationalized industries. At present the only real yardstick for bodies such as BR is their financial bottom line. As is now becoming very plain, BR is prepared to sacrifice almost everything to achieve the financial targets set by the Government. This is no way to achieve a user directed service. The nationalized industries that remain are not there primarily to make money but to provide a service. Thus performance indicators should become the primary measure of how well that industry performs. For example, BR should be set quality of service requirements on an annual basis that could cover items such as reliability, overcrowding, cleanliness, quality and quantity of service. This should be the basis of its client/contractor relationship with the Department.

This is not to say that efficient business management and practices are not needed. The industry should meet its objectives as cost-efficiently as possible. In practice, setting these performance measures would be an iterative process with the cost of achieving different levels of performance informing the choice of target. For example, BR could achieve 100 per cent reliability and 100 per cent punctuality, but it would cost a great deal. Achieving 99 per cent would cost less, and achieving 98 per cent even less. It would be for BR to prepare the 'menu' of options and for the Secretary of State to select which was required (and which could be afforded), probably after consultation with user representative bodies such as a National Transport Forum or OFRAIL (see below). In particular, user representatives' involvement in the preparation of such a 'menu' of options could be important in ensuring that the needs of women, the elderly, children and people with disabilities were outlined and met.

In this way, public attention would be focused on very clearly defined service delivery. 'BR fails quality targets' should be the newspaper headline, not 'BR makes loss'. The same type of clear performance targets could be set for almost all the quangos, although, for the purely advisory bodies, they might have to be couched in slightly different terms.

Appointments to nationalized industries and quangos need to be scrutinized. Since 1979, Conservative Governments have pursued a consistent course of giving priority to Conservative Party members and supporters. They have also provided a cosy home for representatives from the institutionalized pressure groups. This has led to inefficient working as the talents applied have not been the best available, or even appropriate, in some cases. The establishment of clear performance targets should provide a different lead on appointments and point up gaps in relevant representation.

REGIONAL AND LOCAL REPRESENTATION

The role of regional and local authorities is not the subject of this chapter (although it assumes that regional authorities would be created). There are, nevertheless, a number of current functions of the Department of Transport which could properly be devolved to regional or local authorities. Most of these concern the work of the Department's regional offices which currently scrutinize local authorities' TPPs and allocate the Transport Supplementary Grant (TSG), while agreeing major road schemes. These powers should all be devolved to the regional authorities.

The DTp regional offices are also responsible for trunk road proposals. Trunk roads (including motorways) should be devolved to the regional authorities and, therefore, planning would also be devolved, subject to overriding policy control by the national transport systems unit in the new Department of Planning and Transport. This would probably mean that the regional offices of the DTp would be disbanded.

Regional authorities should also be given powers to determine local rail services in their areas, although it is likely that the conurbation would be the primary level for public transport planning in urban areas. Vehicle inspection and bus and lorry operator licensing could also be carried out sensibly at regional or local level as part of the general trading standards operations.

The Department of Planning and Transport would still be able to exert influence over the regions. It would set objectives for national transport systems, environmental, safety and energy targets. It would also set the format for regional structure plans. Regional policy would feed in to structure plans as guidance. The original relationship between structure plans and transport policies and programmes (TPPs) should also be reinstated, whereby the TPP became the vehicle which would indicate the programme for implementing the structure plan's transport provisions, including public transport and local safety schemes. Best practice guides on a variety of issues and general guidance, particularly on links between transport and land use, would also be made available for the regional authorities. Although regional authorities would take some time to establish, joint approaches by existing authorities, over things such as TSG bids, could be encouraged immediately.

In the same way that much of the work now the responsibility of the Department at national level should be devolved to regions, other transport powers could be devolved to counties (if they remain in existence), districts/boroughs or even parishes. There are two arguments here: the first is simply the general principle, used within the EC, of 'subsidiarity' – under which decisions and action should be taken at the lowest possible level of government (i.e., the level closest to the people affected); second, transport policy-making has a long history of overvaluing the minority of long-distance journeys (passenger and freight) at the expense of the majority of local journeys, especially those made on foot, bike or bus. Management of local roads and streets should be devolved so as to give priority to these local journeys and to the many other actual and potential uses of streets (as communities, shopping centres, residential and play areas).

In general, the responsibilities of regional authorities should be confined to co-ordination, policy and funding, leaving detailed executive functions to districts. Where appropriate, powers could even be devolved to parish/community councils. Whether or not this is done, attention must be paid to the question of how best to secure local input, at neighbourhood and town level, into local decisions that would, otherwise, be made by regional and borough councils. Community involvement in decision-making should become an integral part of decision-making in transport as a whole. Current public involvement techniques in transport lag a long way behind best practice in planning and other professions, and the use of 'planning for real' and other techniques should be adopted in transport planning.

THE LINKS TO EUROPE

Europe is going to become an increasingly important focus for decision-making in transport issues. But at present there is very little involvement in European decision-making by all but a few outside national government. It should be a major part of the Department of Planning and Transport's role to open up this process of information and consultation. There are a number of steps that it could take to achieve this.

First, the Department should actively consult on and publicize proposals from the Commission at an early stage when proposals are being formulated. At present these are given little publicity and few organizations are approached directly. The Department should also encourage the Commission itself to canvass more widely and publicly. Second, the Secretary of State should consider more carefully any appointments to European consultative bodies, such as the Economic and Social Committee, to ensure that Britain's appointees are genuinely representative. Third, the Department of Planning and Transport should actively co-ordinate bids for European funding on transport issues and work to ensure that the sums are maximized and that the effect is not just, as at present, to reduce the need for central government funding under 'additionality' rules.

Britain as a whole also appears to be consistently poorly represented at official meetings, with civil servants from Britain attending where other countries' ministers are involved. Such poor participation does nothing to improve the weight which British views carry. The Government should, therefore, also ensure that Britain is participating to the full in European decision-making.

ENVIRONMENTAL INPUT

It is essential that the new Department of Planning and Transport ensures that environmental considerations feature prominently in all aspects of its work. There are two main proposals for this.

First, the environment section of the Department would prepare methods for environmental appraisal and environmental objectives which would not just become part of the Department's own proposals, but which regional authorities would also be obliged to adopt. The appraisal techniques should ensure that proper assessment of environmental factors is taken into account and would be prepared in conjunction with the DoE and the Environmental Protection Agency. The objectives would set targets for issues such as emission quantities and transport energy use. Much in the same way as there is a formal safety target in the DTp at present, the environmental targets would override other considerations. Targets would need to be set in absolute terms not just in relative terms. For example, there would need to be an overall target for CO_2 emissions in the transport sector, not just a target per vehicle or per vehicle mile.

Second, the Landscape Advisory Committee should be replaced with a more wide-ranging and powerful body covering both the built and natural environment. This would bring together interests such as English Nature and the other country nature conservancy bodies, as well as other environmental bodies, and would both monitor the Department's activities in this area and put forward policies on issues such as SSSIs, transport and the urban form, and National Parks.

CONSUMER INPUT

Improved consumer input is essential in developing transport policies, and is considered in detail in chapter 4. Within government responsibilities, though, there are specific proposals that can be made for enhancing consumer input at both central and local levels. There are three broad ways of achieving this. One is by means of formalized consumer bodies; a second is through increasing formal consultation; and the third is by specific consumer appointments on the boards of executive agencies. These three approaches are not necessarily mutually exclusive, but complement one another. For effective consumer input elements of all would probably need to be included.

At local levels, consumer input would be required at all levels of decision-making. Development of local, conurbation and regional transport plans would be required, statutorily, to include proper measures of advertisement, participation and consultation by all interested parties. Regional authorities should also be required to establish formal consumer bodies, subject to rules set out by the Quality Commission. They should, in this way, take over the regional TUCCs. It is likely that these bodies would be general in nature, but have sub-committees to deal with public transport, airport and traffic issues. While the operation of some official consumer bodies has not been perfect, there is evidence that, if properly resourced and established, they can be effective at presenting, quite single-mindedly, the users' view. The London Regional Passengers' Committee is a good example. Effective user participation should also be encouraged by informal events such as bus user forums, pioneered by 'BusWatch'. Co-options of voluntary sector and user group representatives onto local council committees may also take place and would be useful, though this is not a substitute for the other methods described above.

At a national level, the position would be different. There may be scope for appointing a consumer representative onto the board of BR, the CAA and other relevant nationalized industries. This would parallel the appointment of worker board members in line with European legislation, and would be useful. But it would not be a complete answer, and the role of these representatives would not be easy as they would also be corporately responsible for the affairs of that organization, along with the other board members. This could well lead to conflicts of interests on occasions.

There are other proposals for formal consumer (or similar) organizations, including OFRAIL and the National Transport Forum. OFRAIL is proposed as the railway arm of a suggested Quality Commission. It needs to have a right of access to information and some powers of direction if it is to be effective. It would need to monitor closely the quality of service offered by BR. Similar offices would be required to cover the work of the CAA and similar bodies, although these may well be smaller organizations. OFRAIL should maintain the CTCC as part of its structure as it would be important in two ways – first, as a link into the regional rail consumer bodies; and second, as a way of bringing in the views of real users. The positions on the CTCC should be advertised widely and filled, *en bloc*, for a fixed term using published criteria rather than relying on the patronage system as at present. OFRAIL would also need more teeth than the CTCC has at present. One option may be to give it powers to make certain types of direction to BR or, slightly weaker, to request the Secretary of State to make a direction on any matter (not just major policy or financial matters).

THE NATIONAL TRANSPORT FORUM

The key to user input at a national level, though, must be the National Transport Forum. This must combine representatives of users, workers, providers and the community to provide across-the-board input on general issues of transport policy. The scope and scale of its tasks means that it would therefore require a small staff to service it.

There are a large number of interests that would have to be represented on the Forum. On behalf of transport workers, trade unions and the TUC would clearly be involved. Transport academics may also be counted as workers in a certain sense, albeit professionals; certainly, their involvement would be needed. Users would include the main public transport groups but also motoring, freight, pedestrian and cycling groups. Providers would include the major transport industries, but also groups such as community transport, which now play an important role. The community section would include representatives from local authorities and major environmental and community groups and also bodies representing women, ethnic minorities and people with disabilities.

As the Forum would be so large, there is a danger it could become a fairly purposeless talking shop. Efforts to limit its size, however, could become divisive, as fairly large sectional interests might feel excluded. To avoid this the Secretary of State, as chair of the Forum, would have to work to focus the issues the Forum as a whole considers. Working groups could be set up to advise on specific topics, as the Disabled Persons Transport Advisory Committee does at present, or to conduct inquiries. In this way it might act as a cross between the Transport Select Committee and groups such as SACTRA. The Forum would also have right of access to the Department for the purpose of its investigations and would thus act as another form of watchdog.

SUMMARY AND CONCLUSIONS

The Department of Transport has a bad reputation and is not seen as providing the right basis for developing transport in Britain. This chapter sets out ways of reforming it. Principal among these is to create a new Department of Planning and Transport which would include, and be led by, government interests in land use planning. The internal structure of the Department would be organized not on producer lines but on functional lines. Particular emphasis in consultative and policy-making processes would be placed on consumer and environmental input, while many functions could be devolved to regional authorities. Put together, these proposals would produce a new, more effective and more highly regarded government transport agency.

9

MARKET FORCES AND TRANSPORT CHOICES

JUDITH HANNA AND MARTIN MOGRIDGE

This paper looks at what role market forces can and should play in transport policy, in particular to encourage users to choose less damaging modes of transport for their journeys. We argue that:

- the price paid by users of transport should visibly signal at point of use the 'true cost' of that choice, relative to other choices available;
- this requires that the prices paid by users of different modes of transport should reflect the marginal cost that journey imposes on the overall transport system;
- the limits of the market should be drawn where the cost of disbenefits identified will not be paid by users (or their agents), to those who lose out (or their agents);
- therefore decisions on supply of transport capacity should be based within a framework of environmental, quality-of-life and other clearly specified objectives, rather than simply left to market forces of supply, demand and price.

This paper attempts to set out some of the practical policy implications these principles entail.

BACKGROUND

> A generation hence, people won't ask what the Government is doing to meet increased demand for transport, any more than they now ask what the Government is doing to meet increased demand for chocolate.
>
> Paul Channon, [former] Secretary of State for Transport, quoted in the *Scotsman*, 11 April 1989.

This paper draws on, and follows on from, Martin Mogridge's work set out in *Travel in Towns* (1990), which demonstrates that in order to optimize the efficiency of urban transport systems, there is a perfectly logical method of optimizing levels of taxation and subsidy. This requires them to be set at that level which forces people to face the costs of consumption of the resources actually used in making the journey, in other words the marginal cost of their journey.

The government's role in relation to the transport market, then, is to ensure that the full costs of the resources actually used to provide for transport are taken into account, and that the costs as users perceive them through the prices they pay accurately reflect the demands which that extra journey, by that mode, imposes not only on the transport system but on other relevant competing activities and on the human and natural environment.

The Pearce Report (Pearce *et al.*, 1989), commissioned by then Secretary of State for the Environment, Chris Patten, introduced into serious political debate the need to take account of the value of environmental resources in national accounts and in planning developments. He recommended, first, setting 'sustainability constraints' to protect irreplaceable natural resources for the benefit of future generations; beyond this he endorsed the notion of seeking to assign real monetary values to environmental values. We agree with the urgent need to define and observe sustainability constraints, but follow John Adams (1974), Michael Jacobs (1991) and others who have argued that attempting to discuss values that are essentially 'not for sale at any price' in terms of monetary equivalence is an unreliable tactic which avoids the hard arguments about the real conflicts of interest at issue. The present cost-benefit analysis (COBA) model used to justify road building schemes has done much to demonstrate the dubiety of applying such monetary values.

The alternative suggested by SACTRA (1987), and more recently elaborated by Keith Buchan (see chapter 2) and colleagues is that a framework of clearly specified performance objectives should be used as the basis for transport planning. It seems to us that such a framework of practical and concrete objectives, widely consulted and debated, is needed in order to define within what bounds an 'optimized' transport system should be required to operate. That is, the objectives set the limits of what is not for sale to transport users. For instance, clean air standards, or targets to decrease deaths on the roads, are factors that most would agree should be subject to regulation for general benefit rather than for sale to satisfy demand for more or faster travel. This discussion draws on a conference organized by Transport 2000 and New Economics Foundation, the papers for which have been published under the title *What Are Roads Worth?* (T2000/NEF, 1991).

Present Policy

Though successive Conservative Governments have espoused a 'free market' policy, many of the arguments against present policy – that it is severely biased and inefficient at delivering real freedom of choice for travellers – can be couched as arguments that present policies amount to a *distortion* of the market. In effect, present policy operates different markets for different modes of transport, run by different rules, and thus distorts the terms of choice between modes. In addition, the Conservative Party has always accepted the need for a range of regulations, for safety, environmental and other social reasons, which (as the libertarian fringe has pointed out) impose limits on market freedom.

The language of the market can provide a useful framework for considering the value obtained by the nation, and by individual users, from public investment and policy. In arguing from the 'market' viewpoint, however, it is important to clarify the limits within which the market should be allowed to operate; these limits are set by deciding what goods or services are, and which are not, available for sale. Hence the need for a clear framework of *objectives* as the basic mechanism for setting the limits of market forces. It is also important that the full costs are reflected in calculating the marginal price travellers actually pay; this is not the case at present. Moreover, current policy, by assuming that everything not privately owned is for sale or indeed up for grabs without compensation or payment, might be said to operate a forced market, rather than a free market.

KEY ARGUMENTS

A Single Market for Transport

The fundamental policy change needed to shift the market framework of choice is the adoption of an integrated assessment and funding framework. The initial quick fix would be to review the DTp's *Roads to Prosperity* programme, applying the existing COBA framework equally to evaluate alternative public transport investment proposals. If the arguments that public transport yields better environmental and safety performance are sound, then rival public transport schemes should yield the better value, even under the existing flawed system.

The argument is not for preferential market treatment for public transport, but that when the full resource and social costs involved in achieving the transport objectives of cheap and convenient access for people and goods are reckoned up, then with fair comparison public transport options will emerge, in many cases, as giving better performance and better value than car- or lorry-based options. For instance, when the present, badly flawed COBA cost-benefit analysis has been applied to public transport investments, a positive justification for the investment has been demonstrated. For instance, a SACTRA study in 1984 showed that rail improvements along the M40 corridor confirmed that the rail options gave a cost benefit ratio which would justify the investment, if assessed on the same basis as used for road schemes. More recently, a cost-benefit analysis of the proposed Manchester Metrolink light rail scheme (Tyson, 1990) demonstrated a high 'net present value' return. By contrast, roads for which the NPV emerges as negative have nonetheless been constructed.

Transport Appraisal and Expenditure Framework

The allocation of government expenditure between modes sets the fundamental framework for infrastructure and service provision, which in turn sets the scope for modal choices at all levels. The different treatment accorded road-building and public transport investment at present is a fundamental cause of the present modal imbalance: the different modes operate in different markets run according to different rules. The case for an integrated approach to public investment in transport infrastructure and services now has support across the political spectrum, from Labour, Liberal Democrat and Green Party policies, to resolutions from Conservative Associations to the 1990 Conservative Party Conference calling for 'an integrated transport policy'. The changes needed for an integrated transport policy would be:

- a common framework of *objectives* for transport policy; these would include environmental, social and access objectives;

- a common *assessment system* applicable to road, public transport, and local access management options, as packages of alternative measures, assessed in terms of ability to meet the objectives cost-effectively. This should, in effect, apply the principle of 'least-cost planning' to transport;

- a *funding structure* for transport investment which does not discriminate between modes but rather in terms of performance in achieving the objectives;

- changes to *user charges* so that travellers would pay, and perceive, 'true costs' of the journey they chose to make.

In market terms, such an integrated system would enable planning and transport authorities to provide an 'optimal mix' of access by different modes. That is, all forms of transport would be operating in a single market, in direct competition with each other, with government (national, regional and local) acting as umpire within a framework of regulations set according to the objectives.

In other words, grants for transport investment should be available on the same terms for the best options, whatever mix of modes they may involve. When it comes to the running costs of local transport systems, then again, the transport network which gives best value across the local authority's total balance sheet should be aimed for. The need is not for more government money to be spent on transport, but for the present roads budget to be released to be used for the best value options to provide necessary access for people and goods (for additional discussion on transport integration, see chapters 10 and 11).

SETTING THE FRAMEWORK OF OBJECTIVES

In the medium term, a system based on a broad framework of clearly specified objectives (environmental, quality-of-life, equal opportunity and accessibility) that identifies which package of transport measures will optimize access, should be developed and introduced. These objectives would have two sorts of rationale. Some would specify what the transport system is for, in terms of achieving access for necessary movement of people and goods. Others would specify limits on allowable damage that transport systems could impose. The 1987 SACTRA report, and MTRU's *Wheels of Fortune* report (1991), suggest how such objectives can be formulated.

It is worth pausing to note how vaguely stated objectives can be misused. The stated objectives of the DTp's Roads Programme are to promote: i) environment; ii) safety; iii) economic growth (DTp, 1989b; 1989c). These are fine objectives, as far as they go. The problems at present are, first, that they are not applied equally to public transport, and second, that there is no yardstick or evaluation of how, or whether, road-building tackles these objectives. No explicit transport objectives are stated. This example illustrates both how actual policies can act against the stated objectives, and that, without benchmarks against which implementation can be assessed, objectives are no more than good intentions.

Practical transport requirements need to be formulated as explicit objectives just as much as the 'externalities' of environmental and social values. This last ought to be too obvious to need stating. But as correspondence between then Roads and Traffic Minister Robert Atkins and Transport 2000 demonstrated, the Department has been unable, when challenged, to say what objectives other than meeting traffic forecasts roads are designed to fulfil. At present the key official measure is of mobility in tonne- or passenger-kilometres. The performance measure needed is of access: how easily and efficiently can goods and people reach their destinations?

The socio-economic and environmental objectives should set out what transport is for: a good transport system provides for the access needs defined, without breaching the environmental framework, as efficiently and cost-effectively as possible. It is only within the framework of how much access and what sorts are provided within the transport system that people can exercise choice. And it is only in terms of what the transport system actually achieves that we can assess whether public spending is achieving value for money.

For instance, if no bus service exists, or if cycling and walking are too dangerous and unpleasant, these choices are ruled out and the effect is to force journeys to be made by car or to be foregone. It seems a fair assumption too that in choosing to drive no one is actually choosing to breathe polluted rather than clean air, or to incur a one-in-two lifetime risk of being involved in a traffic accident; though these are real consequences of modal choices, they are left out of the present framework of choice.

Modal Shift and Reduction in Travel

Modal shift is not in itself a primary objective, but necessary to achieve other objectives agreed to define an optimally efficient transport system. That is, the scope for modal shift, and extent of modal shift needed in different areas, should be defined in terms of such other, generally acceptable targets at national, regional and local level. These objectives would also relate the transport sector to other areas of activity. In particular, attention to the transport generating impacts of land use and planning decisions will be vital. Objectives and measures to reduce progressively the travel distances to basic facilities should supplement those aiming to produce a more efficient, economical modal split.

Modal shift towards cycling and walking for the short local journeys which make up most trips is equally vital. Here, the user imposes little demand for construction of extra space, nor imposes pollution, danger or noise on others, so the costs required from the walker or cyclist to cover their impact on the transport system are very low if not free. But as Cleary and Hillman point out (chapter 17) pedestrians and cyclists suffer immensely from danger, pollution and unpleasantness caused by motor traffic.

Market philosophy breaks down here. Motorists do not 'buy' from anyone a lease or ownership that entitles them to poison the air others breathe, or subject others to risk of death – nor could any government say openly that these 'qualities' were up for sale. Nor do motorists pay compensation into any fund. Still less do pedestrians or cyclists receive any rent or compensation for the damage done by motorists to these unownable qualities. There is no 'market' in safety and environment: those at the losing end don't want to sell and aren't being offered real money anyway. Those who want to consume others' share in the common good aren't being asked to pay any price. If they were, the terms of choice in everybody's transport decisions would be radically different.

If environment and safety are not up for sale, then in market terms there is a stringently limited supply of these factors available for consumption, for transport or other purposes. The limits to supply can be enforced through regulation – e.g., air quality standards, speed limits – and also through pricing. In a free market, prices for goods in limited supply and high demand rise to a high level. Walking and cycling impose no such unsustainable demands and can be provided for at very low cost.

Even at present most journeys made are very short: the modal length of car trips is between two and three miles. One third of all journeys are under one mile; half are under two miles; three quarters are under five miles. Most such local journeys could well transfer to foot, cycle or better bus provision.

But in effect government transport policy has been subsidizing the luxury and 'bad-for-us chocolate cake' of car comfort at the expense of the healthy 'fresh fruit and veg' of foot and cycle travel. The real differences in cost of provision, and in sustainable supply, are not reflected in any market pricing structure. It may well be neither possible nor desirable to set such a price structure, for in proportion to the infinitesimal costs imposed by cyclists and pedestrians the relative marginal costs of motoring become immense. In that case, non-market measures come into play.

The conclusions of the Oxford University 'Transport and Society' discussion project, published as *The New Realism* (Goodwin *et al.*, 1991) reached a not dissimilar conclusion, which they couched in terms of the need to manage demand, recognizing that it is not possible to satisfy demand for ever faster mobility within the natural and economic resources available.

How Much Modal Shift?

There are two ways that targets for the amount of modal shift needed can be set. Progressive shift of x per cent per year reduction in car or lorry mileage or trips is one approach. The other is to define the wished-for end result (optimal modal split), first as overall national objectives, from which more detailed targets would be derived: for example, no more than 5 per cent of personal trips under 2 miles by car, 15 per cent by bus, 40 per cent each by cycling and walking; this sort of disaggregation in terms of specific trip type would be essential. The two approaches can and should work together: progressive shifts towards a target split.

Setting the targets, and the rate of change which policies should aim for, are political decisions to be taken at national level, and within national objectives, by local government. Experts can set out the implications of adopting, or not adopting, specific targets, but the decisions about the objectives actually adopted are for public debate and the democratic political process.

The 'Netherlands Travelling Clean' study (referred to by Holman and Fergusson in chapter 3) found that in order to achieve environmental targets 90 per cent of all non-work trips made by car would need to transfer to other modes (commuting counted as non-work). To achieve this required investment in public transport and reduction of travel distances. For this last, 'mobility' became redefined as 'many destinations in close reach'. A transport policy to achieve the environmental objectives would not cost more than the present roads-based policies but less – £360 per household per year less (Schoemaker, 1991).

WHAT INFLUENCES INDIVIDUALS' TRANSPORT CHOICES?

Market mechanisms are just one way of shifting the terms of choice. Convenience seems to be the principal factor in people's choices: once the decision to make a particular trip to a given destination is taken, travel time is a major factor in the decision of which mode to use – if more than one is available (Mogridge, 1985). Travel time itself depends on the quality of provision for each mode or mix of modes: for example, the frequency of public transport services and speed at which they are able to travel; the supply of uncongested road and parking space. Quality of service factors (i.e., comfort), and the availability of information about alternative modes, are other factors contributing to convenience. More diffuse socio-psychological perceptions of factors like relative status of different modes (e.g., company car versus bus), or of safety risks, also enter into modal choices. Relative price levels are balanced against these factors.

Market research (e.g., Hallett, 1990; Lex Motoring Surveys) suggests that many motorists do not think that better public transport or other alternatives will persuade them out of their cars. This is the case even where the same survey (MTRU, 1989) shows support, including by motorists, of the need for traffic restraint measures and better public transport. Other evidence suggests that demand for car travel may be relatively inelastic to changes in price – unless the price rise is extremely sudden. Price rises sufficient to change behaviour will certainly be unpopular: it has been suggested by the Cambridge Econometrics group that a 375 per cent carbon tax would be needed in order to keep fossil fuel use at current levels. Therefore the market mechanism of higher price alone does not seem a practicable policy. Changing behaviour towards a more sustainable modal split will certainly require a combination of pricing, alternative provision, regulations, and educational publicity measures.

To make restrictions and higher charges on motoring acceptable people must see a clear gain in exchange. In practice, this means, for instance, regulatory measures to deliver the attractive environmental gains of 'car-free' centres of various types, and for tram and bus roads and lanes. Since in practice there will always be some people able and willing to pay whatever charges may be imposed to discourage or restrain use, delivering 'car-free' benefits will require local bans, which local authorities already have powers to impose. Several recent surveys, such as the RAC's *Green Drivers* show that more car users prefer total bans to increased prices.

Ability to use cars will remain biased in favour of the rich, as is so much of life. However, the benefits of car-free areas, better public transport, cycling and walking facilities would be available to and usable by all. The less well-off, who are less likely to be car owners, would gain most; car owning households would also share in the environmental, safety and amenity benefits which are the objectives of modal shift from car use.

ASSESSMENT OF COSTS AND SUBSIDY

At present, road lobby organizations and Department of Transport tend to assert that motorists and lorry operators pay more in road tax than the costs of road-building, road accidents, and road maintenance. On the one hand, road tax is unhypothecated general taxation rather than a 'payment' for road use, which is otherwise free. That is, it has been suggested, the cry of 'Where are the roads our road taxes pay for?' is akin to demanding 'Where are the pubs our beer taxes pay for? Where are the casinos our gambling taxes pay for?' Nonetheless, the question of whether motorized road users do 'pay for' their road use needs to be addressed: some ways of assessing some usually ignored wider costs of car use are noted in *Transport Retort* (1990). Specific direct and indirect costs can, and need to be, calculated for many of the currently ignored side-effects of traffic and the road programme, if the market is to operate fairly.

On example of real road traffic costs which are not currently met by the transport sector is the English Heritage's (1990) report *Roads For Prosperity: The Archaeological Impact*, which does not attempt to put a monetary value on the significance of the sites threatened, but simply calculates the direct cost of rescue excavation in advance of construction for the approximately 800 affected sites at over £70 million. In 1990 the DTp allocated £500,000 pa, an increase from just £100,000 pa, which over the fifteen-year planned duration of the programme might cover one-tenth of the direct archaeological costs imposed on English Heritage. Just as developers are under planning law required to pay the costs of rescue archaeological investigation in advance of construction, so should road-builders and, equally, railway builders. But a 'sustainability constraint' to require routes to avoid scheduled or historically valuable sites would be a quite separate primary objective.

Many similar cases can be identified: for instance, extra land-take for road traffic and parking at the expense of competing uses, loss of property values due to traffic noise and pollution, pollution damage to health and buildings, health damage from road crashes. All these impose real costs, which are at present borne by other sectors of the public budget rather than met by the travellers for whose speed and convenience these costs are created.

Subsidy, Revenue and Road Tax

Where does the money go? Hypothecation or into general revenue? A fundamental question is whether the charges paid for different forms of transport should be treated as taxes, which would not be 'hypothecated' for specific uses but accrue to the Treasury as part of the general public purse, or whether money raised from transport users should be treated in the same way as public transport fares, and be used to cover the expenses involved in keeping the transport system running.

The key distinction we believe useful to make here is to distinguish clearly revenue to cover direct costs, against a tax accruing to general revenue. In general there is clearer public understanding and acceptance of the need to pay to cover necessary costs; and this is the basis on which the arguments for the payments to be levied have, in general, been made. This implies that charges levied on the basis of a calculation of direct costs should be spent on meeting those costs. After all, the implication of having identified a real cost is that money needs to be spent on meeting that cost; if money is charged against an identified cost or damage, then not spent on dealing with it, the implication is that either some other money must be raised from elsewhere as 'subsidy', or that expenditure which is needed for the benefit of society is being neglected.

However, if the direct costs have included the full range of effects of transport behaviour: on health and safety, on local economy and amenity, on environment; then such hypothecation back in order to cover those impacts should provide a fair social income towards those areas of policy, accurately reflecting the costs they must meet (e.g., treatment and compensation of accident victims, air clean-up, land compensation). This need not preclude an element for general taxation to cover unallocatable expenditure, or as a tax on consumption (e.g., carbon tax) if the levying party were to decide that this were necessary or desirable.

So a logical consequence of a system based on market forces is that revenues based on covering identified costs should accrue to meet those costs, thus eliminating the need for a subsidy from general funds. The crucial question here is in calculating the relevant costs, and any offsetting savings, and relating these to the marginal cost of each extra journey by that mode.

At present 'subsidy' is seen as a soft option. This has become so because it is not clear what subsidy is actually for, other than some vague social good. Clearly specifying the objectives as measurable performance standards, against which proposals can be evaluated and by which the performance of systems can be monitored, is essential. In this framework, a 'subsidy' should, in practice, produce overall savings in terms of the total bill for public provision of services. For instance, savings in health authorities' special transport and on residential places needed, balanced against extra spending on staff to assist public transport passengers, and investment in improving accessibility of footways and public transport should – even leaving aside the values of well-being and independence – mean a real saving in overall local authority expenditure.

At the same time, such broad accounting (or auditing) of social and environmental effects should mean that socially or environmentally beneficial transport expenditure accrues similar credits from other sectors. Cross-sectoral savings and imposed costs are real effects which need to be taken into account. In the long run, it is undesirable for travel by any mode to be 'subsidized': the theoretical ideal would be a broad accounting which can specify at least the direct costs and benefits accruing to other sectors of activity, and present these as part of the overall balance of benefit.

Cross-sectoral Costs and Benefits: Health

A major field where transport decisions can impose real costs, or offer potential savings, is over a range of *health impacts*. For instance, road accidents are reckoned to cost the NHS at least £3bn a year. According to Mackay (1990) 'traffic injury consumes an estimated 10 per cent of total hospital resources, excluding the cost of rehabilitation and the care of long-term and permanent disability. These costs represent a substantial economic burden, being approximately 10 per cent of all of the costs of traffic accidents.' Respiratory damage from exhaust pollutants, according to Holman, may affect up to 20 per cent of the population. People who are ill or disabled may find that being unable to get about independently on local streets or public transport worsens their condition, imposing added personal costs to them and further costs to the health services. This may extend to making it necessary to take into residential care people who might otherwise be able to continue living independently in their own homes, an option both far more expensive to provide and correspondingly less satisfactory as quality of life.

To take another example, public transport vehicles and stations inaccessible to disabled and elderly people mean greater demands on special services, which are very much more expensive per journey to provide, and the costs of which fall on health authority budgets. More accessible vehicles and improving accessibility of stations could enable many of those now dependent on special transport to use less expensive mainstream transport; the recent *Buses for All* (London Dial-a-Ride, 1990) survey of Dial-a-Ride users in Ealing and Hounslow found that 50 per cent were able to use the wheelchair accessible mainstream bus services recently introduced. The 'cross-sectoral benefits' of accessible public transport services are documented by the Disabled Peoples Transport Advisory Committee (DPTAC, 1990) which cites a figure of £3-4 per trip to make mainstream public transport fully accessible – contrasted with costs to health and social service budgets of £97 a week for providing care at home, £183 a week for care in a nursing home or £294 a week for hospital care.

SPECIFIC POLICY RECOMMENDATIONS

Various charges are used to recoup from users some of the expenses of providing transport. This section runs through some of the main types of charges in use, or potentially available. It does not aspire to be a comprehensive run-down, since other papers will be dealing in greater detail with the types of transport operation to which each of these charges pertains.

Public Transport Fares

Public transport users at present pay at point of use, through fares, the full costs of their travel, the price they pay reasonably accurately reflecting the costs of providing that capacity. However, the fares are not calculated to optimize the overall use of the system. Nor are the savings that could be produced – to overall expenditure and resource use by greater use of the more energy-efficient, space-efficient, safer and less polluting high-capacity system – taken into account.

The 'single market' approach to transport assessment argued for above provides a basis for calculating the appropriate fare level, relative to motoring costs for similar journeys. An optimizing approach might produce higher fares for peak hour travel, when extra capacity is expensive to provide; and lower (or possibly even free) fares for off-peak travel to encourage economical use of capacity, that would otherwise be unused, through transfer of journeys from modes or times more expensive to cater for.

'Polluter Pays' Principle: Taxing Fuel Use

The principal objective of taxing fuel use is the need, made urgent by 'global warming', to increase energy efficiency and achieve absolute reductions in the amount of fossil fuel used over all spheres of activity. There is clear agreement across the political spectrum that a 'carbon tax' on fossil fuels is needed. In addition, there are direct costs of pollution damage to health and buildings. However, increased fuel prices on their own are unlikely to reduce mileage sufficiently or to induce modal shift. This is because people will react by buying more fuel efficient cars, and forcing manufacturers to produce them, so that traffic levels gradually recover back to their original levels, although perhaps over a fifteen-year period (it takes that long for manufacturers to react to produce new models and for the existing stock of cars to be replaced). A fuel tax policy is thus in that sense an energy conserving policy.

Driver Licensing

Either as a tax on fuel, or as an annual levy on driving licence (as in Australian states) or on MOT, drivers might also be required to cover safety costs of treatment and compensation of road casualties, calculated in terms of accident rate per mile of driving (unless drivers are to be held absolutely individually responsible for compensation for any injury they cause). Policing costs of enforcement of traffic law might also be included. A charge based on the safety and health expenses (e.g., costs to the NHS, and the costs of a right to compensation) might focus greater driver awareness of the costs to society of road injuries, at the point where the decision to use a car is made, at the same time transferring the cost burden from health budgets to revenue raised from those whose convenience imposes that damage.

Vehicle Tax

Shifting car owners' preferences to more fuel efficient, less polluting vehicles may be aided by imposition of heavier taxes on bigger engined, fuel extravagant vehicles, with lighter tax burden for cars that use less fuel. As in the US, the standards for fuel efficiency should be reviewed regularly as a continuing incentive for manufacturers to improve progressively the fuel efficiency of the cars they produce. In the interests of encouraging purchase of safer cars, a tax break for cars fitted with speed governors might be considered.

Car Ownership

Though car use creates more problems than car ownership, the sheer presence of large numbers of stationary cars, particularly in densely settled urban areas, amounts to a nuisance at public expense. Cars occupy large areas of public land, which is then not available for other, competing uses. The high prices charged for land are a measure of its value for those other, competing uses, and land for transport should not exempted from this value. To do so, as is currently frequently the case (Adams, 1989), is a distortion of the land use market. However, though purchase or rent on land values should be included as a direct cost to transport systems, this direct cost is not a substitute for clear objectives about, for instance, types and amounts of public or other land that should not be taken over for traffic or rail lines.

In some other densely populated small countries, clear objectives limit the number of cars which may be owned to the space that can be made available for traffic. Singapore has found it necessary to impose a quota on the number of cars that may be owned on the island; ownership licences are sold by auction to the highest bidder, ensuring the best market price is obtained. There, a 'what the market will bear' revenue raiser operates within the regulatory framework. In Tokyo, prospective car buyers must show that they have a parking space before they can own a car. There, the ownership through purchase or rental at market price of the necessary space to keep a car where it won't be a public nuisance at public expense acts as the rationing agent.

Car Parking

At present, free provision of public car parking amounts to a massive subsidy to car owners, at the expense of their non-car-owning neighbours. This applies to resident on-street (or frequently and illegally, on-footway) parking as much as to town centre parking. For instance, counties in the south east of England spend more on providing car parking than on public transport services. It has been informally suggested that if a local authority were to exempt non-car-owning households from community charge payments, the resulting reduction in number of cars demanding road and parking space would mean a saving in local authority expenditure.

Nor are the demands on public space (in urban areas) the only public impact of increasing car ownership. Cars parked along streets pose safety problems: some two-thirds of accidents to children involve parked cars preventing them seeing or being seen by traffic. The eventual disposal of cars and used tyres is another cost imposed on the public sector. There are also the costs of licensing and traffic policing, of vehicle inspection (including the pollution monitoring of exhaust emissions). These are fixed costs contingent on possession of the vehicle, rather than marginal costs increasing with use.

In urban areas, the simple presence of cars is more of a nuisance and public charge than in rural areas. There is a case for allowing local authorities to levy a car ownership charge to meet the extra costs imposed by urban car owners. This might be implemented as a charge for resident parking facilities. These costs at present fall equally on non-car-owning residents who suffer all the nuisances of traffic without themselves having the luxury of a car.

Road Pricing

In terms of the market framework, it is clearly logical to charge road-users for their occupancy of valuable space, and for the traffic nuisance they constitute. Road pricing in central areas, when coupled with 'car-free' areas and tram and bus only roads and lanes, will have the benefit that the revenue from the cars continuing to use the roads can be used to improve the public transport service for those restrained, thus speeding up travel for everybody. By forcing car-drivers to pay the marginal costs of their travel – i.e., the costs imposed on everyone else by their presence on the roads – and by subsidizing public transport so that passengers likewise pay the marginal costs of their travel on the bus, tram (or train), the most efficient transport system will result. This cannot be done under the present system of fiscal pricing, where congestion results in slower travel for everyone.

Rural Areas

In rural areas, none of these extra charges would apply, except when rural dwellers are actually using high-demand urban space to which parking or road pricing charges had been applied. The tax incentives to purchase fuel efficient cars would equally apply, and since the greenhouse effect of a gallon of petrol combusted remains the same, so should the price charged for fuel. Local objectives, balancing access considerations, both local and for longer-distance travel, against valued countryside, village amenity and safety standards, would determine whether traffic-calming constraints on road space might be appropriate.

In many cases, the objectives framework together with a broad accounting of the full costs and savings, might well justify better provision of public transport. In other cases, environmental criteria might suggest that where protection of sensitive landscapes requires limiting numbers of visitors (e.g., Lake District, parts of Peak National Park) this could be done by limiting car access and parking with visitor numbers rationed by public transport service provision and those prepared to undertake the exercise of long-distance walking or cycling.

Evans and Bannister (chapter 13) further argue that, by encouraging urban workers to buy up country cottages, easy cheap car access has severely damaged local urban economies.

Freight

As Whitelegg (1990) has argued, at present road freight pays far less than its full costs. Though UK lorry taxes are higher than in other European countries, they do not fully cover the massive road damage their weight inflicts, some 200,000 times more damage for a 38-tonne lorry than an ordinary car. Local frameworks of transport objectives might well produce more local bans and controls on lorry access to certain roads at certain times. The prevalence of illegal overloading, speeding and other offences against safety and environmental regulations in order to cut costs unbalances the competitive position of rail against road freight. In addition, while present rail freight charges cover a share of infrastructure and fixed costs of the rail system, road freight is not required to contribute similarly to infrastructure or fixed costs of the road system. Again, a 'single market' with infrastructure investment on the same basis for each mode, against a framework of objectives which specify limits to the tolerable damage from, in this case particularly, heavy lorry traffic, is needed for fair competition.

The effect of the present underpricing of road freight transport is to encourage extra freight movement. The growth of 'just-in-time' distribution systems is in part a result of businesses making savings on warehouse costs by imposing extra lorry mileage on the transport infrastructure, with concomitant extra noise, pollution and inti- midation imposed on people along the roads affected. Transport statistics which show that lorry tonne/km moved increased by some 43 per cent while tonnes lifted increased only 5 per cent provide a measure of the extent to which although amount of freight has grown little, transport has increased. At present trucking costs amount to an insignificant proportion of transport costs, reckoned at between 2-4 per cent.

Whitelegg suggests introduction of a lorry weight distance tax, a measure currently used in ten US states, in France (since 1968), Portugal, and New Zealand (since 1978). He argues:

> The suggestion for a Europe wide weight-distance tax ... is not designed to increase cost recovery, nor is it designed to make lorries pay for the damage they cause. Both of these things might well happen as a consequence of WDT but the main reason is to turn off the tap on a process which fuels higher and higher levels of lorry use and imposes a spatial logic on society which is intrinsically damaging in every conceivable way.

Business Travel

Potter (chapter 10) looks in detail at the market distortion of the company car subsidy, with its damaging effects. There seems no justification for any tax subsidy to business travel. Whatever forms of government support to business might be desirable, it seems inefficient to provide any incentive that would simply encourage unnecessary extra trips or distances.

The most far-reaching government strategy to encourage environmentally sensitive business travel is that introduced in Los Angeles as part of its South Coast Air Quality Management plan: employers are required to demonstrate a progressive contribution to reducing the excessive car use which has created appalling pollution and congestion; that is, to draw up and implement a policy which is monitored for compliance with local transport policy objectives. Each company must appoint a transport policy manager with responsibility for the environmental impact of all aspects of the company's transport activities.

Also in the USA, developers are required to 'buy in' to local infrastructure, rather than coming aboard as free riders on past investment. Where a development imposes need for extra capacity, developers pay either a contribution towards or the full cost of consequent works. A UK system of 'development gain', which has been resisted by the 1987-92 Conservative Government, provides a basic mechanism which could be developed further as part of a broad system. In Paris, businesses are required to pay a *versement transport* levy to the public transport system, in recognition that they derive from it an essential service, for staff travel, customer access, and the general healthy functioning of the city. The 1987 submission to the Monopolies and Mergers Commission enquiry into Network SouthEast, made by the City Commuter Services group of City employers which was convened by the Governor of the Bank of England, stressed the dependence of the City financial sector on efficient public transport access. Since then, there have been suggestions from business interests that a similar business contribution to public transport operation might be acceptable in this country.

One simple measure which might be promoted is for a standard business mileage allowance to be paid, applying to any modes. The effect would be an incentive to employees to use the cheapest mode available for the journey.

Where Does the Market Come In?

First, what supply of transport is available? The role of public policy is not necessarily to run the transport services, but to set the framework of what can be supplied in relation to other values, activities and expenditure. The question from the market perspective may also be formulated as: what form of market provides people with the greatest freedom of choice in meeting access needs? (These are not the same thing as travel demand – see the Paul Channon quotation at the head of this chapter.)

Again from the market perspective, it is clear that each traveller should pay the 'real cost' of the travel they consume. This hinges on being able to define the 'real cost' of each extra journey by each mode, the 'marginal cost' of that travel. Without knowing this 'real cost', then the 'fair price' cannot be determined. With users meeting more of the cost of their journeys, and of associated costs for damage caused, the burden on public expenditure should be reduced.

What is also necessary is for the prices of the different modes available for choice to be set in terms of the same framework of objectives, as a single market. That this is not the case at present is the most fundamental and far-reaching anomaly in the transport market. An incoming Government in 1992 should review decisions on transport investment in roads and public transport, applying the same assessment criteria to both to ascertain which give best value.

Though market forces can and should be harnessed to signal the relative prices users should pay, in proportion to the costs each extra journey by that mode imposes on the system as a whole, market forces cannot, in practice, form the whole basis for an optimal transport system.

Frameworks of objectives should be formulated, setting limits on the supply of different forms of transport that can be provided. The process of establishing the objectives might also establish and quantify the broader impacts of transport provision, or lack of provision. This is not a matter of putting monetary values on environmental or social values, which is a difficult and unreliable matter. Rather, what is urgently needed is to quantify some of the direct costs not currently taken into consideration in assessing the economic value of transport provision.

As a result motorized travel would be more expensive; cycling and walking free as at present. The level of public transport fares relative to motoring should be fixed in relation to the overall saving to the transport system of modal shift induced.

Determining the overall supply of capacity by different modes is the fundamental task for the transport strategy and policy. The market for transport, and the prices charged, follow from decisions on the supply that can be made available. The supply of transport capacity in turn should be derived from a framework of objectives, social and environmental, specified in terms of measurable and timetabled performance targets.

Only within the sustainable supply of transport capacity which can be made available, at prices which send a clear signal about the 'real price' of travel choices, can the individual exercise real choice.

10

INTEGRATING FISCAL AND TRANSPORT POLICIES

STEPHEN POTTER

This chapter examines fiscal measures that will address transport policy objectives within the basic requirement to raise revenue effectively from the transport sector. Historically, fiscal policy has hardly been used this way and measures will generally have to be phased in with careful evaluation and consultation.

Road transport taxation, company car policy, parking provision, measures to promote accessibility and to assist public transport are considered. However, fiscal measures can only affect certain aspects of the transport system and need to be part of a co-ordinated policy package.

TRANSPORT AND FISCAL POLICIES

Transport policy can be implemented in broadly three ways: by regulation, by fiscal incentives/disincentives, and by direct intervention, the funding of which also has fiscal implications. This chapter deals with fiscal incentives/disincentives.

Historically, fiscal policies have only been used to raise money for government finances and as part of broad economic and employment intervention. Only very rarely have fiscal measures been used to promote transport policy goals, even though their impacts on transport are substantial. Transport taxation is basically for revenue-raising purposes, and even the much publicized tightening of company car taxation has been driven by the goal of fiscal equity – to try to tax income-in-kind at the same rate as income-as-cash.

There are, however, a few exceptions. From 1980, in an attempt to stimulate the development of electric vehicles, they were exempt from Vehicle Excise Duty (VED). The transport policy reasons for this were unclear, but vaguely related to a concern that a replacement for internal combustion engined cars would eventually be necessary. More recently, Vehicle Excise Duty has remained frozen at £100, while fuel taxes have increased, so there has been a gradual shift towards taxing vehicle use rather than ownership.

The most substantial transport policy use of a fiscal measure in recent years occurred in 1989. This was the decision to have a lower level of fuel tax on unleaded petrol as opposed to leaded petrol. The rationale for this is somewhat unclear. The environmental benefit was marginal because the largest reduction in the lead content of petrol had already been achieved using regulatory control. Additionally, with a poorer fuel consumption, unleaded petrol actually increases emissions of all other pollutants.

Furthermore, cars fitted with catalytic converters can only use unleaded petrol. Under the requirement for the fitting of catalytic converters to all new cars from 1992, the growth in use of unleaded petrol is assured. It appears that a tax concession was introduced just when the problem had been addressed by regulatory control.

Overall, therefore, Britain has very little experience in using fiscal measures for transport policy goals and the few examples that exist appear to have had somewhat vague and confused objectives.

The Labour Party, in their document *Moving Britain into the 1990s*, have committed themselves to using fiscal measures for transport (and environmental) policy purposes. The document notes that:

> Labour will review the whole system of transport taxation. The present system is outdated and in urgent need of review. It takes little account of the need to promote energy efficiency or more environmentally friendly forms of transport ... Our aim in this review will not be to increase the real financial burden on transport users overall. Rather it is to overhaul the system completely so that it takes full account of environmental, safety and economic factors.

The basic principle is that revenue can be raised efficiently from the transport sector in a way that also addresses transport policy goals.

The Liberal Democrats share this viewpoint. They advocate a tax 'on primary energy sources ... varied according to levels of pollution caused' (Liberal Democrats, 1991: 13) together with 'the removal of all remaining tax privileges for company cars, and the phasing out of Vehicle Excise Duty ... steady annual increases in real terms' in petrol duty, road pricing, strong pollution control regulations and investment in public transport and pedestrianization also feature in order to 'create significant disincentives to use private cars'.

Government advisor, Professor David Pearce, is well-known for the development of environmental economic theories that seek to use market mechanisms to take into account the environmental impacts of human activities. In particular, Pearce favours fiscally neutral carbon taxation (Pearce, 1991: 22). However, at the time of writing, not a single policy measure has been announced by the Government embodying his environmental taxation principles. Indeed, in their observations on the recommendation by the Energy Committee, the Government gave a very non-committal response to the Committee's strong advocacy of Pearce-type measures to restructure taxation policies in the transport sector. All this consisted of was a statement concerning the freezing of VED and the tightening of company car taxation, with no reference at all to the economic or environmental principles of fiscal policy in the transport sector. Nevertheless, it was stated that 'the Government accepts that the transport sector will have to play its part in meeting any greenhouse gas targets' (House of Commons Energy Committee, 1991: paras 29 and 31). It appears, therefore, that there is a commitment to reduce greenhouse gas emissions from the transport sector but no coherent fiscal, regulatory or investment plan as to how this will be achieved.

What, therefore, is the scope of fiscal measures to promote environmental and transport policy goals? How could such measures be practically implemented?

PRINCIPLES

Clearly, the main purpose of fiscal measures is to collect revenue for government expenditure. Any proposal to address transport and environmental goals needs to accept the general constraints of an equitable and efficient revenue-collecting system. This consideration needs to be added to the principles and goals of transport policy considered earlier in this book (see chapter 2's discussion of transport policy objectives).

It must be remembered, as noted above, that fiscal measures are only one possible way in which transport policy goals can be addressed. In particular, because taxation is very much concentrated on road vehicles, tax changes can only indirectly promote other positive transport policy measures. Therefore, fiscal measures are not free-standing in their own right but need to be part of a co-ordinated package including investment and regulation.

TRANSPORT TAXATION AND ENERGY USE

The amount of energy used to travel a given distance varies considerably according to mode of transport and how efficiently that

Figure 10-1: Primary Energy Requirements of Different Travel Modes in the UK.

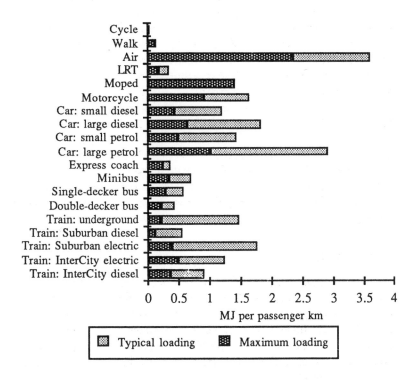

Source: Hughes (1992), updated

mode is used (Figure 10-1). Large petrol cars and air travel are the least energy efficient, with all forms of ground public transport being roughly comparable. They use about half the energy per person than cars. Fiscal policies can be used both to encourage the use of the more energy efficient transport modes and also to increase the efficiency of the more energy intensive travel methods.

Using the taxation system to internalize the external environmental costs of transport via a variety of 'polluter pays' measures is advocated by several economists including Pearce and Cairncross. In addition there are other externalities such as the social costs of isolation for non-car users and a variety of other indirect impacts, which could also be taken into account in such a fiscal framework. A similar comprehensive view is presented in the American report from the National Academy of Sciences (1991), which advocates a price for energy 'including all social, environmental and other costs' which 'would provide consumers and producers with the appropriate information to decide about fuel mix, new investments and research and development'.

Although the principle of 'polluter pays' taxation has achieved wide acceptance in economic theory, there has been little by way of practical proposals on applying such ideas to the transport sector. In order to avoid negative economic effects (on growth, international compe-titiveness and inflation) Pearce advocates 'revenue-neutral carbon taxation', with the overall tax yield remaining the same while being redistributed to reflect the 'polluter pays' principle.

The Labour Party's *Moving Britain into the 1990s* adopts a narrower definition of revenue-neutral which requires the overall yield *from transport taxation* to remain the same. Such a constraint would reduce the effectiveness of any fiscal measures and would make resolving the economic and equity problems of such measures more difficult.

For example, Barker and Lewney (1990) examined a (general) revenue-neutral carbon tax designed to reduce Britain's CO_2 emissions by 18.5 per cent by 2005. In this the carbon tax would be balanced by a reduction in VAT from 15 per cent to 11.9 per cent. Used in this way, the measure would have no noticeable effect on GDP growth due to the economic efficiency gains from lowering VAT. Cairncross (1991: 114) also notes that any inflationary impact of carbon taxes can be offset by reducing other taxes.

Besides this there are the economic benefits of the transport policies themselves. For example, reducing congestion, accidents and road damage, improving health and agricultural production. In a Norwegian study, Glomsrod et al. (1990) estimated that additional CO_2 taxation would produce economic benefits amounting to over 70 per cent of the additional tax burden. Thus a revenue-neutral fiscal package would actually produce substantial net economic benefits.

Barrett (1991: 35) also notes that carbon taxes are less regressive than many other proposals to reduce CO_2 emissions and both he and Cairncross (1991) point out that the distributional impact of carbon taxes depend very much on how the revenue raised is used. To this must be added the point that, unlike the case in most other sectors of the economy, a carbon tax on transport would be progressive in its own right as the amount travelled is positively correlated with income.

It would be possible simply to redistribute taxation whilst maintaining the same overall yield from the transport sector, but such measures would be constrained by economic and distributional impacts. The reform of transport taxation with the goal of tax yield for the system *as a whole* being fiscally neutral, rather than at the level of transport taxation alone, represents a more thorough and effective approach.

The following section provides a series of suggestions about how transport taxes could be restructured. In most cases the restructuring could be revenue-neutral within the transport sector (though accepting the lesser effectiveness of such an approach) or revenue-neutral in terms of public finances as a whole, allowing for counter-balancing reductions in other taxes (such as VAT or income tax) to compensate fully for the economic and distributional effects of increasing transport taxes.

At the moment it is difficult to estimate the effectiveness of different policy measures. Barrett (1991: 37) suggested that taxes be restructured 'accepting the resulting emission reductions instead of setting a particular reduction target'. In other words, using the fiscal system to achieve non-fiscal goals is such an uncertain area that it would be expedient to introduce measures and adjust them as their effectiveness is determined.

FISCAL ENCOURAGEMENT OF ENERGY EFFICIENCY AND CONSERVATION

In the short term, the fiscal measures that will have the most impact will be those that reform the car to make it more energy efficient and less environmentally damaging. This is because policies aimed at, for example, reducing travel need, promoting significant modal shifts, encouraging less transport dependent lifestyles and so on, tend to have a longer lead-time than the impacts of tax changes on our vehicle stock. It is easier and quicker to reform our *use* of the car while at the same time introducing more fundamental transport conserving measures.

However, it is important to use short lead-time policies in order to provide time for medium and long-term measures to take effect. There is a danger that such reforms could become a policy in their own right, particularly if judged by narrow criteria. This is what has happened in the case of Los Angeles. The regulatory requirement for catalytic converters and the CAFE fuel economy regulations were initially successful in improving air quality (Greene, 1990), but the unremitting growth in traffic meant that all these measures did was buy fifteen years before pollution again became as bad as it ever was. Of the many lessons that Britain can learn from the Californian experience, the chief is essentially one of failure – despite some useful reforms – due to an unwillingness to tackle the basic problem of over-dependence upon the car (see Deakin, 1990).

There is a general need for government to provide clear signals to the motor industry as to what policies are being pursued. For example, in the 1970s the CAFE regulations in California provided a clear lead that fuel economy was to be a major policy objective. Today, the targets that the Californian authorities have set for cars powered by alternative fuels mean that the car industry knows that such a market will exist and the technology is worth investing in. It is this action that has led, after years of getting nowhere, to electric cars becoming a serious proposition.

The Californian obsession with alternative fuels is not appropriate for Britain and there is a real danger that the 'clean car' myth could dangerously divert attention from the real long-term need to reduce car dependence (see Hughes, 1991: 156; and Gwilliam, 1991). More appropriately, the signals to be sent to the car industry must be ones of energy efficiency and, for the interim at least, the development of high-mpg vehicles. The lack of a government lead has discouraged car makers from developing this market. As Hughes (1991: 150) points out:

> In the last two decades, research by motor manufacturers has yielded considerable improvements in the efficiency of cars ... However, these advances have generally been used to improve the performance of new cars rather than their fuel economy. This is confirmed by the popular association of technologies such as turbocharging, fuel injection and multi-valve cylinders with high-performance machines, rather than economical ones. Such features can be used either to enhance the fuel economy of an engine (by reducing the cylinder capacity) whilst keeping its performance the same; or to raise the maximum horsepower of a given engine size, allowing owners to 'trade up' to more powerful models with the same resulting economy. In practice the latter has been the dominant effect.

The net result is that the average fuel economy per vehicle mile in the UK improved by only 5 per cent in the ten years from 1977 to 1987 as owners have been encouraged to 'move up' to more powerful cars. Even today, fuel economy rarely features in car advertisements, whereas acceleration rates and top speeds almost inevitably do.

Encouraging demand for energy efficient vehicles could be undertaken by means of a variety of fiscal measures. At the moment a number of transport taxes are levied that fail to relate to the amount of travel undertaken – for example, Vehicle Excise Duty, Car Purchase Tax, VAT on cars and much company car taxation. Given a greater emphasis on environmental and energy goals it would be appropriate to alter taxation to vary proportionally with fuel efficiency, while ensuring that the other objectives for transport policy are still met (see Potter, 1991a). Such restructuring would also encourage a shift to more energy efficient modes as the perception of the marginal costs of car travel are lower than they really are (Cousins, 1991).

There are a number of alternative measures that could be introduced with this aim of relating taxation to fuel efficiency. Differences in administration will probably be a significant factor; some measures could be introduced quickly, with more radical reforms left until later. Broadly the following ideas are divided between those that modify the existing vehicle taxation system (and thus could be introduced relatively quickly) and those that would require the tax system to be restructured.

- *Fuel efficiency rebates and surcharges* – The motor vehicle taxation system could be left essentially as it is, but vehicles that hit a certain target for fuel efficiency would qualify for a rebate of car purchase tax, VED and (if possible) VAT. Those that fell below a minimum level would be subject to a surcharge. For cars and light vans there could be an overall standard, or standards could be set for engine size bands.

  A similar method could be used for freight vehicles. This could either take the form of mpg per unit of laden weight or standards for different sizes/weights of vehicles.

  In order to encourage the further improvement of fuel efficient technologies, the fuel efficiency standards would have to be periodically revised. This is the principle used in California's DRIVE + programme. In this a sales tax deduction is offered on cars and light trucks with lower than average air pollution and carbon dioxide emissions and is paid for by a sales tax surcharge on vehicles with higher than average emissions (see Levenson and Gordon, 1990). So the system is revenue-neutral. Interestingly the DRIVE + surcharges are based on a Pearce-type analysis of the cost of planting trees to absorb the carbon dioxide emitted. This produces a figure of $200 surcharge or deduction in sales tax for each 0.1 gram of carbon dioxide per mile above or below the average.

  The main advantage of such a proposal is speed of introduction. It can also be introduced in a revenue-neutral form within the transport sector or over public finances as a whole.

- *Restructuring taxation according to fuel efficiency* – A more thorough development of the above system would be to create official fuel consumption categories for all cars using the DTp fuel consumption figures. This would take some time to establish. Cars could be allocated into, say, five or six fuel consumption categories and all car taxation varied according to these categories.

  The fuel consumption categories could be used to redistribute existing fixed rate road transport taxation according to fuel efficiency and so promote the development of energy conserving vehicle designs and technology and encourage the purchase of more fuel efficient vehicles. For example, car purchase tax is currently a flat 10 per cent. This could be varied between nothing for the best mpg category through to (say) 25 per cent for the worst mpg category. Vehicle Excise Duty could also be varied by fuel efficiency category: the best category could be exempt, rising to £250 or more for the worst mpg category. Equally there could be a VAT rebate for the most fuel efficient category alone balanced by a VAT surcharge for the worst category.

Simply abolishing VED and replacing it with additional tax on fuel (as was proposed by the last Labour administration and is advocated by the Liberal Democrats) would be an example of this principle. However, retaining VED and relating it to fuel efficiency categories would allow for a greater grading than is possible by simply shifting taxation to fuel. This would also be a clearer signal to consumers and the car industry that fuel economy is an important policy objective.

A variation on this concept, requiring less legislation and administrative change, would be to vary VED by car engine size categories. This could be introduced quickly pending the setting-up of fuel efficiency categories. But it would be important to establish a separate diesel categorization of engine sizes, because diesel engines have a large cylinder capacity for a given power output and therefore combining diesel and petrol cars for tax purposes is unfair. This principle could also be applied to goods vehicles, as was discussed above concerning the less radical rebate/surcharge scheme. Measures of energy efficiency per unit volume for lorries could be used as a basis for a variable VED rate.

These policies could be introduced in a revenue-neutral form either within the transport sector or in public finances as a whole.

Alternative Transport Fuels

The fuel efficiency rebate/surcharge in the first scheme, or the new fuel efficiency taxation categories in the second, more radical scheme could include categories for fuels other than petrol or diesel. With environmental objectives in mind, the system should be adjusted to allow for the primary fuel used and its carbon content. For example, Liquefied Petroleum Gas (LPG) produces 25 per cent less CO_2 per unit of energy than petrol (see Barrett, 1991: 37). Electric vehicles would be allocated to categories reflecting the energy use to generate the electricity on a primary fuel basis. (Because energy losses in electricity generation are high, this must be taken into account in allocating electric vehicles into a taxation category.) If this is not done there is a danger of promoting 'dirty' technologies that simply shift pollution back up the energy production chain. This appears to be what is happening in the USA (Hughes, 1991: 156).

Road Pricing

The principle explored above is to turn fixed rate transport taxes into marginal taxes. A related subject is *road pricing*. In areas where the cost of catering for traffic is particularly high, this externality can be internalized by charging drivers of vehicles to enter the road pricing zone or, as is the case in the Cambridge proposal (see Hills, 1991) to charge when congestion is experienced. In principle, road pricing is simply that – a method of internalizing an external cost. The cost of congestion and the cost of providing road capacity is not uniform throughout the country. Where these costs are particularly high, mainly in the centres of cities, road pricing is a way of reflecting the additional costs of motor vehicle use.

Some concerns have been expressed regarding the principle of road pricing. These focus on the point that such a strong market mechanism would not reflect the need to use vehicles in such areas, but would reflect the ability to pay. For example, most peak time traffic in central London is company-subsidized (GLC, 1986) and such motorists could easily afford any road pricing fee, whereas people with a greater need to use cars in central London (particularly those with disabilities) are among those least able to pay.

The central London situation is probably exceptional, but it would be wrong to suggest that road pricing is an effective policy tool if used alone. It needs to be combined as part of a package of policies to promote sustainable transport patterns – traffic calming, parking policies, public transport investment, promotion of local access etc. (see MTRU, 1991). The great strength of road pricing is that, as part of such a package, it is capable of generating significant income; its distributional impacts would depend on what is done with such income. In the Cambridge study, for instance, the revenue generated from road pricing is estimated to be sufficient to build the city's light rail system. Road pricing can be a crucial element in providing a self-financing package of transport policy measures.

Perceptual Road Pricing

Road pricing and the restructuring of existing transport taxes would charge road users on a marginal basis. Cousins (1991) suggests that instrumentation could be used to increase the driver's perception of the marginal cost of car use. The cost of fuel, servicing, repairs and so on are not associated in the driver's mind with journeys made. Perceptual road pricing (PRP) is simply a display in the car of these marginal costs on a dashboard instrument such that these costs can influence travel decisions and mode choice. The instrumentation could be required by regulation, plus fiscal incentives to retrofit existing cars. Cousins feels that PRP may be particularly important as the level at which conventional road pricing needs to be set to achieve a given result would be lower with PRP than without it and could enhance the political acceptance of conventional road pricing.

COMPANY CAR POLICIES

Although the undertaxation of company cars remains an issue (see Potter, 1990b; 1991a; and Fergusson, 1990), the impact of company motoring subsidies upon congestion, pollution and road casualties are issues that are attracting increased attention. Fergusson (1990) estimates that company cars are responsible for over 22 per cent of the carbon dioxide emissions from British cars, of which 8.5 per cent is generated as a result of their larger engines and higher mileages. The accident rate for company car drivers is 50 per cent higher than that of non-company motorists (Potter, 1990b) and most motorway speeding is also by company motorists (Home Office, 1989).

Company Car Taxation

The existing income tax system for company cars is based on the use of a 'scale charge', which is what a company car is considered to be worth for taxation purposes. It is added to a person's cash income and the employee is then taxed at their appropriate marginal rate. The scale charge varies according to the value, engine size and age of a car.

This system could be reworked to be fairer and, on average, to tax income-in-kind at the same rate as income-as-cash. At the moment the undertaxation is unevenly distributed since the scale charges benefit users of larger cars and the rich at the expense of smaller company car users on lower incomes. In 1989/90, the scale charge for a 1.4 litre car averaged 88 per cent of the true value of the car; for a 1.4-2.0 litre car it was 77 per cent and was only 61 per cent for a car of over 2 litres (Potter, 1990b: 5). Increases in the scale charges have preserved this imbalance. As 'genuine need' company car users tend to have smaller cars and 'perk' users larger cars, the system works to the advantage of income-in-kind company car users and against company car users with valid travelling needs.

A rapidly applied and administratively simple modification, therefore, would be to adjust the scale charges to remove the heavier taxation upon smaller cars and then apply a fuel efficiency

Table 10-2: Illustrative Example of a Rebate/Surcharge System for Company Car Taxation.

Engine size category	Scale charge increased by 25 per cent if car's mpg is below:	Scale charge decreased by 25 per cent if car's mpg is above:
Up to 1600cc	35	50
1600-2000cc	30	45
Over 2000cc	25	40

Note: The mpg would be a simple weighted combination of the urban, 90km/h and 120km/h figures as used in the CAFE legislation in the USA.

rebate/surcharge method as outlined above in connection with restructuring vehicle taxation in general. The table above is an illustrative example.

Such a scheme would also partly remove the disadvantage currently suffered by diesel-engined company cars caused by their being categorized with petrol engined cars. This helps to explain why more fuel efficient diesel cars are used less in Britain compared with elsewhere in Europe. Even were the existing scale charge system to be retained in the interim, a separate set of tables for diesel cars would be necessary.

Corporate Taxation of Company Cars

Successive Chancellors have viewed the undertaxation of company motoring entirely in terms of personal benefit, whereas there are considerable corporate taxation advantages (see Ashworth and Dilnot, 1987; and Potter, 1990b). Indeed, it could be claimed that companies gain more than the users of company cars. The 1991 Budget marked a significant shift with the taxation of employers' National Insurance Contribution (NIC), although employees' NICs are still excluded.

The latter would be administratively difficult to include, although simply allowing for NIC in the income tax scale charges would address this situation.

Corporate taxation of motoring could also be varied with fuel efficiency in a number of ways. For example there could be a rebate/surcharge system on employers' NIC, using the same thresholds as for the employees' scale charges outlined above. Company car expenditure can be set against liability to corporation tax, but this too could be subjected to a rebate/surcharge system. For example, the figure to set against Corporation Tax could be increased by 25 per cent if the car was above the mpg threshold or the figure could be reduced by 25 per cent if the car's mpg was below the minimum threshold.

Reforming the Scale Charges System

One stage on from the slight modifications to the existing company car taxation system would be to reform it so that the engine size categories were replaced by the fuel efficiency categories. The administrative implications of this would need to be investigated and this must be viewed as a medium-term measure.

This practice could be coupled with a more radical view of the distribution of the benefit of a company car. In this the most fuel efficient category is considered to fulfil 'genuine business need' and anyone receiving such a car and undertaking a minimum business mileage would be taxed very lightly. High mpg cars are already available that could fulfil legitimate company car needs (for example, Rover's diesel Montego and 825 diesel). This addresses the point that there are a large number of legitimate company car users and it is unjust to categorize them together with 'perk' company car users. For genuine company car users tax payments would be *reduced*.

It could then be assumed that the entire difference in value between this 'basic company car' category and all other cars in the poorer fuel efficiency categories represents income-in-kind. In other words, if people want their companies to give them more powerful and luxurious cars than is necessary for company business then this rightly should be treated *entirely* as income-in-kind.

The above has assumed the retention (though with major modifications) of the scale charge system. Some consideration could be devoted to replacing it altogether. Advances in computerization since the scale charge system was established in 1976 make it administratively possible to tax people on the individual use of their company car. This would require individual vehicle instrumentation to log business and private mileage. The individual would be taxed on the non in-course-of-work proportion. The technology for such instrumentation is well established and is inexpensive. This would be advantageous for a number of other reasons, among which are safety (company motorists driving for too long and too fast) and, particularly, clamping down on 'clocking' frauds, for which high-mileage and relatively young company cars are notorious.

Fuel Scale Charges

Fuel scale charges apply if a user of a company car is given free fuel by his or her employer. This is presently a flat amount per car, so there is every incentive to 'use up' the amount for which the company car user is being charged. Above this there is no taxation of free fuel. This is compounded by the practice of company car users trying to add as much mileage as possible to their vehicles in order to get them replaced with a better model.

The fuel scale charge could be varied according to the mpg of the car using the fuel efficiency categories outlined above. This would reinforce the attraction of energy efficient cars. A fairer method, and one that would address the problem of the scale charges acting as a 'target' to exceed, would be to tax fuel on an individual car basis. In-course-of-work and total annual mileage would be declared and fuel used for private purposes would be taxed as income-in-kind. In-car instrumentation would make this option easier to implement and reduce the potential for fraud.

Company Cars, Employees' Rights and Health and Safety

Even today, a large number of employees would be better off if paid in cash rather than in cars and motoring costs. Before the 1991 Budget, according to the regular Monks survey of company car practices in firms, 17 per cent of companies offered cash as an alternative to a car. Although successive Chancellors have been trying to equalize taxation on perks and cash, with the overt intention of eliminating the use of company cars for tax avoidance, in practice Inland Revenue and Customs and Excise rules are making it difficult for firms to swap from cars to cash.

In 1991, the Trustee Savings Bank tried to phase out 'perk' cars while retaining them for employees with a genuine business travel need. This plan was abandoned because the Customs and Excise ruled that if the option were offered, those who retained cars would be charged VAT on the contract hire charge (up to £1200 a year). In consequence the TSB scrapped the whole plan (Kemp, 1991). Another example concerns the Inland Revenue, who have ruled that if, in order to pay an employee cash, a company values a car above the scale charge previously paid, then all other employees who retain cars are liable for tax on that higher sum. Not surprisingly, the staff relations problems this causes have also discouraged employers from replacing company cars with cash (Griffiths, 1991).

Clearly, the Inland Revenue and Customs and Excise rules need to be harmonized with policies to discourage the use of cars and motoring costs as income-in-kind. Additionally legislation could be introduced requiring firms to:

- provide employees with an annual statement of the value of the motoring provisions given them in that year, how much tax they have paid on that income-in-kind and how much tax they would have paid had that income-in-kind been paid in cash;
- give employees the right to elect to be paid in cash to the same value as motoring income-in-kind.

Company cars are not adequately catered for by Health and Safety at Work legislation. This is of particular concern given their poor speeding and safety record. One option is that, in the same way that work machinery has to be fitted with devices to improve and monitor safety, this should also apply to company cars. One method would be regulations requiring the equipping of all company cars with a speed limiting device (as currently fitted to coaches and lorries) to ensure that they are not used in an illegal manner. Such an instrument could also be combined with a monitoring device to check the safety performance of drivers (of particular use if they are involved in accidents). A further idea might be that if people who buy ex-company cars keep the speed governor, they would qualify for a VED rebate.

Mileage Rate Expenses

There is a danger that, should company car taxation be tightened up, then firms would simply pay employees a high mileage rate and so income-in-kind would continue to be paid in a different way. With larger cars qualifying for higher mileage rates, this could also encourage fuel inefficient vehicles. A similar principal to the 'basic' company car level could be applied. There could be an official maximum car mileage rate for all cars of whatever size (for example, equal to the standard class fare by rail). Any company paying above this rate would be required to report to the Inland Revenue the amounts paid and to whom. The amount in excess of the official mileage rate would be treated as income-in-kind. In practice the administrative inconvenience involved would probably result in most companies paying only up to the official rate. Schemes to subsidize the purchase of private cars would also need attention.

PARKING PROVISION

Company-provided parking provision is not treated as income-in-kind. In some areas of major congestion (such as central London), the value of the parking space can exceed that of a company car. This is an issue that is much wider than that of company cars alone, for company parking is provided for all types of employees. It would be administratively easier to deal with this fiscally via the employer rather than through taxation of the individual employees.

Consideration could be given to fiscal arrangements that might discourage commuting by car and/or encourage funding of public transport such as those in France and the USA. In France there are specific employer taxes to support local public transport and in southern California large employers are required to take a major role in shifting work journeys to more environmentally friendly modes.

This is one area where local authorities and the new regional authorities could play a major role. For example, local taxation measures could also be applied, with there being a higher valuation than at present for non-residential car parking above a certain ratio of parking spaces to employees. The ratio could be determined locally depending on local transport plans. Car parking for people with disabilities should be excluded from the ratio calculations. In principle, a 'carbon tax' on parking spaces is a logical extension to that on fuel.

Local council tax relief would be allowed for companies providing public transport assistance, season ticket loans, bicycle lockers, provision for people with disabilities, and so on. It is important to include the positive encouragement of energy efficient and congestion reducing modes as well as measures to internalize the external costs of the car.

At the national level, consideration could be given to varying Corporation Tax, with expenditure on car parking above the ratio agreed being non-allowable against Corporation Tax and expenditure on public transport assistance, bicycle lockers etc., qualifying for an additional allowance.

This is an area which needs careful study and application, and can only be properly implemented as part of a wider reform to the structures and financing of local authorities.

PUBLIC TRANSPORT

A local employer tax to fund public transport certainly deserves consideration. Although hypothecation of transport taxes for transport expenditure is difficult at the national level, at the local authority (and regional) level it is more easily achievable. However, an additional local tax could have negative economic and equity impacts unless other fiscal adjustments were made in the taxation system – for example, the local employment tax being eligible to be set against Corporation Tax liability. There are other possible sources of funding. Road pricing would yield a significant income, but only in larger urban settlements. But it is in larger urban settlements where investment in public transport is expensive and where modal shift from car trips is most viable.

The problem of an ageing bus fleet could be addressed by fiscal incentives for new bus investment with, for example, lower rates of VAT and increased Corporation Tax allowances. These could be combined with regulations for new buses to meet transport policy goals (e.g., standards of access for people with disabilities) and/or fiscal incentives linked to environmental goals. For example, Passenger Service Vehicle (PSV) VED rates could be fuel consumption related, as could be VAT on new buses. Any measures for new bus grants could also include similar requirements, thus integrating fiscal, regulatory and state funding policies.

Season Ticket Tax Relief

At the moment the cost of commuting is not allowable as a deduction against income tax, although it is well known that many company car (and self-employed company car) users effectively manage this.

There is the danger that a tax allowance for public transport commuting would only further reinforce the trend towards long-distance commuting. Even if a ceiling on tax relief were introduced, this would make both short and long distance commuting cheaper and still encourage more long distance journeys to work. In Germany, a tax allowance against the cost of commuting has been available since 1920. This has particularly favoured car commuting and has become Germany's tax-dodging equivalent of our company car problem (see Blum and Rottengatter, 1990). Any general tax relief on public transport commuting would have several adverse transport and environmental policy effects.

Public transport income tax relief could be introduced without producing adverse consequences if it was only allowable on short distance commuting (say on season tickets for journeys of 5 miles or less). This would provide a real incentive to reduce commuting journey lengths. At a corporate level, the provision by companies of such short-distance season tickets could also attract tax concessions.

AIR TRAVEL

Martin and Shock (1989), using a 'business-as-usual' scenario, forecast a 186 per cent increase in the amount of domestic air travel and a 67 per cent increase in energy use (Table 10-3). Capacity restraint at UK airports is encouraging airlines to use larger and more energy efficient aircraft, but air travel remains very energy intensive (Figure 10-1).

Table 10-3: Index of Projected Increase in Passenger Kilometres and Energy Use in UK Domestic Flights, 1986-2010.

	1986	2010	Increase (%)
Energy use for flights within the UK	100	167	67
Passenger km	100	286	186

Source: Martin and Shock (1989).

A carbon tax, by encouraging energy efficiency, would both reinforce the development of more fuel efficient aircraft and promote transfer to less energy intensive forms of travel. The proper integration of high-speed rail links to UK airports would be an important complementary measure.

ACCESSIBILITY

An area that could still be explored concerns fiscal incentives to promote local facilities and reduce the general need to travel. Possibly there could be a reduced business rate or tax allowance for small local shops (below a certain floorspace or turnover), particularly in rural areas. The reform of Sunday trading, a subject of justifiably heated debate, could be focused more on helping small local shops rather than the recent attempts to provide a carte blanche for large out-of-town DIY and other retailing stores (see Potter, 1991b). This is a subject where other measures to promote local access (particularly planning policies) will have a role to play and into which fiscal policy could be integrated.

CONCLUSIONS

Not only is it possible to introduce fiscal measures to address transport and environmental policy objectives in a fiscally neutral or beneficial manner, but in actual fact the scope for action is extensive. In this chapter a number of areas have been explored and it is clear that several options exist in each of these, varying from a simple redistribution of taxes in fiscally neutral fashion within the transport sector to the introduction of more radical measures within a wider, fiscally neutral, public finance package.

The main areas of uncertainty relate, on the one hand, to how much reform is needed to achieve environmental targets and, on the other, to the general public/political acceptance of each type of measure. As far as the former is concerned, price elasticities in transport are notoriously fickle, vary with time, and are cross-influenced by a variety of other factors. It is with this reality in mind that this chapter has examined a range of measures in each fiscal area – from minor reforms through to more radical ideas.

This problematic relates to the latter question of acceptability, which also contains a number of unknowns. The measures in this chapter have been required to be equitable and fair. To be acceptable they need to be phased in progressively and neither be part of a sudden 'gut' reaction, nor left until the transport crisis has worsened further. Equally, they need to be part of a package of transport investment and regulatory measures.

It is a simple fact of life that continued growth in traffic and car use is physically and economically impossible as well as environmentally unsustainable (Goodwin, 1991). A rationing process is going to occur whatever policies are adopted, but unless rationing is planned, it will be by the costly and inequitable means of congestion. Whether planned reforms win acceptance or not, traffic restraint is inevitable. If we baulk at using fiscal measures to plan restraint in an efficient and equitable manner, this traffic restraint will come in a way that is socially, economically and politically unacceptable.

11

FUNDING AN INTEGRATED TRANSPORT POLICY

STEPHEN POTTER AND STUART COLE

The present bias in resource allocation between road and public transport cannot survive comparable investment criteria methods or the introduction of an integrated transport policy. Major public transport expenditure can be achieved without increasing public expenditure. This can be done by:

- relaxing Treasury rules to permit private funds to be used by state authorities for transport investments, and providing a policy context in which the private sector has more confidence in investing in public transport schemes;

- redirecting about half the Department of Transport's existing roads budget to public transport investment, area-wide traffic calming, traffic-reducing measures etc. The results would be more cost effective than current plans as well as fulfilling the wider and more stringent goals of an integrated transport policy.

There is an important role for private sector funding: an integrated transport policy should provide an environment in which the private sector is more willing to invest than at present. Investment appraisal methods need to be reformed and although there is room for a cost-benefit approach, this should not be the only appraisal method. A method focused on transport objectives, integrated with a system to evaluate externalities, would seem more appropriate than trying to adapt cost-benefit methods to a situation they were never designed to cope with.

INTRODUCTION

Transport policy has certainly risen up the political agenda in the last few years. Traffic congestion and its effects on economic efficiency have resulted in business disillusionment with government transport policies. Global environmental issues have brought new policy objectives to light with no actual policies to achieve them (Hughes, 1991); light rail is the flavour of the month, but there is no money to build more than two or three schemes before the next century. At the time of writing, Transport Secretary Malcolm Rifkind appears to be in major disarray, announcing a pro-rail policy while at the same time cutting back resources to rail and then adding a £2.8 billion M25 widening scheme to the already substantial roads programme. No wonder Britain's transport 'policy' is the laughing-stock of Europe.

How resources for transport investment are allocated and the investment appraisal procedures used by the Department of Transport have both come in for severe criticism. There is a general consensus now that there is a heavy bias towards road-building and that the whole system of transport investment allocation and appraisal is in urgent need of reform.

A particular target for criticism is the use of cost-benefit techniques to assess public investment in the road-building programme whereas public transport investment is generally appraised on an internal financial basis. Even when wider criteria are occasionally included, allowances tend to be lower than for road-building schemes and the methodology flawed. So, for example, a new motorway is evaluated by means of a cost-benefit analysis where the benefits (or returns) are relief of congestion, reduced journey time, reduced vehicle operating costs, reduced accident costs and environmental benefits to people where traffic noise and intrusion are reduced on existing roads. A new rail line on the same route, however, would be evaluated on *purely commercial terms*. InterCity receives no revenue subsidy from the government and has an objective of earning a 5 per cent financial (cost/revenue) return on investment and assets it uses. Usually the Treasury desires a higher rate of 7 or 8 per cent for public transport investment.

Such a discrepancy makes the implementation of an integrated transport policy very difficult. A public transport investment alternative to road-building cannot be evaluated and real difficulties are encountered if consideration is given to, say, a loss-making low-fares scheme as an alternative to a capital project like motorway widening.

A 'NEW REALISM' IN TRANSPORT INVESTMENT?

The physical, economic, social and environmental unsustainability of present transport trends and policies has led Goodwin *et al.* (1991) to suggest that a 'new realism' is emerging in Britain and that even the most ardent factions of the road lobby are accepting the need for effective measures to restrain traffic growth. The CBI (e.g., CBI, 1991) is now advocating regulations and fiscal measures to improve fuel efficiency (including a system that would penalize less fuel efficient company cars), and the enhancement of public transport to reduce the use of cars. Many pro-road organizations are advocating measures that a few years ago they would have fought tooth-and-nail.

This emerging consensus is perhaps illustrated by a recent statement organized by Transport 2000 (1991) calling for more public transport investment, traffic restraint and management, pedestrian and cycle priority and a common appraisal system for road and public transport. This statement not only attracted the predictable support of pro-public transport organizations, but also that of previous anti-public transport campaigners such as the Automobile Association and the RAC. The statement proposed that:

- The government should assess public transport investment schemes on the same basis as road schemes: the strictly commercial 8 per cent rate of return which the government demands from most new public transport investment at present should be replaced by a broader assessment of social, economic and environmental costs and benefits.

- A long-term investment programme for public transport should be established as with roads, linked to overall government economic, environmental and road safety objectives. This programme should be backed by capital grants to operators and local authorities.

- The government should be prepared to consider public transport investment and subsidy proposals as elements in packages of measures to ease local transport and environmental problems. Such proposals should be considered and planned together with those involving other transport modes, such as traffic restraint and management, pedestrian and cycle priority schemes, parking and roads.

The statement continued:

> We consider it particularly important that the potential environmental benefits from public transport development are recognized and that funding to reflect these benefits is made available.
>
> We recognize that substantial sums of money are already being spent on public transport. However, much of this is replacing worn-out assets rather than investing in new capacity and a decreasing share of the funding for public transport is coming directly from public funds, in contrast to the public transport investment plans of other European countries. We believe that investment in improving the quality and quantity of public transport is essential if economic, transport and environmental problems are to be properly addressed.

This chapter examines current methods of appraising state investment in public and private transport and examines ways in which investment appraisal could take place in the context of a sustainable transport policy.

ROAD AND PUBLIC TRANSPORT INVESTMENT

Proposed spending on trunk roads and motorways was announced in May 1989 (Department of Transport, 1989c). This amounts to a £17 billion programme, to which other schemes (such as the £3 billion

Table 11-1: Motorway Schemes in Preparation at 1 January 1990. Estimated Works Cost (£ Million November 1987 Prices).

	£ million 1987 prices	1990 prices*	%
Widening	4195.4	5189.9	58
Junction Improvements	1786.0	2209.2	25
New Roads	1034.5	1290.8	14
Bypasses	157.0	194.2	2
Climbing Lanes, Diversions & Separated Junctions	21.6	26.5	<1
Total	7203.5	8910.6	100

* Figures uprated by using the RPI, yearly average inflation rates.

Table 11-2: All Purpose Trunk Road Schemes in Preparation at 1 January 1990. Estimated Works Cost (£ Million November 1987 Prices).

| | £ million | | |
	1987 prices	1990 prices*	%
Bypasses	2144.8	2653.1	31
New Roads	1954.6	2417.8	29
Improvements	1742.9	2155.9	26
Junction Improvements	511.2	632.3	7
Motorway Conversions	220.0	272.1	3
Dualling	108.4	134.0	2
Separated Junctions, Diversions, Widening and Climbing Lanes	106.1	131.1	2
Total	6788.0	8396.7	100

* Figures uprated by using the RPI, yearly average inflation rates.

widening of the M25) have subsequently been added. The breakdown of expenditure for the English part of the 1989 programme is given in Tables 11-1 and 11-2.

Although the bypassing of towns and villages is frequently mentioned as a major rationale for the roads programme, expenditure on such projects amounts to only 15 per cent of the total schemes in preparation. In actual fact the vast majority of expenditure is to increase motorway and trunk road capacity.

British Rail and London Underground

By way of contrast, most of the recent investment in British Rail (BR) has not been to increase capacity, but merely to replace old stock and infrastructure. Each year the government sets British Rail an External Financing Limit (EFL) which puts a limit on the amount of funding the railway can obtain from borrowing together with central government grants. Objectives set in 1986 by the Secretary of State for Transport, for achievement by 1989, have meant a continued decline in the PSO grant, a slight rise in the EFL by 1991/92 followed by a reduction by 1993/94. Planned investment expenditure has been set to increase to just under £1.5 billion by 1992/93, falling back to £1.1

billion in 1993/94. Table 11-3 shows recent EFLs, together with plans for the years 1992 to 1994.

In the 1991 DTp report it was estimated that BR would be able to invest £4 billion over the next three years across all parts of the railway, but this depends on the Board's success in reducing losses and improving efficiency.

Table 11-3: Recent and Planned EFL for British Rail.

	1989-90 Actual	1990-91 Est.	1991-92 Planned	1992-93 Planned	1993-94 Planned
EFL	635*	700*	1122	1072	706
Outturn	673	846			
1989-90 prices					
EFL	635	648	980	894	569
Outturn	673	783			

* Increased in the course of the year.

In 1991, the Secretary of State for Transport announced an additional £400 million grant for British rail to cover additional losses in 1991/92. The recession has seriously reduced British Rail's property income and there has also been some reduction in passenger income as well. This extra funding will allow British Rail to proceed with some planned investment, particularly the international passenger route improvements in Kent, which is a crucial part of the Channel Tunnel project. However, it is clear that much of the investment programme will be delayed or not take place. By mid 1991, British Rail was facing the embarrassing situation of having Department of Transport authorization to order a fleet of Networker trains for Kent services, but not actually having the money to pay for this key investment.

It is estimated that possibly over half of the £1.5 billion in EFLs in 1991/92 will go towards underpinning loss making and socially necessary services, leaving only £800 million for British Rail's investment programme. That programme was planned at £1300 million. Furthermore, £200 million of the additional EFL is a loan to be paid back – not a grant. It is thus not surprising that throughout 1991 the extent of British Rail's investment crisis was beginning to emerge as project after project was postponed. Even key investments, like the upgrading of the West Coast Main line and increasing the capacity of London Commuter lines, are now threatened.

London Transport is facing similar difficulties. The modernization of the Northern Line will not now take place until the next century. Indeed, it is likely that the investment crisis will result in much money being wasted. Some signalling is in need of urgent renewal, so rather than a new system for the whole Northern Line being installed, some piecemeal replacement will have to go ahead only to be torn out in a few years time when the full modernization scheme goes ahead.

The investment plans for both British Rail and the London Underground are basically to modernize their systems. Although some schemes (mainly those involving central London) will result in an enlarged carrying capacity for rail, the investment programme basically presumes rail having a broadly similar market share of travel demand as at present. To finance realistically this 'business as usual' situation would therefore require EFLs of at least £2 billion a year. For rail to adopt a larger role, as particularly desired for freight operations by the Secretary of State for Transport, would require further investment on top of that to maintain current operations.

Light Rail

Until 1980, London was the only city in Britain with a metro system (although Glasgow did have a very small underground line). The Tyne and Wear Metro pioneered a new concept in urban railways – the use of upgraded tram technology which makes a metro system viable in cities much smaller than those where the conventional 'heavy rail' is used. Throughout the 1960s and 1970s dozens of such Light Rail Transit (LRT) or metro systems were built in continental Europe. Britain is thirty years behind in this process of updating its urban public transport systems.

By 1988, the Tyne and Wear Metro had been joined by the Docklands Light Railway. The exceptional development of London's docklands had caused this project to be authorized, but with an extremely tight budget of only £77 million for the entire system. It is now being considerably expanded. Only two further LRT systems have been funded – Manchester's Metrolink, the first phase of which opens in the spring of 1992 and Sheffield's Supertram, which will follow in 1993. Faced with the problems of urban congestion and with both the

Table 11-4: Proposed Light Rail and Trolley Bus Schemes and Planned Funding.

LIGHT RAIL

Manchester Phase 1	Light Rail	£110m	PTA/Private
Sheffield	Tramway/		
	Light Rail	£230m	PTA/Sec 56 grant/Private
West Midlands	Light Rail		
Line 1		£81m	Sec 56 grant/EC/Private
Line 2		£238m	
Line 3		£120m	
Avon	Light Rail	£192m	Private/Sec 56 grant
Cambridge	Light Rail	£68m	County Council/Sec 56 grant
Edinburgh	Light Rail	£184m	Sec 56/EC/Private
Croydon	Light Rail	£80m	To be investigated
Chester	Light Rail	£13m	LA/Sec 56/Private
Glasgow	Light Rail	£500m	CC/Scottish Office
Leeds	Light Rail	£150m	Private/public/Sec 56
Middlesbrough	Light Rail	£120m	LA/Sec 56/PSO saving
Nottingham	Light Rail	£50-60m	LA/Sec 56/Private
Portsmouth	Light Rail	£65m	Private/LA/Sec 56

TROLLEYBUS AND BUSWAY

Bradford	Trolleybus	£5m	PTA/DTp & operator
Doncaster	Trolleybus	£2-8m	None yet
Luton	Guided		
	Busway	£2-3m	Private/public

impossibility and unacceptability of road-building to tackle this, many city authorities have seen Light Rail systems as the key to local transport planning. Table 11-4 lists the schemes receiving serious attention.

However, money for further LRT schemes is now very tight and, although the intention was to authorize a scheme a year, by early 1991 it had become clear that no more government money was likely to be available until 1996.

The method that has been used to provide central government funding for LRT schemes is the Section 56 grant. Section 56 grants are currently made available by the government for large, new public infrastructure projects and only those of exceptional merit qualify, as funds are very limited. To be eligible for a grant, projects need to represent a substantial addition or improvement to local public transport facilities and need to be large enough for it to be reasonable that the costs are spread beyond users and local ratepayers.

As the system stands at the moment, local authorities face considerable costs and other obstacles even before the construction process is started. It has been estimated that scheme promoters may face costs of up to £3 million for undertaking the necessary detailed studies, providing justification and winning parliamentary approval, in order to be in a position to compete for funding. Generally speaking local authorities (and many private companies) are not in a position to spend this amount of money, especially when it is considered that the scheme might not get the go-ahead.

If local road projects were dealt with in the same way, it is doubtful if many would be built. The risks involved mean that the private sector has been generally unwilling to invest in this sort of enterprise.

FUNDING SOURCES

Three primary sources are available for all transport infrastructure; these are:

- the Treasury;

- private capital;

- revenue from fares, tolls or from asset sales.

Most public sector transport schemes are currently funded exclusively by government sources. There has been an increasing trend towards public/private sector partnerships, particularly for public transport schemes. These have included the Jubilee Line extension in London, funded by London Transport and Olympia and York, the developers of Canary Wharf in London's Docklands, the Heathrow rail link, funded by British Rail and BAA, and the proposed Channel Tunnel Rail Link. Both Manchester's Metrolink and Sheffield's Supertram have involved a private/public funding partnership.

Private capital schemes entirely in the private sector include the majority of freight depots, bus company garages and bus stations, as is the case with investment by airlines and airport authorities. Except in the latter instance, the investments do not have major strategic transport planning implications. In recent years there have been a few, very large, entirely privately funded road infrastructure schemes. These have been in cases where, due to the very large anticipated flow of traffic (together with a certain amount of monopoly power), the schemes are capable of producing a commercial return. These include estuarial crossings (Dartford Bridge and the Second Severn Crossing) and the Channel Tunnel.

Revenue is available from public transport fares or from tolled river/estuary crossings for the road network. In both cases such revenue can only make a relatively small contribution to infrastructure costs. Indeed for many years the tolls from the estuary road crossings (the Severn, Humber and Forth Bridges, and the Dartford Tunnel) failed even to pay the interest on the capital loans used to build them!

Road pricing, as noted in chapter 10, has the potential to generate sufficient income to make a significant contribution towards transport investment projects. The financial framework for local road pricing income to be used on local transport projects would need to be examined (there are problems with such hypothecation even at a local level), particularly as the popular acceptance of road pricing could be linked with users knowing that the charge was being used to improve transport rather than being just another tax.

For rail, property sales have provided an important source of income for rail finances. Indeed, the financial crisis faced by British Rail and London Underground in 1991 was due to the recession hitting their property sales more than their mainline business.

The Role of Private Funding

Given the objective of an integrated transport policy, with the intention of taking into account the social, economic and environmental impacts of transport's operations and development, how can private funding be incorporated within such a structure, and what investment criteria should be used in planning the overall system and its component parts? Quite clearly, because transport investment decisions from the private sector are only part of an overall system to be optimized, a planning framework is needed which ensures that the contribution of the private sector is a positive one.

An operational example of this would be in a reform of the structure for bus services. At present, under the deregulation provisions of the Transport Act 1985 and earlier legislation relating to long-distance express coach services, any company outside London with appropriate technical and financial quality standards may register a commercial bus service with the local Traffic Commissioners. The County Councils (or PTEs in conurbations) may then put out to tender for other services they consider necessary, constrained by total funding available.

The consequence of deregulation has been instability within local networks and an accelerated rate of loss in bus patronage – a decline of 16 per cent in the first two years (AMA, 1989b), which has continued. However, the majority of the objectives of deregulation – competition, reduced costs, value for money – could best be achieved by supply-side competition rather than demand-side competition and also serve a comprehensive integrated transport policy. For bus services this could consist of private companies tendering to the local transport authority in a similar way to that which presently exists in London. In place of a free-for-all with its accompanying instability for customers, competition would take place within a framework provided by the local transport authority, whose policies could take into account the full range of transport objectives.

For capital investment, there clearly is a role for private investment and, as discussed above, this has been realized in a number of situations. The crucial matter is to provide a policy context in which that investment takes place. Indeed a policy which, for example, provides a long-term commitment to developing the public transport systems of Britain's cities is more likely to encourage private sector confidence and investment than a 'non-policy' that says public transport systems will be developed only if the private sector finds it worthwhile to invest and if the economy booms sufficiently for there to be enough public top-up money available.

However, new ways of involving private sector funding need to be explored. In particular, Treasury rules that inhibit British Rail from borrowing private capital for its own projects (as opposed to entering into sometimes difficult 'partnership' agreements) need to be relaxed. For example, similar rules restricting the borrowing of New Town Development Corporations were abolished in the mid 1970s. This resulted in integrated planning goals being achieved with a much lower commitment of government funds and with the private sector very willing to invest heavily in these previously state dominated ventures.

As discussed by Buchan (1990), in most public/private sector 'partnerships' in the present state of affairs, the balance of power is strongly against the planning authority and the public body. This leads to the strategic transport objectives of schemes tending to be sacrificed in favour of direct financial gains.

INVESTMENT APPRAISAL CRITERIA

Historically two types of appraisal criteria have developed for transport investments. For schemes entirely in the private sector a straightforward financial appraisal is obviously used. However, as widely noted in this book, transport has impacts beyond that of its users and providers. So even entirely private financial appraisals may be influenced by regulations or grants which are designed to reduce transport's social, economic or environmental impacts. Aircraft engine noise limits, the requirement for catalytic converters, safety standards and so on, are all examples of regulatory control. The Rail Freight Facilities (Section 8) grant is a good example of a grant made to influence a private financial assessment on the basis of the environmental impacts of heavy lorries.

Because transport services involve market mechanisms (the users pay fares to use the service), even for state provided services the core appraisal system is financial. This has been true since the early days of municipal trams and buses, which, though provided with wider goals of 'public service' in mind, basically had to pay their way. The problems of loss making public transport forced policy-makers to consider ways of justifying subsidies for non-quantifiable externalities such as the social needs of low car-owning groups. In the end it has really come down to a political decision as to how important the bus services are regarded and how much money should go into supporting loss making services.

Somewhat improvized methods have thus gained a strange legitimacy. Local authorities have to decide what are 'socially necessary' bus services not provided commercially by bus operators. How much money they have for this, however, is not decided by an evaluation of 'social necessity' but via the basic horse-trading of local authority finances. For British Rail, following the discredited Serpell Report in 1983, the decision was made to maintain the exisiting rail network and 'general' level of services, but a cost minimization policy was introduced so that investment to maintain the system must show that it is the cheapest way of doing so.

So rail and bus investment is considered initially on a financial return basis and if the service is loss making and judged still to be necessary, the cost minimization principle applies. Financial rate of return is required for InterCity, Freight and Parcels services. Network South East is expected to be in profit by 1993 while the Regional Railways subsidy is planned to be reduced gradually over the next few years.

Investment in roads, on the other hand, takes place in a non-market context. Road users are taxed but there are no 'fares' to use roads and the tax income is for general purposes. A market in roadspace might exist if the road system were entirely privatized, with residents and businesses paying for the roads they are located on and all local and long distance roads and motorways being subject to tolls to their private operators. Such a system has never existed; the closest we have ever got to it being when the Turnpikes existed in the early nineteenth century.

Since road-building has never operated within a market mechanism, other methods have been developed to determine the amount of resources devoted to the road system and to evaluate individual road schemes. From the early years of this century, simple demand for roadspace has been used as a rationale for allocating resources to road-building. As noted by Potter (1982): 'The demand for roadspace by vehicles is treated as a market force by the state, even though it occurs under non-market conditions. And this attitude, established over fifty years ago, persists to this day.'

So the evaluation of new roads is carried out on a cost-benefit basis where the 'returns' on investment are user benefits – relief of congestion, reduced journey time, reduced vehicle operating costs and reduced accident costs and so on, rather than fares. There is no other area of state transport involvement that has anything approaching the history of unquestioned legitimacy that road planning and construction enjoys. Road engineering departments in counties and the Department of Transport have at least a sixty-year history behind them. Yet the basis on which road-building plans are undertaken has no theoretical credibility. There is a clear need to achieve an equitable system of investment appraisal. To use different forms of analysis means that optimum resource allocation is unlikely to be achieved.

The Department of Transport has decided to review the appraisal methods for public transport capital investment, moving towards more of a cost-benefit approach. The Central London Rail Study (DTp *et al.*, 1989) moved in this direction as it contained a development strategy for improving services to rail passengers, forecasts of demand, a list of strategic choices and packages of measures whose costs are justified in terms of both revenue and benefits external to the railway. However, there are concerns that the reforms within the Department of Transport could *worsen* the current situation. Their proposals involve further discrimination against public transport investment as user benefits of public transport schemes are treated as a rationale to raise fares (and so reduce demand), whereas for roads user benefits simply strengthen the case for a road to be built!

Clearly, an integrated transport policy must be able to evaluate the most effective deployment of resources. An ability to compare not just public transport and roads investment, but also revenue against capital schemes is needed. The evaluation method must include the criteria of the integrated policy, which includes environmental objectives, targets and constraints as well as economic and social impacts to both transport users and affected non-users. Whether this broad, policy-led assessment can be based upon existing cost-benefit techniques is uncertain. These have been developed with road schemes alone in mind and in a totally different policy context. Perhaps rather than adapting inappropriate tools from a discredited past, we need to develop new appraisal tools geared more to achieving the transport policy objectives (see chapter 2).

So, for example, rather than taking any reduction in transport casualties as a 'good thing', a policy objective to reduce transport casualties to a certain level would then require any particular transport scheme to hit a certain casualty reduction target. Equally, if the road transport sector is to reduce emissions by an internationally agreed target, then individual road schemes will have to prove they contribute to this target. Alternatively, the transport sector could be allocated 'pollution permits' and investment schemes would have to keep their outputs within such limits, perhaps trading off a reduction in one scheme for an increase in another.

So although the comprehensive systems approach of cost-benefit analysis is appropriate for an integrated transport policy, this approach needs to be refocused on the goals of policy rather than serving the goalless, demand-driven status quo.

FUNDING SUSTAINABLE TRANSPORT

Given the financial crisis faced simply to modernize existing public transport capacity (let alone the financial problems experienced in trying to expand it, epitomized by the plight of the LRT projects), how could funds be made available for such crucial investments?

Simply to provide a decent modernisation programme for British Rail and London Underground would require EFLs of £2 billion per annum (an increase of about £1 billion). Expansions of existing metro systems such as the Jubilee Line extension, the Chelsea-Hackney line, and the Docklands Light Rail extensions in London, plus Newcastle's Metro extension, would cost another £7.5 billion. But much of this has already been funded, simply because such key London-focused schemes attract government concern and have the potential to attract private sector funding.

The eighteen provincial LRT and trolley bus projects have a much more limited potential for private support and will be looking to Section 56 grants as a vital element in their funding package. Together these would require £2.7 billion – much less than the politically favoured financing of the London schemes. With an average LRT scheme costing £147 million, starting two or three per annum would probably only require grants totalling £200m a year, possibly less.

In developing a green transport policy for Britain, it is important to realize that a redirection of existing state transport expenditure must take place. Trying to 'add on' green policies in an attempt to counterbalance existing 'non-green' projects would not only require more public finance, but would also fail to produce the desired results. A green transport policy must reappraise the government's whole transport investment programme.

An analysis of the road programme (see Tables 11-1 and 11-2) shows that £6480 million (at 1990 prices) is intended for new roads and widening schemes, plus a further £5000 million from the trunk road programme which is for new roads, motorway conversion, dualling and widening. Two-thirds of total roads expenditure (£11,480 million) is basically to allow for traffic *growth* while only a third (£5800 million) is for bypasses and other work essential to cater for the impacts of *current* traffic flows.

An integrated transport policy with clear objectives for environmental sustainability, personal mobility, economic efficiency and safety would be very unlikely to devote such a large proportion of government spending towards catering for road traffic growth. A goal-focused appraisal system would certainly release funds from the existing roads programme to be better spent elsewhere. The wasteful use of public money brought about by the lack of an integrated transport policy is illustrated by the M1 widening programme. Costed at over £1400m it is over seven and a half times as expensive as the electrification and upgrading of the parallel Midland Mainline (see Tables 11-5 and 11-6). The latter has real potential to reduce motorway congestion as part of a carefully planned programme, and would do so at a lower cost to the Exchequer. This option has not been explored.

The amount of public money devoted simply to increasing road capacity is very large (see Table 11-7). If half of these proposed widening schemes were cancelled, over £2500 million could be made available for use on other transport modes by local authorities. For example, it would be enough to fund fifteen to twenty LRT systems. Such a commitment to a programme of urban public transport development would encourage private sector investment which, together with road-pricing funds becoming available in some areas, would mean that it would be possible to provide every town and city of 250,000 people or more with a modern LRT system *at no additional* cost to the taxpayer.

Table 11-5: M1 Programme Schemes in Preparation at 1 January, 1990. Estimated Works Cost (£ Million November 1987 Prices).

	£ million	
	1987 prices	1991 prices
Widening	995	1244
Link Road	100	125
Junction improvements	13	16
Climbing lanes	10	13
Diversions	10	13
Total	1128	1410

Source: DTp (1991)

Table 11-6: Midland Mainline Electrification Costs (£ million).

	1989 prices	1991 prices
Electrification	93	107
Track improvements	10	11
Locomotives	30	30
Coaches	30	30
Total	163	187

Figures taken from Railway Development Society, Briefing Paper No.8, 1989.

Table 11-7: Motorway Widening Programme.

	£ million (1990 prices)
M1:	£1230.8
M2:	£ 59.3
M3:	£ 51.0
M4:	£ 362.3
M5:	£ 280.7
M6:	£ 998.2
M11:	£ 100.1
M20:	£ 117.5
M23:	£ 37.1
M40:	£ 137.5
M25:	£1237.0
M42:	£ 228.8
M56:	£ 28.4
M62:	£ 295.7
M63:	£ 24.7

CONCLUSIONS

Overall it is clear that the bias in resource allocation between road and public transport cannot survive comparable investment criteria methods or the introduction of an integrated transport policy.

Major public transport expenditure can be achieved by redirecting the Department of Transport's existing budget. The results would be more cost effective than current plans, as well as fulfilling the wider and more stringent goals of an integrated transport policy.

There is an important role for private sector funding, and an integrated transport policy should provide an environment in which the private sector is more willing to invest than at present.

Investment appraisal methods need to be reformed and although there is room for a cost-benefit approach, this should not be the only appraisal method. An appraisal method focused on transport objectives, integrated with a system to evaluate externalities, would seem more appropriate than trying to adapt cost-benefit methods to a situation with which they were never designed to cope.

12

LEARNING FROM THE REAL EUROPE

JOHN ROBERTS

This book lists many deficiencies in transport policy and provision in Britain. Can corrective lessons be learnt from mainland Europe? This chapter suggests there are many positive concepts lying alongside others which are incompatible with environmental salvation. Among these contradictory examples are supply-led situations, like (western) Germany's very high investment in both road and local rail, when reduction in travel should be the paramount goal. In terms of government policy, the most useful lessons are to be found in methods of effecting shifts from car and air passenger travel, and road freight, towards the 'greener' modes of transport, and in the integration of related means of transport. Simply to ape European developments in infrastructural provision is unlikely to be effective in enhancing quality of life.

INTRODUCTION

While researching *Quality Streets* (TEST, 1988), data availability and their effective translation to Britain were ever-present problems. Britain has a quite good set of transport data, though changes in their structure from time to time do not help with continuity, and some areas like retailing are surrounded by the specious secrecy that is endemic to Britain. Most countries had population, density, and employment data for the cities we investigated. Most had a clear idea of roadspace and public transport facilities. But only Germany and Austria had systematic small area retail turnover data, available to the public. Little publicly collected data was available in Italy, though just after our study of Bologna that city established a statistical office.

Research on Groningen in the Netherlands was facilitated more by the university than the public sector. Denmark had little data; Sweden excellent data in some areas, none in others.

Our response to these difficulties was to provide whatever was available as an economic indicator in each of the countries – not the best way into comparisons with Britain. Five years earlier we had studied several European rail systems' investment and fares policies, and had backed these up with a general overview of the performance of each national rail system (TEST, 1984a). We made great attempts to standardize the data, first by converting all monetary figures into real terms based on inflationary rates in each country, and second by using ECUs as the standard form of currency.

Given these cautionary remarks, what format has been adopted for this chapter? It seemed sensible to concentrate on those areas where Britain performs poorly: not because it lacks skills or innovatory people, but because these are under-exploited in the face of political dogma. Poor performance might be encapsulated in terms of *quantity* and *quality*. This chapter will discuss supply and demand (quantity), and later look at the reasons why the 'green modes', through quality of provision, moderation in charging for those with fares, and high standards of interchange, attract high use. Where information is available, it examines research initiatives, both nationally and supra-nationally, to illuminate the advent of particular transport policies. Comparisons with Britain will frequently be interwoven with this commentary. The characteristic political consensus on transport issues in mainland European countries will be shown to contrast with Britain where virtually any transport issue becomes polarized, and may be a significant reason for Britain's often retrograde performance.

The reader will perhaps not be surprised that most of the policy recommendations made by other contributors to this book reflect actions already underway in mainland Europe; this chapter does not make policy recommendations, though it would tend to accept the influence of European practice where it approaches the attainment of chapter 2's objectives. It should also not be considered comprehensive: such a prospect would require encyclopaedic dimensions, rather than the few thousand words here. It is introductory. It is also critical, and refuses to see mainland Europe through rose-tinted spectacles – after all, some of their policies are unwittingly *encouraging* travel, while others fit my concept of a 'placebo effect' (i.e., where some action is taken to make it apparent that a government's policies are firmly pro-environment, but where the results belie this). For example, 'pedestrianization reduces accidents' – of course, in the immediate locality; but it is likely that accidents are merely displaced outside the pedestrianized area, according to TEST's work in Groningen and Sutton. 'Catalytic converters dramatically reduce polluting emissions from vehicles' – yes, but they do nothing about CO_2, in fact they slightly increase its emission. 'Traffic calming improves environments' – yes, but it frequently leads to additional on-street parking spaces, which is the opposite of improving the environment.

SUPPLY AND DEMAND

A characteristic of many mainland European nations is that they have more of a particular commodity than Britain does. In descending order, Germany, the Netherlands, Denmark and France have more traffic calmed streets than Britain (see, for example, Wiedenhoeft, 1981). Germany has more kilometres of freeway than Britain. Most mainland European countries have more motor vehicles per 1000 inhabitants than does Britain. Six European railways have a higher

Table 12-1: Passenger Car Stock in Various Countries, 1970 and 1987 in Thousands, and Cars and Taxis/1000 People in 1987 (Some 1988 Rates/1000 may be Found in Table 7-1).

Country	1970	1987	Percentage increase 1970-87	Rate/1000 1987
USA	89,244	137,736	54	575
FRG	13,941	27,908	100	450
Italy	10,191	22,719	123	419
Switzerland	1,380	2,733	97	416
Netherlands	2,465	5,118	106	411
Sweden	2,288	3,367	47	398
France	12,280	21,970	79	397
Austria	1,197	2,685	124	352
UK	11,802	19,799	67	331
Denmark	1,077	1,594	47	312
Spain	2,378	10,319	331	·258
Hungary	–	–	–	176

Sources: ECMT (1990), DTp (1989e), UNEP (1991)

proportion of their network electrified than Britain. Cycleways abound in Germany, the Netherlands and Denmark (see Brog *et al.*, 1984). The examples are numerous. Table 12-1 reinforces these broad statements.

The growth rate of Spain started from a low base; that country still has fewer cars and taxis per 1000 people than any of the other countries listed (except Hungary). Denmark and Sweden, on the other hand, had equal lowest growth rates, but Sweden started from a high base, and Denmark has maintained a relatively low base, largely because all its vehicles are imported and subjected to high import taxes. Perhaps the rate/1000 figures are the most significant. Germany and Luxembourg (not shown, 446/1000) had the highest European rates (ominously creeping up on the US rate), and the UK among the lowest, taking eighth place among the eleven European countries shown.

The supply of road and rail infrastructure is more difficult to display because of the different areas and populations of European countries. Our own Department of Transport (1989e) shows road and rail km per 1000 square km which goes some way to resolve this difficulty. In Table 12-2 this measure has been used; the Table also contains a track *per capita* measure, and the percentage of rail track which had been electrified, all for 1987.

The commentary for Table 12-2 is for the capitalist (as opposed to the erstwhile communist) countries. It shows that the quantity of road and rail (km/1000 km2) is proportional to population density, with the exception of France. (Pre-unification) Germany registers high for both road and rail, the result of deliberate policy rather than being geographically determined. On a km/capita basis, the sheer size of a country raises its rail profile – the USA and Sweden for example – but this is less clearly demonstrated than for road (though there Spain is an anomaly). Rail electrification is high in the main hydropower countries, Switzerland, Sweden, Italy and Austria, but the Netherlands does not fit this pattern.

The UK is about average on quantity of road and rail track. But when viewed as km/capita it is third lowest in the table for both road and rail. It was also poorly placed in terms of rail electrification, being below any European country except Denmark. However, recent East Coast MainLine electrification, and a variety of smaller schemes connecting with Cambridge and Hastings, for example, will have improved Britain's position.

Table 12-2: Road and Rail Infrastructure 1987.

| Country | km/1000 km2 | | km/1000 People | | Percentage Rail Electrified |
	Road	Rail	Road	Rail	
USA	668	23	25.8	0.91	0.8
Austria	1282	76	14.2	0.84	51.6
Denmark	1630	57	13.7	0.49	8.0
France	1480	64	14.6	0.06	33.4
FRG	1975	125	8.0	0.51	38.1
Italy	999	66	5.3	0.35	52.3
Netherlands	2430	69	6.8	0.19	67.9
Spain	297	28	3.9	0.37	45.1
Sweden	476	26	25.5	1.39	64.1
Switzerland	1693	124	10.6	0.77	100.0
UK	1537	69	6.6	0.30	24.7
Bulgaria	333	39	4.1	0.5	48.0
Czechoslovakia	571	102	4.7	0.8	25.2
DDR	435	132	2.8	0.9	16.3
Hungary	975	84	8.6	0.7	24.3
Poland	195	78	1.6	0.6	34.1
Romania	206	47	2.1	0.5	25.8
Yugoslavia	227	36	2.4	0.4	37.3

Source: UN (1986), DTp (1989c), UNEP (1991)
Note: Calculations for the final seven countries should be treated with some caution: population is for 1990, road data for 1988 (one is 1987), and rail data for 1984 (one for 1983). The DDR, of course, no longer exists. Further data for its European member nations may be found in OECD (1989) but these environmental statistics *only provide road data*.

Examining Table 12-3, again it is necessary to separate low from high bases. Thus the USA would be expected to be among the lower growth rates and Spain to be the highest, in terms of passenger car-km. It is interesting to note Denmark's low growth, paralleling its equally low car stock growth in Table 12-1. The freight numbers provide some surprises: first that the USA, from a high base, should have the highest growth rate of all the countries shown; Germany makes an apposite comparison with Italy and France, for it is the only one of the three that intervenes in the freight market, determining that a proportion

Table 12-3: Road Passenger and Freight Volumes, bn v-km, 1970 and 1987 and Percentage Change.

Country	Passenger Cars 1970	1987	Percent. Change	Freight 1970	1987	Percent. Change
USA	1434	2133	50	346	860	151
Austria	16	29	81	6	11	83
Denmark	20	27	35	3	6	100
France	165	295	79	42	80	90
FRG	201	357	78	27	36	33
Italy	123	226	84	23	44	91
Netherlands	38	71	87	6	10	67
Spain	25	64	156	10	20	100
Sweden	32	49	53	2.4	2.3	−4
Switzerland	21	38	81	3	7	133
UK	141	257	82	35	50	43

Source: ECMT (1990)

must be carried by rail. Sweden's negative growth must be connected with a particular national freight policy.

THE CONSTITUENTS OF QUALITY

A general transport policy based on excellence emanates from aims and objectives which concern service to the user and security of the users' environment (as in most mainland European nations), rather than corporate profit (as in the UK). In the same way, the aims and objectives will tend to be politically consensual, rather than politically divisive. In fact, it is often a source of surprise that Britain regards itself as the only one in step, despite its record of being the one European nation to sell off nearly all its public assets, to drive on the left, not to be metrically dimensioned, to have a loading gauge designed for pygmies, and to have the highest priced public transport (there are always exceptions to a general rule, as with the good-value London Travelcards). These are undeniably claims for uniqueness, but being different on principle is usually regarded as simply being perverse.

However, not all mainland policies are ideal merely by virtue of being different to UK policies. For example, (western) Germany set out to satisfy demand, an aim which many other nations have deemed impossible, particularly if meeting environmental standards is regarded as important. Germany is the arch-mobilizer: there has been vast investment in autobahn construction (in pursuit of a long-standing objective that no house should be further than 5 km from an autobahn). This led to a massive increase in car and truck movement, which then produced a fuel tax to pay for a comparable, if not quite so dramatic, increase in public transport infrastructure, particularly in rail systems. France pays for its public transport investment through the *versements transports*, a payroll tax payable by employers with ten or more employees in towns and cities with a population of 30,000 or more (Simpson, 1987).

The German actions, described in the last paragraph, can of course be measured, though it is more difficult to achieve international comparisons where there are different population and/or track densities. Table 12-2 showed this to some extent. Table 12-4 takes the argument further, and should be read in conjunction with Table 12-5, which makes some comparisons between transport investment in Britain and Germany.

Table 12-4: Passenger Transport in Britain and Germany, 1966 and 1986, bn p-km.

	1966 GB	FRG	1986 GB	FRG	Percentage change 1966-86 GB	FRG
All surface public transport	97	93	78	116	−20	+25
All surface private transport	249	290	476	512	+91	+77
Distance travelled per capita, all surface modes, 1000 km	–	–	10	10.28	–	–

Sources: Der Bundesminister für Verkehr (1987), DTp (1976, 1989c)

Table 12-4 shows that while the (western) Germans have been more supportive of public transport, and the British of private means of transport, in 1986 the *per capita* distance travelled by surface modes was very similar. Table 12-5, though it is full of inconsistencies, shows that the Federal Republic was investing considerably more on transport than the whole public sector in Britain, and federal spending on public transport was likely to be very much greater in Germany than it was in Britain in 1986. These differences in investment partly explain the differences in public transport use in the two countries – an increase over ten years in Germany and a decrease over the same period in Britain.

Table 12-5: British and German Transport Investment 1986, Converted to £m, on the Assumption That 3DM=£1.

| | | | Million £ | |
| | | GB | | FRG |
	1976/77	1986/77	1976	1986
All Federal (national)				
expenditure			6532	8463
of which, capital			3070	4316
Percentage capital of total			47*	51*
All public (national and				
local) expenditure	2719	5574		
of which, capital	1012†	1871		
Percentage capital of total	37.2†	34†		
Total spent on:				
Trunk/major roads	466†	859	1933	2066
Public transport (capital)	148	89		
Rail (capital)			2879	4477

* Germany shows a consistent proportion of its Federal transport budget allocated to investment: over the period 1976 to 1986, the proportion had a mean value of 48.4 per cent. The same comparison appears difficult to achieve in Britain as overlapping transport statistics (DTp, 1982; 1989c), used to cover the period from 1976 to 1986, disagree.

† Proportion of capital given for England, but not for GB: therefore an estimate was used to achieve a GB figure and percentage.

Sources: Der Bundesminister für Verkehr (1987), DTp (1989c).

Perhaps the most important finding from Tables 12-4 and 12-5 is that while Germany's prodigious expenditure on transport is having some effect on modal choice, in the end people are travelling similar distances in the two countries. It can be said, however, that in German public transport they are journeying more comfortably, reliably and expeditiously than in Britain, and at a lower direct cost to the user. But should not this high investment be having a greater influence on modal choice? Or is that limited because there are few restrictions on car use?

There does seem to be a policy lesson for both countries in this analysis. Britain should spend more on public transport, Germany less on roads. Having done that, both should intervene to restrain the motorist's freedom and so ensure their spending policies bear a rich and pollution-free fruit. Neither should be investing in *mobility*; both should be judiciously spending money on *accessibility* in order to reduce the need to travel.

WHAT INHIBITS PROGRESS TOWARDS THE MILLENIUM?

If the millenium – in the sense of a future time of peace and happiness – is defined by successful adherence to the objectives laid out in chapter 2, then abuse of the car must be a major inhibitor. In a world more concerned with the common good than the supremacy of the individual, cars would be used to access the places that other transport cannot reach, rather than as status banks, footwear prolongers, human relationship laboratories, or the *raison d'etre* of environmental health

Table 12-6: Company Cars as a Proportion of the National Car Stock and New Cars.

	Company cars as Percentage of all cars	Company car sales as Percentage of all car sales	Year
Australia	–	35	1980
Belgium	8	10-12	1989
Netherlands	10	–	1983
Norway	16	45	1989
Sweden	9	38	1985
UK	16	63	1989
USA*	3	14	1987
West Germany	15	34	1988

* Cars registered in company fleets of ten or more.
Source: TEST (1991a)

departments. So, for the moment excluding people with special needs, they would not be used to visit the corner shop or convey a letter to the post box, nor would they be used to reach work, or to travel about within work time. These last are the real enemy, whose support for transport policy may be found in two broad areas: the parking space provided at work, and other company subsidy of motoring. Britain certainly has a high rating in the second, if not the first, area.

In terms of parking spaces at the workplace, a special study in England (TEST, 1991c) showed that it was not simply a matter of company provided or supported cars receiving a parking space: a high proportion of these spaces was occupied by private car owners who received no other 'perk' from their employer. It was often a valuable perk – in provincial towns like Sheffield and Swindon the annual value of the space to the employee was £300-400; in the City of London it could be at least £3500. And, since 1989, these parking perks have not been taxed in Britain. Ironically, one case study was of British Rail's offices in a major railway centre, Swindon. Its 10,220m² of offices had been allocated a total of twenty-two spaces as part of the planning consent; it then rented a further 381 spaces in a private car park nearby. While these are British examples, it seems likely that car use is similarly encouraged through the provision of free parking spaces at workplaces in some mainland European countries. Notably, in offices of, and surrounding, the European Commission in Brussels, several floors of basement parking resulted from requirements of the planning permission.

/ These examples of car dependency are not, however, the universal rule. The Dutch National Environmental Programme (see chapter 3) endeavours to cut car travel. Geneva permits central office development only if it *does not* have in-built parking, and Bern has only 3500 parking spaces in a centre with 5000 residents and 30,000 jobs; in France, employers are required to contribute to the cost of employees' travel cards, thus encouraging public transport use; in Germany, employers are now permitted to substitute expensive car parking provision with subsidies of their employees' public transport costs; and, at the Swiss chemical company Ciba Geigy, over 200 employees took up the offer of a company bicycle instead of a car, and another new car park was avoided.

In other instances Britain's disdain for rationality shows not so much through disregarding the lessons from mainland Europe, as in the time it takes to introduce them. Light rail (in the form of the tram, which some still confuse with true light rail that is segregated from other road traffic) abundantly served the British for a long period of time, before being removed not long after the second world war. In some cases this was probably because of the power of the road lobby, for the tram's inflexibility was seen to inhibit movement of other vehicles: this argument was certainly used for the removal of Montreal's trams, and those in Los Angeles were bought out by car manufacturers. Morissette (1990: 113) shows how General Motors, Exxon and Firestone started plotting in 1932 to buy out and eliminate a hundred tramway companies in forty-five US cities. Most mainland European towns and cities retained theirs, and gradually upgraded them. Gothenburg in Sweden, which claims it originated light rail, has been extending its network ever since, and converting trams to true light rail (in a city with the main Volvo car plant and among the highest levels of car ownership in Europe). Very much the same has been happening in Hanover. Stuttgart has been converting its narrow gauge trams to standard gauge light rail for some years. Vienna has gone further – several of its streetcar routes have gone underground, upgraded to form a new U-Bahn network. In contrast, Britain's only light rail achievements in the last fifteen years have been the Tyne and Wear Metro and Docklands Light Rail in London; Manchester's Metrolink is under construction, as is Sheffield's first route. To be fair, there has very recently been a flood of other projects, but these must all wait in line for parliamentary time and government money.

Similarly, pedestrianization in Britain had to await Alfred Wood's courageous initiative in Norwich in 1967. As we have seen at the start of this chapter, Germany predated this by fifty years. Traffic calming, practised in Germany for perhaps twenty years, with 200 schemes operating in Stuttgart alone by 1980, is appearing in Britain with a flurry of activity in the early 1990s.

Transport integration too was a concept little practised in Britain until, again, Tyne and Wear showed how bus and rail could be complementary and, much later, an integrated approach was suggested by MVA for Birmingham in the late 1980s (see May, 1990). Long before this, integration was an accepted principle throughout mainland Europe and Scandinavia (Stockholm had been in the vanguard, as had Switzerland for forty years or more).

Positive attitudes towards cycling in other European cities are another example to review in this dismal roll-call of 'where they do it better than us'. Bicycle use differs widely: in 1990 65 per cent of daily trips were by bike in Shenyang, 50 per cent in Groningen, 43 per cent in Delft, 26 per cent in Erlangen, 20 per cent in Basel and Copenhagen,

8 per cent in Manhattan, 6 per cent in Perth (Australia) and a pathetic 2 per cent in London (UNEP, 1991). Britain has long had an intuitive response to cycling – the poor chocolate workers in York, the bike makers in Nottingham, rich students in Oxford and Cambridge, all adopted the bicycle for different reasons and thus kept cars in check in their cities. But where in Britain are the Erlangens and Munsters – perhaps the two most bike-friendly towns in western Germany which had 45 million bikes as against 26 million cars in the mid-1980s according to UNEP (1991) – and the many Dutch and Danish towns that have made specific provision for cycling with special routes, safe road crossing signals, ways through parks, space for bikes on buses and railways, and parking facilities? They are just beginning to arrive in Britain, at a time when most mainland European cities are turning their attention to other problems which may only be recognized in Britain by the year 2000, and acted upon five to ten years after that!

PATRONAGE AND SERVICE QUALITY

Public transport in France, Germany, the Netherlands and Switzerland, as particular examples, can be characterized as having high service quality, good interchange with other modes, lower-than-British fares, and high use. The erosion of public transport provision in the form of deregulation of British provincial buses has made the contrast sharper still: service quality is often poor or erratic, with some routes quite inadequately served, buses not being replaced with new stock, fares higher than when the services were regulated, interchange often not a high priority of bus operators, and all capped by an unsurprising reduction in demand.

British Rail, however, does experience high use and makes an efficient provision of services. But many parts of the country are inaccessible by rail, and there is a limited supply of track and services in relation to demand. Its 'popularity' is often attributable to the lack of an alternative, and to a lesser extent to the provision of 'saver' schemes. But inherent imbalances frequently lead to acute discomfort in overcrowded trains, and anger at large numbers of empty first class seats. It does appear that there is scope in Britain for a substantial transfer from environmentally malign modes like the car to public transport, particularly if good service conditions, reliability of interchange and sensible fares policies suddenly re-emerged, and if there was the investment to match.

RESEARCH

Supra-national research on transport is carried out by the European Conference of Ministers of Transport, the OECD, the Commission of the European Communities, the International Union of Public Transport, the International Union of Railways, various pressure groups, Universities and Polytechnics, and some consultants. Most airlines, and some railways (e.g., the SNCF with its TGV ambitions, including the umbilical cord between the Channel Tunnel and London) look at Europe with an international eye.

Each European nation (and some regions like the Länder in Germany) have research programmes, though they differ considerably in scope and quality. It may be that the proliferation of supra-national studies curbs national enthusiasm for research. Certainly in Britain government sponsored transport research has been cut back from the respectable level it once enjoyed. Theoretical and policy-based research, which one would have thought was pre-eminently appropriate to the locale of central government, seems to be passing to private bodies: this was the case, for example, with the initiative of the Rees Jeffreys Road Fund to examine 'Transport and Society' which commissioned some thirty discussion papers, some of which led to more detailed research.

Discussed elsewhere in this book are the innovations of the Netherlands ('Travelling Clean'), where substantial cut-backs on CO_2 emissions are called for from all sectors of society, and Sweden with its attempts to make Stockholm less car-dependent and more aware of its excellent public transport system. The Dutch initiative is embryonically echoed elsewhere in Europe, with the environment group Transport 2000's 'UK Travelling Clean' study and the European Transport and Environment Federation seeking funding to co-ordinate Europe-wide activity. Various Cantons of Switzerland are taking serious action against over-use of the car: Zurich with its new S-Bahn and 'barometers' at tram stops showing how many travellers were persuaded to transfer from car to bus and tram during the previous week; Bern with severe restrictions on parking in the city centre; and Geneva with permission only given to new office construction without in-built car parking. North Rhine Westphalia has attempted car restraint on a broad front, which includes clarifying the full implications of the fuel costs of motor traffic.

Occasionally, transnational research is commissioned by amenity societies, particularly in Britain where until recently there was a dearth of knowledge on 'How might it be done differently?' The Anglo-German Foundation has compared bicycle safety in Germany and Britain (undertaken by Environmental and Transport Planning). The same Foundation and others have examined children's freedom to travel unaccompanied by adults in Germany and Britain (Adams, Hillman and Whitelegg). Transport 2000 commissioned from TEST studies of six European railways' investment and fares policies; the Rees Jeffreys Road Fund supported TEST's studies, in eleven European cities, of the hypothesis (ultimately endorsed) that reduced vehicular traffic in cities' main activity centres would increase their economic performance.

Two studies of the relationship between land use and travel demand are current in Britain in early 1992: one is sponsored jointly by the Departments of Transport and the Environment; the other was independently originated by TEST, two years before the official study. The official study is mainly based in Britain with some linking to other countries' experience, while the TEST study is biased toward countries outside Britain. The TEST study is sponsored by a wide range of bodies including the Commission of the European Communities, the OECD, the ECMT, London Transport and others. It is notable in this key area of the causes of travel demand that Britain, after many years of exemplary and careful development control, has suddenly taken its hands off this particular steering wheel and is allowing many out-of-town centres – just at the time when Germany and France particularly have been through the impact of *laissez-faire* policies on their existing town centres, and legislated against the out-of-town developments (see TEST, 1989a).

CONSENSUAL CONCLUSIONS

My examples have shown that while consensus bridges political opinion in mainland European countries, the bridge is incomplete in Britain. This creates not just a range of policy frameworks and initiatives which frequently conflict, it means a stop-go situation in which the passenger's unsteady progress is partly attributable to bewilderment and partly to inhalation of preventable vehicular pollution.

Island Britain and mainland Europe have been examined and compared. While the mainland is often thought to contain a cornucopia of answers to transport questions, in fact it can also lead us astray, especially with misguided attempts to satisfy travel demand.

Nevertheless, given the range and scale of transport issues that Britain faces, an intensive course in mainland European problem-solving should be mandatory for the UK's policy-makers.

13

URBAN TRANSPORT POLICY: A LOCAL RESPONSIBILITY

PHIL SWANN

The main thrust of a new government's policy in relation to urban transport should be to ensure that local and regional authorities are able to formulate and implement policies designed to meet the needs of the areas they serve. A new government has a responsibility to promote transport policies which will help to protect the environment, but at the same time it should ensure that financial and regulatory restrictions which currently frustrate innovation are relaxed. A partnership between central and local government must be established, backed up by a financial regime which positively encourages the adoption of an integrated approach to transport planning.

INTRODUCTION

The starting point for any attempt to rehabilitate the ramshackle structure which currently passes for decision-making in urban transport must be the central role of local and regional government. Urban transport facilities often meet regional and conurbation level transport needs. But the local environmental impact of such facilities is considerable, and the vast majority of journeys meet local needs. The organizations best placed to balance the environmental, economic and social factors arising from transport policies must be regional and local authorities. The issues involved are such that these organizations must be democratically accountable and should either have land use planning responsibilities or close links with planning authorities. They should also have an ability to influence and formulate policy in relation to all urban transport modes.

A new government's plans for local and regional government will therefore be central to the effective formulation and delivery of urban transport policies. The requirements of transport policy will be only one of a number of factors influencing the shape and responsibilities of regional government, and the allocation of functions between regional assemblies and town halls. Two broad principles are, however, extremely important:

- The enormous local impact of transport decisions lends added weight to the general principle that decisions should be taken at the lowest appropriate level of government and that the functions of regional government should be devolved down from the centre rather than being absorbed from local authorities.

- Given geographical fact and the nature of transport need there is likely to be a continuing role for some form of conurbation-level decision-making on transport policy even with regional government. This is likely to depend on close working between district and borough councils rather than the establishment of another tier of government.

The precise allocation of responsibilities for transport functions between regional government and urban authorities has received relatively little attention to date and is not addressed in any detail in this paper. An attempt at an initial allocation was set out in the AMA's urban transport policy document *Changing Gear* (1990) and is reproduced in Table 13-1. Whatever the precise allocation, close working between local authorities and regions will be essential.

Table 13-1: Allocation of Responsibilities for Urban Transport.

DISTRICT/BOROUGH LEVEL

1. Highway construction and maintenance responsibilities.
2. Highway planning/policy in relation to all non-strategic routes.
3. Traffic management and regulation, including parking enforcement, with requirement to consult at conurbation level in relation to strategic routes.
4. Consultee in relation to provision of rail and bus services.

INTER-DISTRICT

5. Formulation of transportation policy linked with strategic land use strategy.
6. Planning and funding of urban rail services (heavy and light).
7. Planning and funding of bus services.
8. Highway planning/policy in relation to strategic bus routes including all-purpose trunk roads.

REGIONAL LEVEL

9. Formulation of regional transportation policy primarily concerned with inter-urban transport.
10. Regional rail services.
11. Strategic highway planning/policy in relation to inter-urban trunk roads.

NATIONAL LEVEL

12. Inter-regional rail services.
13. Planning/policy in relation to motorways.
14. National transport policy – concerned primarily with inter-regional transport, linked to industrial and regional policy.

Note: in relation to London, conurbation and region are treated as being the same.
Source: AMA (1990).

Given the importance of local and regional level decision-making, the main objective of a new government in relation to urban transport should be to establish an environment in which local and regional authorities can formulate and implement policies designed to meet the needs of the areas they serve. The current government has shown that it is possible through tight control over financial mechanisms to influence directly local transport policy. It will be tempting for an incoming government simply to change the criteria and use the same mechanisms to secure a different set of policy objectives. But this approach would run counter to the objective of ensuring that transport policy reflects local and regional needs and aspirations.

That is not to deny a legitimate role for central government in a number of important respects:

- National legislation will remain important in terms of, for example, the regulation of the bus industry and highway and traffic regulation legislation.
- Insofar as local authority capital investment is grant-aided by

central government, it is legitimate for the centre to steer that investment in a way which reflects its priorities.

- The environmental impact of transport means that the establishment of national targets in key areas is essential, and local and regional authorities should be required to work towards achieving them.
- There should also be an important role for central government as an enabler of innovative ideas and approaches.

URBAN TRANSPORT POLICY: A PARTNERSHIP

If this balance of national, regional and local interests in urban transport policy is to work effectively it must be perceived as a true partnership. Targets and standards set for local and regional authorities must be discussed and formulated in conjunction with them rather than being imposed on them without any prior involvement. This could be achieved most effectively through the establishment at a formal political level of a consultative mechanism between central and local government on urban transport issues. The increasingly moribund National Annual Consultative Meeting between the Secretary of State for Transport and the Local Authority Associations and the Regional Consultative Meetings could provide a basis for this mechanism. Issues to be discussed and agreed through this mechanism would include:

- the expected contribution of urban transport policies to meeting national and European level environmental targets;
- identification and achievement of quality targets in relation to, for example, road safety, highway maintenance, accessibility and urban public transport;
- involvement of transport users in urban transport policy formulation and implementation;
- central government financial support for local and regional urban transport investment;
- establishing trial and experimental schemes.

Finance
Central to the problems facing transport authorities under the current government is the fact that over 80 per cent of their capital investment is directly controlled by central government. Combined with tight central controls over the total volume of current and capital expenditure this means that authorities' ability to develop and

implement innovative transport strategies is severely limited. The problems of the metropolitan Passenger Transport Authorities have been exacerbated by their position as levying rather than precepting authorities.

Problems have also arisen as a result of the existence of separate grants, budgets and appraisal mechanisms for highway and major public transport schemes. Another problematic feature is that locally important but non-strategic schemes such as bus priority measures and highway improvements on purely local roads have fallen through the funding net.

The policies of a new government in relation to local government finance as a whole will have major implications for urban transport. But there are a number of important principles which should be reflected in the new arrangements:

- Where transport responsibilities remain with single-purpose authorities, those authorities should have tax-raising powers.
- Central government should continue to grant-aid local and regional transport capital investment. The grants should be designed to support major infrastructure projects and conurbation-level transport strategies; to encourage innovative and experimental schemes; and to support central government priorities.
- Transport authorities should have more freedom to borrow in order to finance transport investment programmes and the cost of approved borrowing should be reflected in revenue support grant.
- The scope for establishing new mechanisms of raising finance for urban transport investment should be explored.

It is important that central government grant and borrowing approval for transport investment is based on an appraisal of transport strategies rather than individual road or public transport schemes. Borrowing powers should not be tied to specific schemes, but to the progressive implementation of a locally formulated package of schemes. And a new government should establish mechanisms to enable grants to be awarded to a group of authorities as well as to individual councils.

A new government should therefore establish in conjunction with local and regional authorities an urban transport investment programme similar to that which currently exists for the national roads programme. It should also develop criteria and an appraisal methodology which can ensure that the best value for money is obtained from urban transport investment without having to rely on the use of different criteria for road and public transport schemes or on a scheme-by-scheme approach.

Public Transport Operations

For at least the medium term, public transport services are likely to be provided by organizations outside the direct control of transport authorities. These will include British Rail, light rail concessionaires, and bus companies – whether private sector companies, or 'arms length' public transport companies. So in order to be able to implement urban transport policies the authorities need to be in a position to:

- plan transport networks – the level of detail should be allowed to vary from area to area and mode to mode, but is likely to include integration between different modes, fare levels and ticketing arrangements;
- finance routes and levels of service over and above those which can be provided commercially while ensuring that the scope for commercial cross-subsidy is maximized and that best value for money for public expenditure is obtained;
- facilitate the provision of comprehensive and up-to-date passenger information;
- ensure delivery of an agreed quality of service, including the use of financial penalties in the case of poor performance. Service standards should include vehicle specification.

Early amendment of the Transport Act 1985 will be necessary to achieve this, together with a review of the basis of the agreements between BR and the PTEs in relation to the provision of rail services in urban areas.

Highways Legislation

Over the next ten years the development of effective urban transport policy is likely to hinge around experimentation with various forms of traffic management and restraint measures. It will be desirable to allow the types of measures used in different areas to vary significantly, both in order to reflect different circumstances but also to allow a broad range of approaches to be developed and assessed.

Existing legislation and procedures tend to discourage this type of approach. There is little discretion available to local authorities, with too many innovative approaches requiring express approval from the Secretary of State. Progress in relation to traffic calming measures, for example, has required authorities being prepared to stretch legislation to the limits and some schemes have not proceeded in the face of cautious legal advice.

A future government should, in the short term, review administrative controls over local authorities' freedom to act. Also in the short term the Department of Transport should adopt a less inhibited approach towards the authorization of experimental schemes. In the medium term legislation should be revised to delegate more responsibility to local authorities, with some form of 'call-in' power to enable ministerial intervention where appropriate.

This legislative review should be accompanied by a commitment to ensuring that investment in this vital area is not squeezed out as a result of a concentration of resources on high profile initiatives. The relaxation of constraints on local authority borrowing, rather than additional grants, is crucial to this area of work.

A new government should also work with local highway authorities to ensure that the recent increase in priority being given to highway maintenance is continued. Priority in particular needs to be given to footway maintenance.

In general, central government needs to adopt an enabling, rather than a restraining, approach to local authority initiatives in transport policy.

14

ACCESSIBLE TRANSPORT FOR RURAL AREAS IN THE 1990s

DAVID BANISTER AND PENNY EVANS

Transport policy in rural areas must be based on accessibility for both residents and visitors. This chapter presents some of the conflicts of policy-making in rural areas and comments on the many inconsistencies which currently occur. It then discusses the range of options available for passenger and goods transport, and for environmental protection in the countryside. Unless positive action is taken now, rural areas will increasingly become accessible only to car users and the objective of balanced communities which are to a great extent sustainable will never be realized.

GENERAL CONTEXT

It is only recently that transport provision has caused a major upheaval and subsequent radical change in rural life. The network of green lanes, byways, footpaths, well-worn country tracks and Roman roads are the testimony to past land uses and until recently travel was by foot or horse along well established footpaths and bridleways. Nowadays these rural routes have been metalled, widened, straightened or even abandoned to provide the fast efficient framework felt necessary for rural, suburban and inter-urban life. The car has become the dominant means of travel and more frequent and longer car journeys have resulted.

Already current travel patterns have taken their toll on the countryside and rural areas. Protected sites are threatened by new or 'improved' roads; small communities are crying out for bypasses usually due to the intrusion caused by the number and size of vehicles; the winding country lane is unsuitable for farm lorries and unsafe for walking or cycling. But predicted travel patterns which suggest an increase in road traffic volume of around 50 per cent by the end of the century make it imperative that we reassess our travel requirements in the country as much as in towns and cities.

First, it is important we no longer concentrate on mobility (i.e., the freedom to move unrestrictedly) but rather on the need for accessibility to necessary and desirable goods or services. Accessibility is important but mobility is not. Travel for travel's sake is not highly prized and most people, rural dwellers and those in towns, would happily reduce travel if they were still able to have the benefits of and access to a wide range of facilities. Therefore, if we can reduce travel distances to these facilities the distances that people need to travel will fall too. It is important then to look at different facilities for employment, for health and education, for shopping, entertainment and sport. In rural areas different facilities are particularly important because they can help to maintain or re-establish a balanced community, where all sectors of society can be represented. This may not sound economically attractive but the true costs of centralizing services have never been compared with the costs of a more dispersed system. These costs should include not only savings to the provider of the service, but additional costs of travel, parking, time, inconvenience and stress incurred by users of the service. If these user costs together with the additional consumption of resources and environmental costs are considered, then the benefits of centralization are likely to become less clear-cut (Banister, 1989).

Second, it is essential that environmental policies, including reduction in the exploitation of resources and waste production, as well as adequate protection of our natural and cultural heritage, are properly integrated with development policies. We can no longer continue to argue for economic growth, at the expense of the environment, as the overriding objective of land use, social and fiscal policies. The environment must be valued and protected. After all, concerns over the quality of life seem to be important across the entire social spectrum.

Radical and positive change is required in policies and programmes in both rural and urban society to establish objectives and meet targets both for the protection of the countryside and for the development of balanced rural communities. Transport provision should play an enabling and not a directive role in achieving this overriding objective of sustainability. The targets would include:

- the outright protection of the 'special' areas – landscapes, wildlife habitat, historic sites – which make up the British countryside;

- a decentralization of facilities and provision of services locally, together with the encouragement of greater diversity of employment opportunities in rural areas;
- the development of balanced rural communities to reduce the need for long-distance car-based journeys.

COUNTRYSIDE PROTECTION AND RURAL SOCIETY

Transport infrastructure has become one of the most intrusive and damaging elements throughout the British countryside. Roads and railways have been built through attractive and peaceful countryside, and although they may provide vital services, the characteristic features of rural Britain (including wildlife, landscape, cultural history and rural society) are destroyed. Hitherto little attention has been given to avoiding or minimizing these impacts. Any transport proposal now must be examined fully to identify its environmental consequences. Indirect effects, such as damage to hydrological patterns, local atmospheric pollution, global warming and increased development pressures need to be identified along with the direct impacts such as land take, noise, visual intrusion, use of resources and damage to sensitive wildlife habitat or landscape. This evaluation does not need to be quantified in numerical or monetary terms but rather to be described and assessed through the effective use of Environmental Impact Assessment (EIA). The skills and practices associated with EIA are developing rapidly following the European Community Directive (85/337/EEC) in 1985, and all transport infrastructure proposals should be subjected to a full EIA. But assessment alone is not enough: the project has to be shaped to minimize the environmental impact just as much as it is shaped to respond to economic evaluation.

Transport policy as expounded by the Department of Transport continues to conflict with countryside protection policies which have been put in place by the Department of the Environment (such as SSSIs and AONBs). There is still a belief that it is acceptable to damage the countryside for the economic benefits which current appraisal methods attach to road provisions. These benefits bias the justification for a scheme to such an extent that they override even the most important countryside – for example, Twyford Down, the White Cliffs, numerous SSSIs and Scheduled Ancient Monuments. Transport policies and provision must be compatible with countryside protection policies (Owens, 1990).

Infrastructure provision consumes vast resources and little effort has been made in minimizing this use of resources; in fact, it often seems that resource consumption by new roads is encouraged. Whole industries exist to provide road-building materials and services, and the new environmental awareness concerning the recycling of materials, and reducing consumption and environmental impact, has yet to affect this sector of industry. It is important that design standards are adopted to reduce land take to a minimum, to promote the use of recycled construction materials and to balance the creation and disposal of spoil. Environmental audits of construction companies' activities would ensure the minimum use of resources, the maximum amount of recycling and raise the general level of environmental awareness.

Construction and design are only two aspects of transport infrastructure. The basic question is whether large-scale construction is the best means, in economic and environmental terms, of meeting transport policy objectives. These objectives and an assessment as to whether the proposed scheme actually meets them should be an integral part of any evaluation (see chapter 2). Alternative schemes, including those which do not involve road construction, should also be presented so that a full comparison can take place.

This is particularly important in the case of bypasses which, despite their name, can often be part of a strategic route across Britain rather than an isolated scheme to resolve traffic congestion or intrusion in a town or village. The latter may be relieved by traffic management packages while the former should correctly be assessed as a complete route, not short stretches of road which 'happen' to link across the country. A good example of this is the Poole to M4 'strategic' link through Dorset and Wiltshire: although there has apparently been no identification of the complete route, it does now include the Melbury Abbas bypass. This bypass has simply the stated objectives of reducing environmental pollution and removing HGVs from the village (with no mention of the strategic route). It is proposed to cut through the peaceful Dorset Downs, an area recorded by Thomas Hardy, designated as nationally important and now liable to permanent irredeemable damage without proper attention to other strategies, such as restriction of HGVs, which might well meet the stated objectives.

As the provision of new or improved roads continues in a vain attempt to provide roadspace to accommodate the growing number of trips and, more significantly, the increasing length of car and truck journeys, the effect of the construction does not stop at the hard shoulder. Better access to rural areas often leads to pressure for housing, industrial or leisure development. Tracts of land previously locked into the rural economy as farm or forest become open for speculative land purchase as attractive locations to entice new development now close to good road infrastructure. Some of this development may be required but some is resisted by the local authority and the local people. Transport planning must be seen as part of the overall development plan for the local area, and both must be compatible with regional planning policy. The alternative would be a continuation of existing policy where new road schemes are generated by the Department of Transport in their Policy for Roads, often with little reference to the development strategies of the local authorities. Transport policy, development policy and concern over the protection of the countryside must all be seen as a whole, so that an appropriate balance can be maintained between the requirements for accessibility and those that relate to the quality and maintenance of the environment (Headicar and Bixby, 1991).

TRANSPORT FOR PEOPLE

The car has been the instrument of change in rural areas. Conservative policy over the last ten years has reinforced its role by dismantling much of the planning framework within which development and public transport had been financed and organized. To the user the car is the perfect means of travel as it offers door-to-door transport at a

Table 14-1: Car Ownership Levels 1985/86.

No. of House-hold Cars	Percentage of Households		Percentage of People	
	Urban	Rural	Urban	Rural
No Car	40	22	31	15
One Car	44	44	47	42
Two or More Cars	16	34	21	42

Note: the definition of rural is 'other areas including urban areas under 3000 population containing about 11 per cent to Great Britain's population 1985/86'. Although no strict definition of rural is used in this paper the general definition is thrown much wider than this narrow census definition with 'rural' being used in a more generic sense.

level of convenience that far exceeds any method of public transport. For those people moving to rural areas it is essential to have at least one car (see Table 14-1).

However, the car has two fundamental limitations. It will never be available to all people as some will be too young, too old, have some disability, or will not be able to afford a car. Others will be dependent upon drivers to chauffeur them around as they are not the prime user of that vehicle or cannot drive. The second major drawback is that there are social and environmental costs associated with the car: these include accident costs, the consumption of resources, pollution and other environmental costs, and congestion costs. Rural congestion costs are increasing as mobility increases: some costs are daily but many relate to weekend recreational and seasonal holiday congestion.

Nevertheless, despite these difficulties, accessibility in rural areas may be greater than in urban areas as the greater travel distances are more than compensated for by higher travel speeds and easier parking. The net effect is that travel times and travel time variability may be less in rural areas. This conclusion is only valid of course for those with access to a car (Banister, 1989).

Dependence on the car may have had other important implications as it has made opportunities for walking and cycling less attractive. The perceived danger of walking or cycling along narrow country lanes is well known and many parents are reluctant to allow their children to use even 'quiet' country roads unaccompanied. Public access onto land adjacent to roads is often restricted and as a result the potential for using the countryside for leisure is not realized. Conversely, many 'honeypot' sites suffer from overuse, so that traffic management for both people and cars is essential. The well publicized Goyt Valley scheme in the Peak National Park is the exception rather than the rule. Policy should be directed at making more of the countryside accessible to people, particularly locations near to cities (e.g., the community forest proposals), and at the same time protecting some of the overused sites and 'wilderness' sites in the more remote areas.

Inaccessibility for those without access to a car is manifest and increasing, whether due to withdrawal of bus services, closure of local facilities (such as schools) or the general trend towards centralization and specialization in the provision of services (such as hospitals). The true costs of centralization and specialization should be estimated to include the additional costs of travel, time, inconvenience and stress to the user, the resource and environmental costs to society as a whole, as well as the savings to the provider of the service. To allow for the development of balanced and sustainable communities these trends may have to be reversed. However, in the intervening period, transport needs for those without access to a car must be considered much more imaginatively:

- The usefulness of each car could be increased through more extensive social car schemes and lift giving, and there may be a considerable role for taxis and private hire cars.
- Public transport still has a crucial role to play and it must move up-market to provide quality services, including minibuses, demand responsive services, post buses, community buses and other voluntary sector schemes (Banister and Mackett, 1990: 189-214).
- Local rail services may have a limited role but as with all services should be integrated into a 'package' of public transport.
- Competition for public transport patronage does not occur in rural areas so bus services should be franchised as a whole rather than on a route-by-route basis to ensure co-ordination and stability.
- Companies employing over ten people should be required to provide a minibus service to bring their workforce to and from work.
- Cycling and pedestrian provision must be improved to include, for instance, rural cycleways along lightly used roads. These roads would in turn have restricted access for cars, road humps and speed limits.
- The concept of the rural transport broker should be developed to help assess local transport needs, to make the best use of vehicles available to local authorities, health authorities, social services and education authorities, and to publicize the range of transport services available.
- Improvement is also required in local consultation processes to identify the exact nature of small scale local needs, and to discuss possible solutions.
- Local authorities should be required to meet the transport needs of rural areas and to assess the means by which local accessibility can be improved either through transport or non-transport alternatives.
- An additional tax could be charged on petrol to allow for the maintenance of public transport in rural areas. Hypothecation of fuel tax would allow public transport support to be guaranteed rather than negotiated each year.
- A stable financial commitment should be made to the voluntary and community sector to assist and encourage them to set up and run

transport and other rural services. These services should complement public transport and be seen as part of the co-ordinated package of services available in rural areas (Banister and Norton, 1988: 57-71).

- Services to people through mobile shops may reduce isolation, and potential exists for more extensive use of delivery services such as postal deliveries, milk rounds and newspaper deliveries. These services could be extended to deliver prescriptions, local information, food and other goods (e.g., videos, books and magazines).

- The potential for use of telematics in rural areas should be explored. Much has been written on working from home together with the dream (or perhaps nightmare) of the electronic cottage (e.g., Miles, 1989), and it has been optimistically estimated that 50 per cent of the workforce could be telecommuting by 1995 (Henley Centre for Forecasting, 1988). Changes brought about by telematics are likely to be much more subtle with modifications of travel patterns, transactions being carried out remotely, and the use of technology for information and other services.

The car is likely to become even more important to those living in the countryside, but it must also be made easy to live there without a car. The difficulty with policies to increase the costs of using the car is that they may cause considerable hardship to low income households who need a car to carry out essential activities in rural areas. Such policies may also reinforce the trend towards the countryside becoming the preserve of the rich. There seems to be an increased polarization between those with access to a car and those with no access to a car. Transport policy in rural areas based on increased accessibility to local facilities, jobs and services, including the provision of imaginative forms of quality public transport would reduce the need for cars and help develop balanced communities as well as maintain the quality of the countryside (Nutley, 1990).

Transport For Goods

Transport costs (including warehousing and storage) have traditionally only formed a small part of total production costs (about 6.6 per cent on average). But, with the move to a post-industrial society and extensive use of technology in distribution processes, industry is now much freer to choose where it wishes to locate. Access to labour, good quality housing and attractive environment all feature in location decisions, and considerable development pressures coincide with opening any new motorway, particularly if it passes through rural areas. Over the next ten years these trends are likely to be reinforced, particularly after 1992 with the Single European Market and with the breakdown of barriers between East and West. Growth is likely to occur through production on a European rather than a national scale, and this will have an impact on all regional economies and labour markets. Within the UK itself, the average haul for HGV lorries has increased from 53km (1970) to 70km (1988). Rural areas will need careful protection from these new pressures:

- Development proposals in rural areas should consider the traffic generation effects and part of the conditions for planning approval should be based on minimizing road goods movements to below specified levels. These specifications could be based on empirically derived trip generation rates but should also consider trip length reductions.
- A national system of designated lorry routes would ensure that the largest vehicles are restricted to the trunk road network, particularly with the likely further increase in lorry weights and sizes resulting from the Single European Market.

THE ENVIRONMENT

The environment is likely to be a major concern during the 1990s with a variety of tax charges being introduced to ensure people are made more aware of the costs of travel and to make firms pay the full costs of transport. In the recent environmental debate it seems that transport has been exempt from much of the discussion as it is seen as being too difficult an area in which to take direct action. However, there do seem to be a series of themes arising from our discussion of transport in rural areas which are common across the complete range of transport policy:

- Policy which might enable communities to become more self-sufficient through the provision of local services and facilities would allow the regeneration of rural society, and result in a reduction in the need to make journeys or at least to move towards shorter journeys. The notion of a sustainable rural transport policy should be considered as part of a green transport policy.
- Green taxes, both positive and negative, are one means by which

users and firms can be made aware of environmental costs. The abolition of Vehicle Excise Duty and an increase in petrol prices of some 40 pence per gallon for leaded petrol would make the user more aware of costs. Tax differentiation could be used to encourage the purchase of cars fitted with catalytic converters, and differential levels of VAT could be use to discourage the purchase of large cars.

- Higher petrol prices may cause hardship to low income households in rural areas, but this needs to be balanced against the greater efficiency of cars in rural areas due to less congestion and the fact that low income households use the car less. Compensation could be made either through the general taxation system or through subsidy to low income car users. Better quality public transport would alleviate some of these problems.

- Public transport is a more effective user of resources than the private car both in terms of energy used and in terms of the levels of pollutants created, particularly if it is used to its full capacity. If the government is reluctant to subsidize public transport because it may reduce the levels of cost efficiency within the sector, perhaps 'green grants' should be paid instead. The basis of the payment would be made on passengers carried per unit of energy used and on the levels of pollution created. Assessment could be made over a year-on-year basis or on the basis of achieving agreed targets.

- Environmental Impact Assessment which conforms fully to the EC Directive (85/337/EEC) should be carried out on all new road schemes and transport programmes as a whole. This EIA would allow full account to be taken of environmental damage to the countryside, ensure that transport policy does not compromise countryside protection policy, and that road construction (where necessary) would use minimum resources.

- Monitoring and careful auditing is necessary to allow empirical comparisons between bypass construction and alternatives such as slowing down traffic within towns and villages. Part of that auditing would cover the redistribution effects of roads, traffic generation and development pressures brought about through new infrastructures. Environmental audits should cover both the schemes which are constructed and the performance of the construction companies involved.

Planning in rural areas is still essential as the market cannot accommodate the complex interactions between accessibility (land use and transport), the question of equity and polarization of opportunity, the full range of transport modes (how one mode impacts on other modes, integration of modes, brokerage), and the quality of environment. Rural areas have been the testing ground for many radical ideas, yet they are basically conservative in outlook. Rural areas have suffered disproportionately from cutbacks in public expenditure and they are now becoming the preserve of the affluent mobile car drivers who are enjoying unprecedented levels of accessibility, not matched in urban areas – these people will never use public transport. Public resources, the hypothecation of petrol taxes and green grants, should be used to ensure that people without access to a car have some opportunity for improved accessibility – these people are the rural deprived, often poor and suffering considerable hardship. Such a strategy would maintain the balance of rural communities, and if transport policy is combined with positive planning and economic development policies these settlements would then also become more sustainable in environmental and development terms.

15

FREIGHT POLICY

KEITH BUCHAN

The problems of road freight are well known, but little has been done to tackle them. Solutions lie in preventing environmental damage, raising standards within the industry and stimulating new freight transport systems. These would capitalize on the energy, safety and environmental advantages of modes such as rail and water, but include local road freight delivery systems with smaller, more environmentally friendly vehicles. These would have favoured status in traffic management proposals. Environmentally unacceptable vehicles should be banned from roads where they mix with people. Road pricing generally would drastically reduce congestion costs to industry, and for heavy lorries help to restructure the freight market.

INTRODUCTION

The movement of goods is a secondary activity, almost exclusively governed by external demands. In undertaking this activity there are two main influences, and these are often in conflict. The freight industry's first objective is that the transport of goods should be carried out at least cost to the customer. From society's point of view there is a second objective: that costs and other disbenefits to third parties outside the 'customer-carrier' relationship, in particular environmental damage, must either be minimized or avoided altogether.

This conflict is often exaggerated by the adoption of entrenched positions by various lobby groups, a lack of interest from transport planners, and a general lack of understanding about the freight transport market. One key problem is that road freight is often studied as though it were one homogeneous whole. In fact, there are two basic functions being carried out: long-distance bulk hauls and local distribution. The heaviest vehicles are used for bulk hauls, but in recent years they have been increasingly used for local deliveries. Road freight accounts for the vast majority of tonne-km (amount carried x distance carried), but little distinction is usually made between these two main elements.

In this context, remarks such as 'rail will never carry groceries to the local shop' are completely irrelevant to the key issues of how large flows of freight should be transported longer distances, exactly what size lorries should be in urban areas, and what environmental standards should be applied for lorries away from motorways.

OBJECTIVES FOR FREIGHT

Within the general objectives set out earlier in this book it is possible to identify a series of operational objectives for freight transport.

- The establishment of a proper career structure (including training), consistent pay and conditions and enhanced manual, financial and managerial skills in the industry. (Economic Development, Safety and Fairness objectives.)
- The removal of the worst mismatches between vehicles and their environment, whether in major conurbations or rural villages. This must entail comprehensive restrictions on access by the heaviest vehicles. (Environment, Safety and Efficiency objectives.)
- The development of new freight systems which will allow area wide bans without excessive cost, and improve on the current efficiency levels of the freight industry. (Accessibility, Environment, Economic/Efficiency objectives.)

FREIGHT PROBLEMS AND THE HEAVY LORRY

The main concerns about freight transport are associated with road transport and its failure to meet environmental, safety and efficiency objectives. This occurs both within the industry (reflected for example in poor training and working conditions) and in society generally (for example, in the damage to quiet countryside, or urban residential and shopping streets). There appear to be four main groups of people affected:

- the local community;

- other road users (including pedestrians);
- goods vehicle operators and drivers;
- public authorities.

The problems associated with road freight are well documented (Buchan, 1980; GLC, 1983; MTRU/SEEDS, 1990) and broadly accepted. What has not evolved is any consensus about the real extent of the problems, or how to make any substantial improvements. The rest of this section focuses on how to make progress in this difficult area.

Long-Distance Haul Versus Local Delivery

The size, safety and pollution disbenefits arising from heavy vehicles, particularly when they mix with human beings in towns or villages, are easily recognized. What is less well understood is the mismatch between the task to be undertaken in these areas (local deliveries) and the size and power of the vehicle used. Larger, heavier, more powerful vehicles, which save money when travelling long distances on motorways, are often extremely inefficient when operating the local delivery part of their journey. These same vehicles cause most environmental damage.

Why do operators not have a better match between demand (in this case the size of a load), and supply (in this case the size of the lorry)? First, operators will tend to buy the biggest vehicle they think they are likely to need if they can possibly afford it. This is why goods vehicle registrations are grouped towards the maximum weight. The second answer is the structure of the industry, with many very small, highly competitive but inefficient operators in the 'hire and reward' sector, and many companies arriving and disappearing in rapid succession. With only a small number of vehicles (sometimes only one), the desire to have the biggest possible is understandable.

The other section of the industry involves highly specialized operations dedicated to a single firm and not available for public hire. Here there is also significant use of the heaviest vehicles, grouping loads together in low-cost out-of-town warehousing, and delivering them in bulk to where they need to be consumed (frequently in narrow urban streets). An example of this type of operation is supermarket distribution. Despite high technical standards, the drive back from the shop is almost always empty, creating high wasted mileage. Of equal concern is where supermarkets are shut because they are too small or inconveniently located to take heavy lorry loads.

How Much Would Bans Really Cost?

In these circumstances there will be many savings, as well as costs, in local areas if vehicle size or weight is controlled. Thus the simplistic response that twice as many vehicles will be needed if the carrying capacity is halved, is completely wrong. This was confirmed by the work undertaken in London using GLTS data by the Wood Inquiry. The Inquiry Panel included industry representatives and agreed a method to test the impact of various bans in London. When this showed that bans would not cost the huge amounts of money previously suggested by industry, their two representatives withdrew their support for the method. The rest of the panel stood by its conclusions.

The method used simply took the loads from any lorry which was to be banned, and put them into the largest lorries permitted. There was no further rationalization into the smallest lorry actually required and this means that a realistic level of inefficiency is maintained in the system. Thus if the load fitted in the maximum size lorry permitted, the replacement was on a one-for-one basis, but because the new lorry was smaller, efficiency (environmental and economic) improved. If the load did not fit, the vehicle replacement ratio was the weight of the load divided by the carrying capacity of the largest permitted vehicle. This gave the following results for vehicle kilometres on and within the M25, following a ban with the M25 as its boundary.

Table 15-1: Effects of Banning Certain Weights of Goods Vehicles Within the M25.

A Percentage increases in vehicle kilometres			
Ban at:	7.5 tonnes	16.26 tonnes	24.39 tonnes
	+ 20%	+ 5%	+ 1%

B Percentage changes in total operating costs and fuel			
Ban at:	7.5 tonnes	16.26 tonnes	24.39 tonnes
Costs	+ 4%	− 1%	− 1%
Fuel used	− 8%	− 9%	− 8%

Source: Wood Report, GLC (1983).

These figures would be different if the journey to and from the M25 boundary were considered, but it does show that for the local delivery part of goods trips, there should be ways to achieve environmental and efficiency improvements at the same time. This is in accord with the earlier studies – for example, the Swindon study of a 3 ton ban (TRRL, 1976). The simplistic notion of doubling the number of vehicles needed if the carrying capacity is halved bears no relation to reality, and there must be considerable scope for town centre depots which would lead to efficient and environmentally acceptable delivery systems. The reason why they are not pursued at present is the lack of area bans on heavy vehicles which also limit access.

IS ALL FREIGHT 'ESSENTIAL'?

Lorries may be environmentally damaging at present, but they perform functions which are the direct result of people's demands for goods and services. Along with buses, goods vehicles are the most obvious examples of what most people would consider to be 'essential traffic'. However, this is not the complete story. The price and availability of freight transport influences where companies put their factories, shops and warehouses, the nature of their products (for example, how fresh and thus how transportable they are) and the amount of packaging they use.

In addition, goods vehicles are used to substitute for other parts of the supplier to customer distribution 'chain'. Examples of this are 'just-in-time' delivery systems, which substitute extra road freight transport for holding stocks, and the specialization of production away from where goods are consumed. For example, a biscuit manufacturer with several factories could decide to make all its digestive biscuits in its Northern factory, and all the chocolate creams in the South. A juggernaut full of chocolate creams for the North will regularly pass a juggernaut full of digestives for the South, probably on a motorway somewhere between London and Manchester. If road freight transport was not so cheap, the production cost savings may not have been worthwhile, a range of biscuits would have been made at both factories, and overall transport costs reduced.

Parallel examples can be found where local manufacturing (such as brewing or baking) has become centralized away from where people consume the products. These two are particularly interesting because recent trends have reversed this process, at least in a small way, with supermarkets baking on the premises, and small local brewers reappearing. The motivation has been product freshness and quality, not transport cost, but it illustrates the ability of the market to adapt to new demands or conditions.

CONGESTION COSTS

There are various estimates of the cost imposed on business traffic in Britain. The most quoted is the CBI estimate of ten to fifteen billion pounds a year. Even if this slightly overstates the cost, congestion is undoubtedly a severe economic, as well as an environmental, cost.

There are two ways to solve this problem. The first is to give priority lanes to essential goods traffic, and issue permits to use them to vehicles which prove need and which meet high environmental standards (including size and road damage). There is likely to be some scope for such facilities without the necessity of permit issuing, but for most towns and cities such a system could never be comprehensive, and would be intensely bureaucratic if need tests were introduced.

Despite this, the use of 'no-car' streets where buses and environmentally acceptable goods vehicles would be permitted is an attractive, if limited, option. Neither should buses be allowed to escape from rigorous environmental safety and other quality standards if they are to mix closely with cyclists and people on foot.

The alternative is to charge vehicles for their use of the road, both goods vehicles (related to size and other environmental damage) and general traffic. This does not have to involve complicated electronic gadgetry. Simple pay and display schemes could also be effective. In the case of goods vehicles, where numbers are smaller than cars and the capital cost far lower, devices which can charge by weight and distance are relatively straightforward. Speed, distance and time measurements are already taken by the tachograph, and speed governors are about to become mandatory.

Traffic restraint by price is the single most beneficial measure which could be applied to help goods traffic. If CBI estimates are correct, the cost to motorists would be easily outweighed by the fall in the cost of goods caused by reduced transport costs. This is, of course, without considering the substantial environmental benefits.

ALTERNATIVES TO THE HEAVY LORRY

The principle of separation between bulk haul modes and local delivery modes permits a new assessment of the role of other modes of freight transport, in particular the railways. This new role would have two main elements. The first would be to compete with bulk road haulage – for example, by running trains between depots which then serve as local delivery/collection centres. The second would be to compete for traffic between industrial and commercial locations which have private sidings or waterway links available.

In safety terms the advantages of rail and water are obvious, particularly in relation to reducing road accidents. The picture is also favourable in environmental terms (TEST, 1991b), but there will be a substantial number of locations where noise is a local problem. For rail, speeding up the change to continuous welded rail will help, but silencing diesel engines and introducing noise barriers at depots should be as much a duty on British Rail or waterway users as it should be on a road freight operator.

Grouping loads together for carriage by rail or water can have major fuel efficiency advantages. Waterways (including coastal shipping and short-distance sea routes to Europe) and pipelines are competitors both with road and rail, and any improved regulatory and financial framework for freight transport is bound to cause changes between modes. However, rail is the key competitor for inland transport, and its future role is considered in more detail in the following section.

A New Operating Environment for Rail

If rail is to offer a positive alternative to road, certain changes will be required to rail freight operations. These can be summarized as follows:

- improved wagons to cope with specialized traffic and to run at higher speeds;
- new freight locomotives and shunters to operate the higher speed services and to marshall wagonload traffic;
- new systems to enable easy handling of goods from rail to smaller vehicles, such as small containers and small trailers;
- a new system for organizing wagonload traffic;
- an enlarged network of private sidings;
- greater compatibility with European operations.

Such changes imply a reversal of current rail policies. The recent decision to drop the Speedlink wagonload service has angered many industrialists who invested in rail on the basis of this service. It leads to a poor competitive position, particularly in conjunction with the trend to fewer, larger depots for trainload freight, which are served by heavy lorry.

A clear example of this is the way in which much of the South East's freight for the Channel Tunnel will have to be driven to a depot in inner London for transfer to through-Chunnel freight trains (MTRU, 1991). In many cases this will involve driving in the opposite direction from the final destination. The obvious question any user will ask is whether it is really worth the trouble. From the environmental and fuel use point of view the use of private sidings and grouping of wagons for full trains would be far preferable.

ACHIEVING PROGRESS

Matching Vehicles to the Environment

The fundamental principle in this section is that vehicles should be better suited to the environment in which they are used. If delivery vehicles are fully 'civilized', priority measures for goods vehicles, parallel to those proposed for buses, could be introduced. Local authorities and freight operators could also be given new responsibilities to provide facilities for drivers away from their base, and to assist small hauliers by setting up depots where they can group together and share facilities such as route planning, return load systems and technical facilities such as weighing and maintenance.

The basic task of separating out the delivery role from the trunk haul does not have one solution which applies to all commodities or all industries. Some firms will wish to reorganize their existing operations to undertake warehousing and transhipment in different locations – most goods undergo some form of transhipment already. In some cases a new local depot may be required, and this would become the interface between the longer-distance, trunk haul goods network, and local delivery services.

Rail Freight

Such local developments could be served by rail, and Section 8 grants should be extended so that local authorities can stipulate rail provision in planning permissions, and apply for grants themselves. The grant system for new rail freight facilities which help the environment has recently been extended (Rifkind, 1991).

However, much more is needed to build up the network of sites served. For example, at the beginning of an expansion programme, sidings will not be well used because insufficient sites will be connected. The number of sidings will have to build up to a 'critical mass' before rail becomes a viable alternative for a wide range of businesses. It is worth noting that France, with similar GDP, has over ten times the number of private sidings as Britain. As a first step, suitable rail freight sites which are under threat of development should be identified by local authorities, so that the option of freight use is not removed by new building.

For European traffic, the Channel Tunnel offers a rail freight opportunity, but to match the continental pattern of operation, the provision of an extensive network of private sidings is essential. The limitations placed on the interchangeability of wagons by BR's smaller width and height clearances is a disadvantage, but not as great as the lack of a sidings network. There are no reliable figures for the cost of upgrading BR track to the European 'Berne Gauge' standard, or beyond (Germany operates an even larger standard). What is required is that new facilities match the largest standard (this will cost little if included at the design stage) and a review of key industries where the change would offer significant improvement. If investment were worthwhile, this infra-structure improvement should be financed nationally.

Environmental Standards and Pricing

In environmental terms, what is required for road is a set of vehicle standards for populated areas limiting size, gross weight, axle weight, noise, air pollution and insisting on safety features such as speed limiters and side guards. There are two alternative approaches to ensuring that these standards are met. First, vehicles could simply be banned if they do not meet standards. On the other hand, they could be charged according to how damaging they are to the environment. The two are not incompatible: for example, a future ban could be phased in by using price; or pricing could still be used to manage overall demand, while vehicle standards were also being strictly observed.

There are other advantages in pricing heavy lorry use in addition to the smooth introduction of tougher overall standards. First is that it encourages rationalization and increases efficiency. For example, it will encourage return load systems which prevent excessive empty running. Providing all operators are treated on an equal basis, there will be a resource cost saving and negligible impact on domestic competition. The tax revenue will be an added cost to industry, but is small in relation to total costs. It will flow back to industry in the form of grants for rail and water facilities.

In addition, in such a system, all essential traffic will benefit very substantially through congestion relief. In particular, any reduction in car traffic achieved by the policies in this book will be of enormous benefit to goods vehicles. This would be even greater if 'delivery vehicle only' or 'no car' streets were introduced following traffic restraint by price.

The second advantage is that the pattern of road freight would change, allowing more equal and direct competition with rail for longer-distance traffic. Raising the price of bulk road freight would have low overall economic impact, and would reflect high environmental costs. Rail would automatically become more competitive on a price basis, and the time/handling cost penalty would diminish as more private sidings were introduced. New wagons would also attract private funding, and this is now becoming popular in Britain, as it has been in Europe for many years.

Shop to Home

In the light of this, and other policies which would inhibit exclusively car-based shopping and leisure activities, it is likely that new home delivery services would spring up. One example is bulky, long shelf-life products which mainly compete on price, such as baked beans, cat food or toilet rolls. New local shopping centres would be encouraged in such a system, in particular offering a variety of perishable products (e.g., fresh foods and newspapers). The recent trend of large weekly or monthly shopping trips with cars used as mini goods vehicles would be reversed, resulting in lower levels of congestion and fuel consumption. It would reduce 'forced' car use, particularly for people with childcare responsibilities.

Funding a New Approach

If road freight transport were to be priced properly, and the implementation of a national sidings network funded, as at present, by Section 8 grants (suitably improved), there is unlikely to be any requirement for a long-term operating subsidy to BR. There may be some transitional funding needed from central government for new investment in rolling stock, improved freight depots, and the development of innovative systems for combining road and rail. At present 'combined transport' has concentrated on the idea of large trailers on rail wagons, which are then unloaded and can cause the same amount of environmental damage doing their deliveries as before. The reduction in mileage is useful, but the development of smaller swap bodies and trailers, easy transhipment systems and plenty of local depots is preferable.

This would help to encourage the pattern of local distribution and collection in smaller, more environmentally acceptable vehicles. These would have local priority schemes in their operating area, and achieve high load factors through radio-computer control – a sort of freight taxi service. Greater specialization would occur between local and long-distance haulage, leading to greater efficiency. Tailor-made solutions for town centres would also evolve, with very sensitive locations supplied by pedestrian controlled electric vehicles. Equipment is readily available and a recent pilot project was only dropped because of lack of funds (Transport Planning Associates, 1989). Resources are needed to explore these new methods through working schemes, either through national or local authorities. Heavy lorry pricing would be a good source of funding.

CONCLUSIONS

The key process at work in this new approach to freight policy is the stimulation of innovation through market regulation – using price or vehicle standards or both. The distribution industry is constantly changing and responding to market change. Providing the rules of the game are changed in a clear and fair way, and everyone is treated equally, there is no reason why ingenious technical solutions cannot be found to achieve environmental and efficiency objectives.

At the moment the lack of enforcement of existing regulations gives a strong competitive advantage to road – European studies suggesting over 20 per cent (Whitelegg, 1990). As well as taking firmer control over the industry on safety and environmental grounds, taxation needs to be restructured to reflect the way that damage rises rapidly with vehicle size and weight. The present taxes mean that smaller vehicles are penalized at the expense of larger ones. Again this depresses freight rates for bulk freight, damaging rail and water freight enterprises, and holding back both pay and investment in the road transport industry.

Proper standards and taxation in road haulage would of itself improve British Rail's competitive position. But the current infrastructure and its use need to be radically altered. Presently, Rail Freight is virtually abandoning the idea of wagonload traffic, and this is quite clear from its plans for the Channel Tunnel. There is no desire from BR to assemble wagonload traffic in a modern system and ship to European destinations, although many of these will be rail connected. There are many instances of new developments next to rail lines which will have no siding. For this reason, extension and simplification of the sidings grant is essential, and intervention to modernize wagonload operations will make Britain fit better with European freight patterns.

16

REGULATING ROAD HAULAGE

REG DAWSON

The quality-based road haulage operators licence system is sound in theory but weak in practice. There are three main faults: the criteria for issuing licences are not stringent enough; too many hauliers guilty of serious road safety and other offences are allowed to retain their licences; and unlicensed hauliers find it too easy to continue to operate.

The most urgent need is the substantial reduction of the leniency shown by the Licensing Authorities to operators who regularly and persistently break the safety and other laws regulating the industry. This could be achieved by relatively minor legislative and administrative changes at virtually no financial cost. But the changes are likely to be fiercely resisted by the Licensing Authorities, and on past form the Department of Transport will be extremely reluctant to impose them.

THE LAW

In Britain road haulage is regulated by the operator ('O') licensing system. (Northern Ireland has its own legislation.) Those wishing to operate a goods vehicle of more than 3.5 tonnes gross weight have to convince a Licensing Authority (LA) that they are of good repute, professionally competent, of good financial standing and have proper arrangements to maintain the number and type of vehicles for which they are seeking a licence.

In 1983 a new criterion – environmental suitability of the operating centre – was added. This was a by-product of a defective planning system, and fits uneasily into 'O' licensing. Problems it aims to solve should be dealt with in an improved land use planning system, and are not discussed here. Nor does this chapter deal with Licensing Authorities' bus licensing work, wearing their Traffic Commissioner hats. Unlike road haulage licensing, the bus regulatory system itself needs radical change.

'O' licences normally last for five years. If operators fail to meet the quality criteria Licensing Authorities can revoke, suspend, terminate early or limit the number of vehicles authorized on a licence. The most common reasons for such action are poor maintenance, overloading, drivers' hours and records offences, and use of vehicles not authorized on the licence. Licensing Authorities' penalties are in addition to any imposed by magistrates or sheriff courts.

THE LICENSING AUTHORITIES

Licensing Authorities are individuals appointed by the Secretary of State for Transport, and hold office until the age of sixty-five. They can be removed earlier only for 'inability or misbehaviour'. They receive an annual salary (in 1990) of around £40,000, plus a non-contributory indexed-linked pension.

Licensing Authorities are independent administrative tribunals. Each is responsible for a geographical district known as a Traffic Area, the number of which has recently been reduced from eleven to eight. Appeals from their decisions go to the Transport Tribunal, a court of record. The law requires them to act under 'the general directions' of the Transport Secretary, but this is widely regarded as a dead letter. In any event, ministers cannot influence Licensing Authorities' decisions in individual cases.

OPERATORS LICENSING IN PRACTICE

Getting a Licence

The figures in this section come from Annual Reports of the Licensing Authorities 1 April 1989 to 31 March 1990 (DTp, 1990).

All holders of the 132,236 'O' licences in force at 31 March 1990 should have been scrutinized by a Licensing Authority before being allowed to operate the 441,656 vehicles authorized under these licences. Few fail this scrutiny. In the year to March 1990, of the 17,158 applications for new licences, only 287 (1.7 per cent) were refused. Another 349 (2 per cent) were authorized to operate fewer vehicles than applied for.

The 15,666 applying to renew their licences fared even better. Only

51 (0.3 per cent) were refused, while 105 (0.6 per cent) got authority to operate fewer vehicles than applied for. Among many other cases this has led, in recent months, to:

- an applicant who admitted operating without a licence for a quarter of a century getting a three vehicle licence;
- another who admitted operating without a licence for over a year getting a two vehicle licence;
- a firm which had not disclosed pending overloading and hours prosecutions to one disciplinary enquiry, and which was about to be called up for another, being allowed an additional vehicle;
- a haulier with a licence for eighteen vehicles and fourteen trailers with no maintenance staff or records having his licence renewed;
- fifteen operators who regularly parked vehicles away from authorized operating centres getting off with a severe warning;
- a tanker operator having the number of authorized vehicles trebled and trailer numbers increased by 50 per cent despite an inspection of five of his vehicles attracting four prohibitions and three defect notices.

While leniency might occasionally be justified, reports in the road transport press show that it is the norm.

Losing a Licence

The initial scrutiny before a licence is issued, and awareness of Licensing Authorities' wide powers should lead to high standards of compliance with the law.

In the year to 31 March 1990, of the 87,134 British vehicles inspected for mechanical condition at the roadside by Department of Transport examiners, 14,587 (16 per cent) had serious faults. Nearly half (45 per cent) of these faults were dangerous enough to justify immediate immobilization. Even pre-arranged checks by appointment at operators' premises found significant faults in 2662 (5 per cent) of the 54,922 vehicles examined.

Of the 286,334 British vehicles stopped for non-mechanical inspections in the same period, 16,578 (5.7 per cent) had faults serious enough to justify prosecution. Of the 109,805 weighed, 6778 (6 per cent) were overloaded enough to justify immediate immobilization.

The percentage of overloaded vehicles is misleading. Empty vehicles, and those which are clearly lightly loaded, are not weighed. On the other hand, enforcement officers allow substantial tolerances –

between 5 per cent and 10 per cent – before prosecuting or prohibiting. Even before CB radio and in-cab telephones, knowledge of a roadside check spread rapidly, leading to drivers with guilty consciences diverting or waiting in laybys until the coast was clear. And lorries moving at night, or using motorways, or both, are underrepresented in the checks.

These statistics are not reflected in those of Licensing Authorities' use of their disciplinary powers. Those were invoked against 463 (0.35 per cent) of the 132,236 licence holders. There were 111 premature terminations, thirty-nine curtailments, twenty-nine suspensions and ninety-nine revocations. 185 (40 per cent) received either a formal warning or no penalty at all.

Even those low figures overstate the extent of penalties. Many revocations are purely formal, relating to operators who have not surrendered their licences when going out of business. Others are used as a warning, accompanied by the simultaneous grant of a new licence. Curtailments often merely delete vehicles on the margin of the licence – those the holder is authorized to operate but does not in fact possess. Premature terminations put the operator to the trouble of renewing his licence earlier than would normally have been the case.

There are also wide variations among the Licensing Authorities in the use of their powers and the severity of their punishments. In the four years ending in March 1990 one Licensing Authority with some 11,000 operators revoked only four licences, but issued 166 warnings. In the same period another Licensing Authority, with some 12,000 operators, revoked seventy-five licences but issued only seventeen warnings.

Evading a Licence

Some hauliers operate without an 'O' licence. This is not just a matter of not having the right disc on the windscreen. Despite its weak administration 'O' licensing provides a net made up of the threads of safety and environmental legislation relating to the vehicle, its driver and its operator. Many unlicensed hauliers fear (with some justice in these computerized days) that to 'join' one system may reveal their illegal status, so they choose to remain completely outside the rules – no annual test, unlicensed drivers working excessive hours with insufficient rest, no tachograph, untaxed or improperly taxed lorries. They are a threat to public safety and provide unfair competition to law-abiding hauliers. Their activities often extend into other criminal areas – e.g., illicit waste dumping, National Insurance or VAT frauds.

In 1978 the Independent Committee of Inquiry into Road Haulage Operators' Licensing, chaired by Professor (now Sir) Christopher Foster, in its report (Foster, 1978) thought the problem serious enough to justify impounding unlicensed lorries, and empowering Licensing Authorities to disqualify an illegal operator from applying for an 'O' licence for a long period (major recommendations Nos 20 and 21). Impounding would present practical problems, but none that is insuperable, given the political will. The DTp took no action. Ten years later the then Metropolitan Licensing Authority attracted public attention by expressing concern on television at unlicensed tipper trucks, and calling for impounding powers.

Such powers are now available to deal with another problem in the Control of Pollution (Amendment) Act 1989. But it is not clear whether they could be used to deal with the problem first highlighted by Foster thirteen years ago.

ENFORCEMENT

Before Licensing Authorities can penalize offending hauliers they have first to be caught. Law enforcement is outside the scope of this chapter. The National Audit Office 1987 report *Regulation of Heavy Lorries* and the subsequent Committee of Public Accounts report criticizes the DTp system in some detail. The recent transfer of more responsibility to the Vehicle Inspectorate Executive Agency may bring about improvement. But one gap needs to be filled urgently.

Foster (major recommendation No. 14) wanted facilities for checking goods vehicles on motorways and high speed roads, and suggested that these should be provided when such roads are built or substantially improved. Stopping heavy vehicles on high speed roads is difficult and dangerous. Some lorries are diverted to weighbridges and other facilities constructed near motorway exits. But such checks are expensive in police time, and in any case are impracticable after dark.

The USA solves the problem by a network of 'truck scales' on high speed roads, preceded by signs diverting vehicles over a certain weight to them. These can be used by day and night. Besides weighing, the sites are used to check other activities, including driving time and rest periods, mechanical fitness, driver and carrier licensing and taxation.

No such network exists in Britain. So vehicles which operate most of the time on motorways and at night are checked much less frequently than those working mostly by day and on local roads. Yet the former perform much higher mileages than the latter.

In addition to safety, this affects inter-modal competition. Rail is most competitive in long-distance traffic. The very limited number of lorry checks on motorways and at night makes it easier for long-distance hauliers to operate illegally if they choose to, knowing that they are unlikely to get caught.

The provision of a network of such stations would be expensive – more expensive than if, as Foster suggested, they had been provided when road construction was at its height. But they could be made an essential element of privately financed roads. And some contribution to the cost could come from their combination with badly needed rest, refreshment and other facilities for truck drivers who, shamefully, are increasingly unwelcome at normal service areas.

THE INDUSTRY'S ATTITUDE

No doubt to the surprise of some, the present situation does not please the haulage industry. The main victims of Licensing Authorities' leniency towards law-breakers are other hauliers. They lose traffic to competitors who undercut them by illegal means. A version of Gresham's Law operates, in that bad hauliers tend to drive down the standards of the good. Hauliers who see competitors persistently breaking the law with impunity are tempted – or forced by commercial pressures – to do likewise, knowing there is little risk of severe punishment if caught.

It would be naive to suggest that most hauliers and lorry drivers, any more than most private motorists, obey all the laws all the time. Most obey most laws most of the time. Still more would do so if most regular and deliberate law-breakers lost their 'O' licences. At present this happens too rarely to be an effective deterrent.

Lorry drivers are often pressured by their employers to break the law, even though it puts their vocational driving licences at risk. So the industry's trade unions support effective law enforcement, as do the industry's two trade associations. Quite apart from questions of principle, the industry's leaders know that hostile public opinion is likely to lead to further restrictive laws, like the recent decision to make speed limiters mandatory.

Early in 1991 the Road Haulage Association (RHA) drafted a legislative amendment which would have made vehicles operating without an 'O' licence liable to seizure. Put down by the Opposition in the Lords, it was withdrawn when the Government spokesperson promised more effective action against illegal operators. Similar promises were made when the Foster recommendation was shelved in 1980. But nothing happened.

THE PALMER REPORT

The present deplorable situation is not new. Statistics for the two decades since the system was introduced tell the same story. Today's Licensing Authorities are merely following their predecessors' gentle habits. The only satisfactory remedies lie in action at the level of the Licensing Authorities. But the DTp has always shied away from any action which would upset them.

In 1989 the DTp appointed John Palmer, then a recently retired Deputy Secretary, to report *inter alia* on the relationship between Licensing Authorities and the DTp. Palmer was an intriguing choice. Until retirement his command had included the licensing system, so his report was based on several years experience of Licensing Authorities' foibles.

Palmer's unpublished report 'Traffic Commissioners and Areas' directly addressed the question of Licensing Authorities' leniency. He wrote: 'The objective of the operator licensing systems is to keep bad operators off the road, in the interests of improving road safety. If that were not being achieved, there would be little point in maintaining the system.' (para 3.6) Despite the unsurprising fact that the Licensing Authorities 'take the view that the present level of disciplinary action is about right' (para 3.9), he concluded that 'there is a tendency to weigh the scales too much on the side of giving another chance to the operator as against the interests of road safety.' (para 3.11)

After that realistic conclusion his preferred solution was modest, possibly because he knew that no radical solution stood any chance of acceptance by his DTp successor. He attributed Licensing Authorities' leniency to the fact that each Licensing Authority 'bears this heavy responsibility alone, as an individual, with no standard to which he can refer' (para 3.11). He then suggested that there should be a national Licensing Authority for the whole country, with the remainder acting as deputies (para 3.20).

Even this anaemic idea attracted Licensing Authorities' hostility. It was watered down by the DTp, who appointed one Licensing Authority as 'first among equals'. As the first holder of this office was the Licensing Authority referred to above who had revoked only four licences in four years this move was unlikely to make much impact. In his annual report to the Transport Secretary another Licensing

Authority (previously head of the DTp Division responsible under Palmer for road haulage regulation) openly welcomed 'the decision not to proceed with some of [Palmer's] more extreme proposals'. However, following the retirement in 1991 of the first 'first among equals', a Licensing Authority with more robust views and reputation has been appointed to the post. It remains to be seen if he has any influence over his colleagues.

Why so Lenient?

But why do Licensing Authorities act so leniently? One cannot take seriously Palmer's 'loneliness' theory applied to the senior military officers and civil servants who traditionally occupy most Licensing Authority posts (six out of the seven in 1991). Palmer also quoted Licensing Authorities as saying that withdrawal of the licence is a very severe penalty since it takes away the holder's livelihood (para 3.9). That is undeniable. But illegal operation also takes away, or at least threatens, the livelihoods of those who stay within the law. And not just livelihoods but lives are threatened if the illegality involves overloaded or badly maintained vehicles, or exhausted drivers.

A further clue to Licensing Authorities' attitudes comes from another remark by Palmer – 'On the whole they think it better to keep the backslider within the system and encourage him to do better.' (para 3.9) This supine insinuation that operating within the system is an option rather than a legal requirement led Palmer to follow Foster in recommending a power to impound unlicensed lorries (para 5.3).

THE REMEDIES

One can only guess why Licensing Authorities are lenient; there are probably as many reasons as there are Licensing Authorities. But certain steps can be taken to reconcile Licensing Authorities' quasi-judicial freedom in individual cases with greater responsiveness to ministerial wishes. Those wishes can be assumed to favour proper enforcement, if for no worthier reason than the general dislike of lorries.

First, the machinery in which Licensing Authorities operate must be changed to discourage their propensity to leniency.

Foster recommended that Licensing Authorities be limited to a judicial role, with Traffic Area Clerks (the senior administrators) and other staff brought under direct DTp control, no longer basking in a Licensing Authority's quasi-judicial independence (major recommendations Nos 42 and 43). Palmer did not favour this (unimplemented) idea when he considered it eleven years later, but he did admit a need to reduce ambiguities (para 6.15).

This is not just bureaucratic shuffling. Ring-fencing Licensing Authorities would fundamentally alter the way in which disciplinary cases were conducted. Each Traffic Area operates in a different way, depending on the Licensing Authority's predilection; Palmer says 'No one can look at the administration of the system without being overwhelmed by the evidence that from top to bottom it is run as eleven [now eight] separate kingdoms.' (para 3.12) Licensing Authorities often personally select the cases which are to be called up for disciplinary hearings. There is no separate 'prosecution' to present the case against the delinquent. The LAs themselves normally examine the witnesses and the offending operators, though the latter may be represented by a lawyer or a lay specialist.

Once freed from Licensing Authorities' control Traffic Area Clerks could select the hauliers to be subjected to disciplinary hearings. More important, they or their staff could prepare cases and present them before the Licensing Authorities. The mere fact that Licensing Authorities no longer prosecuted and judged the same case should make it easier for them to decide the appropriate penalty. But this would only be a start.

Second, the law should be changed to give the DTp the right of appeal to the Transport Tribunal against any decision of the LA.

At present almost all appeals are by an aggrieved operator or would-be operator, biasing the system still further in the direction of leniency. On average about half the goods vehicle appeals succeed (Lord Chancellor's Department, 1987; 1988). A succession of Tribunal judgments in DTp appeals against what it sees as leniency would set standards against which Licensing Authorities could measure their penalties. And if the DTp thought the Tribunal's penalties were too lenient it would have to consider amending the basic legislation.

Third, Licensing Authorities should be recruited from a wider public, as suggested by the Council on Tribunals, and on a different basis.

The present criteria were designed to attract the former DTp officials and military officers who are appointed to most Licensing Authority posts at an age when many men are seeking a quiet life. (There has never been a woman Licensing Authority.) Appointments for a fixed term – say five years – rather than until the age of sixty-five should increase their responsiveness to ministerial wishes without trespassing on individual judgments.

Fourth, there should be an intensive drive to catch and prosecute unlicensed operators, and impound their vehicles.

This might be preceded by a brief amnesty.

Fifth, the Secretary of State should issue a general direction to Licensing Authorities to refuse licences to applicants who have been operating unlicensed vehicles within a period of, say, one year before applying.

A substantial minority of new applicants admit operating without a licence. This would test Palmer's doubts about the effectiveness of such directions (para 3.14).

Giving the DTp the right of appeal to the Transport Tribunal would require primary legislation. Palmer (para 5.3) thought that the Control of Pollution (Amendment) Act 1989 already provides the necessary powers for impounding, though the RHA amendment mentioned above makes this seem unlikely. But even if both measures – and perhaps a clarification of the power of general direction – needed legislation they would provide a neat and popular package for the DTp to offer to an MP who has come high in the ballot for Private Members' Bills and is seeking a topic.

CONCLUSION

These recommendations have been mainly directed at ridding the industry of unsatisfactory operators. This is the most urgent need, in the interests of road safety and of the industry itself. But in the longer term entry standards should be raised to the levels of the Netherlands. In the Transport Act 1968 Britain after all pioneered the move from quantity to quality road transport licensing which is now almost universal. 'O' licensing and related legislation have significantly raised the industry's standards.

But quality costs hauliers money. And unless high standards are general throughout the industry competitive forces will exert inexorable downward pressure. Hauliers who regularly fall below acceptable standards must regard loss of their licences as a real threat. At present, thanks to the leniency shown by Licensing Authorities, they do not.

This can be remedied at practically no cost to the government or to those hauliers who observe high standards. But it will demand political determination to overcome traditionally stubborn resistance from the Licensing Authorities, and equally traditional Department of Transport reluctance to take them on.

17

A PROMINENT ROLE FOR WALKING AND CYCLING IN FUTURE TRANSPORT POLICY

JOHANNA CLEARY AND MAYER HILLMAN

For too long walking and cycling have been treated as the Cinderellas of transport policy in the UK – at best, parsimoniously, at worst, ignored. Non-polluting, almost universally accessible, healthy, cheap, versatile, and largely accident-free in a vehicle-free environment, these modes clearly have many societally desirable attributes. However, the overriding obsession with the car has led to a decline in their feasibility, attractiveness and safety, and to oversight of their significance for land use, travel studies and forecasts for future planning. There is an unarguable case for radical reorganization of central and local government priorities, placing these benign modes at the heart of transport policy.

INTRODUCTION

Anyone given the task of devising a transport strategy aimed at promoting patterns of travel for the future to reflect the wider public interest rather than narrow and short-term self-interest would have to conclude that walking and cycling are the transport modes deserving the highest priority. Quite simply, their characteristics offer a panacea for most of the adverse consequences of Britain's love affair with the car – increasing danger, pollution, community severance, road congestion, noise, vibration, visual intrusion, and land take.

As current trends in car-oriented patterns of travel are first arrested and then reversed, as is increasingly being seen as necessary, an alternative strategy must be developed. This will have to take account of the needs and desires of the individual set within the needs and desires of the wider population. It can no longer be assumed that individuals' decisions concerning their personal travel should be made without reference to the effects of that decision on other members of society. The guiding principle on which a future strategy should be based must be to maximize accessibility while minimizing social costs. Many reasons can be put forward to support the proposition that pride of place be given to walking and cycling as a means of contributing significantly to satisfying that principle.

WHY PROMOTE WALKING AND CYCLING?

In order to justify the elevation of walking and cycling to the dominant modes of the transport system, their advantages and disadvantages, particularly for urban travel, need to be recognized.

Social Equity

In theory, most trips, especially for non-discretionary purposes such as to school, to work, to the shops and so on, are made – or, in a safe environment, should be capable of being made – by people travelling on their own. Surveys reveal that nearly all the population have the ability to walk (Hillman and Whalley, 1979); 99 per cent of men and 87 per cent of women over the age of fifteen can cycle (Mintel, 1989); and, as 90 per cent of junior schoolchildren own cycles (Hillman, Adams and Whitelegg, 1991), at least that proportion are able to ride one. On the other hand, less than two in five of the population have the optional use of a car because they do not satisfy the prerequisites for driving their own one – being old enough to do so, having adequate income and a desire to do so, and sufficient competence to pass the driving test and maintain a licence to drive. In spite of these statistics, planners, engineers and politicians have tended to make decisions on the assumption that virtually everyone has *access* to a car. This has led to a growing divide between the convenience and safety of those who do have a car and those who do not.

Independence

It has also led to a reduction in the personal autonomy of a substantial proportion of the population whose opportunities for leading lives that do not depend upon being driven or accompanied to and from desired destinations have thereby been limited. Parents feel obliged to impose increasing restrictions on their children's unaccompanied travel which, in the main, is on foot or cycle, because the skills required in order to cope with traffic have become ever more demanding. As a result, most young children are denied a basic element of their freedom during a crucial stage in their social development to adulthood. Many old people have also sustained a decline in their capacity to meet their daily travel needs conveniently compared with *their* parents at an equivalent age. Few of them have cars, whilst for the rest, there are now greater demands made on their declining faculties when walking – their primary mode of travel also – owing to the rising speed, ubiquity and severance effects of high volumes of traffic.

Versatility and Journey Time and Length

Walking and cycling can provide 'transport' at any time, obviating the frustration of relying on public transport, or the adverse effects of car travel. Notwithstanding these considerations, both walking and cycling can be easily combined with other modes, especially train travel, for longer journeys, and in many urban areas, cycling can offer faster journey times than other travel modes for journeys of up to 10 kilometres (Hudson, 1978).

Currently, the average journey time for trips is between 20 and 25 minutes. This suggests that people are prepared to spend this length of time on journeys and that therefore trips of five kilometres or less should be within the capability and tolerance of most people. At present, 62 per cent of all trips are within this distance band, but over 60 per cent of them are made by motorized means (Banister, 1990), indicating scope for a significant transfer from motorized to non-motorized transport, as illustrated in Table 17-1.

Table 17-1: Modal Distribution With all Motorized Trips of Less Than Five Kilometres Made by Cycle.

Mode	current distribution (%)	new distribution (%)
Car	50.6	29.9
Walking	34.1	34.1
Bus (local)	8.4	4.2
Bicycle	2.5	28.4
Train	1.6	1.5
Motorcycle	0.8	0.5
Other	2.1	1.4

Source: Banister (1990)

Fuel Conservation

It is clearly preferable for journeys to be made with the minimum use of resources. A greater take-up of walking and cycling would satisfy this condition. The fact that four out of five people travelling to work by car carry no passengers illustrates the wastefulness of current travel patterns (Clarke, 1988). While pedestrians and cyclists do not draw on the world's finite fossil fuel reserves, cars now consume 90 per cent of the oil used for personal travel. By contrast, a bicycle travels 1600 miles on the energy equivalent of one gallon of petrol and the energy source – food – is of course renewable. The 1990/91 Gulf crisis and war has again brought into sharp focus the necessity of reducing dependence on fossil fuels, especially where these have to be imported from politically unstable regions of the world. However, the contribution of walking and cycling to the goals of energy conservation is significant, though rarely acknowledged in policy documents (Hillman and Whalley, 1983).

Land Take

Pedestrians and cyclists require far less space to get about than car-borne travellers. For example, a 4m-wide cycle path can carry five times the number of people catered for in cars on a road twice as wide (Clarke, 1988). Pedestrians leave no unattended vehicles, while ten bicycles can be parked in the space required by one car. The inequitable consumption of public space by private motor vehicles is evident in central London: while only 16 per cent of people travel to work by car, they take up 85 per cent of the available road space.

Community Severance

Walking and cycling facilitate social interaction. By contrast, the presence of large numbers of motor vehicles degrades the physical and psychological environment in urban areas in terms of the noise, vibration and visual intrusion they cause. Research during the 1970s demonstrated the inverse relationship between community interaction and traffic volume (Appleyard and Lintell, 1975). In heavily, as compared with lightly, trafficked streets, residents' privacy and their network of acquaintances were reduced, their sense of personal territory restricted, and their activity in the street curtailed by the streams of motorized traffic.

Health Considerations

While there is clear evidence of the major preventive role that daily exercise can play in lowering the incidence of both heart and respiratory diseases (Morris *et al.*, 1990), and increasing longevity (Paffenbarger *et al.*, 1986), research also reveals that only a small proportion of adults get sufficient exercise to maintain their fitness (Vines, 1990). Brisk walking, jogging, cycling and swimming are all acknowledged as ideal ways of keeping physically fit. However, walking and cycling are the most appropriate because of their wide scope for take-up across all sections of the population, and because they can be maintained throughout life as they are more readily tied in to the daily routine of travel to school, to work and so on. On the other hand, current patterns of traffic and planning, which induce stress as well as fear and anxiety about the risk of an accident occurring, actually deter people from keeping fit in this potentially convenient way.

Air Pollution

A related consideration stems from the pathological impacts on health of pollution from motor vehicle exhausts. These emissions have led to a deterioration in air quality, with harmful effects on human health which increase morbidity and mortality (Lave and Seskin, 1977). Ozone levels in urban areas frequently exceed WHO guidelines (World Health Organization, 1987). Efforts to reduce pollution from motor vehicles have limitations, though these are as yet largely unacknowledged: for example, the lead taken out of petrol is replaced by benzene which is carcinogenic (Marriott and Dickson, 1990); and catalytic converters do not operate on cold car engines and thus are ineffective for the majority of car journeys which are less than 8 kilometres. Indeed, any reduction in emissions as a result of 'technological fixes' are likely to be more than offset by the government forecast of increases in motor traffic over the next thirty years (Fergusson, Holman and Barratt, 1989). Needless to say, walking and cycling are non-polluting means of travel – a positive benefit overlooked in policy on reducing pollution from transport sources.

Public Expenditure and Economic Vitality

The infrastructure necessary to cater for pedestrians and cyclists places a minimal demand on public funds in terms of costs of provision and maintenance. Currently, central government spends about £2500 million each year on road-building (Department of Transport, 1990c), but such insignificant sums are spent on cycle facilities that they do not feature in public accounts. Yet clear economic gains have been shown to result from reducing the volume of traffic in urban centres while facilitating walking and cycling. A cross-European study has shown that, as volume decreases, the remaining mix of pedestrians, cyclists and mass transit modes stimulates economic activity, especially in city centres, as measured in terms of increased retail turnover; and employees' productivity is improved in a working environment which has grown in attractiveness and vitality (TEST, 1988).

Traffic Danger

Travel by motorized means, especially by car, is detrimental to the safety of pedestrians and cyclists whereas, of course, the reverse is not true. This can be seen in relation to the effect that motorized travel has on the risk of physical injury in traffic accidents, and to the psychological impacts of distress and bereavement resulting from these accidents. About two million people have been killed or seriously injured in road accidents in Britain in the last twenty years (Department of Transport, 1990d). Of these, 25 per cent were pedestrians, and 6 per cent were cyclists – thus victims of nearly one in three of these accidents, though only accounting for about one in fourteen of all mileage travelled. Schoolchildren account for one in three of all pedestrian and cycle fatalities and serious injuries, mostly as a result of being knocked down by a car, but represent only about one in six of the population. Indeed, on an average day, five pedestrians and cyclists are killed on the roads in accidents involving cars, lorries and motorcycles. Bearing in mind the fact that there is a considerable level of under-reporting, it can be calculated that a further seventy-five are sufficiently seriously injured to be included as in-patients in hospital, and over 300 are treated in hospital casualty departments.

Whilst there is concern about the disturbingly high pedestrian accident rate among children, neither politicians nor the general public are aware of the fact that, as Table 17-2 shows, the rate is much higher among elderly people. Indeed, analysis of data from road accident statistics and the National Travel Survey shows that the fatality rate for young pensioners per kilometre walked is about twice as high as that among children, and the rate for old pensioners is about *ten* times as high (Hillman, 1989).

Although the incidence of accidents causing death and serious injury has been falling in recent years, the relative risks between travel by different modes have not stayed constant. Table 17-3 shows a wide disparity between the casualty rates for the main modes of personal travel: for example, in 1978, the fatal and serious injury rate per kilometre for cyclists was nine times higher than that by car whereas, by 1988, it was seventeen times higher.

Table 17-2: Pedestrian Fatality Rate per Kilometre and Per Capita, by Age Groups.

Age group	Pedestrian fatality rate per 100 million kms	per 100,000 population	Percentage of population
0-4	4.6	1.6	
5-9	8.4	2.7	18.8
10-14	5.1	2.8	
15-19	3.7	2.3	7.9
20-59	4.5	1.7	52.5
60-64	8.7	3.3	
65-69	10.7	4.3	20.8
70-74	22.5	7.3	
+75	66.4	12.0	
All	7.9	3.1	100.0

Source: O'Donoghue (1988), and further analysis of road accident statistics.

Table 17-3: Casualty Rates per Billion Person Kilometres by Mode of Travel, 1978 and 1988.

	1978	1988	Percentage change 1978-88
Walking			
killed	97	70	−28
seriously injured	757	645	−15
Cycling			
killed	62	46	−26
seriously injured	867	938	+ 8
Car users			
killed	7	4	−41
seriously injured	92	53	−42
Bus or coach passengers			
killed	1.0	0.3	−70
seriously injured	21	20	− 8

Source: calculated from annual volumes of Department of Transport, *Road Accident Statistics Great Britain*, HMSO.

Table 17-4 shows that, other than motorcycling, walking and cycling have the highest casualty rates per kilometre travelled. Indeed, the fatality rate for walking is eighteen times higher than that for car travel. It can be seen too that motor traffic, especially cars and lorries, is associated with the great majority of pedestrian fatalities and, moreover, that it is these types of vehicle which are increasing in number at the fastest rates.

Table 17-4: Fatality Rate per Kilometre Travelled by Mode, Vehicle Involvement With Pedestrian Fatalities, and Traffic Volumes, 1977-87.

	Fatality rate per 100 million kms travelled	Percentage of pedestrian fatalities associated with one vehicle	Percentage change in traffic volume 1977-87
Transport mode:			
Motorcycle	13.1	7.1	+ 6
Walking	7.9	0.0	n/a
Bicycle	6.4	0.5	−14
Car	0.5	68.7	+45
Lorry	0.3	15.6	+28
Bus/coach	0.1	4.4	+17

Source: Department of Transport (1988), *Road Accidents Great Britain 1987*; and (1988), *Transport Statistics Great Britain 1977-87*, HMSO.

Owing to their lack of protection, pedestrians and cyclists are especially vulnerable to injury when they are involved in a road accident. This is illustrated in Table 17-5 which shows the ratio of deaths to deaths and serious injuries combined for each road user group and for three individual years with a gap of a decade between them. It can be seen that, in spite of their relatively low speed, the ratio has remained highest among pedestrians, clearly by virtue of their high involvement in accidents involving motor vehicles.

Thus, if one takes each of the elements affecting the conditions in which people can make their journeys on foot and by cycle, and therefore their predisposition to doing so, one can only acknowledge the manifold benefits of the non-motorized modes but conclude that

Table 17-5: Ratio of Fatal Accidents to Fatal and Serious Injury Road Accidents Combined, Great Britain, 1968, 1978 and 1988.

	1968	1978	1988
Pedestrians	11.3	11.4	9.8
Cyclists	6.6	6.7	4.6
Two-wheel motor vehicles	5.1	5.4	5.3
Car users	7.0	7.1	7.3
Bus passengers	3.1	4.7	1.7
All road users	7.7	7.6	7.4

Source: Department of Transport, annual volumes of *Road Accidents Great Britain*, HMSO.

most of their attractions have steadily deteriorated. Ironically, pedestrians and cyclists who are most at risk of injury and most exposed to air pollution are the ones making the least contribution to these public hazards.

THE ROLE OF WALKING AND CYCLING IN CURRENT TRANSPORT PATTERNS

Insofar as an understanding can be gained from official survey sources of changes in patterns of travel over the past twenty or thirty years, it is clear that the use of walking as a transport mode continues to decline, and cycle use has fallen dramatically. In 1953, 10 per cent of total travel mileage by mechanical modes was made by bicycle, the majority on commuter journeys, whereas only 1 per cent – of a much larger total – is made today, and accounts for less than 2 per cent of journeys (Hillman, 1990b). Table 17-6 shows the changes in the proportion of personal travel made on foot and cycle between the last two National Travel surveys covering the ten years from the mid-1970s to the mid-1980s. It can be seen that the use of the two modes has fallen overall among all of the social groups examined, except for men of working age.

Despite the general trends of increasing availability of cars and a reasonable level of public transport for the majority of the population, walking and cycling still cater for over one-third of all journeys. The Table shows that, at present, they cover over a half of all children's

Table 17-6: Percentage of Journeys on Foot or Cycle, by Age and Sex, 1975/76 and 1985/86.

		National Travel Survey 1975/76*	1985/86†
Children	walk	55	47
	cycle	6	4
Elderly	walk	47	41
	cycle	3	1
Women (16-59)	walk	41	34
	cycle	2	1
Men (16-59)	walk	23	23
	cycle	3	3
All	walk	39	34
	cycle	4	3

* special tabulation from the National Travel Surveys.
† special calculations from published figures (Department of Transport, 1988).

journeys (though the great majority of children live in car-owning households), over two in five of the journeys of everyone over the age of sixty, and a quarter of the journeys of men below this age (though over three-quarters of them are licence holders). So significant does walking remain as a mode that, for the average person in the mid 1980s, it was accounting for three times as many journeys as by all forms of public transport combined.

Walking and cycling would play a far more significant role if safe and convenient provision were made for them. With respect to cycling in particular, there are also indications of mounting suppressed demand: although the road environment for it deteriorates, both the number of cycle-owning and multi-owning cycle households are growing (Morgan, 1987). A recent survey found that nearly three in five households are cycle-owning (Mintel, 1990) but, in marked contrast to the car where 94 per cent are used every day (MORI, 1990), only one in three bicycles are used in a typical week (Morgan, 1987). From these observations, it can be deduced that walking and cycling have the potential to satisfy a much higher proportion of travel needs than is currently the case. In order to realize this potential, it is necessary to recognize and then remove existing deterrents to their use.

DETERRENTS TO WALKING AND CYCLING

There are a number of factors which explain the decline in walking and cycling, and over which central government has some influence through its fiscal and regulatory policies. These include the widening access to cars, increasing danger on the roads, and the rise in pollution from motor vehicle exhausts.

Access to Cars

First, there is the ownership and use of cars. The changes in this that have occurred are apparent from the figures set out in Table 17-7. These show that, whether analysed on the basis of household, per adult, or simply licence holding, there has been an apparently inexorable growth in access to cars. The proportion of multi-car-owning households has risen in recent years at as rapid a rate as the proportion of households without cars has declined. Nevertheless, it can be inferred from the figures that just under three in five adults do not have the *optional* use of a car and two in five do not hold a licence.

Table 17-7: Adult Access to Cars in Great Britain, 1968, 1978 and 1988.

	1968	1978	1988
Household car ownership:			
per cent with one or more cars	49	57	65
per cent with two or more cars	6	12	21
Cars per 100 adults	27	35	50
Licence-holding adults	38%	49%	62%

Sources: Department of Transport, annual volumes of *Transport Statistics Great Britain 1968-1978* and *1978-1988*, HMSO and Office of Population Censuses and Surveys, volumes of *Population Trends*, HMSO, London.

Road Safety

The second important deterrent to walking and cycling is attributable to the detrimental effects of motorized traffic on the quality of the environment. In assessing the changes in exposure to road accidents over the years, it is necessary to pay attention to the changes in the *risk* of accidents occurring as well as those that do occur: a plausible explanation for the fairly steady fall in deaths and serious injuries in road accidents over the years is that the rising volume and speed of traffic have obliged people to exercise greater care in the face of the more *dangerous* traffic environment and that this has also resulted in people being discouraged from travelling on foot or cycle: the massive growth of traffic has not led to more safety but more danger.

Some indication of the increase in the levels of *danger* on the roads can be inferred from comparison of the findings of surveys carried out in schools in Britain in 1971 and 1990 (Hillman, Adams and Whitelegg, 1991). This shows a dramatic decline in the proportion of children allowed on their own to go to school, to visit friends, to cycle on the roads and so on. The principal justification for the restrictions which their parents have imposed on the latter-day children is a heightened fear of them being injured. Indeed, whereas 90 per cent of junior schoolchildren now own bicycles, only 1 per cent use them to go to school.

Pollution From Motor Vehicles

A third deterrent to walking and cycling on which action can be taken is pollution from motor vehicles. It has been noted earlier that vehicle exhaust fumes have harmful effects. They represent a health risk to pregnant women, young children and old people, all groups in the population which are more sensitive to lowered oxygen levels and, as has been seen, are more exposed to air pollution because they are more reliant on walking in their daily patterns of travel. Yet, the volume of many of these pollutants from road transport sources – carbon monoxide, hydrocarbons and nitrogen oxides – has risen by more than 50 per cent above its level twenty years ago: nitrogen oxide from transport sources now represents 45 per cent of the total man-made production, and carbon monoxide 85 per cent (Department of Transport, 1990c).

To add to these hazards, there is no doubt that traffic noise lowers the quality of the pedestrian and cycle environment, particularly when people wish to converse. However, although there are surprisingly no surveys of changes in noise levels over time, the dramatic rise in the number of motor vehicles on the roads, and their spread by place and by hour of day and night – not to mention poor enforcement of the limits – is very likely to have increased these over and above the reductions attributable to the regulatory limits introduced in recent years.

A DIAGNOSIS OF THE LOWLY STATUS OF WALKING AND CYCLING

What is the explanation for the fact that walking and cycling have not been accorded the role that they so obviously deserve, and for the fact that the environment in which people travel by these modes has been allowed to deteriorate so much?

Much of it appears to stem from a lack of appreciation of the relevance of these modes to a sane, equitable and sustainable transport policy, and from the inadequacy of the lobby to promote such a policy. It derives too from a poor understanding of the latent demand for the green modes, especially cycling, and a lamentable perception of the benefits of such an approach. Many reasons could be suggested for these outcomes.

Self-centred Behaviour

The opportunity for a job entailing long-distance commuting by car is accepted as the marginal costs are low (and commuting in any case can be a fairly pleasant activity, that is seated comfortably listening to the radio), even though the regular use of the car for this purpose makes life marginally more dangerous, noisier and the air more polluted for everyone on every day along the route taken by that car commuter.

It is seen too as legitimate in that car ownership is reaching a larger proportion of the population. But, it cannot be stressed too strongly that such an apparently logical course of action flies in the face of all the evidence that the growth of traffic, whilst apparently reflecting public preference, actually lowers the quality of life in all the ways noted earlier. Already the average distance travelled by every man, woman and child in the country is over 100 miles a week (Department of Transport, 1988b), having increased by nearly 50 per cent in the last twenty years, and the Department of Transport predicts increases by the year 2025 of up to one and a half times higher than the present levels as justification for a major road building programme to accommodate this new 'demand' (Department of Transport, 1989c).

Inadequacy of Monitoring

Walking is largely overlooked in policy because the principal use to which the findings of the National Travel Survey are put record it in order to be able to recognize trends in the demand for *motorized* travel and therefore in order to plan to accommodate this in the future road-building programme. For this reason, the NTS report concentrates on travel *distance*. In an easily overlooked Note prefacing the latest report, it is pointed out that journeys of under a mile only account for 3 per cent of all personal travel mileage and that 'most of these are walks' – with the implication that they are of little consequence (Department of Transport, 1988b), even though this chapter has shown the non-motorized modes are the ones that are most in the public interest to promote.

The omission of these 'very short' (*sic*) journeys leads to a very different image of the distribution of journeys by mode: Table 17-8 compares this distribution for each of the main modes, including and excluding journeys of under a mile. It can be seen that their omission results in the significance of the non-motorized modes, particularly those on foot, being seriously under-represented. Thus, of all journeys, the proportion made on foot is reduced to a third of its actual level, whilst the proportion for those by car is increased from half to over two-thirds.

Table 17-8: Distribution of Journeys by Mode Including and Excluding Journeys of Under One Mile, 1985/86.

| Mode | Journeys of under one mile | |
	Percentage included	Percentage excluded
Walk	34	11
Cycle	3	2
Bus	9	11
Car	51	69
Other	4	7
All	100	100

Source: special calculations from published figures in Department of Transport (1988).

Moreover, as Table 17-9 shows, on average, over a third of the journeys that people make are over distances of under a mile, with nearly half of the journeys of children and nearly two-fifths of people over the age of sixty years being made over this distance. It can be seen too that roughly three-quarters of these shorter journeys are made on foot or by bicycle. To compound the NTS error of judgment, the most widely used sources of data on patterns of travel do not incorporate figures on these shorter trips, thereby providing meaningless and distorting bases for the formulation of a sensible transport policy (Department of Transport, 1990c; 1990f; and Central Statistical Office, 1989).

Table 17-9: *Percentages of Journeys by all Modes and by Walking and Cycling, Over Distances of Less Than one Mile, by Age and Sex, 1985/86.*

| | Journeys under one mile | | | | |
	children 0-15	elderly 60+	women 16-59	men 16-59	all
Percentage of all journeys	45	38	33	22	33
Percentage of these on foot or cycle	78	78	79	69	76

Source: special calculations from published figures in Department of Transport (1988).

Oversight of the Implications of Land Use Changes

Reference to the two modes is rare, particularly in the context of planning. Where it is made, evidence and discussion of their role tend to be limited. It is almost as if those who draw up policy, or compile documents in which this would be highly appropriate, consider that they have to do so but that it has very little bearing on *real* transport issues.

This can be illustrated by reference to a recent Department of the Environment document aimed at directing local authorities towards public interest decisions on patterns of shopping provision. The document relied on published 1985/86 NTS figures (Department of the Environment, 1988) and therefore reports on walking playing only a very minor role, overlooking the fact that nearly half of all shopping trips are made on foot. Having incorrectly overrated the significance of longer journeys, mostly by car, the document then emphasizes for local authorities the importance of providing sufficient parking space for car-borne shoppers, and goes on to give policy guidance on large stores and the 'now well-established form of retail development, clearly meeting strong customer demand for convenient car-borne weekly household shopping'. In turn, these planning changes have exacerbated the main disadvantages associated with the non-motorized modes, especially of course walking, namely their limited range and increased exposure to the adverse environmental impacts noted above.

Exaggeration of the Relative Importance of Public Transport

As can be seen in Table 17-10, journeys on foot are, on average, three times as frequent as those by all public transport modes – a ratio that has not changed in the ten years from the 1975/76 NTS to that of the 1985/86 one. The Table also shows that, in spite of the decline in the use of walking and cycling noted in Table 17-6, the ratio is highest among children and rising, but is still high and fairly constant for all adults.

Table 17-10: Ratio of Number of Journeys on Foot to the Number by Public Transport, by Age and Sex, 1975/76 and 1985/86.

	National Travel Survey	
	1975/76*	1985/86†
Children	4.5	5.2
Elderly (60+)	2.9	2.9
Women (16-59)	2.7	2.8
Men (16-59)	2.7	2.6
All	3.1	3.1

* special tabulation from the National Travel Survey.
† special calculations from published figures in Department of Transport (1988).

Omissions From Traffic Forecasts

The significance attached to walking and cycling in public policy in recent years can also be established by checking through other official documents on transport in which it could be expected that they would feature. Such an examination reveals that few mention them, and those that do typically categorize them in effect as 'also rans'.

This could be cited as a further explanation for the unsatisfactory outcome as forecasts made in the process of determining plans for meeting future transport demand, and expenditure on the plans, extraordinarily exclude walking and cycling. It would appear that only motorized travel is worthy of consideration. Yet, the relevance and reliability of this forecasting process would be considerably improved, and the focus of policy sharpened, if it were simply acknowledged that in the year for which predictions were made, close on 100 per cent of the population will be able to walk and the great majority will be able to cycle, and would welcome wider opportunities for doing so if proper provision were made for them in the form of safe networks. In this way, a future role for walking and cycling would be recognized and policy adjusted accordingly.

A further instance of the loss of perception of any future role for walking and cycling is apparent in an ECMT report (European Community Ministers of Transport, 1988). This incorporated a set of papers on demand for future travel but only one of them referred to walking or cycling. It can be seen too in a published document on statistics on transport in London which is compiled and written without reference to walking (Department of Transport, 1989d). Even in the Secretary of State for Transport's 1989 Policy for London, cyclists and pedestrians are consigned to eight paragraphs in an appendix describing his 'approach towards the operation and development of London's transport systems', even though one of these paragraphs cites the significant finding that 'over one third of all the journeys undertaken in London are made on foot' (Department of Transport, 1989a).

Oversight of the Low Costs of Provision for Non-motorized Travel

Again, the low cost of making provision for walking and cycling compared with motorized travel appears to be totally overlooked, and rendered unlikely to be noticed because of the absence of meaningful figures on them. The only figure is the absurdly high 12 per cent of the total capital and running costs of public expenditure on roads which is 'assigned' to pedestrians in the published statistics (Department of Transport, 1990c).

WALKING AND CYCLING AS CENTRAL GOVERNMENT CONCERNS

Some may question the place of walking and cycling in a National Transport Policy Document on the grounds that these are not 'real' modes of transport but rather modes out of which 'advanced' industrial societies grow. Others may hold the opinion that unless provision incurs high levels of public expenditure, it does not warrant attention by central government. There are, in fact, three clear reasons to justify their inclusion within its ambit of responsibilities.

First, any attempt to redress the current transport crisis must include efforts to reduce dependence on the private car and to increase concomitantly the use of other modes. These must be considered and promoted in a holistic way that reflects the relative benefits and disbenefits of each. Cycling and walking are two important alternatives that have tended to be overlooked: as noted earlier, changes in the modal split have not come about by transfers between public transport and the car. Recent increases in car use represent a move away from cycling and walking to a far greater extent than they have represented a transfer from public transport.

Second, a corresponding shift in public opinion is required away from dependence on cars towards acceptance of the desirability – even necessity – of walking and cycling as the dominant transport modes. Only central government has sufficient power, influence and resources to effect such a change in attitudes.

Third, if walking and cycling are to play their optimal part in a future integrated transport system, they must be considered alongside other modes at all levels of the government decision-making process. The current situation in which local authorities are largely left to decide for themselves how, or indeed if, they intend to accommodate pedestrians and cyclists is unsatisfactory. In particular, it takes no account of the pertinent constraints imposed on them, such as:

- Funding allocations – what is spent and how it is spent – are significantly influenced by central government. To illustrate this point it can be noted that Transport Supplementary Grants have only recently been made available for small-scale safety engineering measures which may include pedestrian and cycle facilities. Until this change, local highway authorities could only apply to central government for grant funding for 'strategic' transport infrastructure proposals which, by definition, are confined to, and thus have focused attention on, major road-building programmes.
- Land use planning proposals framed by central government currently favour a dispersal of development and therefore encourage a dependence on private transport.
- Local authorities must work with speed limits and other inflexible traffic management regulations which are, again, set by national government.

Policy Implications

An equitable national transport strategy would rest on the foundation that modes are prioritized according to the extent to which their use improves a person's quality of life without diminishing the quality of other people's lives. To determine a framework within which decisions on this basis could be made, an initial task would be to research and document the comparable characteristics of different modes. Mindful of the analysis in the earlier sections of this chapter, such an exercise would undoubtedly reveal walking and cycling as the transport modes deserving the highest priority.

There are two prerequisites for the success of any attempt at realizing a modal shift in their favour: these modes must be made more 'useable' and attractive. In other words, future trends must be towards keeping journeys within walking and cycling distance by increasing the proportion of activities that can be organized at the local level; and the main deterrents to walking and cycling such as danger, discomfort and negative social attitudes must be ameliorated. Measures to achieve these objectives can be grouped into two categories. First, those that with political consent could be readily implemented and could have immediate effect. And second, those that, by entailing longer-term strategies, may take time to bring into operation either because current trends stand in the way of their implementation, or because they require the consent or co-operation of individuals or parties over which the government has relatively little control.

Immediate Objectives

A wide range of actions can be quickly taken by a government committed to prioritizing walking and cycling within a coherent transport strategy. One of the first would be to establish a hierarchy of responsibility among the different tiers of government. This is not to say that different tiers would be responsible for different modes, but rather that each tier would take charge of particular aspects of all modes. For example, one element of the remit of central government would be to win acceptability for walking and cycling by increasing public awareness about the private and public consequences of travel by each mode. Regional government would act as a filter, interpreting central advice and local knowledge to formulate workable policies.

Meanwhile, local government would represent the interface between theory and practice in both implementing policies and providing a forum for public participation in the decision-making process. This structure would be more of a continuum than a hierarchy of authority with a two-way flow of information and ideas between all tiers. Notwithstanding this, each tier would be accountable for its particular sphere of responsibility.

Concomitant with the success of such a structure would be the allocation of appropriate resources in terms of suitably qualified staff and adequate financial resources. In contrast to the current arrangement, future responsibilities would be allocated to incorporate walking and cycling as strategic modes.

DIVISION OF RESPONSIBILITIES FOR POLICY ON WALKING AND CYCLING AMONG THE TIERS OF GOVERNMENT

Central Government

Current situation: Walking and cycling are viewed principally as a road safety problem. Their promotion as means of transport is not seen by the Department of Transport as lying within its remit and thus they are rarely mentioned in policy documents or statements. In spite of the fact that they impose the lowest costs on society and have the scope for catering for the travel needs of the majority of the population, current transport policy effectively discriminates against them. There is little formal liaison by the Department of Transport with other departments of government regarding the interactive effects of policy decisions on the attractiveness and feasibility of walking and cycling.

Future proposals: *Broaden the remit of the Department of Transport to cover all policy areas surrounding the facilitating of walking and cycling, and locate these modes at the centre of transport policy. Set up a consultative process between the Department of Transport and the main relevant government departments whose policies and programmes impact on transport decisions, e.g. the Treasury (fiscal incentives); the Department of the Environment (land use planning and pollution); the Home Office (laws and their enforcement); the Department of Energy (the conservation of fossil fuels); and the Department of Health (the promotion of health). Ensure that due consideration is given to walking and cycling in transport documents and statements.*

Current situation: Decision-making is heavily influenced by pressure groups, such as the roads lobby, which have vested interests in the outcome. The degree of their influence reflects the financial resources at their disposal and the scope of their political contacts rather than the merits of their proposals. This can be seen in the national road-building programme which is based on the unattainable and undesirable objective of matching demand from traffic growth with the supply of road capacity, and in road safety policy which tends to result in the onus of responsibility for behavioural change being placed on the victims of road accidents.

Future proposals: *Decision-making should be based on the interests of society as a whole. Transport modes should be promoted in accordance with the extent to which they confer freedom on the individual and reduce the harmful effects of motorized traffic. The onus of responsibility for reducing road accidents should be placed on those who generate danger on the roads.*

Current situation: Limited staff and expenditure are devoted to walking and cycling as transport modes, and insufficient policy guidance or financial incentives are given to local authorities to encourage provision for these modes. The focus of consultation with the general public is largely confined to proposals on reducing congestion by road-building or measures aimed at managing traffic to keep it moving. There is very little government research undertaken on aspects of walking and cycling other than those pertaining to safety.

Future proposals: *Appoint suitably qualified and resourced teams to deal exclusively with the various elements of a national policy on these modes and its implementation. Through the medium of demonstration projects, directives and advice, and fiscal allocation, encourage local authorities to favour walking and cycling in their policies and programmes. Adopt a public education programme aimed at promoting the benefits both to the individual and to society of a modal shift towards walking and cycling. Establish a research team to undertake a rolling programme of projects aimed at facilitating that shift.*

Regional Government
Current situation: Vague statements acknowledging the existence of walking and cycling can be found in regional policy documents but there are rarely proposals or commitments on promoting these modes. Little if any attention is paid to the impact of regional transport and land use proposals on the attractions of walking and cycling.

Future proposals: *Regional policy documents should focus on the needs and considerations of pedestrians and cyclists, with clear policy commitments supported by viable programmes for implementation and backed by suitable financial resources. Careful consideration should be given to the effect of all regional transport and land use proposals on the viability of walking and cycling, particularly the severance effect of motorways and trunk roads and the accessibility of regional retail and business parks.*

Current situation: The Department of Transport's Regional Cycling Officers (RCOs) are charged with ensuring that the needs of cyclists are met in all central government road proposals, and with liaising with local authorities on the provision of cycle facilities. But these responsibilities constitute only a very small element of their work load. In practice, RCOs have proved to have neither the resources, incentive nor qualifications to fulfil this remit satisfactorily. Moreover, there is little communication of ideas and information between the tiers of government, among RCOs themselves, and between RCOs and non-governmental interested parties, e.g. sports, tourist and health bodies; cycling pressure groups; and the general public.

Future proposals: *Regional cycling groups comprising representatives from relevant fields working on this tier of government – e.g., planners, surveyors, engineers, recreation tourism officers – should be appointed. Their task would be to ensure that central government's pro-cycling advice and directives are implemented at the regional level; that the activities of local authorities are co-ordinated; and that a forum for the exchange of ideas and information is provided between central and local government. Formal channels of communication between regional cycling teams and relevant bodies need to be established through the medium of national conferences, seminars, and advisory committees.*

Local Government
Current situation: Relevant policy documents, such as structure plans, local plans, and Transport Policies and Programmes (TPPs), invariably pay scant regard to the needs of pedestrians and cyclists, and tend to assume that the majority have access to a car which people should be able to use provided that there is sufficient capacity on the roads. Provision, particularly for cyclists, is dependent upon an *ad hoc* approach in the allocation of resources and is dependent on the personal attitudes of sympathetic officers and councillors.

Future proposals: *All local authorities should be required to ensure proper provision for walking and cycling and that these are treated as the dominant local transport modes. Local planning policies should aim to reduce the number and length of car journeys.*

Current situation: There is little opportunity for the exchange of ideas, concerns, constraints and lessons about facilitating walking and cycling either with other government tiers, other local authorities, non-governmental interested bodies or with the general public. There is also a general dearth of expertise, manpower and financial resources in relation to planning for pedestrians and cyclists. Where appointments are made, these tend to be at a relatively low grade.

Future proposals: *Formal channels of communication should be established for the exchange of information through the medium of conferences, symposia, technical guidance notes, publicity material and so on, on provision for pedestrians and cyclists. Each local authority should appoint pedestrian and cycling project teams with responsibility for comprehensive provision of appropriate facilities, and to liaise with neighbouring authorities on a co-ordinated approach.*

Once this reorganization of responsibilities in the transport field has taken place, the second course of action would be to develop a symbiosis of land use and transport planning. Because of the extent of the effect that decisions regarding land use have on travel patterns, the role of the two disciplines must be integrated at all government levels. In view of the strength of the arguments to support a reduction in car travel, there must be a presumption in future in favour of developments that are either primarily accessible on foot, bicycle and public transport, or which generate demand for travel by these modes.

In practical terms, advances in telecommunications and home-based working methods should be exploited as a means of substituting for much extraneous travel. Similarly, activities that require daily trips, for example to offices, shops, schools and recreation facilities, should be decentralized to the neighbourhood level.

As a result of the long honeymoon enjoyed by the private motorist, official thinking has come to focus almost entirely on the needs of this particular section of the travelling public, to the extent that governments in recent decades have been accused of having a Ministry of Roads rather than a Department of Transport. The third course of action would therefore be to redress the imbalance that has developed. The composition of government departments with responsibility for transport issues must reflect more equitably the full range of modes. A change of attitudes and reassessment of values among relevant public servants will be an integral part of this process. Work undertaken by the government's transport research bodies, such as the Transport and Road Research Laboratory, must similarly respond to the need for this change. In particular, to compensate for years of neglect, activity should be stepped up in the field of research on improving the safety, convenience and feasibility of walking and cycling.

Furthermore, to arrest the current preoccupation of planners and engineers with car-based transport systems, all relevant educational training programmes should also be reassessed and, where necessary, altered to accommodate new thinking in the field of transportation where the primary objectives are a reduction in travel and a prioritizing of modes in favour of walking and cycling.

Having established a framework for more equitable decision-making, attention should be turned in the next stage to the formulation of policy. In any future assessment of travel patterns, all trips, including those of less than one mile, must be included. On this basis, a truer measure of the significance of walking and cycling in daily travel patterns will be recognized. Notwithstanding this, it will be necessary to formulate policies that stimulate use of these benign modes still further. To this end, all transport policy statements or documents need to contain clear commitments to walking and cycling. Such commitments should be at the heart of local transport strategies around which all other considerations are oriented. Thus, for example, Transport Policies and Programmes should state that walking and cycling are the dominant modes of transport in urban areas and will be developed accordingly.

Perhaps one of the most challenging, but no less important, tasks for a government committed to the promotion of walking and cycling would be to swing public opinion, much of which is firmly wedded to the car. Central government should embark on a campaign aimed at increasing public awareness of the costs and benefits of travel by each of the modes, and should prevent anti-social driving behaviour from being glamourized in car advertisements. To this end:

- Motor vehicle access would be limited and speed limits sharply reduced in all areas where pedestrians and cyclists are circulating.

- Road traffic laws would be rigorously enforced to ensure that motoring offences such as speeding or drink-driving are no longer socially acceptable.

- Company car subsidies would be removed while the motorist generally would be presented, as far as possible, with the full costs of their transport decisions. The onus would therefore shift onto those who cause accidents, environmental degradation, create pollution, generate noise, and so on.

- Meanwhile, government bodies would set a precedent in awarding financial incentives to those who utilize walking and cycling in acknowledgement of their contribution to society in choosing these particular modes, for example, in reducing the risk to other road users by opting for non-motorized travel. Such incentives could take the form of mileage allowances weighted heavily in favour of the benign modes, and zero-VAT rating of bicycles.

LONG-TERM OBJECTIVES

The massive increase in car ownership in the last few decades and the government response to this has led to the current situation in which land uses and infrastructure have developed largely around the requirements of the car. Many industries and retail and leisure facilities have been 'rationalized' and decentralized to accommodate the massive parking requirements of a predominantly car-borne clientele, while new roads have been constructed to service such developments. Such trends will take time to reverse as the matching patterns of travel are de-coupled. As noted earlier, the initial task will be to stop this type of land use and give priority to future proposals that reduce the need for motorized travel. As a longer-term objective, it may be possible for 'out-of-town' developments to become central business districts in the future, with the land surrounding them zoned for new housing. Access from residential areas to these commercial areas would be designed for the pedestrian and cyclist, and their surrounding car parks turned over to a diversity of land uses to complement the existing ones and meet the needs of the 'new' community.

Some of the key deterrents to walking and cycling – danger, discomfort and inconvenience – may be attributed to a lack of adequate or appropriate provision. To redress this situation, a network of safe, convenient, well maintained routes will need to be developed in all urban areas and, where appropriate, between built-up areas. Such routes need not entail the provision of extensive infrastructures, but rather an identification of the main preferred directions taken by pedestrians and cyclists, clear signposting, engineering measures at potential trouble spots and, most importantly, a reduction in conflict points with motor vehicles.

To complement such initiatives, particularly in areas where vulnerable road users must continue to share road space with motor vehicles, traffic calming techniques will have to be widely implemented. Traffic calming utilizes a variety of physical measures such as road humps, chicanes and textured surfaces to encourage low speeds. Experience on the Continent has shown that areas treated in this way suffer fewer and less severe road accidents and lower levels of noise and air pollution, while pedestrians and cyclists enjoy a less intimidating environment (Cleary, 1991).

Finally, while walking and cycling could satisfy a significantly greater proportion of travel needs than is currently the case, it would be utopian to assume that they could meet all personal travel needs. For example, the length of some necessary trips will remain beyond the scope of a pedestrian or cyclist. For such journeys, public transport should be promoted as the primary alternative. Nevertheless, it should be borne in mind that longer journeys are often multi-stage. Thus, public transport termini should be served by adequate pedestrian access and good facilities for the storage or hire of cycles, and public transport vehicles should be better adapted to carry them.

CONCLUSIONS

The last forty years have witnessed a considerable increase in the volume and speed of traffic. This has steadily eroded the quality of the environment generally, making walking and cycling less pleasant. During this period too the land use planning changes that have been associated with it have reduced their role as convenient means of serving public travel needs. This situation will worsen without a radical reappraisal of the objectives of transport policy which at present reflects the judgment that the widening ownership and use of cars both reflects public preference and the wider public benefit. The changing role of walking and cycling and the lack of attention paid to them in transport policy suggest that such a reappraisal is urgent.

In 1979, the Policy Studies Institute (PSI) published a report exclusively on the subject of walking (Hillman and Whalley, 1979). It called for walking 'to be included in tests of social, environmental, financial and energy performance, and judged on the same criteria as the motorized modes'. A parallel examination of cycling could well have led to the same recommendation. The report concluded:

> Are people in fact better off or worse off if they make more of their journeys by motorized means rather than on foot, or if their daily travel needs are met over increasing distances? Or would the community benefit from people being encouraged to adopt life styles which become more walk-oriented? Indeed, how can transport and planning policy be appropriately determined without establishing the advantages and disadvantages both to the individual and to the community of all the major methods of travel as well as of changes in the balance of people's patterns of travel – including walking.

At a PSI conference in 1980, the then Secretary of State for Transport, acknowledged that 'walking undoubtedly serves all and that is going to be an increasingly important central government objective'. He stated his Department's intention of taking 'a real interest in policy for pedestrians ... to see what changes or improvements might be made', and of producing a Discussion Paper on pedestrian policy later that year (Hillman, 1980). The following year, he reiterated this intention. But in 1983 the Minister at the Department of Transport at the time decided not to do so 'in view of the lack of significant new data on the subject which are likely to be of interest to the public'.

Some policy analysts may draw comfort from the gradual 'greening' observable in statements and actions by Transport Ministers in the last few years, reflecting growing recognition of the importance of walking and cycling. One of these former Ministers was quoted as stating that 'for too long, people on foot have been the 'Cinderellas' of road users, in spite of the large number of journeys that involve walking.' Technical guidance is now given to local authorities on how to create pedestrian priority areas, introduce traffic calming measures, and install speed humps. Criteria for crossing facilities and phases on traffic lights have been revised in favour of pedestrians and 20mph speed limit zones are now planned for residential areas.

Thanks to an EC initiative, there is now the prospect of a considerable reduction in pollutants from motor vehicle exhausts, albeit not until the end of the decade. In addition, a wide range of bodies representing transport interests at the national and local level have produced reports which now acknowledge the role and significance of walking and cycling (National Consumer Council, 1988; Transport 2000, 1988; Association of Metropolitan Authorities, 1989a).

It would be timely to produce a policy document on the non-motorized modes soon; and it would be difficult to find a better source for its content than that contained in the 1988 European Charter of Pedestrians' Rights drawn up on behalf of the European Parliament's Committee on the Environment, Public Health and Consumer Protection (European Parliament, 1988). This includes the following clauses:

I. The pedestrian has the right to live in a healthy environment and freely to enjoy the amenities offered by public areas under conditions that adequately safeguard his physical and psychological well-being.

II. The pedestrian has the right to live in urban or village centres tailored to the needs of human beings and not to the needs of the motor car, and to have amenities within walking or cycling distance.

III. Children, the elderly and the disabled have the right to expect towns to be places of easy social contact and not places that aggravate their inherent weakness.

IV. The pedestrian has the right to urban areas which are intended exclusively for his use, are as extensive as possible and are not mere 'pedestrian precincts' but in harmony with the overall organization of the town.

It would be easy to draw up a comparable Charter of Cyclists' Rights.

It is apparent that the necessary measures that need to be taken to reflect fully the significance of walking and cycling and the greater role that they should play in the future require a far more ambitious approach than has been seen to date. A precursor to such an approach must be a Government Green Paper on this subject.

The case for promoting walking and cycling is considerably strengthened by reference to the huge increase in traffic forecast for the next few decades for this flies in the face of the policy implications, which are perhaps ecological imperatives, of taking action to avert global warming. It seems highly probable that international agreement will have to be reached on this, bringing in its wake many of the attendant public interest benefits noted earlier. It will require setting markedly low *per capita* quotas for fuel consumption in the developed world. This is very likely to be a key policy agenda item for the 1990s.

Fortuitously, one of the most obvious means of achieving dramatic cut-backs in carbon dioxide production from man-made processes lies in this transport sector of the economy by promoting walking and cycling, and at the same time reducing dependence on cars. Indeed, any attempt to formulate a coherent transport policy for the future which does not place these modes at the centre of that policy rather than at its periphery, is doomed to failure.

Some sections of this Chapter draw heavily on a Paper by one of the authors written for the Rees Jeffreys Road Fund research project *Transport and Society*, published in 1990.

18

BUS POLICY DEVELOPMENT: DEREGULATION IN A WIDER CONTEXT

LAURIE PICKUP

In 1989, the Department of Transport published its traffic forecasts for the period 1988 to 2018. The implications of these forecasts were clear; there will not be sufficient road capacity to cope with forecast growth in mobility. Past policies have also demonstrated that further road-building to cope with greater traffic volumes only serves to increase traffic, not reduce it. It is therefore clear that the key elements of future transport policies in British towns and cities will be public transport and traffic demand management.

Improving the quality of public transport will be a key issue in combatting the dominance of the private car. Much has already been achieved in many European countries to develop integrated transport systems in which bus and rail modes play key roles. In the UK, partly as a consequence of the traffic forecasts, there is now a resurgence of interest from local authorities in integrated transport studies and many are looking to Europe for suitable models to apply.

The quality of public transport in European states is maintained by a variety of operating regimes. Most systems are operated under public ownership; others such as in France, additionally plan networks and franchise the operations to private operators. Investment in improved quality is achieved in most states by high public subsidy (up to 80 per cent of operating costs in some states), or by other forms of direct public transport funding such as the French *versement transport* on employers. Under this latter system, quality and service stability are assured by central planning and financing, or by the conditions placed on franchises in those areas where competition is sought (see also chapter 12).

The position in Britain since 1985 has been that public transport operations maximize the ability to compete for business, with quality benefits hopefully accruing from this competition. Competition exists both for services defined as commercially viable by operators (where operators have the ability to plan, register, operate and change routes as part of normal competitive practice subject to safety and competition regulations), and for services not covered by commercial operators but defined by local authorities as being 'socially necessary' (where authorities seek tenders for defined routes over specified time periods). The ability of planners to adopt integrated policies will be hampered by their lack of control over most of the bus network in marked contrast to other European states where control over the scale of operations does exist.

In some European cities, public transport patronage is increasing despite a continued growth in car ownership. In the UK by contrast, patronage continues to decline as car ownership increases. Research has shown that investment to improve the quality of public transport must offer substantial improvements to attract motorists in significant quantities. Work by Bly (1980) has estimated from a review of studies that the elasticity of demand with service quality changes could be as high as 0.3, i.e. the same level of elasticity as for fares. The longer-term elasticity of service quality could be even more favourable as improvements in quality affect people's travel habits on a permanent basis.

Cars also have important psychological advantages: they represent personal space for their users, an extension of the home, an extension of personality, and drivers feel in control of their journey; particularly important for many women drivers, cars represent a safe and defensible space. These factors have been important aspects of the success of cars in society (Marsh and Collett, 1986). Public transport of whatever quality, finds it difficult to compete with these factors, especially in the face of heavy advertising and conditioning of people from an early age. It is likely that the policies required to improve substantially the quality of public transport would need to include positive restraints on car users to counteract the (often erroneously) perceived advantages of cars, and to give priority to public transport modes. It would be insufficient to finance better quality public transport provision without parallel action in these other areas.

In arguing for the benefits of such an approach, the rest of this paper looks at the development of public transport policy before and after deregulation in Britain. It concludes with the lessons of our experience in the context of an emerging new transport policy consensus.

THE RISE AND FALL OF PUBLIC TRANSPORT FROM 1930 TO 1985

Public modes of transport have changed radically over the century. In the inter-war years, public transport was the main focus of the growth in urban mobility. However, between 1950 and 1970, demand declined as car ownership grew and the car became the preferred vehicle of mobility, both at the urban and inter-urban level. In Britain, the main focus of public transport from 1950 was the bus and that remains the case today and for the medium-term future. On mainland Europe, there was greater investment in urban rail modes rather than buses, which were used more as local feeder links rather than on main transport corridors.

The reasons for the decline in public transport use from 1950 were not solely the availability of a newer, faster, more attractive and higher quality mode of travel. A key factor was economic. The car captured a larger number of fully-employed persons who had previously used public transport. As a result, there were reduced resources to meet the industry's growing financial problems. Cars were becoming part of a new lifestyle for many middle income families, but primarily for the use of male heads of household; women remained reliant on public transport. Policy and investment programmes were providing more roadspace to satisfy this growth in car mobility. Thus the social and financial impacts of rising car ownership were more significant than the absolute numbers of people involved: those switching from buses to cars were the financial core of the public transport market. As a result, from the middle 1960s, subsidies were required to bridge the gap between public transport revenues and costs. Subsidies grew annually to become a key political issue in transport in the 1970s and 1980s.

The pattern of public transport decline since the 1950s is often referred to as a 'vicious circle'. Higher incomes increase car ownership and use which in turn reduces public transport provision. In the short term, increased congestion from cars reduces bus speeds by a proportionately greater amount than cars. In the medium term, this changes the economics of bus operations – increasing fares, cutting service levels or both, which further reduces bus use. The policy often implemented in this context of 'cutting services in line with demand' is not a neutral response. By so doing, waiting times or walking distances for remaining public transport passengers are increased, thus reducing their travel quality. Over the longer term, the urban structure has been changing in response to rising car ownership and has dispersed to a pattern which is more difficult for public transport to serve. Accessibility by public transport has been reduced by this process and cars become not only desirable but necessary, which provides a further boost to the spiral (Pickup et al., 1985).

For many transport professionals up to the early 1970s, when a series of reports such as that of the Independent Commission on Transport (1974) and the work of Mayer Hillman (e.g., Hillman et al., 1973) were published, there was a tendency to think of this vicious circle as inevitable: the UK would follow the trend of the USA in terms of its growing dependency on the car. However, it was also clear that the vicious circle, during the 1950s and 1960s, had been accelerated by policy actions, whether deliberate or consequential. Public transport journeys continued to decline at roughly 3 per cent per annum from a relatively high initial rate compared to those of other European states (Webster et al., 1985).

The 1970s and 1980s have been a period of reflection and a search for new policies; these developed on political lines. In the previous twenty years, a policy consensus had been based on the proposition that car ownership would increase, justifying a large road-building programme. From the mid 1970s, the costs of road infrastructure, the destruction of residences for road-building, the impacts of policies on those reliant on public transport use, and the beginnings of a concern for environmental issues, removed the consensus which had existed and produced the search for new policies.

It was clear during this period that the quality of public transport required improvement: the cities turned to the European model of integration with investment in urban rail systems (Strathclyde, Merseyside, Tyne & Wear). The key issue at this time was the level of government subsidy required to fuel the investment needed to improve public transport quality. The academic and political debate on subsidy increased in the late 1970s and was central in the move to deregulation in the early 1980s. At the same time, population, unemployment and car ownership all continued to move in directions which were unfavourable to public transport operations.

The subsidizing of bus services was justified on three basic grounds:

- to meet social objectives;
- to accrue economic benefits by reducing the external costs of using cars;
- to maintain investment to retain a longer-term market.

Those arguing against subsidy stressed the amount which was being lost or 'leaked' into higher wage settlements in the industry at the expense of better quality services – as high as one third of subsidy introduced (Webster *et al.*, 1985). This was inefficient use of resources, it was argued despite the good intentions of those favouring subsidy on social grounds. Countering this argument, the pro-subsidy lobby underlined the fact that public transport quality had improved with subsidy; furthermore, the public transport industry had to pay a market wage to attract appropriate staff so the 'leakage' argument was untenable. It was also felt that those arguing against subsidy did not fully account for social benefits in their assessment of its efficiency of use.

Despite these counter arguments, the leakage proposition won political credence and became part of the argument for proposing deregulation of bus services in the 'Buses' White Paper of 1984. It was touted as a way of improving service quality without the need for further public investment in operating subsidies; the investment was to come instead from profits gained in a competitive bus market.

BUS SERVICE QUALITY SINCE DEREGULATION

The 1985 Transport Act was accompanied by fierce political and academic debate. The basic proposition was that the bus market was a contestable one and that competition could provide travellers with better quality services. The proponents of deregulation argued that deregulation would lead to more buses, lower fares, more competition and higher patronage, while opponents argued that the opposite would happen. In hindsight, neither the greatest hopes of the proponents, nor the worst fears of the opponents have been realized. Limited market contestation has resulted, but in a market where some operators have a distinct advantage. By 1991, it is clear that deregulation has neither reversed the decline in bus patronage nor provided noticeably better quality services.

In 1986, a higher than expected proportion (of the vehicle miles that had been operated in 1985) were registered as commercial services (about 80 per cent as opposed to tendered services). This arose due to a degree of hidden cross-subsidy with operators aiming to retain their pre-deregulation operating territory rather than reduce their economically marginal services. The commercial and tendered services thus became interrelated.

The industry was restructured for deregulation with the splitting up and privatization of the National Bus Company, the establishment of private Passenger Transport Companies (under semi-public control) in the cities and municipal areas, and the splitting up and eventual privatization of the Scottish Bus Group companies. The old small independent companies which had operated contract services for local authorities prior to 1985, now either registered them commercially or operated them as the successful tenderer. Because of this registration, the number of companies operating services apparently increased – figures often quoted by local authorities to demonstrate the Act working in their area. However, in nearly all cases, this statistic is misleading for there are few new companies. The major companies have retained the majority share of mileage operated. Other smaller operators have increased their share of services, but from a small base and in such a way as not to be too threatening to the larger operators (such as an infrequent service on a heavily patronized route). Most have concentrated on tendered services or commercial services in niche areas.

From 1988, there was the realization by the larger bus operators that the best way to avoid competition was to purchase the competing company. A large number of mergers and buyouts followed, producing local monopolies in many areas by 1990. Thus, by 1991, deregulation had not produced a substantial shift in the structure of the industry in terms of the relative sizes and market shares of companies. The relative roles of small and large companies were similar to the pre-deregulation situation with two important exceptions: first, the subsidy was smaller; and second, the investment in better quality services now crucially depended on generally low profit levels in a declining market.

The low investment levels in the bus industry witnessed in the immediate pre-deregulation years have become significantly worse since 1986, particularly with regard to the replacement of fleets (White, 1989). In the drive for profitability from a position of substantial operating subsidy (about 40 per cent), bus companies had to make large reductions to their costs and, in some metropolitan areas in particular, large increases in fares. For example, in Merseyside, fare levels on new commercial services doubled in October 1986.

The 30 per cent operating cost reductions which the Government argued were achievable in 1986 have been broadly attained, but the reductions were mostly of a one-off nature related to a restructuring of labour in the industry and a reformulation of working agreements (Pickup and Goodwin, 1989). The cost reductions achieved via more efficient operations were marginal relative to these other savings.

One impact of competition has been to increase the number of bus vehicle miles operated. However, this has not increased the number of bus users, they have declined. The additional mileage has concentrated on the busy radials at peak and inter-peak times, at some expense to other areas and fringe operating periods. Concentration of mileage in this way has led to cases where operators have been accused of 'over-bussing' routes. Furthermore, the tendency under competition was for services to bunch, rather than provide the traveller with a smaller service headway. So more buses did not mean a more frequent service.

The increasing provision of minibuses by many operators did increase headways on radial routes and also enabled operators to maintain a better suburban route penetration. Importantly, they also enabled operators to employ staff aged eighteen to twenty-one and to tap new labour markets, such as part-time women on new working conditions and substantially lower wages, without provoking the trade unions. Minibuses have been shown to possess both good and negative features for service quality. The use of minibuses also made a substantial contribution to the overall increase in vehicle miles operated without substantially increasing the provision of seats to the public; they were seen by operators largely as a mechanism of competition to deter entry by others on their routes. In Greater Manchester, for example, by 1989 vehicle mileage had increased by 25 per cent while seat mileage due to the introduction of minibuses only increased by 3 per cent.

The main effect of deregulation has been the reduction in the number of people using buses. Patronage fell faster nationally after 1986 than it had in previous years, but the fall was particularly marked in the metropolitan areas where it had been rising prior to deregulation. Loss of patronage was related to fare increases and also to new factors associated with journey quality. The main factor to emerge was the instability in services as a result of commercial operators being able to alter services at six weeks' notice. As operators made many initial changes to their services at the onset of deregulation, patronage fell rapidly and never recovered ground. Again Merseyside, for example, lost one third of passenger journeys by bus in the first year after deregulation. Subsequently, the level of service changes reduced during 1987 but still remains at a significantly high level as a permanent feature of deregulated operations.

Instability has meant that passengers have had greater need for good service information (which had not been essential before 1985 when services changed less frequently), but the instability in services which has become part of deregulated operations has made it more difficult for authorities to provide it in a comprehensive and up-to-date form. Lack of certainty about services continues to be a major problem for bus users and the need for better means of information provision a major problem for local authorities.

Bus services since October 1986 have thus become both more and less efficient than previous regulated operations: more miles operated for less financial input (more efficient); more miles operated but fewer passengers and less revenue (less efficient). The final equation appears to be that the industry now operates more miles for a lower staff input, at lower wage costs with lower central government subsidy. However, the potential benefits of these cost savings have been reduced to the margin by the lower number of passengers produced by fare increases and service instability.

As a consequence, profit levels in the industry are dangerously low and this will fuel further merger and takeover activity (Price Waterhouse, 1990). It will also continue to keep investment low with inadequate fleet replacement.

In the medium and longer term, the main effect of deregulation will be the way in which it has removed buses from the planner's tool box. They have no control over commercial bus networks and this makes the task of designing an integrated transport system more difficult. Work by Banister and myself, comparing the fortunes of the metropolitan areas under deregulation and London which was not fully deregulated, but where networks were defined by the authority and put out to competitive tender, showed that London achieved most of the cost savings of the other cities through competitive tendering while ensuring service quality was maintained through tender conditions and without the instability in services which followed from full deregulation (Banister and Pickup, 1990).

BUSES AS THE CORE OF A FUTURE TRANSPORT POLICY?

Despite the growth in light rail proposals in recent years (emulating the

European experience), the medium-term policy future for public transport in Britain will depend on bus operations. At present, following the faster than average decline in patronage in the immediate years following deregulation, patronage now declines at the rate witnessed in pre-deregulation years. The 1985 Transport Act has therefore failed to halt the 'terminal decline in the industry'. However, as the introduction pointed out, the public transport market in many European states is increasing not shrinking. Furthermore, it is increasing against a background of rising car ownership and where the rate of increase is above the European average. A situation in which public transport breaks out of the 'vicious circle' is certainly possible in present circumstances.

Given the current traffic forecasts, the bus must be the centre of future transport policy. In many ways the decline of the bus as a mode of transport reflects an introspective view of the British bus industry with its low levels of investment, wages and profit. Attention needs to be focused away from operator 'A' competing with operator 'B' towards the real competitor, the private car. It is also clear that the bus industry will require more assistance than it can currently receive from the deregulated market in order to face the formidable challenge of the next ten to twenty years.

According to the traffic forecasts, the saturation level for car ownership will be reached in 2030. In the two years since the forecasts were published, a major shift has been witnessed in the policies of the main actors in transport and with unprecedented speed. It has resulted in a realignment of a 'strong' roads lobby and a 'weak' public transport lobby. Recent work for the Rees Jeffreys Foundation by Goodwin *et al.* (1991) underlines the nature of a new consensus which includes organisations previously anti-public transport. It focuses on integrated transport policies and, in their view, has five main characteristics:

- a very limited role for new road capacity;
- greater emphasis on an expanded role for public transport;
- traffic calming and pedestrianization schemes to enhance city centres;
- advanced traffic management to provide bus priority;
- some professional support for road pricing to pay for quality improvements on public transport.

In this scenario for the 1990s and 2000s, public transport is not marginalized but is centre stage and competing with other modes under fair rules. If this occurs, public transport quality will require substantial investment. But if implemented, the consequent growth in patronage could equal that witnessed earlier in the century.

One issue which remains is how a deregulated system would provide such a level of investment, given the experience since 1985. Additional finance would need to come from another source to achieve the objectives of the new policy consensus. Many in the profession argue that road pricing is the way forward, in which a proportion of the income is fed directly into improvements in public transport quality. If road pricing becomes politically acceptable as the alternative taxation source for transport (in addition to its traffic demand management functions), then the required investment in bus and rail systems could be achievable. There will, however, be a fairly long lead time in which the systems will require finance prior to pricing being introduced. At present there is no mechanism for handling this situation in a deregulated system.

This chapter has charted the development of public transport policy in Britain, pointing to the unequal situations under which public transport has competed with the car in past decades. In contrast to this situation continuing, integrated transport strategies in the future would need to maximize the efficiency of public transport provision over cars. Quality of provision could be improved by dedicated, unbroken bus priority lanes, sensible traffic calming schemes which deter car use, park and ride schemes, maximum use of transport telematics to improve system efficiency for public transport, and possibly road pricing options which would provide requisite revenue. Local solutions will involve a mix of these features as appropriate. Such objectives could feasibly be attained by either a regulated or deregulated bus regime. However, changing the legislation to introduce network control via forms of franchising would improve the position of the planner, stabilise the services provided to users, and achieve the benefits which accrue from competition while ensuring that safety and social conditions are met within the franchises offered.

Some of the research summarized in this chapter comes from a study undertaken for the Association of Metropolitan Authorities and the Passenger Transport Executive Group by Oxford University Transport Studies Unit (Pickup *et al.*, 1991). I would like to acknowledge the contributions of the co-authors of that report: Gordon Stokes, Shirley Meadowcroft, Phil Goodwin, Francesca Kenny and Bill Tyson.

19

A TRANSPORT POLICY FOR LONDON

GAVIN SMITH

It is proposed that prior to the re-establishment of an elected planning body for London, unified control of London's transport planning be vested in a Minister, working in tandem with a committee drawn from the London Boroughs. Specific proposals are made with respect to: the control of bus and rail services in London; the creation of a fully accessible network; and a coherent and unified investment programme.

INTRODUCTION

London's transport is in a mess. Congestion is worsening both on the road and rail networks. Bus services are under-utilized and under constant threat of disruptive reorganization. Service standards on public transport are falling. We are witnessing a transfer to the car as the preferred means of transport in both inner and outer London – to the obvious detriment of road safety, the environment, road congestion, and the quality of life of those without access to a car or taxi. Over the last two or more decades the governmental response has been the same: the road capacity is increased to meet the 'demand' for increased car usage. Rail freight depots meanwhile have shrunk; the freight and deliveries sector in general has become ever more unco-ordinated.

Only recently has the alternative – a public transport oriented approach more closely matching policies in continental Europe – received even passing governmental recognition.

The Labour Party's *Moving Britain into the 1990s* (1990) makes particular mention of London. The document's proposals include a new directly elected body with responsibility for co-ordinating transport in the capital, policies to improve public transport and freight movement, and the reduction of car usage. Most independent observers would be in concord with this general perspective, which is one of a number of London overviews now in print.

There are, however, at least three principal areas where a coherent policy for London requires further thought:

- the organizational issue of what to do from day one of a new government – i.e., before it is possible to re-establish an elected London planning body;
- the question of equality of access to transport;
- a fuller concept of how public transport might develop in London.

ORGANIZATION FROM DAY ONE

A new government, determined to follow green and equitable policies, must have a plan of action ready to be implemented without delay. There is as yet no agreement on such a plan. Below are its possible outlines.

There should be a *halt to the privatization* of any parts of London Transport or British Rail. Privatization is *not* the only way to generate more investment, and carries with it the strong risk that transport inequalities would be increased. Asset-stripping (of garages, land resources, etc.) has been one highly undesirable side-effect of recent privatizations in this sector (e.g., in bus companies outside London).

A *London-wide planning authority* should combine both transport and land-use functions. It should be democratically controlled by the London electorate as soon as practicable. These two reforms would bring London back into line with the norm in Britain, where, though land use and transport planning are too frequently pursued independently, at least they are overseen by a single metropolitan county (or in Scotland, regional) authority.

In the interim, the London planning powers held by the Department of Transport, the Department of the Environment, London Transport and British Rail, should be transferred to a Minister with responsibility for London's planning and transport. However, this Minister should work in tandem with a *London Boroughs Transport Committee* (LBTC) comprising one representative from each of the London Boroughs – an executive arrangement already pioneered by the London Boroughs Grants Committee (LBGC). Within two years this Committee should take over full power from the aforesaid Minister. It should operate (like the LBGC) on the basis of majority voting.

Given the experience elsewhere, *buses in London should not be deregulated*. This is in contradistinction to the ill-thought out policies floated in the latest Department of Transport paper (1990b).

It has been suggested by some, that the best option is to retain the existing London Transport tendering procedures – indeed, that these offer a model for the rest of the country. The argument is that tendering can be reformed, by full public access to information, by contract compliance clauses (e.g., on staff conditions), firm monitoring and provision for the cessation of contracts, and effective controls against the emergence of ownership cartels (already a feature of the national bus industry).

However, it is equally possible that tendering itself – which was introduced as a half-way house to privatization and deregulation – is in reality unreformable. The essence of tendering is cost-cutting. Most cost-cutting is achieved through wages reduction, backed up by the sale of assets. Even if garages are not sold or buses parked in the open air (a pollution and land use issue), tendering very frequently leads to the inefficient practice of running empty buses to and from distant depots. Wage reduction leads to an alienated and unstable workforce, and has involved a variety of abuses including illegally long driver hours, higher accident levels, and the employment on tendered contracts of drivers retired by London Buses as medically unfit.

What London needs is a strong, stable bus service. This might be best achieved by not renewing tendered contracts when they end, but instead drawing the services back into the London Bus subsidiaries. These subsidiaries, rather than becoming independent (as intended at present), should revert to the central control of a single London Buses Ltd – thus enabling the removal of a whole tier of newly multiplied upper and middle management. Individual garages could instead be given an enhanced self-management role. One essential feature would be liaison with local Borough officers and passenger groups – something traditionally lacking, and something most unlikely under a deregulated welter of competing, cost-cutting private companies.

The priority as always is the development of a substantial integrated, accountable public transport system in London. Within such a strategy, the rapid expansion of *co-ordinated* bus services is virtually a precondition.

London Transport should retain its planning functions (and expand them, by taking over, for example, the power to institute bus priority traffic management), but be subject to the higher control of the

Minister/LBTC.

Those services of *British Rail Network SouthEast* that do not extend beyond the former GLC boundary, should likewise be subject to the planning control of the Minister/LBTC.

Again in contradiction to government proposals, the *London Regional Passengers' Committee* (LRPC) should retain its role as statutory passengers' watchdog with respect to rail, Underground and bus services. (The Department of Transport [1990b] proposes the LRPC's remit over bus services be restricted.)

London's public transport should be *funded to average European levels*. Specifically, let us define this as approximately 50 per cent revenue support, though the figure could be higher. (Current government policy is to reduce London Transport and Network SouthEast support to zero.)

In view of its strategic importance to Britain's future in Europe, the Minister should announce immediately that meetings will be held between British Rail and the Minister on the *Channel Tunnel* (concerning especially its links to London, and its termini). We would envisage that (contrary to policy at the time of writing) a fresh approach would be found. If adequately funded, the favoured route probably would be a dual-purpose passenger/freight link between the Channel Tunnel and Stratford (Newham) via the north bank of the Thames, and thence (in tunnel where necessary) either to Kings Cross or direct to the rail routes north out of London. In parallel should be considered the recommended but delayed CrossRail scheme (a Stratford to Paddington British Rail tunnel).

There should be a coherent approach to *road congestion*. Current makeshift policies and suggested policies – Red Route no-stopping routes, in-car traffic jam avoidance computer systems, selective 'road pricing', and of course the continuing massive road-building programme – should be put on ice for two years. During this period, the Minister should require of the Department of the Environment that its policies be reviewed under the umbrella of the public transport focused policies outlined above.

The net effect should be the emergence of a pedestrian/cycle/bus priority programme, whose outlines are indicated in this chapter. It is anticipated that this would lead to work on almost all of the Department's present policies for London being terminated. New work would be initiated on central London parking policy, advice and standards for grant-aided Borough 'traffic calming' programmes, and a London-wide lorry policy involving road improvement at specific congestion points on a lorry-route network that has yet to be identified. The Department's role as effectively the highway authority for London would be transferred first to the Minister and thence to the LBTC.

EQUALITY OF ACCESSIBILITY

It should be a basic principle that London's public transport is accessible to all. This is not the case at present. In various ways, women, pensioners, children, people of ethnic minorities, and people with disabilities, are denied full access. The following strategies are suggested to bring this situation to an end. (See also chapters 5 and 6.)

Transport Police statistics show fluctuating but still high numbers of assaults and even murders at and in the vicinity of stations. At the same time, both London Underground and British Rail are decreasing their staff coverage at stations. *Stations should be staffed* at all times that trains are running. Staff could progressively be removed from ticket offices as the ticketing system is reformed, and into Help Points and other roles directly accessible to the public. Human resources alone can create a railway characterized by operational safety and personal security – features ebbing away at present, and leading to a declining attractiveness of the system for many potential and former users.

In this same vein, the Labour Party's proposed retention of *bus conductors* is to be welcomed. In addition, *train guards* should be present on each Underground and British Rail train, though with a movement towards a revised job description following the successful precedent of the Docklands Light Railway 'train captains'.

The Minister/LBTC should ensure that *service standards* are defined, and thence achieved, monitored and enforced. Such standards ultimately should be national; in the interim, London standards are required. They should include: geographical accessibility; accessibility for people with disabilities; frequency; punctuality; vehicle design; information; fares; and ticketing. In the absence of such standards, there can be little movement towards either an accessible or an integrated system.

The government's Citizen's Charter concept of passenger compensation for faulty service might look a step in the right direction, but is valueless in the absence of both publicized service standards and adequate investment in public transport.

Concessionary fares for pensioners, and the *Taxicard scheme* fares reduction for people with disabilities, are London initiatives that must not be lost. Ideally, they should be operated as a national policy, funded by central government via the local authority.

In the interim, the Minister/LBTC should fix the terms for London; these would be mandatory for all Boroughs (some being tempted to save on this measure). Concessionary fares should apply equally to British Rail services, and ought to be extended to the unemployed (for whom expensive travel is a hindrance in the search for work).

Mobility Buses (wheelchair-accessible bus services running regular public routes) and *Dial-a-Ride* (equivalent membership-only vehicles) should continue to be planned and controlled by London Transport, but with an expanding budget that recognizes the currently low level of service. (Mobility buses commonly run only once a week, while waiting times for Dial-a-Ride are in some cases weeks.)

Buses accessible to people with disabilities will become near universal in London (as they are in New York) only if legislation or policy demands they do so. That all vehicles meet Diptac standards, is a first step only – and one that is threatened by bus deregulation. A national strategy is required, perhaps for completion by the year 2000.

It should be national policy also that all *stations be accessible to people with disabilities*. London's could be so by the year 2010.

A DEVELOPMENT STRATEGY

The desire for a coherent investment programme can be realized only if an agreed programme exists in some detail. This is not the case at present, and must be rectified. The elements of such a programme might include the following.

A *land use and planning team* of high calibre must be assembled and deployed by our proposed LBTC (staff shortages are today a major impediment to transport and land use planning, both at Borough level and London-wide). The team's work must be fully open to the public.

Bus priority: since the demise of the GLC, and in contrast to Europe, bus priority policy has languished in spite of enthusiasm (but no power) on the part of London Transport. The Department of Transport has been consistently obstructive, at least until the advent of the Department's experimental Red Routes scheme. Red Routes should be rethought to become *Green Routes*, on the model currently pursued in West London by a consortium of five Boroughs, the London Planning Advisory Committee, and London Transport, and along the Archway corridor by Haringey Council together with local groups.

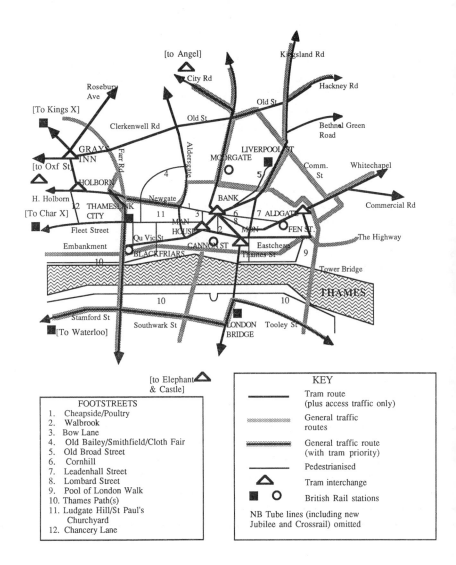

Figure 19-1: Central London – A Proposal for Tram Routes and Footstreets in the City and its Environs.

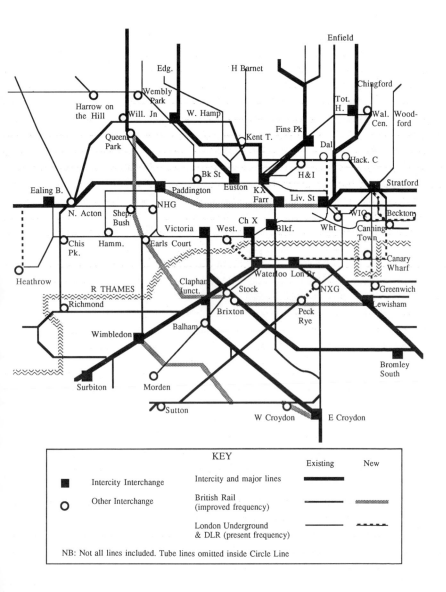

Figure 19-2: Interchange Stations – A Proposed Network.

It should be announced that within a short time-table, *all tickets will be fully transferable between modes* (i.e., buses, rail, Underground, and hopefully in future, trams). This is commonplace in Europe, but goes far beyond London Transport's discussion in their recent consultation document (1991).

The Minister should announce the intention that there be a comprehensive network of 'bus, cycle and access only' streets (later convertible to tram routes) in *Central London*. Again these are common to the more progressive European cities. There should be a parallel expansion of 'pedestrianized' streets (i.e., time controlled 'access only', with cycle access where appropriate). See Figure 19-1.

A valuable European feature is the *interchange station*, where passengers may make easy transfer between bus and rail, or rail and rail – an essential characteristic of a comprehensive public transport system. A network of interchange stations should be determined by the Minister and the London Transport Committee. There should be between two and five per Borough (see Figure 19-2) which should:

- be identified in Borough Unitary Development Plans;
- be made fully accessible to people with disabilities by the year 2000;
- be a focus around which local bus and cycle routes are planned;
- be provided with well serviced taxi ranks;
- provide cycle parking/hiring facilities.

The Minister should announce immediate research into the potential in London for on-street modern *trams* (plus trolleybuses, mixed-mode vehicles, etc.) of European type. The concept should be that Green Routes (see above) would form the first phase of a programme leading to the development of a tram network (see Figure 19-1). This presents the single greatest potential for relieving pressures on the Underground system. A pilot route should be initiated at the earliest possible date.

Light rail, especially as a conversion of existing British Rail track, has received some publicity. However, conventional *rail and Underground expansions*, although far more expensive, are appropriate in some situations (e.g., as linkages or extensions to existing services, or where sharing track with goods trains). After bus priority and trams, rail developments represent the third biggest potential area of expansion of London's public transport. Today's *ad hoc* initiatives should be welded into a coherent programme, which would include:

- the Croydon Light Rail System (already approved by the Government, but not funded);
- the East London Line extensions north to Dalston and south to East Dulwich (for which approval is currently being delayed);
- a frequent passenger service on British Rail's West London line – Clapham Junction–Willesden Junction (a scheme which received British Rail's blessing until disrupted by the confusion over Channel Tunnel routings);
- a frequent passenger service on Britsh Rail track between Lewisham and Clapham Junction – a new 'South London line' (which, like the West London line, has the support of local Boroughs and until the Channel Tunnel fiasco, that of British Rail also);
- the Docklands Light Railway extension south of the river to Lewisham (which again has approval, but has not been funded).

Note here that: the Croydon Light Rail would be a pilot conversion scheme; the East, West and South London lines, with an improved service on British Rail's North London line, would effectively bring into being the 'Outer Circle' concept advocated by the Labour Party in 1991; the Docklands Light Railway is a technology isolated from the rest of the system, and should not be replicated further.

More expensively, the recommendation of the government's own *Central London Rail Study* (DTp/BR/LT/LU, 1989) should be clarified, prioritized, and entered into a defined construction programme. The first priority would likely be the Paddington to Statford BR tunnel, serving both Docklands and the potential Stratford Channel Tunnel terminus.

CONCLUSION

The above 'package' represents something of a coherent strategy, and one likely to receive ready public approval. It could proceed only under the aegis of a similarly unified funding programme. The most practical financial strategy (to be used in tandem with higher government investment, and the freedom of planning and operating authorities to raise funds), would be a special London transport tax. This could be a local employers' tax (of the type in operation in Paris), or a redirection of the existing London business rate (as advocated in 1991 by the Association of London Authorities). Its form would have to be decided by the Minister, in consultation, and pushed through

Parliament. Such a tax would seem to have a measure of tacit support from the Corporation of London in their paper on *London's Transport* (1990). The London Boroughs Transport Committee would control the fruits of this tax, with London Transport and British Rail acting as agents (a relationship similar to that enjoyed by metropolitan Passenger Transport Executives elsewhere in the country).

We are here advocating an essentially London solution. However, this might mesh very nicely with the European Commission's intended 'green' fuel tax. Vehicular fuel would be taxed to its true cost in resource use and environmental pollution – a reform which could only lead to an enhanced emphasis on public as opposed to (vehicular) private transport. Some of the income from any 'green' tax should go towards building up a sustainable 'green' infrastructure, in which a decent public transport system for London would figure largely.

20

PLAYING TRAINS

PAUL SALVESON

Playing trains is fun, and many people in the transport industry still have a tendency to treat running a railway a bit like operating a Hornby Dublo train set. The main thing is that the trains go round and round, and occasionally stop and start to add a bit of extra interest. The big difference between a train set and real life is that *people* use public transport, and many of them depend on it to live their lives. The country's economy depends on an efficient transport system to move goods and raw materials. All too often, the social, economic, and environmental dimensions are left out of our transport planning.

This chapter explores some ways in which Britain's railways can serve people and their communities more effectively, and make a stronger contribution to improving the country's economy and protecting the environment.

BRITISH RAIL – KEEP IT PUBLIC, KEEP IT SAFE

The quality of some of BR's services, particularly in the Regional Railways (formerly Provincial) and Network SouthEast sectors, have suffered because of grant reductions by the Conservative Government and poor quality management in some areas.

The lack of investment and revenue support for keeping the trains running has been condemned by bodies as respectable as the Central Transport Consultative Committee. Further cuts and eventual privatization will lead to line closures, and fares would rise to such a level that people are priced off trains and forced to use a car, if they can afford one.

Privatization is a non-solution to the problems of an underfunded railway. BR's business sectors are already operating on a commercial basis, and it is difficult to see what privatization would achieve other than higher fares to increase profit levels, loss of co-ordination, and operational chaos as competing trains try to gain access to an overcrowded network. Its one possible advantage, that it would free the railways to make their own investment decisions and allow them to spend their own money without having to ask the government's permission, could be achieved equally well under a publicly owned structure, but with the railways having more autonomy from the government. (For a more detailed comment on rail privatization, see my *British Rail: The Radical Alternative to Privatization*, 1989.)

SET OBJECTIVES AND CHANGE THE STRUCTURE

Britain's railways need to remain under public control: they are a vital part of the country's infrastructure and can contribute, positively or negatively, to the way Britain works. Some change is needed – both in how Britain's railways are structured, and in the management culture of the railways.

Government involvement in running the railways should be limited to the setting of a number of general objectives, covering financial, commercial, quality, social, employment, environmental, and safety objectives (see the end of this chapter for some suggestions). All of BR's existing business sectors should be expected to run commercially. Subsidies should be targeted to achieve specific objectives, and should be part of a programme to reduce dependence on public support. The infrastructure of Britain's rail network should become the responsibility of the government in the same way that the strategic highway network is.

The Labour Party's plans for regional government have some major implications for BR, particularly in the Regional Railways sector, which has three distinct markets: the intensive suburban networks, mostly provided on contract to the metropolitan passenger transport executives (PTEs), the rural or semi-rural branch line network, and lastly the longer-distance 'express' services, most of which are now operated by new 90mph trains. The first two market areas should be separated out from direct BR responsibility, and be given to new regional transport authorities (RTAs), which would be accountable to the new regional governments. If the RTAs took over the suburban and semi-rural networks BR could still provide the actual train services but on a contractual basis similar to the present arrangements with the

PTEs. Closer integration could be achieved with other forms of local transport, including fares and ticketing, information, and actual services. BR's Regional Railways would be left to supply high quality inter-regional services which connect into both BR InterCity services, and RTA-supported services. The slimmed down Regional Railways should be able to run on a commercial basis, without subsidy. Subsidized services should become the sole responsibility of the RTAs for which Regional Railways could, if the RTAs wished, provide services on a contract basis.

CREATE A TRACK AUTHORITY

The structure of BR has undergone considerable change in the last few years. The 'Organizing for Quality' (OFQ) restructuring exercise has led to the establishment of BR's sectors as virtually separate companies: InterCity, Trainload Freight, Railfreight Distribution, Network SouthEast, Parcels, and Regional Railways. Each sector takes bottom-line responsibility for its infrastructure, permitting other sectors to use its track on an 'avoidable cost' basis – in other words paying for extra wear and tear, as well as any extra infrastructure which may be required.

The project has met with some severe criticism from within BR management. The danger of loss of co-ordination, excessive dependence on accountants working out who is responsible for what, and a loss of economies of scale and corporate control are some of the dangers which have been highlighted. Having several different bodies responsible for infrastructure is likely to cause continuing headaches for BR managers as OFQ becomes fully established.

On the positive side, new energy has been brought to many services which were once the poor relation within BR, notably the Regional Railways services. Despite a serious lack of revenue funding, investment in new trains has been substantial, and there has been a very heartening new era in co-operation with local authorities – not just with the passenger transport authorities and their PTEs, but also with many shire counties and Scottish regions.

The directive from the European Commission to separate rail infrastructure (track and the rest) from operations (the actual running of trains) has major implications for BR which could prove very positive. In some countries like Sweden this separation has already happened, and many other countries are following its example. In Sweden, the government takes responsibility for the infrastructure, and Swedish Railways, and other operators, run the trains on a straightforward commercial basis without worrying about finding money for major investment in new lines or stations. This is part of a very advanced approach towards transport planning in which all forms of transport investment – road and rail – are evaluated using the same criteria, and all modes pay for their full external costs. Some local passenger services are subsidized by local authorities. The model allows for other operators to run trains in addition to the state-owned railway.

This approach would be better than the existing BR structure where there are at least four bodies (the main sectors) responsible for infrastructure. Planning any major new investment project would have to be co-ordinated between the railway operators and the track authority, in the same way that today's business sectors collaborate with civil engineering, and signal and telecommunications departments, on future projects such as electrification.

The British Railways Board and its civil engineering and signalling and telecommunications organization, should become an infrastructure authority which is a part of the Department of Transport. To avoid confusion with the 'old' BR, it could be called BriTrack. It would take responsibility for:

- permanent way (track, bridges, tunnels, etc.);
- signalling and telecommunications;
- basic station infrastructure;
- train control.

The business sectors would own their own locomotives and rolling stock, depots, and some station facilities (mostly passenger services such as booking office and information services, buffets and restaurants, etc.). They would have the option of sharing some resources, including depots and workshops, and could enter into arrangements for borrowing locomotives or rolling stock. They would employ their own staff, including train crew, platform staff, and other customer-service personnel.

The sectors should maintain their independence as publicly owned companies, and run their services on a commercial basis. Socially necessary services would be paid for on contract by the RTAs. The sectors would then pay to use the track on the basis of the marginal cost, with responsibility for capital investment resting with BriTrack. The costing structure would take into account the impact on the environment, and the same formulation would apply to all other forms of transport.

This structure would make it considerably easier to make investment decisions based on common criteria applied to road and rail: for the first time in Britain, all transport investment would be judged on an equal basis, with the best mode chosen to achieve particular objectives. It would also make it easier for other approved operators to have easy access to the rail infrastructure because of the transparency of costs.

There are two areas where such a development would be potentially positive. The first is in rail freight. Already some companies like Tiger, and Charterail (the BR-GKN joint venture), are running what are essentially private trains on BR tracks. The wagons are privately owned, and maintained to BR's high safety standards. In most cases they use BR locos, and in all cases BR drivers. There is tremendous interest in the private sector in developing more such initiatives, and BR itself has teamed up with several companies to form Combined Transport Ltd.

The second area is in local commuter networks. Some of the metropolitan PTEs have already bought their own rolling stock for use on their passenger services contracted from BR. If regional transport authorities are formed which have access to greater resources than the existing PTEs, many new possibilities begin to open up, including RTAs running their own trains, or contracting other companies to run them (as in parts of Sweden) providing that stringent quality and safety standards are met. This could provide better integration with bus and light rail networks provided locally, but it would be important to maintain co-ordination with the main BR network. By facing real competition for RTA contracts, BR would be forced to improve the quality of its own product.

The RTAs would work in close conjunction with BriTrack to help finance new investment in local and regional projects such as electrification, new lines and stations, and improving the accessibility of the regional network.

A PEOPLE-CENTRED RAILWAY

Catering for the needs of all passengers should be a major priority of Britain's railway operators. Considerable effort has been put into making trains and stations more accessible for disabled passengers, but further work needs to be done to reduce disabled passengers' dependence on BR staff assistance. A start would be to identify a core accessible network, similar to that achieved on Swiss railways. A geographically spread network of 110 'support stations' have been established following discussions with disabled peoples' organizations. In Britain, we have a big potential advantage over most of European railways because platforms are higher: level or near-level access to trains is comparatively easy.

Resources need to be focused on station facilities, and making sure that the trains themselves are accessible for all forms of disability, including passengers with sight or hearing difficulties. National transport policy should see the development of a 'transport chain' in which railways are only part of a chain of accessible transport services for disabled travellers. Buses, taxis and trams should provide another part of an integrated accessible network. A new 'accessibility grant' should be available, based on the existing Section 106 of the 1985 Transport Act, which is available to all public transport agencies to help make infrastructure and vehicles more accessible, and to improve information and other customer services for disabled people.

Other customers have their own particular needs: for example, parents with children need to have better facilities on trains and at stations. People whose first language is not English should have much better assistance in provision of information. Cyclists should no longer be treated with a mixture of contempt and exasperation.

Many travellers, particularly women, but also elderly people, find using all forms of public transport at night intimidating. The problems are greatest at unstaffed stations, often situated in out-of-the-way locations. The policy of de-staffing stations should be reversed and new categories of rail staff introduced at smaller stations, with a wide range of commercial duties.

AN ENTERPRISING RAILWAY?

Most rail facilities have a lot of untapped commercial potential which could make rail travel more attractive. The passenger sectors could set up a 'Rail Enterprises' which could take a broad and imaginative look at ways of generating new forms of income. A lot can be learnt from the example of Japanese railways, where stations have changed from being dismal places where people come and go to catch trains, to busy commercial and cultural centres. Shops, cafes, restaurants, and other facilities attract people who aren't actually using the train, but are perhaps more likely to when they realize its convenience. Stations become more people-friendly, and less intimidating at night-time because there's a lot going on.

Major stations should have the equivalent of a 'chief executive' whose job it is to promote the station energetically, exploit commercial opportunities, and develop community liaison. All station staff should be trained in customer care, and this should include language training, disability awareness, and methods of how to defuse potentially violent situations. All passengers, whether Regional, InterCity, or Network SouthEast, should get the same quality of service, from the same staff. Booking office and information staff should be 'handling agents' for other sectors and operators when there is a mix.

Main stations should form the hubs of transport activity in a town or city. The RTA should ensure that local bus and tram networks converge on them, with good taxi provision. Cycle hire facilities, as well as secure storeage, should be available at all major stations, as in cycle-friendly Holland.

Business opportunities on trains themselves should be exploited, with a wider range of consumer goods available including newspapers and magazines, and, where the market justifies it, a range of consumer services.

A NEW BRANCH LINE AGE

One of the biggest of BR's problems is loss-making branch lines. A strategy could be developed which not only helps to revitalize the lines, but which also breathes new life into small communities. Years ago, the local station was often the focus of village life. This era could return, through a joint approach between BR, local authorities, and the communities themselves – with help from rural development agencies. Particular branch lines should have 'trusts' formed to promote them, involving representatives of all the above bodies. Money should be put into developing each station as a centre of small-scale economic activity: workshops, offices, and specialist shops, some of which could cater for tourists. On my own branch line, from Truro to Falmouth, one idea could be to involve students from the local art college in re-designing local stations in co-operation with the local community, particularly young people. The trains themselves could have internal re-designs which identify them as being specifically Cornish, reflecting Regional Railways' promotion of its Cornish Railways network. The point is to use the talent within each community, and apply it to the local line.

RAIL FREIGHT: A CHANCE IN A MILLION

The conflict between rail and road freight transport is collapsing. Intermodal technology, where freight containers or vehicle bodies can be transferred quickly from rail to road (and vice versa) has forced road and rail operators to start talking to each other. Rail freight's traditional handicap in being confined to an island, within which only relatively short journeys could be made, is about to be overcome by the opening of the Channel Tunnel. It's a chance in a million for BR to improve decisively the position of freight movement.

The much-delayed regional terminals for the Channel Tunnel should be hubs for feeder rail and road services which provide a country-wide network for European freight services. Rail freight users are pressing for further improvements to the existing Freight Facilities Grants which is designed to encourage the transfer of freight from road to rail on environmental grounds. The grants should be easier to obtain, and the total budget for the grants should be enlarged. Loans, or capital grants, should be made available for buying intermodal equipment. The weight limit for intermodal vehicles should also be raised to the European standard of 44 tonnes, giving rail/road a major competitive advantage. Fiscal measures, such as reducing the vehicle tax on intermodal vehicles to zero, would also help the switch to rail for long-distance freight. In many areas, existing private terminals could be developed much more, possibly in collaboration with local or regional authorities. Integrated strategic planning should play a crucial role, with industrial development being directed towards locations with existing depot facilities, or the potential for them.

As traffic through the Channel Tunnel builds up during the 1990s, serious problems will arise because of insufficient capacity in the tunnel, and possibly in the feeder rail network. Other options for freight movement to mainland Europe will have to be seriously explored. The idea of a trans-Pennine rail link between Ireland, northwest England and the East Coast, is gaining support. It could feed into a North Sea train ferry to Germany or the Netherlands, and would serve a distinct market in northern and eastern Europe giving manufacturers in the North a better range of options for the export of their products. Other rail and sea routes will have to be encouraged, including a Scotland-Scandinavia sea and rail corridor.

Railfreight Distribution (RfD) needs to evolve as a very flexible business-oriented organization developing a range of relationships with the private sector, including manufacturers, freight forwarders,

271

wagon manufacturers, and others. It should collaborate more closely with local authorities who are increasingly keen on the idea of supporting rail freight: the example of Grampian Regional Council which is promoting a freight terminal near Aberdeen is one worth copying elsewhere. Improved facilities for rail freight should be a key part of any regional economic development strategy.

One of the biggest problems facing RfD's international freight services is BR's loading gauge limitations: it is far more restrictive than on the continent, where railways generally conform to the 'Berne Gauge' standard, so only certain wagons can enter the country. While some people have argued for an entirely new, segregated Berne-Gauge spine running up to Scotland, the cost and operational complexity of it would be enormous. It would create a two-tier rail freight network, and the more restricted part of the network would eventually wither and die. BR's own solution of developing smaller-sized wheels for Channel Tunnel wagons which can operate over most of the network, and gradually extending the existing loading gauge, seems to make most sense, though no one would say it's ideal.

NEW PROJECTS

Many countries around the world are promoting exciting rail projects – whether it's new high-speed lines, freight arteries, light rail systems, or electrification projects. With the qualified exception of the Channel Tunnel, we have nothing to match the progress in France, Germany, the Netherlands, and even the United States. Part of the problem is lack of imagination! But that lack of imagination is reinforced by the highly unfair rules on investment appraisal criteria used by the Department of Transport. It's vital that the rules are harmonized, so that rail investment criteria can take account of environmental benefits, safety improvements, and effects on regional economic development.

As argued earlier, the 'track authority' approach is the best way to achieve this. This ought to be linked to a fiscal system in which all forms of transport are charged for the full costs they incur, which would include the impact of road, rail, air and water transport in terms of pollution, accidents, and other areas of the environment. A balanced investment strategy will be achieved at regional level through the new regional transport authorities: as well as being responsible for public transport, they should also have responsibility for the regional highway network.

Money for investment in transport could be raised through forms of road pricing in city centres, increased taxes on petrol which discourage long-distance driving, and an employment tax, where employers pay a certain amount per employee, as in France, which goes into supporting public transport. Cities such as London could have higher tax bands to cope with more serious problems.

Such a dramatic policy change would place rail in a very advantageous position for major new capital projects, but the money would still have to be found from somewhere. The traditional solution of asking the Treasury for every penny is no longer adequate. Big national projects like the Channel Tunnel, or major modernization projects, should be supported by central government funds acting as a catalyst to encourage support from the private sector and European sources.

Costly local projects promoted by RTAs – such as new light rail schemes – should be able to qualify more easily for central government assistance. Financial support from the EC should be additional to any assistance from central government.

A new mechanism should be introduced where firms which benefit from a new project are obliged to pay something towards the capital cost, which could, using some methods, be partially repaid from future revenue. The simplest way is to use the 'employment tax' favoured by the French.

The Transport Act 1985 (the deregulation act!) allows for experimental transport projects to get government funding. It makes sense to try out a range of projects: light rail systems, from monorails to low-floor trams, guided bus-ways, trolleybuses, and other ideas including forms of road pricing and traffic restraint.

Britain can learn a lot from looking at other major investment projects in Europe, America, Japan, and elsewhere, though solutions adopted need to fit the social, economic, and geographical contours of our own country. The British InterCity network needs a long-term programme of upgrading involving further electrification (Aberdeen, Penzance, Swansea), increased line speeds through track realignment, junction fly-overs and re-signalling, new lines, and a reappraisal of tilting-train technology for use on existing main lines with a large number of curves.

THE RAILWAY INDUSTRY

Today, the British railway industry is in better shape than it has been for a long time. It is smaller, but healthier. Most of it is part of large multinational companies such as GEC Alsthom and ABB, but there is also a large number of small and medium-sized companies which are designing and manufacturing railway products for the world market. The industry would be a lot stronger if its home market was in better shape. The manufacturers want a clear, long-term investment strategy from Britain's railways – a cry echoed by BR management but stifled by the Department of Transport. If British manufacturers were sure of a rolling programme of investment they could tool up accordingly and be in a strong position to win orders in a competitive market. Unlike many European firms which up to now have been cushioned from competition, firms like Brel (formerly BR Engineering Ltd) have been fighting hard, and successfully, for survival.

Government can help the industry. The Department of Trade and Industry (DTI) could do more to co-ordinate international marketing, in conjunction with the Railway Industry Association.

A closer relationship should be encouraged by the Department of Education and Science (DES) between railway manufacturers and academic institutions. Universities and polytechnics should work alongside firms' research and development sections, with an emphasis on the more innovative areas of research and design. Research grants should be available for these purposes, either from the DES or DTp.

BRITAIN'S RAILWAYS IN THE WORLD

The British railway industry should develop a new role for itself in the world community, as part of a wider reassessment of Britain's place in the world. It needs to assert a new role, aimed at a positive partnership with the developing world. An important area is help with expertise, through BR's consultancy arm Transmark, and through the Railway Technical Centre, based at Derby.

Britain could provide high quality training to railway staff in developing countries, in a manner which is sympathetic to their needs, rather than imposing a western 'solution'.

A QUESTION OF CULTURE

In recent years BR's management culture has emerged from a highly conservative tradition of production oriented management which laid little stress on either business opportunities or customer needs. The old mentality has been replaced by a new culture in which business targets are central – and many aspects of the new commercialism should not be derided. Problems remain with the new approach, which needs some refinement. The profile of BR managers remains depressingly monochrome – smiling white males from nice middle-class backgrounds. 'So what?' you might ask, as long as they have the right approach to running a railway. But what, in the 1990s, does running a railway mean? It's got to have at its centre a very strong emphasis on meeting customer needs.

Putting aside the equality issues of why more women and black people aren't getting jobs in BR management, there is the issue of management perspective: that is, how people actually view the world they're in. If there are hardly any women managers within BR, issues which have a business impact get ignored or played down – like personal safety on unstaffed stations, and facilities for babies and young children on trains. The lack of people with personal experience of disability can lead railway management to neglect the needs of disabled passengers. A further neglected area is the need to recruit from lower ranks within BR, to overcome the traditional ignorance and often suspicion between management and workers, as well as to make better use of the skills and talent among the so-called 'lower grades'.

Greater cross-fertilization between rail managers and other public and private sector management would also be positive: the tradition of gradual progress up the management ladder within the railways tends to award the less enterprising and more cautious people, while the brighter risk-takers go elsewhere. Britain's future railway management needs a combination of both.

Training is vital to achieving a safe, high quality, customer-oriented railway. French National Railways (SNCF) devotes 9 per cent of its total salary budget to training which involves every employee undertaking at least one course each year. Britain's railways should co-operate with educational agencies to get a top quality training programme for every member of staff.

The logic of such a programme is the eradication of the nineteenth-century distinction between 'wages' and 'salaried' staff on the railways, to allow easy progression to higher graded posts. This should not be dependent on length of service: if the railways are to get the right person to do a job, promotion should be on merit, not on seniority.

If all staff are to have the same chances, this also requires greatly improved childcare facilities for workers with small children, and improvements to buildings, rolling stock, and other facilities so that disabled people have greater access to a range of jobs. Staff, particularly managers, should not be forced to move every few years in the latest reorganization: women managers bear the brunt of such changes, with enormous disruption to family life.

WORKERS AND MANAGERS

A rethink is needed in BR's industrial relations machinery. Improved communication is probably crucial to this, but so is direct employee involvement in how the railway is being run. The old idea of workers' control of industry may have been crude and simplistic, but at least it pointed to the genuine need for greater worker participation in the workplace. Local 'quality circles' for staff in each business sector could be a step in the right direction, with direct contact between the responsible manager and his/her staff.

The machinery of negotiation and consultation within BR goes back to 1907 and reflects out-of-date divisions and structures. It should change to reflect the needs of good industrial relations in the 1990s, instead of the 1890s, and give greater priority to ways of improving the working environment, staff welfare, training and career progression, childcare agreements, wider educational opportunities, as well as the traditional stress on wages and narrowly defined conditions. How it does that is a matter for the trade unions themselves to determine, in discussion with management.

BR IN THE COMMUNITY

It is important to develop a new culture among public enterprises which places them firmly as part of the communities they serve. This makes commercial sense, as well as being a sensible social obligation for a public body. The railways should do more to sponsor cultural and sporting events, support community activities, and be involved in bodies like the Training and Enterprise Councils. Part of procurement budgets should be set aside for 'community business' which could include women's and black people's enterprises as is common in the United States among both private and public companies.

CONSULTATION AND REGULATION

BR must consult widely on its day-to-day services, and also on its broader strategies. The proposed new regional transport authorities will be important vehicles to ensure that this happens, on a number of levels. The RTAs could be means by which local elected politicians have an input into rail services, but they could also help to develop flexible forms of consultation at local level. Many of the existing PTAs have done this already: in Greater Manchester the PTA funded the Greater Manchester Transport Resource Unit, which helps local community groups to lobby for improved public transport. BR itself, as well as the RTAs, should not only have well staffed community liaison departments which deal with day-to-day complaints, but also have a wider and more positive role in promoting links between BR and the community.

Formal processes are needed, and the existing Transport Users' Consultative Committees (TUCCs) form the basis. However, these regional committees are appointed by the government, and are not representative – despite the good job they do! Their terms of reference also tend to be severely circumscribed. Membership of the TUCCs should be on the basis of election from a range of organizations including line user groups, trades councils, business groups such as local chambers of commerce, and community groups representing, amongst others, women, disabled people, and pensioners.

As BR evolves towards a more decentralized structure with other operators using its track, greater involvement by local authorities in rail services and more stress on the rights of the customer, some form of regulatory body will be needed. This should be independent of BR and supported and resourced by funds from central government. At regional level, it should be part of the RTA structure.

CONCLUSION

The arguments about the need for greater investment in BR have become unanswerable. Capital investment in new trains and improved infrastructure is vital, and so is money to keep trains running on lines which currently make a loss. A major reassessment is needed of the role of different modes of transport, with a new approach which recognizes the total contribution, both positive and negative, which particular modes of transport make to the environment, safety and the economy. The government should take over responsibility for the rail infrastructure, and develop and maintain it in the same way it does the highway network. Rail managers should be guided by a series of objectives laid down by the Secretary of State for Transport, but with the freedom and encouragement to seek out commercial opportunities.

The railway sectors' own relationships should evolve towards closer co-operation with local and regional authorities, community agencies, and a wide range of interests in the public and private sector in Britain and indeed the rest of the world. The railways should develop, in conjunction with the Department of Transport, a twenty or twenty-five year investment programme based on providing a top quality rail service for passengers and freight. Where necessary, they should have the freedom to borrow without government interference to finance major projects, as well as being able to spend their own money.

A possible set of objectives for Britain's railways could include those suggested below. They would apply to the separate business sectors, InterCity, Regional Railways, Network SouthEast, Railfreight Distribution, Trainload Freight and Parcels – all where appropriate. The infrastructure/track authority – BriTrack if you like – would, as the custodian of the country's railway infrastructure, be bound by a series of legislative requirements which would include making the best operational use of railway assets, and with clear guidelines for charging, and access, to the railway infrastructure by rail operators.

Financial Objectives

- All publicly-owned railway companies should run on a commercial basis without a general subsidy. Specific subsidies on social grounds will be in the form of contracts from other public agencies (e.g., regional transport authorities).
- Each railway company will be set financial targets each year by the Secretary of State for Transport.

Commercial Objectives
Each company must:

- maximize revenue by energetic promotion and marketing;
- explore potential joint ventures with other companies, both public and private;
- except where specifically provided for by other agencies (e.g., transport authorities), develop a fare structure based on commercial considerations;
- pursue closer relations with other railway administrations in Europe and the world.

Quality Objectives
The passenger businesses should be set a series of quality objectives covering at least:

- punctuality;
- operating the advertised timetable;
- overcrowding;
- accessibility;
- frequency of service;
- information;
- co-ordination with other transport services;
- personal safety on trains and at stations.

The precise standards should be developed in discussion between the railways, the government, and consultative groups.

Social Objectives
The passenger businesses must:

- provide socially necessary services for local or regional authorities on a contract basis, covering fares, timetables, rolling stock, and other matters agreed between the authority and the railway;
- maximize opportunities for community involvement;
- consult widely on service provision and policy.

Employment Objectives
Each business must:

- produce a comprehensive training and development programme for all staff;
- ensure a barrier-free promotional ladder for all staff;
- practice a rigorous equal opportunities policy;
- develop new forms of staff involvement;
- negotiate and consult with the recognized trade unions on all aspects of policy affecting staff.

Environmental Objectives
Each business must:

- provide services on the basis of the most environmentally positive means; minimize pollution; safeguard energy resources;
- pursue ways of transferring goods from road to rail through intermodal technology;
- promote research into environmentally positive technology.

Safety

Each business must:

- recognize safe operation as a prime responsibility to staff, customers, and others affected by railway operations;
- integrate current safest and best practice into all new technology;
- progressively implement automatic train protection equipment on all trains;
- provide safety training for all staff, from induction to retirement.

21

RAIL'S CONTRIBUTION TO IMPROVING TRANSPORT AND THE ENVIRONMENT

JOHN WHITELEGG

INTRODUCTION

The image of rail in Britain is poor and the reality is not far behind, especially when comparisons are made with other European countries where rail has figured centrally in national transport policies and public expenditure decisions. In many ways this is not surprising. The growth in car ownership and the worship of motorized transport with its individual mobility over ever-increasing distances is not a rich environment for rail support strategies to take root. Land use changes which relocate workplaces, shopping centres and homes also diminish the utility of a fixed track system. Large expenditures on new roads while rail support is reduced add a further layer of difficulty, perhaps compounded by lorry deregulation in 1968. Britain has the highest number of vehicle kilometres run by road goods vehicles in Europe (55.1 billion compared to an EC *total* of 189). These figures (Department of Transport, 1990a) from 1987 show [formerly West] Germany as producing 35.8 billion vehicle kilometres and Italy 43.5. This shows, first, that Britain has largely abandoned its railways for serious freight movement; and second that this is not the result of some immutable law but rather the consequence of policy.

The demand for freight, like the demand for passenger travel, is large and leaves substantial market opportunities for the rail industry. These opportunities are not pursued because of inadequate funding of transport infrastructure, wildly discriminatory regimes between rail and road investment when decisions have to be made, a free market fetishism which produces anything but a free market by loading rail with enormous fiscal, social and safety obligations which road can side-step, and a complete lack of integration of environmental and transport policies. The result of all this is a rail industry with enormous *potential* to deliver high quality public transport and real gains in welfare, as well as real progress towards sustainability. The failure to realize this potential is mirrored in rising car ownership and use, rising pollution and rising dissatisfaction with rail travel.

The consequences of this disappointed potential are serious both on large geographical scales and at the local level. On the large scale (i.e., Britain and Europe) rail is failing to deliver reductions of greenhouse gases and other auto-induced pollutants, and is failing to rescue an ailing economy by delivering the goods (literally) to the rest of Europe in a way which emphasizes the local connections to rail. For this, it would also need to guarantee in an absolute and unequivocal way that freight can be shifted over distances like Milan-Glasgow with complete reliability. At the local level rail, is failing to move enough people around with similar absolute guarantees of quality, and is thus making its contribution to the loss of rail traffic and the growth of road traffic. This is best seen through the specific geographical filter of corridor evaluations.

Currently there is an abysmal service on the Leeds-Lancaster line – reminiscent of BR's determined attempts to get rid of passengers and income on the Settle-Carlisle line in the early 1980s (Abbott and Whitehouse, 1990), an experience that has taught BR very little. At the same time, the A65 road (Leeds-Kendal) is in receipt of millions of pounds of 'investment' to bypass Settle, Skipton, Gargrave, Burley-in-Warfdale and Ilkley. The existence of these bypass schemes means that there is a great demand for movement on this trans-Pennine corridor. Bypasses are 'sold' to local residents on the basis that they will remove through-traffic, particularly lorries, when in fact a large (and often unmeasured) proportion of the traffic and hence the problem is local demand. Solutions presented by rail and by local measures such as traffic calming and lorry bans are ignored. There can be no effective rail policy or strategy for improving environmental quality in towns and cities until there is a fundamental review of demand for transport and how that demand can best be met through a combination of new infrastructure, land use changes and policy initiatives which reduce the demand for longer-distance movement.

All kinds of passenger and freight movement need to be carefully monitored and evaluated on specific corridors and targets set to reduce the volume of movement by environmentally damaging modes (i.e. road). Rail has the potential capacity to take the increase in freight and passenger movement, especially if it is phased over twenty-five years with the appropriate investment.

In discussions of rail – essentially a technical, economic and engineering subject area – it is easy to neglect important social goals and the value of rail (of all kinds) in nurturing communities and providing safe, reliable transport for all those sections of society who do not have or do not wish to make use of a car. The needs of women, the elderly, young children, the mobility impaired, the nervous, those with bikes and those with a well developed environmental orientation, are paramount. This is another way of presenting the case for high quality, integrated public transport at affordable fares and this will be discussed below in a little more detail. Rail, however, will not work alone and will not make a contribution to urban environmental quality and to the quality of life of all the varied social groups in urban areas (including the poor, however defined), if it is not available at a price which reflects the benefits to society at large of a trip transferred from car to public transport, or from any mode to walking and cycling.

THE CASE FOR RAIL

The case for rail is eloquently made by TEST (1991b) which explains in some detail the relative environmental impacts of road and rail transport. It is very clear that our consumption of land, air quality, water and biological diversity is now so intense that we are tripping critical and possibly irreversible thresholds in terms of the planet's ability to recover. Motorized transport plays a significant role in the consumption of non-renewable resources, pollution and the emission of greenhouse gases; rail offers considerable advantages in reducing this impact. Table 21-1 shows the relative impacts of rail and road modes in freight transport on a range of environmental variables and Table 21-2 does the same for passenger.

Table 21-1: *Differential Impact of Road and Rail Freight Transport on a Number of Environmental Variables.*

	Unit, pro tkm	Lorry	Rail
Primärenergie	9 SKE	98.40	23.70
Endenergie	g SKE	85.00	11.00
CO_2	kg CO_2	0.22	0.05
NOx	g NOx	3.60	0.22
NOx 1993	g NOx	3.18	0.16
CO	g CO	1.58	0.07
CxHy	g CH	0.81	0.05
Staub	g Staub	0.27	0.03
SO_2	g SO_2	0.23	0.33
SO_2 1993	g SO_2	0.17	0.12
Unfälle	Verungl./Mrd tkm	248.00	10.00
Fläche	m²/Jahres-tkm	0.007	0.0025

Source: Teufel (1989a)

Table 21-2: *Differential Impact of Road and Rail Passenger Transport on a Number of Environmental Variables.*

	Car	Car with 3-way cat.	Air	Unit
Land use	120	120	1.5	M²/person
Primary energy use	90	90	365	g coal equiv. units/pkm
CO_2 emissions	200	200	839.5	g/pkm
Nitrogen Dioxide emissions	2.2	0.34	6.4	,, ,,
Hydrocarbons	1	0.15	1.4	,, ,,
CO emissions	8.7	1.3	8.1	,, ,,
Air pollution	38,000	5900	95,000	Polluted air M³/pkm
Accident risks	11.5	11.5	1.4	Hours of life lost/1000 pkm

	Rail	Bus	Bike	Ped.	Unit
Land use	7	12	9	2	M^2/person
Primary energy use	31	27	0	0	g coal equivalent units/pkm
CO_2 emissions	60	59	0	0	g/pkm
Nitrogen Dioxide emissions	0.08	0.2	0	0	,, ,,
Hydrocarbons	0.02	0.08	0	0	,, ,,
CO emissions	0.05	0.15	0	0	,, ,,
Air pollution	1200	3300	0	0	Polluted air M^3/pkm
Accident risks	0.4	1	0.2	0.01	Hours of life lost/1000 pkm

Note: pkm = passenger kilometre
Source: Teufel (1989b)

Environmental goals coincide with social and community goals. A public transport system in a city with heavy or light rail (as appropriate) at the centre and frequent buses feeding in to rail corridors has the potential not only to transfer passengers from cars to public transport but also to reduce accidents and injuries dramatically. Such a modal shift would assert the advantages of accessibility over the disadvantages of mobility, for all social groups. An efficient public transport system at the urban level can enhance labour market efficiency and generate traditional economic benefits, as well as improve social and recreational opportunities for all groups. It can offer safety and security to women and the elderly (through efficient, clean, reliable and well staffed trains and buses) and accommodation for bikes, pushchairs, wheel chairs and whatever is necessary to make public transport and its rail core genuinely accessible to all users.

Dieter Apel, working at the *Deutsche Institut fur Urbanistik*, has compared the private and social costs of car traffic in Berlin with local public transport (Apel, 1988). Local public transport is heavily dependent on buses and the underground (*U-Bahn*). Apel shows that the motor car costs Berlin (i.e. public and private costs) DM 4.470 billion per annum and local public transport DM 1.478 billion pa. This works out at DM 0.64 per passenger km for the car and DM 0.38 per passenger km for public transport. It makes fiscal as well as environmental sense to move people by public transport as opposed to the car. Apel's conclusion is important:

If, in accordance with the principles of the market economy, the total economic costs of local transport were to be fully borne by users of the respective modes and if for car traffic, for example, this were to take place by raising the duty on fuels, the present rate of tax would have to be raised approximately fivefold.

It makes even more sense to enhance the possibilities for moving people by foot and bike and a secure public transport environment will help this to be achieved. Trains and buses that carry bikes help enormously. In the Ruhr area of Germany the *S-Bahn* (heavy rail) carries bikes but with some time limitations and some buses are adapted for the same purpose for recreational trips. In San Jose, California, the Santa Clara County Transit Authority allows bikes on buses and light rail, and in Aspen, Colorado bikes are carried in summer and skis in winter!

A well used public transport environment produces a well used urban environment, enhancing safety and security for all users. Traffic calming and extensive pedestrianization schemes (as in some German cities) help pedestrians and cyclists particularly where light rail (trams) are an integral part giving high quality access to non-car users whether on foot, bike or on the public transport vehicle.

The Public Transport Users Association of Australia (PTUA, 1991) have shown for Melbourne how new tram routes, new heavy rail routes, new bus-rail interchanges and a priority system for public transport can reduce the share of travel by car by one-sixth and increase public transport's share of demand by a factor of 2.5. This produces a substantial contribution from Melbourne to achieving reduction in greenhouse gas targets and substantially improves air quality and quality of life.

THE WAY FORWARD

Since the majority of travel is very local it seems sensible to begin with this basic manifestation of the demand for transport. Over one third of all journeys are under one mile and of these 84 per cent are made on foot (Potter and Hughes, 1990). More than half of all journeys are under two miles in length. Rail accounts for 2 per cent of all journeys compared to 48 per cent by car (passenger and driver). Much of this car share is potentially divertible to walking and cycling (see chapter 17) but much can also be diverted to rail, particularly rail serving cities. Rail accounts for 11 per cent of all journeys over 25 miles in length

(Potter and Hughes, 1990: Table 11) and here the potential for increasing market share is even greater with considerable environmental gains from the reduced demand for long distance road travel.

Table 21-3 shows the relative intensity of use of car and public transport modes for two very basic journey purposes compared to all purposes.

Table 21-3: Journeys per Person per Week by Mode and Purpose.

Main mode	To and from work	Shopping	All
All car	2.09	1.68	9.11
All rail	0.17	0.04	0.33
All local bus	0.37	0.46	1.56

Source: Department of Transport (1990c), *Transport Statistics Great Britain 1979-1989*.

Note: Walking is not listed in this table becasue the DTp ignore walked journeys of less than one mile in their tabulations.

Most of the work and shopping journeys must be regarded as transferrable to integrated public transport – bus and rail working together in a reliable manner with optimal interchange possibilities and built-in design features to enhance walking and cycling modes (for example, room for bikes and best possible access for bus and tram stops, compared to cars which can be limited to car parks some distance away from prime sites). This is feasible given some simple prerequisites:

- adequate mechanisms for land use and transport planning emphasizing local access;
- adequate investment and local democratic control;
- total priority for public transport vehicles and new LRT schemes in as many cities in Britain as can demonstrate the need by meeting predetermined conditions and targets;
- restoration of a legal basis for complete integration of public transport;
- provision of a sound legal basis for setting fares at levels which do provide an incentive such as the '*Umweltkarte*' (Environment

Ticket) of Berlin and Bremen costing around DM 60 for a month's travel on the complete public transport system and justified by environmental accounting of the kind suggested by Apel (1988);

- realistic controls on cars in cities – reduced car parking, poorer access for cars, traffic control systems which ensure that trams and buses can beat car journey times at any time of the day.

Such systems already exist in most respects in Zurich, and in many respects as far as integration and fares are concerned in Berlin, Bochum, Dortmund and Essen. No great insights or technological leaps are needed to advance rail as a major contributor to urban public transport. The commodity in shortage is political will and political vision.

Britain can support thirty-fifty 'Zurich-like' systems at a cost of approximately £100 million pounds each. Besides giving a much better deal than high speed rail and paying for itself in ten years it will transform our currently clogged and unhealthy cities. Rail is the key to such a transformation: rail can move the millions of extra trips that can be brought on stream by investment, reorganization and effective, integrated planning.

500 trips by public transport are made each year for every 1000 Zurich residents and no capacity problems have been found. New rolling stock with double deck trains have been introduced and these can carry 60 per cent more seated passengers than a conventional train. For a city of 360,000 people with 300,000 workplaces, 200,000 use the stations every day and are expected to rise above 350,000 over the next ten years (Finkbohner, 1990).

POLICY OPTIONS

Over the next ten years some very important decisions must be made. Some of the most important are not easily tagged as support for road or rail but involve major reorientations of perceptions and priorities. Key areas can be identified:

- There is an urgent need for urban transport policies which will deliver social, accessibility and environmental gains. This involves a recognition that people and their needs must be catered for by a basic design objective: the shape and size of public transport vehicles and their relationship to kerbs and pavements and stops and facilities (and each other) are more important than other planning objectives. Such an emphasis will also require major land use initiatives to counter the consumption of distance as a free good and a determined effort to create sustainable cities. Rail is crucial to the achievement of these objectives with a massive expansion of light rapid transit (trams) and of integrated public transport on the Zurich model. Only the highest quality is acceptable.

- There needs to be an immediate reform of the fiscal system to bring about a substantial shift in travel demand from motorized to non-motorized modes and from longer-distance trips to shorter-distance trips. The principles of ecological taxation reform are described in Whitelegg (1991) and motorists must expect to be paying at least five times as much per passenger kilometre ten years from now; at the same time, public transport journeys costs would be 50 per cent cheaper in real terms compared to 1991. Walking and cycling will remain as very low-cost modes (to society as a whole). Public policy needs to work to a ratio of total costs to society as a whole of 1:10:50 where 1 is the cost of walking and cycling modes, 10 of all public transport modes operating as one highly co-ordinated and integrated whole, and 50 the cost of private trips by car.

- The lorry problem must be tackled swiftly. The lorry (see Table 21-1) is a major fiscal and environmental drain and has no place in urban areas, on trunk roads through towns and on bypasses. The European single market, which confers such enormous advantages on the lorry, offers as much potential for rail if enough investment in intermodal transport and rail-connected activities can be produced. Lorry costs need to go upwards to exceed the costs of rail or combined operation by at least a factor of five and lorries must be controlled to observe every detail of loading, speed, driving hours and mechanical condition regulation. Rail, though not the only alternative to the lorry, will have to take up a substantial share of the demand for freight movement.

- The concept of high speed rail for passenger travel must be rejected as a policy option. High speed rail is a curious fetish by which longer-distance travel is given greater priority than shorter-distance travel. The consequent pressure on land uses and energy consumption is entirely opposite to that needed to achieve sustainable goals and environmental quality. Higher speeds will encourage longer distance journeys including commuting trips with their attendant planning and housing difficulties. Higher speeds are intended to substitute for air trips but much of the travel would be newly generated; and the demand for air trips also continues to grow, encouraged by the release of domestic or short haul slots for longer haul slots and tourist traffic. High speed travel does not address the urgent problems associated with railways and substitutes a misplaced political ambition to realize the technological challenge of high speed rail for basic service improvements across the system: it is disingenuous to suggest that much needed improvements in urban rail, rural rail and cross-country routes will come about after high speed rail. The likelihood is rather closure of less profitable lines and a two-tier rail system ripe for privatization. These arguments are spelt out in more detail in Hulten and Whitelegg (1992).

- The structure and organization of the rail industry has to be one that can deliver clear results to its users and even clearer results to society as a whole. Rail has to work in close co-operation with local authorities and with user groups. It is unlikely that any environmental and social gains can be made by a rail industry which is either in part or in total privatized or, indeed, run as a state monoploy deprived of funds and oblivious to the needs of users, potential users and elected bodies.

22

AVIATION POLICY

ROBERT CAVES

Air transport policy changes are constrained by international trends and obligations and by the ability to resolve conflicting goals. The economic growth versus conservation and local versus national goals are so conflicting that they can only be resolved by long-term changes in planning methodology, incorporating an open forum and rolling plans.

In the short term, fair competition for airports, airlines and air transport, should be ensured. This requires sufficient capacity to allow competition. High quality InterCity rail access to airports, early clarification of the EC internal market changes, a fundamental research programme and an independent transport safety board are also needed.

INTRODUCTION

In a very short review of a subject which fills many books, it is necessary to take many aspects of aviation and of policy for granted. The policy stance taken here is that, in a free market economy, government policies should be concerned mostly with the relationships between aviation's own interests and those of its users and of other UK citizens. They should be less concerned with the management of aviation. The policies should therefore deal with standards of service and safety, with regional disparities, with the use of resources, with striking the balance between the needs of the aviation industry and aviation's impact on the rest of society. However, aviation is an important sector of the UK economy and, to that extent, its interests are the nation's interests. So policies should also be directed to ensuring that UK aviation does not meet unfair competition from foreign carriers or from other modes of transport within the UK.

This review of aviation policy starts with a brief description of the UK's aviation industry, identifying its roles, its product and its regulation, and thus implicitly identifying the constraints on policy formation. The review then proceeds to analyse the more important policy areas, before attempting to draw the threads together with some suggestions for a revised policy framework.

THE AVIATION INDUSTRY

The industry consists of the airlines, other aircraft operators, the airports and air traffic control and all suppliers to these activities including aircraft manufacture. This review will focus on policy with respect only to the provision of public air transport service.

There is a very strong international dimension to UK air transport. Only seven per cent of the 70 billion passenger kilometres flown on UK scheduled airlines, and almost none of the 50 billion passenger kilometres flown on UK non-scheduled services, were on domestic flights in 1989 (CAA, 1990a). Although twelve million out of a total of sixty million passengers borne by UK airlines were domestic, probably a half of these were flying to join an international service. The total distance travelled by domestic air transport passengers represents less than 1 per cent of inter-urban passenger kilometres. Some 30 per cent of all domestic passengers at the London airports were feeding into the international services of UK and foreign airlines in 1987, of whom almost half were connecting to Europe and some 20 per cent were connecting to North America (CAA, 1989). Furthermore, foreign operators accounted for 30 per cent of the almost 100 million passengers handled at all UK airports in 1989 (CAA, 1990b); while just over half the passengers at Heathrow in 1987 were foreign (though only 30 per cent of Gatwick passengers and 10 per cent of Manchester passengers were foreign).

While there is a balance of international passengers between UK and foreign scheduled airlines, the same cannot be said for charter airlines, mainly because the UK does not seem to have the same attraction for Europeans that the options of sun and snow have for UK residents.

Although air transport is becoming the preferred mode for business people at a much shorter trip length than leisure passengers (OECD, 1977), it is predominantly used for non-business purposes. Even at Heathrow, with virtually no charter operations, some 60 per cent of both UK and foreign international passengers are non-business, almost half of whom are visiting friends and relatives (CAA, 1989). On charter flights, virtually all the passengers are non-business: since approximately 85 per cent of charter passengers use UK airlines (CAA, 1990b), at least this proportion is likely to comprise UK citizens taking holidays abroad. Even on domestic flights, approximately a third of passengers are non-business.

UK's aviation product is very large *per capita* compared with most other countries, reflecting the historic world role of the UK and the presence of the English Channel. Yet the annual 5 per cent growth matches that of other advanced countries. Within the UK industry, the distribution of traffic among airlines and among airports is very uneven: BA alone accounts for 60 per cent of the tonne-kilometres and is among the world's top five airlines. The group of airports owned by BAA accounts for 70 per cent of passengers handled at UK airports, Heathrow alone handling 40 per cent of the total. Even on a route-by-route basis the same pattern emerges. Only four routes account for 40 per cent of domestic passengers; and similarly four routes account for 20 per cent of international scheduled passengers, all from London. In contrast, ten routes account for 20 per cent of charter passengers, four of the routes being from Manchester. Concentrations of this nature are very common everywhere except in the USA.

The regulation of the industry is as internationally based as the traffic using the system. The industry's safety and security regulations and standards of infrastructure provision follow directly from the UK being a member of the International Civil Aviation Organization (ICAO). If ICAO standards and recommended practices were not met, foreign airlines might refuse to enter UK airspace. The Civil Aviation Authority (CAA) not only ensures that UK standards exceed these minimal levels, but in fact contributes significantly to the formulation of the ICAO regulations. They have also played a major part in the formation of common European standards. Due to CAA expertise and industry conscientiousness, UK air transport has one of the best safety records in the aviation world. Similarly minimum standards for aircraft environmental impact are set by ICAO, though the cumulative impact at any given airport is not legislated for in the UK. An uneasy peace is maintained by compensating agreements between an airport operator and its neighbours and by the imposition of controls on the airlines' operations: in addition, the government can designate an interest in an airport and thus take powers to control the aircraft movements.

Economic regulation of UK international air transport is based mainly on separately negotiated bilateral agreements with other governments. While UK negotiators have, since the early 1980s, attempted to develop a liberal approach to the regulation of route access, fares and capacity along the lines indicated in the Civil Aviation Act of 1982 and now being taken for the post-1992 internal services of the EC, the attitudes of other governments have meant that on most routes these factors are still subject to close control. The unregulated charter industry arose partly in response to the requirement to balance scheduled capacity in an unbalanced market. Domestically, the CAA retains ultimate authority on route access and fares in order to protect thin routes and small operators against predatory action, while maintaining a liberal stance. Government control of the airlines' economic behaviour is now largely in the hands of the Monopolies and Mergers Commission (MMC) and the Office of Fair Trading (OFT), though the CAA dictates the proportion of equity which can be in foreign hands.

Since the Airports Act of 1986 privatized BAA and required the majority of the airports owned by local authorities to be recognized as public limited companies, there is also little central control of airport investment or planning. The CAA is simply required to monitor airport charges, as it does air fares, in an attempt to protect consumers from any potential monopoly profits and to protect smaller independent airports from unfair competition through cross-subsidy within BAA.

The CAA itself, almost uniquely in the world, is required to be self-financing, not only in its regulatory duties but also in its provision of air traffic control. It therefore requires a 100 per cent cost recovery from the industry for any service it provides. Yet it is almost a monopoly provider, being subject to competition only in the training of air traffic controllers and the provision of air traffic services at airports.

With this background, suggestions for changes in policy are given. The close detail of the reasoning behind the suggestions is given elsewhere (Caves, 1991).

THE ISSUES AND THEIR REQUIRED POLICIES

The Policy Framework

The respective roles of the CAA, the DTp, DoE and the 'watchdog' bodies in the interpretation of policy should be reviewed. The CAA's interpretations are stated publicly, but all too often it is left in the position of having 'responsibility without power'. It is capable of overriding advice from the MMC on BAA charges, but its own advice to DTp is frequently not taken. The DTp's and Secretary of State's interpretations of policy are often perfunctory – the wider issues concerning the national role of aviation are therefore not aired and clarified in the same way as occurs within the aviation community. It should not, however, be expected that merely gathering all the functions into an umbrella organization will resolve the problems. The joint responsibility of the CAA for national air traffic services (NATS), for regulation of the industry and for advice on the provision of airports has not noticeably improved the provision of air services.

Policy goals and objectives with respect to transport in general and air transport in particular must be expected to contain incompatible elements. Resolution of the conflict requires that the issues be faced squarely. A National Air Transport Forum, as a sub-committee of a general Transport Forum, would encourage open debate of the conflicting issues which make the interpretation of policy so difficult. Some of the more important conflicts requiring attention are those arising from the need for a strong national presence in aviation and the need to promote competition; to conserve resources; to encourage regional growth; to protect the environment.

Any debate can only be productive if it is well informed. The Forum should, therefore, commission urgent research on the implications of inter-airline competition for extra system capacity and for consumer benefits; on the value of air transport to communities and to the UK; on the resource implications of modal switching, given that an integrated approach to transport is necessary (Labour, 1989a); on the need for safety initiatives and their implications; on the need for equality of opportunity for access to air transport; on the establishment of environmental capacity rules; on improving strategic forecasting.

A framework is required which will ensure continuity of policy, rather than allowing it to be subject to sharp and damaging reversals of national or local attitudes. This is especially the case in the provision of infrastructure. Some form of rolling plan should be introduced which would be effectively embodied in legislation from time to time and which would require further specific legislation to unravel. The whole plan should go through a modified form of public inquiry procedure, but most of the issues should have been previously reconciled in the Forum.

Planning Methodology

Even in a liberalized and privatized setting, planning is necessary for efficient provision of adequate infrastructure. A systems approach to planning should be adopted, so that aviation's role within society may be properly reflected. The Transport and Air Transport Forums should be an invaluable aid to this approach, providing not only the essential objectives but also setting criteria for capacity provision and operational performance and then the performance monitoring of the system. However, given the international nature of air transport, the EC should be encouraged to recognize the need for a systems study of the future of European aviation. This could build on earlier OECD work (OECD, 1977), but consider the shape and extent of the future network under a variety of scenarios covering the implications of future policy options. Factors which need examining in the systemic methodology are:

- the accessibility needs of the UK regions as the EC progressively centralizes, and the ways in which the accessibility should be provided;
- the Air Traffic Control capacity needed to encourage regional links and to allow competition: airspace design requires a very long lead time – properly informed strategic planning should have been undertaken already;
- the effects of an internationally agreed carbon tax and modal competition on demand;
- airline strategic responses to competition and to the infrastructural limitations;
- the value of aviation to regional, national and EC economies;
- the impact of aviation on the troposphere;
- the establishment of Community goals for the environment, for accessibility, for resource consumption; the testing of the air transport options against the goals.

It could soon be too late to institute the new start which some believe is needed in European aviation, but for which no planning has yet been done because a systemic approach has not been taken (Eggers, 1989). To this end, attention should be directed urgently to the opportunities and the threats of new technologies: the studies should not treat their impact as adjuncts to the present system, but assess their potential when the system has been restructured around them. Technology options assessed should include short take-off and landing

(STOL), very large aircraft, advanced navigation concepts, closely separated runways, fuel-efficient aircraft, hydrogen powered aircraft.

Economic Regulation

The industry and its consumers are broadly agreed that competition is the key to a good service. The CAA has been pursuing this policy for some years. The EC Commission directives to liberalize the Community's internal transport should also be fully supported (House of Lords, 1990), because UK airlines are very capable of competing with their EC counterparts and because any improvements in air travel opportunities represent the best way of ensuring that the regions have adequate links to support their economies. However, it should not be expected that much extra demand will be stimulated by liberalization (Poole, 1986; Caves and Higgins, 1991), and there are dangers – of variable service; of industry concentration; of excessive use of scarce runway capacity by multiple airline, high frequency services on the dominant routes; of the erosion of the UK's effective status as a European gateway by any joint negotiating stance by the EC with non-EC countries; of false competition with airlines from other EC countries who do not fully liberalize; and of false competition within the EC with other modes whose fares do not fully represent their long-term resource costs. All of these issues should be monitored carefully. The most helpful action which could be taken without negotiation would be to encourage provision of extra capacity at the UK's congested airports and airspace, without which the UK industry cannot maintain its comparative advantage.

The Structure of the Industry

It will take some time to apply the recommended changes in the policy framework and planning methodology and to develop a properly researched long-term policy for aviation. Yet there are problems which need solutions in the short term if UK aviation, which has proved itself of economic and social value to the UK, is not to be in danger of failing to provide those benefits.

The UK industry's world status should be protected by further strengthening the role of the London area airports. In a privatized and competitive setting, this would happen most naturally if the three BAA airports were under separate ownership, so providing fair competition with Luton and any other potential airport. Some extra capacity is essential: it may well be that the best ratio of incremental user gain to non-user disbenefit would be achieved by a third short runway at

Heathrow (Caves, 1990). The entrepreneurial competing options, which present policies rely on, need firm objectives to be stated before thay can be properly developed.

In a strongly liberalized environment, the role of the regional airports is determined primarily by airline competitive tactics, though constrained by government policy on bilateral agreements and on access to Heathrow. The developing trend for regional traffic to grow faster than London traffic should be encouraged, not so much to take the strain off the London system (CAA studies [1990c] show the futility of attempting to do this), but to give regional travellers more convenient access to air services. As the overall base of travel grows, the scheduled market should expand into the regions in the same way that the charter market has already done. This should be encouraged by negotiating bilateral agreements which favour the use of regional airports and by encouraging foreign airline involvement when UK airlines do not come forward to fill the role.

The regional airports should be able to compete fairly with the London airports. They too should therefore be in private hands and able to draw on the money markets, with MMC control over mergers: capital will become critical (Lovett, 1990). Those local authorities who feel that planning law is not strong enough to limit the environmental impact to acceptable levels could be allowed to retain a 'Golden Share'. Where the regional boundaries realistically capture the catchment area of the airports, regional versions of the proposed National Air Transport Forum would be useful in striking the balance between the environment and provision of air services.

There will always be many destinations which it would not be viable to serve at a reasonable frequency from most regional airports. Regional travellers will continue to require good access to London (and continental) airports to reach these destinations. At the moment, these access trips are mostly made by air or by road because rail trips are very inconvenient. The high percentage of passengers reaching Gatwick by rail shows that rail services dedicated to air passengers with a convenient airport interchange can satisfy the access requirement in many cases. Maximum effort should be directed at providing direct InterCity services into the major airports in order to alleviate the use of scarce capacity and resources by air feeder services. This would also benefit locally based passengers and workers, so reducing the main source of pollution around airports – namely, (vehicular) ground transport.

Many domestic services will, however, continue to be needed. Some rail access journeys will be too long or inconvenient and there will always be passengers whose perceived value of time causes them to choose aviation for internal trips. It would be unwise to adopt policies which would curtail these services until it is certain that the passengers' choices do not lead to the minimization of resource (including social) costs.

Airports' managements can only plan and operate efficiently if the rules they have to follow are clear and stable over time. Early resolution is therefore required for the nature and timescale for implementation of EC proposals on points of entry, on classification of intra-EC passengers; on security requirements; on Special Branch requirements; on duty-free allowances; on VAT charges; and on harmonization of airport fee structures.

Similarly, the airlines' managements need to know the timescale and extent of liberalization of route entry, and the EC's attitudes to mergers. They also need to be able to compete fairly with one another: this cannot happen while the smaller airlines are denied access to the major markets because of lack of capacity at the major airports. Even if extra capacity is provided physically, there is a high probability that it will be taken by strong foreign carriers unless some protection is afforded to the smaller operators.

Safety and Security
An independent body should be created as an aviation safety watchdog, along the lines of the US National Transportation Safety Board, though not necessarily within the DTp. The safety record is good, but there is some evidence that the travelling public would pay more for a lower exposure to risk. (A Mori poll conducted a few months after the fatal fire on a Boeing 737 at Manchester in 1985 suggested that more than half those asked would pay at least 5 per cent more for added safety.) Even if the system compensates for added economic pressures in a liberalized environment, the supervisory role will become more important. The CAA's responsibilities for both the safety and the economic health of the aviation industry make it more difficult to act on the advice of independent bodies such as the Air Accident Investigation Board.

The new safety body should be aware that unilateral imposition of more stringent safety regulations may be economically damaging for the UK industry and may not be justified in economic as opposed to emotional terms. Analysis of accidents and incidents shows clearly that the two areas requiring attention are human performance relative to the tasks to be performed, and adherence to the present regulations. The former requires research, the latter requires a review of the quality of training and inspection of all aviation-related personnel, including CAA staff. In this area, CAA performance indicators of licences granted per employee are likely to be a counter-indication of safety.

Aviation security should be a national police responsibility. The issues are of a trans-modal nature and action is required in the sphere of both EC and global harmonization. The main issues not currently being given adequate attention are where the security cordon should be drawn at individual airports, which airports should have given levels of security precautions, and the identification and vetting of staff allowed access to aircraft.

CONCLUSIONS

This short review of UK aviation policy has concentrated more on strategic rather than operational issues. It concludes that, where it is possible to consider the industry's and the consumer's interests in isolation, there are few areas where policy needs to be improved. Unfortunately, in many important areas aviation cannot be considered in isolation.

The present policy framework quite properly then involves the DTp and other branches of government in decisions in the areas of new runway location, and bilateral negotiations. In contrast to the CAA's relatively transparent interpretation of its policy guidelines, the interdepartmental discussions and interpretations of advice from inspectors of public enquiries evolve in a more opaque way and are less open to challenge. Yet the issues are often of greater national importance, perhaps too important to be influenced by intensive lobbying. It is suggested that a more open forum is needed for the consideration of such issues as: the role of airports in regional and national development; the balance between growth in traffic and damage to the environment; the advantages of competition compared with the costs of providing the infrastructure to give it free expression; the integration of all modes of transport; Community goals for longer-distance transport; the integration of UK and EC policy with respect to non-EC nations; and methods of monitoring monopolies.

The most severe problems facing the industry are lack of physical capacity, environmental constraints and the medium-term implications of fuel scarcity. The infrastructural requirements depend on the balance achieved between these constraints and the attractiveness of aviation to the consumer and to society at large. Correct decisions on infrastructure provision and the mode's regulation can only be made after deep research into these matters. The resulting policy can only be implemented within a planning framework which recognizes the long response time for infrastructure provision and for instituting changes in the industry's technology.

23

THE ENVIRONMENTAL CAPACITY OF AIRPORTS: A METHOD OF ASSESSMENT

MOYRA LOGAN

The public demand for improved quality of life encompasses, *inter alia*, two conflicting objectives – high standards of environmental and amenity protection, and more air transport services. In an attempt to deal with this problem, this chapter proposes a means by which an airport could become more socially acceptable and a more predictable planning unit – something which would benefit aviation as well as the local environment and quality of life.

The chapter proposes a framework in the form of a common assessment methodology for establishing the appropriate environmental fit for any airport in any situation, taking account of a wide range of impacts. It suggests a matrix of the factors to be assessed, as well as listing provisional strategies available to airports for reducing the adverse effects of airport use. The benefits which would follow from such an approach and the way forward – through a research project designed to fill gaps in the data and to develop and test the methodology – are set out.

INTRODUCTION

Throughout the 1980s, it became increasingly clear that concern for the environment had reached a critical level. Until then, it had sometimes seemed that those raising environmental issues were a rather esoteric minority; but by the end of the decade, the public had shown – through the media, opinion polls, the ballot box and direct action –

that protection of the natural and built environment was an issue demanding a positive response from governments and at all levels of society.

Aircraft and airports have become one focus of these concerns. Aircraft noise, local air and global atmospheric pollution, ecological damage, land take and airport infrastructure impacts are all identified issues. They encompass the wish to preserve the health, welfare and quality of life of those living close to airports, as well as a sound earth for future generations. In short, as with all other sources of adverse environmental effects, the reduction or removal of the damaging aspects of the use of aviation at the fastest achievable pace is seen to be in the general public interest.

However, the parallel public demand for air transport clearly creates a conflict with environment-friendly objectives. This is nowhere better demonstrated than in the actions commonly taken to deal with the problem of aircraft noise for airport neighbours. Measures tend to involve constraints of variable intensity on the number of aircraft movements, through limits on numbers, or on times of day or night, and on the types of aviation activity permitted. But current and future growth trends set targets for the expansion of the industry, and underline its wish to plan for future capacity. A balance, a constructive compromise, between the two conflicting interests, has become an urgent priority.

In dealing with noise, the first line of approach is to tackle the source – in the case of aviation, to make aircraft quieter. The international regulatory bodies have undertaken to provide a framework of progressive standards which have to be met over a specified period. Currently, legislation to phase out the older, noisier aircraft worldwide is in the process of being established. But air transport is widely predicted to double by around the end of the century. Although there are a number of airlines in Europe and elsewhere which are taking the initiative and investing in new or re-engined aircraft, the indications are that, by itself, the noise certification programme will not be able to guarantee generally acceptable airport noise exposure levels. A deteriorating noise climate would make more airport authorities and also governments, under the pressure of public opinion, feel the need to limit airport capacity to compensate.

Some airport authorities, taking a responsible attitude to protection from aircraft noise or complying with local regulation, have already developed strategies to establish a suitable 'environmental capacity' for their airports – an approach intended to provide a more acceptable local noise climate. These examples give an important lead, and can achieve significant improvements, but individual solutions like these at airports can provide variable standards of environmental control, as well as logistical problems for the airlines. The use of different noise packages at different airports also introduces competitive inequalities: any airport's ability to compete is affected by site-specific factors, such as the political influence of the local environmental, or airport, lobby. The Airfields Environment Federation (AEF) and the European Environmental Bureau (EEB) are therefore urging the development of criteria for determining the 'environmental capacity' of any aerodrome or airport, which could be applied universally: a common framework of standards of environmental protection within which the industry would operate, avoiding the constant need among airlines and airport authorities to examine how to respond differentially to environmental considerations.

The first task in developing such an approach would be to establish the basic framework of an assessment tool. According to the methodology presented here, the experience and expertise of both aviation and environmental interests (among others) could assist in the construction of a complete strategy. (In addition, substantial further research would be required to provide a valid data-base for the construction of this assessment tool.) Set out below are: matters which could be taken into account in surveying a site and assessing its 'environmental capacity'; an approach to the evaluation and interpretation of the results; how these may be translated into a score which in turn could be used to provide a picture of the local area in relation to the impact of the airport; and finally suggested methods of implementing the strategy.

The assumption, on which this concept of the 'environmental capacity' of airports is based, is that the use of aircraft has implications, good and bad, for people's quality of life: any optimization of the relationship should allow for both the positive and the negative aspects to be taken into account. Currently, decisions about airport development tend to involve just such an assumption but are made largely on an *ad hoc* basis.

In developing this concept, the tasks involved would include the definition of data required to apply the assessment tool, for example:

- the noise climate associated with airport use – in outline, the total noise exposure due to aircraft activity associated with the airport site and that due to other airport use, including other forms of transport, together with an assessment of the sensitivity of the area affected;

- the needs of the locality in which the airport is sited (e.g., employment needs, infrastructure development, housing provision);
- the airport's contribution to the locality in these contexts;
- the value of the airport in a national/regional context (e.g., in terms of demand, and government strategy/policies, its role in public transport, training and sporting needs);
- the airport's effects on ecological and environmental quality.

In summary, the matrix of factors to be taken into account might be:

- aviation capacity;
- planning and land use – land take, local planning policies, soil quality, infrastructure, severance;
- environmental considerations – noise and vibration, emissions and effluents, conservation, visual amenity, special factors (e.g. archaeology);
- economic and socio-economic factors – local income and tax base, employment.

These are some of the headings which might underpin an evaluation, providing an assessment of the position of any airport in relation to its site, but taking account of the value of its role in a wider context.

DEFINITION OF THE TOOL

Following screening to decide which factors to take into account, the method would involve rating and weighting of the matters for assessment in order to achieve a score. In developing this method, we would take the view that the allocation of values should be the subject of consultation and expert statistical advice. The conclusion should be based on weighing in the balance economic and ergonomic efficiency and social justice and equity.

Over a map of the area around an airfield (the dimensions of the land to be assessed would have to be defined), a grid would be overlaid. Each segment of the grid would be subjected to the assessment and a total numerical score applied. To make reading the picture which emerges easier, these numbers might be assigned grading by colour. This procedure could be designed to be interpreted as reflecting the acceptability or otherwise of the score; or it might provide a type of noise contour – based on existing knowledge of noise exposure and community response, each colour (or numerical band) could be assigned a noise emission limit which must not be exceeded. Either approach results in a set of 'contours' tailored to each individual airport.

This method of developing a picture of an area which describes its particular qualities and characteristics clearly lends itself to computerization. Such an approach is already being used for other purposes in the environmental and planning fields. One important asset would be the ability to employ a 'What if?' approach, making it possible to try out the effects of changes in strategy on the computer before carrying them out.

IMPLEMENTATION

The airport authority would be responsible for ensuring compliance and designing the means of achieving the stated targets. Improvements in the score would have implications for increasing the airport's capacity. Measures to achieve this could include increasing the positive inputs in the assessment, such as:

- purchase of noise-sensitive properties and conversion of such properties to non-noise-sensitive commercial or public service uses, as appropriate;
- insistence on the use of quieter aircraft – the quantifying of the contribution made by individual aircraft or types of aircraft to the overall emission levels can now be readily established by computer models based on the certificated values, so the calculation of the fleet changes necessary to achieve compliance is accessible;
- improved approach and departure routes, improved circuit patterns and rota arrangements, aircraft operating procedures and other commonly used methods of reducing local disturbance;
- avoidance of the more sensitive periods in the 24-hour day, and where appropriate, days of the week; and/or selection of the quieter types of aircraft for use at such times;
- concentration on uses for which there is a national or local need;
- insulation of noise-affected properties where appropriate;
- involvement of local communities as neighbours in consultation on the implementation of the strategy;
- organization of activities within the airport involving noise from

static sources or ground-running so as to minimize their contribution to the score;

- implementation of strategies to minimize, or reduce to prescribed target levels, air pollution from all airport sources;
- landscaping and airport design for noise reduction and for visual amenity;
- conservation and ecological land management (e.g., preservation of flora and fauna, control of water run-off and wastes etc.).

Implementation which includes day-to-day measurement of noise and pollution levels at sensitive locations around the airport offers a means of ensuring that limits are being observed. Up-dating of other inputs would maintain the accuracy of the assessment.

The AEF's view is that there is likely to be a need for supervision of such a strategy: one approach would be a licensing authority with the responsibility to oversee the implementation, to hear appeals for variation of the limits set and so on could be set up along the lines of similar bodies required by current legislation to regulate activities which have environmental impacts. The AEF has already undertaken a project to examine and propose a viable method of instituting and running such a licensing body. Local residents would continue to fill a monitoring role. Alternatively, if the methodology were used to inform and implement government policy for airports, other strategies for securing co-operation or compliance might be involved.

It would be very important for public acceptance of this method that the matters to be taken into account, the loadings and the way in which they have been reached and the adjustments to the permitted score, could be readily accessed and understood. Transparency rather than a 'black box' methodology would be a key objective.

Of course, such an approach is not without its difficulties. A research project to take forward this concept would be expected to tackle those areas where more information is necessary, as well as establishing the assessment techniques and testing them in real situations at real airports. The benefits of making it work are very attractive.

THE BENEFITS

The essence of the method is that it could be used to evaluate the environmental capacity of every size of airfield from the small grass strip to the international hub airport. It provides a flexible and sensitive means of achieving the balance between the positive and negative aspects of the presence of an airfield in any site – a balance which may be said to be the aim of environmental control for improved quality of life.

If the 'environmental capacity' of an airport were described in terms of a set of contours indicating acceptability or otherwise, or contours interpreted in terms of noise exposures appropriate to that airport but which must not be exceeded, airport operators would be given the freedom to determine how to achieve that target. The use of cleaner, quieter aircraft would be encouraged implicitly, as a means of optimizing airport use within the limits set.

Such a strategy would be particularly apt for use in the context of the liberalization of air transport now being introduced by the European Commission. It would act as a flanking policy to protect people and the environment from any adverse effects of that liberalization, and ensure the removal of competitive inequalities arising from varying approaches to environmental controls between countries and between individual airports within the Community.

One of the great advantages of such a system is that it would be possible to identify those airports with scope for expansion, giving a very useful indicator of its capacity and investment potential, as well as those where intensification would not be acceptable. It would also identify those where the noise exposure is already inappropriate: in these cases, a programme for its reduction within a specified time scale could be applied. The evaluation would be particularly suited to assisting with the selection of airport options when development within a region is proposed by local or central government.

The need for planning regulation by local authorities and by central government would be unaffected, but the application of the new assessment method would contribute to speed, consistency and technical soundness in decisions about airfield and airport development. The guidance provided to local planning authorities about the potential of the airport would inform their planning policies and decisions within the areas affected. Sensitive developments constructed *after* the establishment of the airport's environmental capacity assessment would not be able to look to the airport for mitigation or change. Sensitive developments already within the environmentally controlled zone would be identified as 'hotspots' and taken account of within the score.

Equally, the local environmental impact implied by development applications sought by an airport could be more readily put into context: planning authorities as well as the local populations could afford to be more relaxed, knowing the parameters within which the overall environmental climate might be altered. Noise is the quality-of-life issue most commonly raised in relation to airport use: the method would prevent intensification of use from worsening the noise exposure levels exponentially; new residents or businesses moving into an area would be able to check the expected aircraft noise and determine in advance whether the noise climate would be acceptable to them or not.

Fresh data and legislation on air pollution or other aspects of the environmental impact of aircraft could be readily incorporated into airport assessments. In advance of any legal requirements, complementary benefits could be passed on to the airlines investing in cleaner technology by the airport authorities which would have the responsibility for not exceeding the total score.

CONCLUSION

By providing universal criteria for the use and development of airfields and airports, the government would remove a great deal of the mistrust and uncertainty surrounding this contentious issue. Research and experience have already shown the importance for airport authorities of securing public confidence: the attitude of the public affected by noise towards the aerodrome or airport and its perception of the care for local communities displayed by the airport authorities are non-acoustical factors which play an important part in determining sensitivity to the noise.

There is a high degree of consensus, between those whose prime purpose is to promote measures to protect people and the environment from aviation's adverse effects and those whose function is to provide the best commercial operating conditions for civil aviation, about the attractiveness of an equitable and universally applicable method of evaluating the impact of airports. This is evidenced by the fact that a co-operative effort between environmental and aviation interests has been directed towards designing a project to move the AEF's idea forward. A small Working Group of members of the IATA's Environmental Task Force and its Infrastructure Action Group and I have designed a project proposal which would enable the necessary research to be done and would involve the evaluation of the approach in relation to real examples. Since the result of this project would have an international application, the aim is to have supra-national financial support for the work, and to have world-class experts to carry it out. A Steering Group, consisting of representatives of the international aviation and relevant planning and environmental bodies, should be appointed to oversee the study.

Probably the best chance of achieving a widely acceptable compromise of interests is through such a co-operative approach: the time is right for aviation and specifically environmental interests to explore the common ground between them – accepting that there is likely to come a point at which our different priorities would work against agreement and when we each would wish to promote our own case, perhaps then calling upon a third party, the government, to make the policy decision.

A system such as this could make a major contribution to removing, in part or altogether, what has been called 'the morass of uncertainty, cynicism and conflict' which has typified the debate on this subject to date. With such an assessment tool, society would be capable of securing an equitable balance between the public demand for air transport (and air sport), and the public demand for high standards of environmental and amenity protection.

24

BRITISH SHIPPING: SALVATION IN EUROPE?

FRANK WORSFORD AND MARK DICKINSON

In this chapter we seek to make a case for the maintenance of a UK registered fleet on the basis of our national interest and for the sake of the environment. In the short term, unless there is immediate government action Britain will no longer have a Merchant Navy of any significance and we will have lost our role as an influential maritime nation. In the long term, the solution to the UK shipping industry's problems must be sought within the European Community whose role in maritime transport will become a crucial one. We conclude by making the case for Britain to take a leading role in negotiating for Community action to halt the decline of EC shipping.

THE DECLINE OF BRITISH SHIPPING

During the period 1979 to 1990 there has been a dramatic decline in the British merchant fleet both in terms of the number of ships and manpower. In 1979, 1305 ships of over 500 gross registered tons (grt) totalling 41 million deadweight tonnes (dwt) were registered in the UK. The table below shows that, in each successive year up to the present, there has been a continuous decline both in the number of ships, and tonnage, sailing under the British flag. By 1990 our fleet had declined to 337 ships of 4.2 million dwt, a decline of 90 per cent in tonnage terms.

Not so many years ago the UK merchant fleet formed a significant proportion of total world shipping. As late as 1979 our fleet represented 7 per cent of total world tonnage, but that same fleet today represents a little over 1 per cent of world shipping – a decline of 82 per cent since 1979 (HMSO, 1990b).

Table 24-1: The UK Registered Merchant Fleet (of Ships Over 500grt).

Year	Ships	Tonnage (dwt)
1979	1305	41,221,000
1980	1272	42,308,000
1981	1118	35,625,000
1982	985	30,399,000
1983	866	24,467,000
1984	777	21,970,000
1985	695	18,596,000
1986	545	11,222,000
1987	482	6,230,000
1988	410	5,619,000
1989	361	5,193,000
1990	337	4,213,000

Source: HMSO (1990).

The age of the surviving UK merchant shipping fleet is now cause for serious concern. Since 1982 the average age of British ships has increased by 62 per cent, from an average of 8.7 years to an average of fourteen years in 1990 (HMSO, 1990a). A modern merchant vessel has a fifteen- to twenty-year working life, which means that 75 per cent of the UK fleet will need replacing by the year 2000. The depressed state of the world shipping industry over the past decade has meant that shipowners have extended the working lives of their ships beyond the limits envisaged by ship designers. This has serious consequences, not only for long-term viability, but also for the environment.

There has also been an equally dramatic decline in the size and age of our seafaring workforce. At the beginning of 1980 there was a total of 64,622 seafarers employed in the UK shipping industry. In the ten year period up to 1990 we have experienced a 71 per cent drop in the number of seafarers employed on our ships (GCBS, 1990). Today, we employ just over 18,000 seafarers under the Red Ensign. Recent research undertaken by the University of Warwick indicates that over half of our Merchant Navy officers are over forty years of age – a clear signal that no new blood has been entering the industry in any significant quantity for years. Not only is the fleet dying of old age, but so is the workforce (IER, 1990).

The share of the UK's trade carried on UK flag ships has continued to decline throughout the 1980s. In 1980 the UK flag carried 34 per cent of imports and exports but by 1990 only 18 per cent of imports and exports were transported in UK flagged ships (HMSO, 1990b). Imagine the scale of contributions to the balance of payments if we could achieve a more respectable percentage share of our own trade? Imagine the benefits for our maritime related industries if we could merely reclaim the share the UK fleet carried at the beginning of the decade?

As we have shown, the industry has gone through a dramatic decline, principally because of the governments *laissez-faire* policies. In the next part of this paper we will discuss why the UK fleet has reached this nadir.

THE REASONS FOR THE DECLINE IN THE UK FLEET

The reasons for the decline of UK shipping are well documented. Suffice to say here that, as a result of unfair competition and lack of government support, many British shipowners have either left the industry altogether or have transferred their ships to 'flag of convenience' registers. The latter enables them to reduce their operating costs by, *inter alia*, employing low wage crews, reducing manning levels and avoiding more stringent safety requirements. In June 1991 (according to the British Chamber of Shipping, 1991) a total of 312 ships of 11.6 million dwt were beneficially owned in the UK, but registered abroad. In other words, more than two thirds of British owned ships are registered outside the UK and sailing under foreign flags. This indicates that something is seriously wrong with government policy towards British shipping. Government action is needed to encourage British shipowners to bring this foreign flag fleet home.

British shipping fares remarkably well considering the advantages of some of our main competitors. The 'free market' – cornerstone of Conservative ideology – does not exist in shipping because all competitors do not have access to the same input costs and revenue. The reasons for this are as follows:

• Government support can reduce the effective cost of capital.

- Crewing costs are less if shipowners can utilize 'cheap labour' or benefit from government employment subsidies.
- Less stringent safety standards available under certain 'flag of convenience' registers can significantly reduce operating costs.
- Access to certain trades is restricted, or cargoes reserved, for national flag shipping.

This is why, in the competitive market place, our long-term decline has actually accelerated and is now so serious. In the past decade successive Tory Governments have been the only administration in Europe not to provide meaningful financial and fiscal aid to the shipping industry. The lack of significant state fiscal aid to shipping since 1984 (when the Government scrapped the 100 per cent first year allowance on investment in new ships) has been at the root of the industry's continued decline.

WHY SAVE THE UK REGISTERED FLEET?

The demand for shipping is set to grow, with world trade forecast to increase by 3-4 per cent per annum up to 2000, and the world shipping fleet is estimated to increase by 33 per cent by the year 2000. However, the worldwide demand for seafarers will outstrip supply by a staggering 750,000 officers and ratings (IER, 1990). This is a unique opportunity for the government to re-establish the UK as a leading maritime nation, but action is required without delay.

The report of the House of Commons Transport Committee in 1988 noted that there were two compelling economic reasons for maintaining a UK registered fleet. They were:

- Given the UK's reliance on sea transport it would be dangerous to allow the fleet to decline to such a level that the UK was almost totally dependent on ships of other nations to move its imports and exports.
- It seems inevitable that a decline in the UK registered fleet will result in a drop in the contribution by the shipping industry to the balance of payments.

While opening of the Channel Tunnel in 1993 will provide a rail link with the rest of Europe, Britain will still be an island. As an island, maritime traditions are at the heart of our economy. Even today 94 per cent of our foreign trade still travels by sea and our Merchant Navy made a direct gross contribution to the balance of payments of almost £4 billion. Half of the world's maritime related services (such as broking, finance, insurance and legal support) is still provided by Britain and produces £1.2 billion of service exports each year (Chamber of Shipping, 1991).

Apart from shipping, maritime transport includes an extensive infrastructure of harbours, ports, waterways and support services. It has been estimated that for each ship in use a shipping company alone needs up to four shore personnel (Lloyds Ship Manager, 1989). The true onshore jobs multiplier is likely to be significantly higher owing to the requirements of pilotage, dockwork, ship inspection, port and harbour maintenance, shipbuilding and ship repair, brokerage, insurance and banking – the list is endless. Maritime transport thus involves a complex range of factors far broader than just shipping, which requires a response that takes into account these broader issues. In this context the importance of linking together shipping, ports, railways, inland waterways, air and road transport in an integrated transport system cannot be stressed too strongly.

Seafarers, shipowners, academics and even a government-backed joint industry report (which claimed that the Merchant Navy was a 'vital national interest') have all warned that further decline may prove irreversible. Put simply, the end of the British Merchant Navy may be just over the horizon. If no action is taken to reverse the decline the required critical mass of maritime industries, seafarers and support services may not be sufficient for the task of recovery. There will be further decline if free market forces are allowed to continue – government intervention is essential if our merchant fleet is to survive and prosper.

In the event of a war or other national emergency our shipping industry would be unable to cope with the demands placed on it. During the Falklands campaign the Government procured fifty ships or 5 per cent of the UK fleet and this stretched the shipping industry's ability to supply sufficient specialized vessels (House of Commons Transport Committee, 1988). During the Gulf War it was widely publicized that the Government was forced to charter in around 127 foreign flag vessels at a cost to the British tax payer of £180 million: according to the *Sunday Telegraph*, the same fleet would have cost only £85 million in peacetime. The availability of sufficient shipping to deal with our strategic requirements is therefore essential for our national security. The maintenance of a core fleet of UK registered roll-on/roll-off ferries should also be considered given the likely adverse effects – in terms of competition – of the opening of the Channel Tunnel.

Safety and environmental considerations must also be taken into account when considering the desirability of maintaining a national flag fleet. In an age of super tankers, huge bulk carriers and large container vessels there is growing concern over the safety of life at sea and the potential threat to the marine environment caused by the ageing of the world fleet and the operation of sub-standard vessels by certain 'flag of convenience' ship operators. We have all become familiar with the damage done to our beaches and fishing stocks through ship losses and accidents involving oil spillage. Given the notorious correlation between incidents of marine pollution and loss of life with certain 'flags of convenience', the UK fleet should be proud of its low loss rate. Statistics compiled by the Institute of London Underwriters (ILU) in 1989 reveal that UK registered ships had the lowest ratio of thirty-six of the world's biggest fleets. This is in stark contrast to the record of 'flags of convenience', which in the same year accounted for two-thirds of all ship losses. If the UK fleet is to maintain its low loss rate we must ensure that it is a modern fleet crewed with competent and well qualified British seafarers.

Unlike the rest of Europe, the UK carries very little of its internal freight on coastal or inland waterway shipping. In some EC countries, despite having cross-boundary road and rail links, up to 25 per cent of all internal freight is carried by coastal or waterway shipping; in the UK the equivalent is 7 per cent (DTp/MDS-Transmodal, 1988a). Government policy has consistently encouraged road freight on an already overloaded road system with dire long-term consequences, for the economy and for the environment. By shifting long-distance internal freight from our roads to more environment-friendly forms of transport such as coastal shipping, and by encouraging short sea trade with Europe, our maritime transport industry and the environment will together reap the benefits.

There have been fundamental changes to the structure of the shipping industry, and as a result our Merchant Navy may never be restored to its historic size. Clearly, however, our dependence on maritime transport will not diminish even with the opening of the Channel Tunnel. If Britain's national interest is ignored, future generations will be entirely dependent on foreign ships for imports and exports and we will have lost our rich maritime cultural heritage, not to mention many thousands of jobs and the prospect of thousands more.

So for economic, strategic, and environmental reasons alone the

UK's national interest lies in the growth and development of our maritime transport industry. In the short term, we must encourage British shipowners, who have registered their ships abroad, to return them home; and those who have remained in the UK not to 'flag out'. We must stimulate new investment in the maritime transport industry, by providing substantial fiscal and financial incentives to ensure that operating a vessel under the UK flag is an attractive proposition. If this is achieved and the government encourages modal shift from road freight to coastal shipping, together with investment in port facilities, one of the main barriers to the UK's economic prosperity will have been removed. However, in the long term, we must look towards Europe for salvation.

THE EUROPEAN APPROACH

The problems facing European Community shipping are the same as those that face British shipping; and the decline of the UK fleet has been mirrored by EC shipping as a whole. In 1975 the fleet registered in the Community amounted to more than 30 per cent of the world fleet. In 1990 the Community fleet accounted for less than 15 per cent (CEC, 1991b). The Commission of the European Communities (CEC) sees this decline as the result, *inter alia*, of the growth of protectionist measures by certain countries and unfair pricing practices. In response to this the European Council of Ministers adopted a package of regulations designed to liberalize Community shipping with the underlying principle being 'free trade'. The organization representing European seafarers disagrees with this principle believing that a commitment to free trade will do nothing to ensure the survival of the Community fleet, preferring instead practical intervention to reserve cargoes for Community shipping (International Transport Workers' Federation, 1990). While European shipowners endorse free trade, they also seek to exempt liner conferences – a fixed service consisting of two or more operators on a specific route with common freight rates (UNCTAD, 1986) – from the terms of the Single European Act. This is contradictory because it restricts access and attempts to eliminate competition between member states.

The CEC has proposed a block exemption for European liner conferences under Regulation 4056/86 – application of the competition rules to the maritime transport sector. If these proposals can ensure the survival of British flagged ships involved and secure the continued employment of British seafarers then they should be supported by the British government.

The importance of a European Community maritime transport policy has now been acknowledged and a number of measures has been proposed to the social partners by the CEC. These proposals are aimed at ensuring a future for European shipping and include the establishment of a European shipping register (EUROS) running in parallel with national ship registers. This would form the basis of a package of financial and fiscal benefits to aid EC shipowners. In addition cabotage trades would be liberalized for vessels up to 6000 grt registered on EUROS, and a programme of research would be set in motion to ensure technical compatibility across the industry. Port State Control would be expanded and a minimum package of the social and working conditions on EUROS ships would be guaranteed.

Unfortunately a consensus opinion on the CEC package has not been possible, mainly because the proposals have not satisfied the employers' group that they give enough financial advantage to EUROS ships to make registration attractive. They have also been criticized by the workers' group for laying insufficient emphasis on safety and employment standards, and on employment opportunities for EC seafarers. Among the social partners, however, there is a consensus of opinion regarding the financial and fiscal benefits that should apply to EUROS ships. These include tax relief to shipowners and seafarers, and exemption from social security payments (without loss of benefits) to reduce employment costs. Flexible fiscal allowances against the purchasing of new and secondhand tonnage is considered by both sides to be essential for stimulating investment in shipping. But one of the main obstacles to the introduction of EUROS is the disagreement over the social measures – specifically that the crews of EUROS registered ships may be made up from non-EC nationals at lower employment standards.

The workers' group insist that crews on EUROS registered ships should be composed entirely of EC nationals on EC conditions with an upward harmonization of living and working conditions on board ship. Job security and continuity of employment should also be guaranteed. The employers' group prefer more 'flexibility', suggesting that the officers only would be EC nationals with the ratings being drawn from the main third world labour supplying countries and paid at local rates of pay. The European Parliament Transport Committee view is that only EUROS registered vessels working between EC ports should be 100 per cent operated by EC nationals, although it would seem ludicrous to invest taxpayers' money in developing our maritime industries without guaranteeing employment opportunities to EC nationals.

The debate in Europe about maritime transport policy raises two main issues: how to ensure the survival and future prosperity of an EC fleet; and how to ensure that safety and employment standards, and employment opportunities for EC seafarers, are maintained and improved. Clearly these same issues underpin the survival and development of the UK fleet – our interests are those of Europe. The CEC will soon publish a White Paper on future transport policy and has set in motion a process of consultation with all those involved in the industry. The British government must be at the forefront of these discussions if we are to have any influence over the outcome.

The CEC argues that maritime issues have become increasingly important in ecological, economic and political terms and has set out the arguments for future action on technical harmonization, safety, the development of maritime infrastructure and intermodalism, training, the environment, the removal of distortive competition etc. To ensure the fullest consultation across the maritime industry the CEC has proposed establishing a Maritime Forum which will, through a network of working groups, collate and analyse the common maritime interests of the Community. The first report of the Forum will be made to the CEC in July 1992 when Britain takes the Chair of the European Council of Ministers. In view of these European initiatives it is essential that the Government of the day takes into consideration the wider European perspective and is prepared to negotiate for our national interest by firmly establishing our special status within the EC as an island nation with a rich maritime tradition.

25

TOWARDS A SUSTAINABLE
TRANSPORT POLICY

JOHN G.U. ADAMS

The central problem of British transport is an excessive, unsustainable level of motorized mobility – of both people and goods. From this stems a host of social, economic and environmental problems. The main objective of a morally, intellectually and environmentally sustainable transport policy must be to reduce the country's dependence on motorized transport. This is an essential pre-condition for building an equitable and environmentally benign transport system.

INTRODUCTION

The social, economic and environmental consequences of present traffic levels, reviewed in earlier chapters, are now well known. Noise and vibration, fumes and dirt, danger, the disfiguring of cherished landscapes and destruction of wildlife habitats, are all costs of Britain's transport system of which no sentient politician or civil servant can any longer claim ignorance. There are other costs not directly detectable with the naked eye, ear, or nose: the social divisiveness caused by growing disparities in mobility between those with cars and those dependent on declining public transport; the stress and anxiety of motorists stuck in traffic jams, and the fears of cyclists and pedestrians contending with a transport system that accords them few rights; the loss of neighbourliness that accompanies high mass-mobility; and the large-scale pollution effects in the form of European-wide acid rain, and the greenhouse effect.

All these costs are either directly perceivable, or have been sufficiently widely discussed to make them common knowledge.

Collectively they make a compelling case for *reducing* our dependence on motorized transport. But the opposite is happening. Transport planning in Britain still rests on the assumption that further large increases in traffic will, and should, occur. Why?

POLICY

The primary objective of the Conservative Government's transport policy has been to 'assist economic growth by reducing transport costs'. (Department of Transport, 1991a: 1). Labour has a similar objective: 'to deliver a transport system which will help to meet the

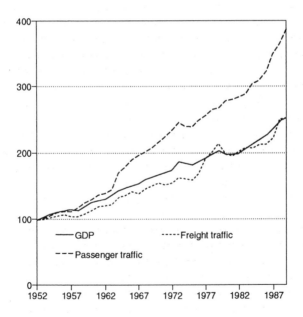

Figure 25-1: Growth Indices GDP, Tonne-kms of Freight and Passenger-kms; 1952=100.

Note: 1952 is the year in which most of the published statistical series for transport begin; 1989 is the most recent year available.
Source: DTp (1990c)

economic needs of the nation – allowing goods to be transported quickly and efficiently and enabling economic growth to be spread more evenly throughout the country' (Labour Party, 1989a). The Labour Party vies with the Conservatives over which can promote the highest sustainable rate of economic growth. Joseph, Lester and Hamer (chapter 8) note that the Department of Transport is the willing servant of this objective. The connection between economic growth and the environmental damage inflicted by Britain's transport system is one that has yet to be addressed by either Party's transport policy, or by the Department of Transport.

Reducing transport costs clearly does assist economic growth as conventionally measured by Gross Domestic Product (GDP). Economic growth in turn generates more movement of both people and goods. Figure 25-1 shows the connection between movement and GDP.

Between 1952 and 1989 the indices of GDP and tonne-kilometres of freight increased by almost exactly the same amount. The correlation between passenger traffic and GDP is also close, although over the same period the rate of increase in passenger traffic was considerably greater than that of GDP. The close relationship between economic growth and freight traffic is not surprising; GDP is an index that summarizes a range of activities that involve gathering together geographically dispersed raw materials, processing them, and redistributing them to geographically dispersed consumers. Personal travel is not only involved in the processes of production and consumption, but is also, as tourism, a form of consumption in itself.

Figure 25-2 shows that as the total amount of travel was increasing there was a marked shift away from the most egalitarian and environmentally benign modes of transport to the most socially divisive and environmentally damaging. Between 1952 and 1989 travel by car increased ten fold, and air travel more than thirty fold. Over the same period travel by bicycle decreased by 80 per cent and bus travel halved. Passenger-kilometres travelled by rail increased by about 5 per cent while the number of rail journeys decreased by about the same percentage; but the pattern of rail travel changed considerably as branch line services declined and the railways concentrated on their inter-urban business.

There is important information missing from Figure 25-2 – the amount of travel on foot. The National Travel Survey estimates that as recently as 1985/86 more than one third of all journeys were still made on foot. Statistics were not collected in the past to permit the decrease in walking to be charted along with the trends in other modes of travel, but the decrease has been substantial. Frequent walking trips to local shops have been replaced by less frequent but longer trips to supermarkets and out-of-town shopping centres. Far more children are now driven to school, and many other social and recreational journeys previously made on foot are now made by car. Other journeys have been replaced by the telephone and television. Popping round to the neighbours is increasingly done electronically, and sitting in front of the box has replaced many trips to the cinema.

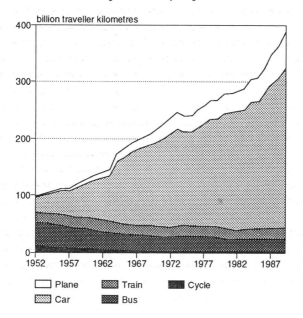

Figure 25-2: Travel by Britons by Cycle, Bus, Train, Car and Plane.

Since 1952 the distance travelled every year by the average Briton has more than trebled. Because of the decline in short, frequent walking and cycling trips, fewer journeys are now made than in 1952; the increase in travel is accounted for not by more trips but by longer trips. In 1952 the bicycle accounted for five times more passenger-kilometres than the airplane. Now the plane accounts for twenty-five times more than the bicycle.

In absolute terms the largest increase in travel since 1952 has been by car. This increase has been associated first, with changes in *activity patterns* and second, with changes in *land use patterns*. When people acquire cars they begin making trips which were previously inconvenient or impossible. They tend to use them for all possible journeys, and they make use of the opportunities afforded to travel at times of day not served by public transport, and to dispersed destinations which are inaccessible by public transport, or too far to reach on foot or by cycle. Over time, as more people acquire cars, the land use pattern responds to their 'needs'. The retail and commercial service sectors, sensitive to the wishes of their more affluent customers, choose sites that are easier to reach by car. Employers respond in similar fashion. The plans of residential developers take account of the high priority that car owners place on ease of parking. The older built environments, whose scale cannot accommodate mass car ownership, decline. Prosperity moves to the suburbs.

Those who cannot afford cars are left behind. The increase in the mobility of the 'average' Briton masks a growing disparity. Those without cars become less mobile as it becomes more dangerous to walk and cycle, and the public transport on which they depend declines. The shops and services upon which they depend become less accessible, as small local facilities are replaced by fewer larger ones. (Chapters 6, 7, 13 and 17 describe this process and its consequences in some detail.) The Department of Transport is familiar with this evidence but, because it has no answer to the problems it raises, simply ignores it.

TRIP GENERATION

Transport planning under both Labour and Conservative governments has deliberately encouraged the trends illustrated by Figures 25-1 and 25-2. The most recent Government White Paper on roads states:

> Higher economic activity and prosperity have led to a large increase in demand for transport and travel ... New National Road Traffic Forecasts published in 1989 suggest that traffic demand could increase by between 83 per cent and 142 per cent by the year 2025, compared with 1988. These forecasts are largely determined by forecasts of economic growth. *They are in no sense a target or option*; they are an estimate of the increase in demand as increased prosperity brings more commercial activity and gives more people the opportunity to travel and to travel more frequently and for longer distances.

Despite its disclaimer that the forecasts are in no sense a target, they are acknowledged to be the direct and inevitable consequence of a target – economic growth. The forecasts continue to be used at public inquiries into road schemes to determine the design capacity of the roads proposed: the Department of Transport argues – in pursuit of its objective of reducing travel costs to promote growth – that new roads should be built to carry the forecast traffic without congestion. Building new roads, chapter 8 shows, continues to be the principal function of the Department of Transport.

For many years the Department has argued at public inquiries that its forecasts are government policy and hence not debatable at local inquiries. More recently its position has shifted; it now argues that it is government policy to rely upon the forecasts. The effect is the same. They are used to justify more road-building, and objectors at public inquiries are not permitted to challenge them. The growth of traffic is treated as an inevitable phenomenon beyond the government's control. A few years ago the Department's principal forecaster told the Royal Statistical Society, 'If we did not believe that there was something inevitable about traffic growth, then we would not be producing the sort of forecasts that we have been' (Tanner, 1978: 14-63). This remains the position: in *Trunk Roads, England: Into the 1990s* the Department argues that 'to stop further inter-urban road improvement would not stop traffic growth, since demand is largely determined by growth in the economy.'

The planning of airport capacity in Britain is also based on the 'predict-and-provide' principle. As with road traffic the main determinant of the forecast growth in traffic is GDP. The Department of Transport produces high and low forecasts of traffic based upon high and low assumptions of economic growth – and then prefers to err on the high side. It observes:

> For planning purposes a point estimate is often required, rather than a range. The usual approach is to assume that the mid-point of the range is the best guess of the outcome. However, this guidance ignores the relative implications of air traffic under- or over-shooting the level for which authorities had planned. Over-provision is considered to be less costly than under-provision so a point estimate above the mid-point of the range is more suitable for planning purposes. (Department of Transport, 1991a).

In the case of air travel Labour does not dissent from the predict-and-provide principle. In fact, it accuses the Government of under provision.

Congestion at airports and in the air is a major problem. This has been made more acute by government cuts and delays in investment in airports and in air traffic control equipment, and in the reduction in numbers of air traffic controllers ... Passenger traffic is expected to more than double over the next fifteen years. We must reduce congestion, increase airport and airspace capacity and improve the access to and from airports.

In the case of surface transport the policies of neither Party confront the environmental consequences of their pro-growth economic policies. The policy-makers have yet to explain how they can achieve the economic growth they espouse while at the same time achieving the reduction that they claim to seek in the harmful consequences of traffic growth. The transport policies of both Labour and the Conservatives are therefore subservient to economic policies that generate traffic growth.

Rarely are the costs of excessive motorized mobility contemplated holistically. Problems are addressed piecemeal and partial solutions are advocated. Individually and collectively these solutions fall far short of what is needed.

SOLUTIONS?

Improved Efficiency?

Better traffic management, computerized route guidance, and cleaner, more energy efficient engines offer the prospect of reducing the environmental impact of a given volume of traffic, but all would be quickly overtaken by traffic growth. Indeed, where improved traffic management and route guidance succeed in squeezing more capacity out of a congested road system they encourage growth by liberating suppressed demand. Catalytic converters can effect large reductions in some harmful emissions, but not for short journeys and only at the cost of increasing the production of carbon dioxide, one of the major greenhouse gases. Lead in petrol may eventually be removed completely, but there is a growing suspicion that the extra carcinogenic benzene added to lead-free petrol could result in one health risk being exchanged for another. And, even if petrol and diesel engines are abandoned, a recent study by the Institute for Environmental Protection and Energy Technology in Cologne indicates that switching to electric vehicles could increase total pollution when all the environmental costs of electricity generation and transmission are taken fully into account.

Holman and Fergusson (chapter 3) note that there is, as yet, no effective technology to reduce CO_2 emissions from engines burning fossil fuels. Their proposed 30 per cent reduction target for CO_2 is a concession to this difficulty, but it should be noted that it is far less than what is likely to be required. Barrett (1992) estimates that for the 60 per cent reduction in CO_2 emissions recommended by the Intergovernmental Panel on Climate Change to be achieved, *and* for Britain's *per capita* emissions to be reduced to the global average, would require a 93 per cent reduction in Britain's emissions. This second requirement cannot be brushed aside: equity has become a significant issue in the international negotiation of national pollution targets. There appear to be no 'technical fixes' for the traffic growth problem.

Road Safety Measures?

For many years the Department of Transport under both Labour and Conservative Governments has produced a steady stream of road safety measures. There is no convincing evidence for the effectiveness of any of them. There is a major unresolved problem with measuring effectiveness: accident statistics provide an unsatisfactory measure (Adams, 1988). The fact that there are now about half as many children killed in road accidents each year as there were in the early 1920s does not prove that the roads have become safer. Clearly, as traffic has increased the roads have become more dangerous. The Department of Transport's road safety campaign featuring the slogan 'One false move and you're dead', is an explicit reminder of the no-go world that modern traffic levels have created for our children. A recent Policy Studies Institute study (Hillman, Adams and Whitelegg, 1990) reported dramatic declines in children's independent mobility as parents, worried about the danger of traffic, have increasingly confined their children to back gardens or in front of television sets. The study also reported large increases in the amount of parental chauffeuring motivated by a concern for safety. As traffic increases the only way of containing the accident toll among vulnerable road users is to separate those on foot or on bicycles from motor vehicles. This generally involves motor vehicles taking space from people. If traffic is allowed to do so, 'safety' will require increasing deference to motorists by cyclists and pedestrians – precisely those environmentally benign travellers that a sustainable transport policy must encourage.

Traffic Calming?

This was a feature of the Buchanan Report of the mid-1960s which recommended the development of 'environmental areas' from which through traffic would be excluded and within which local access traffic would be made to respect the presence of pedestrians and cyclists. However, environmental areas were presented as part of a package which also included a network of high-speed, high-capacity roads which were to avoid residential areas and shopping precincts, and from which pedestrians and cyclists were to be excluded. The main reason so little progress has been made with the idea in Britain is that large parts of the built environment pre-date high levels of car ownership, and nowhere can be found to build the network for through traffic. As a result, where traffic calming schemes have been proposed, they have usually been criticized, rightly, as 'muck-shifting' measures – the traffic that is moved out of the traffic-calmed neighbourhood is transferred to some other less fortunate area.

A study of *Verkehrsberuhigung*, the German version of traffic calming, has shown that they have failed to stem the rising tide of traffic (Whitelegg, 1990a); and in re-designing residential streets to discourage through traffic, *more* parking space has been provided (TEST, 1989b). From the time of its introduction in the Buchanan Report to the present, traffic calming has been seen as a way not of curbing traffic growth, but of accommodating it. Most trips begin and end in congested urban areas. There can be no by-pass solutions for such areas so long as traffic continues to grow.

Relief Roads

The justification now most frequently offered for new road schemes is 'environmental relief'. In a policy paper entitled *Roads for Prosperity* the Conservative Government asserts that 'new roads take traffic away from places where it should not be ... For these reasons many communities are anxious to have by-passes.' Labour concurs, and insists that the programme should be speeded up: 'The local by-pass programme – given proper local consultation – could offer towns and villages relief from congestion. Yet it is years behind schedule.'

With growing traffic the relief provided by new roads is either temporary, or at the expense of some other community, or both. The policy of taking traffic away from areas where it should not be assumes the existence of sufficient areas where it should be. Such areas are in short supply.

Electronic Road Pricing?

At present, among professional transport planners, this is probably the most popular of the fiscal measures discussed by Stephen Potter in chapter 10. It is a way of restraining traffic in the most congested areas and during the most congested times of day. Its advocates propose that the revenues collected by charging motorists for the use of selected parts of the road network during rush hours could be spent on improving public transport. They propose a set of sticks and carrots to encourage motorists, principally commuters, to shift to public transport.

There are three main objections to the measure: it would require an enforcement system based on Orwellian-style electronic surveillance; its management would be technically complex and not readily susceptible to democratic control; and it would encourage dispersal to the suburbs (Adams, 1990a).

Traffic growth has already virtually ceased in urban centres because they have reached capacity. The Department of Transport now concedes that traffic cannot continue to grow at the forecast rates in urban areas. It says that the national forecasts 'are an average; in some areas [cities] growth will be substantially lower, in others [the suburbs and rural areas] higher.' Targeting urban areas for restraint while still pursuing policies of accommodating traffic growth elsewhere would promote a further shift toward low-density, car-dependent land use sprawl. The need for restraint by pricing is in those areas where traffic growth is fastest – in precisely those areas *not* targeted by electronic road pricing.

Electronic road pricing appears to have growing support among transport planners and academics but to date has yet to gain official approval by the Government or the Labour opposition. The reluctance of politicians to support the idea is, ironically, not because the restraint it proposes is too limited, but because they judge it to be too severe.

Improved Public Transport?

One of the clearest differences between the Conservative and Labour transport policies is in the support they offer public transport. With the departure of Mrs Thatcher the Conservative Party has begun to pay more lip service to the environmental benefits of railways, but Labour has a large and well established lead as the party of public transport. Good public transport is the central plank in Labour's policy to reduce the environmental impact of road traffic. It argues for greater subsidy for public transport, citing the example of European countries:

> Compared with other European countries, Britain has a relatively low level of car ownership. However, the use of cars in Britain is high and the proportion of travel by car is higher than any country with our level of car ownership. For example, West Germany has 36 per cent more cars than Britain – per head of population, but their owners use them less and travel is less car dominated. (Labour, 1989a)

This is misleading. Certainly government support for public transport on the continent is more generous, fares are lower and services are superior, and more widely used. But the average German, and Frenchperson, travels farther by car every year than the average Briton. The same holds for freight. The Germans and the French move more freight by rail, water and pipe than the British, but they also move more by road. Labour promises to 'encourage a significant and continuing shift from use of the private car to public transport' (Labour, 1989a). As Roberts and Pickup note in (chapters 12 and 18 respectively), the European example shows that it is possible to have simultaneously an increase in the proportion of travel by public transport, and an absolute increase in car traffic.

The frequent assertion that the solution to the present transport mess is to get people out of their cars and back into public transport is facile. As Figure 25-2 shows, they were never in public transport. *All* the passenger and freight traffic now carried by rail is equivalent to less than the *growth* in traffic in 1988 and 1989. Most of the increase in travel by car does not represent a shift from public transport to cars. It consists of new, longer trips between widely dispersed origins and destinations – trips that cannot realistically be served by public transport.

The car and the lorry benefit from enormous environmental subsidies – environmental damage for which the motorist is not charged. Attempting to counter these subsidies with subsidies for public transport simply generates more environmentally damaging traffic by all modes of travel. The recent argument over a fast rail link to the Channel Tunnel has revived the long-running road *versus* rail debate. What has been lost in this debate is that Kent is not being offered an environmentally damaging railway in place of even more environmentally damaging road traffic. It is being offered both.

This book contains numerous proposals for improving public transport and shifting freight from road to rail. So long as traffic continues to grow at its forecast rate these proposals can best be described as necessary, but not sufficient conditions for a sustainable transport system.

More Cars?

What must not be ignored is that the main solution currently offered by the Government to the deprivations of those without cars is *still more* cars: 'the Government welcomes the continuing widening of car ownership as an important aspect of personal freedom and choice.' (Department of the Environment *et al.*, 1990b: 73) Labour does not dissent: 'Labour is clearly not opposed to car ownership' (Labour, undated). In addition to all the problems discussed above, there are three further reasons why increased car ownership should not be seen as a solution to the problems of those without cars:

- As car ownership increases, the deprivation of those without them also increases. The proportion of the population who can never qualify as car drivers because they are too young, too old, or otherwise disqualified, is about 35 per cent. They will remain second class citizens, dependent for their mobility on the goodwill of car owners or the withered remains of the public transport system.
- Leaving aside the difficulty of providing sufficient roadspace for them to move about, there is an insoluble parking problem in the older parts of the built environment. The Department of Transport's forecasts envisage an additional 27.5 million more vehicles in Britain before everyone capable of driving has a car. It has been estimated that they could all be accommodated, if stationary, on a new motorway stretching from London to Edinburgh – if it were 257 lanes wide.
- The environment debate has now become global. Traffic is one of the main contributors to pollution that threatens the stability of the world's climate. The contributions of individual countries to this threat are now being negotiated in international forums. Were the whole world to achieve the level of car ownership that the Department of Transport forecasts for Britain there would be an eleven fold increase in the world's car population (Adams, 1990b).

For the air travel disparities between rich nations and poor are even greater. The average North American uses over fifty times more aviation fuel every year than inhabitants of Asia or Africa (Barrett, 1991) – and the growth of air traffic in North America is much faster than that of surface traffic. The rich world cannot continue to increase its consumption of the world's energy and atmospheric resources and then sign a non-proliferation pact excluding the rest of the world. Britain's advice to the Third World on environmental housekeeping will only be heeded if it sets an example of self-restraint.

A SUSTAINABLE TRANSPORT POLICY

A comparison of Labour and Conservative transport policies shows that both are attempting to treat the symptoms of excessive mobility while encouraging more of it. Labour's policy, with its greater enthusiasm for public transport, might be described as the lesser of two evils: under a Labour Government pursuing current Labour transport policy Britain's transport problems would get worse more slowly.

The main objective of any transport policy that purports to be intellectually, morally and environmentally sustainable should be to *reduce* the demand for motorized transport; merely stopping growth will not suffice. Traditional transport planning seeks to predict demand and then accommodate it. The focus of its methodology is the estimation of 'trip generation'. Inherent in a given distribution of population, income, shops, offices, factories, warehouses and other facilities, is a demand for transport. The distribution is calculated to generate a pattern of trips. The job of transport planning has been to serve this demand in the most efficient way possible. In so doing, by reducing the cost of transport, it has itself increased demand, and made yet more work for transport planners.

The challenge now is to reverse the process by which we have become dependent on an unsustainable level of mobility. The skills of transport planners should be turned to the task of 'trip degeneration' – reducing the length and number of motorized trips.

The task for politicians is more difficult. In a democratic society, they argue, they have a duty to respond to the wishes of the electorate. They insist that people want cars and the freedom to drive them wherever they wish, and there is considerable evidence from opinion polls to support this view. How then, they ask, can they deny this aspiration and get re-elected?

First, they must stop fostering unrealistic aspirations. If people who do not own cars because they cannot afford them are asked if they would like to have them, they almost always say yes. This is the implicit opinion poll to which Britain's political parties are responding with their transport policies. But this question tempts people with the impossible. The longer that policy attempts to deliver the impossible, the greater the damage that will be done. If asked if they would like to live in the sort of world that would result from everyone's wish coming true – a bleak, dirty, noisy, dangerous, socially polarized, fume-filled greenhouse – people say no.

There is a third, more positive question that can be asked: would you like to live in world in which it was safe for children to play in the streets and walk or cycle to school on their own, in which women and old people were not afraid to venture out at night, in which conversation was not drowned out by the roar of traffic, in which there were, once again, local shops and efficient home delivery services ... in a safer, more beautiful and harmonious world? It ought not to be beyond the wit of politicians to persuade people to trade in their cars for such a prize.

Consider again the pro-growth alternative. Each week last year in Britain we travelled on average – every man, woman and child -about 250 kilometres. And feeding our appetites for material goods involved the movement each week of 60 tonne-kilometres of freight for every one of us. The Department of Transport assumes that before growth ceases, these numbers will more than double. Would we be happier and feel richer? I doubt it. Would Britain be a greener and more pleasant land? Impossible.

REFERENCE BIBLIOGRAPHY

Abbott, S. and A. Whitehouse (1990), *The Line That Refused to Die*, Leading Edge Press, Hawes.

Adams, John G.U. (1990a), 'Road Pricing in London: Diversion or Focus?', Paper presented to PTRC Conference on 'Practical Possibilities for a Comprehensive Transport Policy with and without Road Pricing', December, London.

Adams, John G.U. (1990b), 'Car Ownership Forecasting: Pull the Ladder up or Climb Back Down?', *Traffic Engineering and Control*.

Adams, John G.U. (1989), *London's Green Spaces*, Report for Friends of the Earth & London Wildlife Trust, London.

Adams, John G.U. (1988), 'Evaluating the Effectiveness of Road Safety Measures', *Traffic Engineering and Control*.

Adams, John G.U. (1974), '... And How Much for Your Grandmother?', in *Environment and Planning A*, Vol. 16.

Allen, S. and C. Wolkowitz (1987), *Homeworking: Myths and Realities*, Macmillan, London.

Anon. (1989), 'Company Car Drivers More Dangerous', *Transnet News*, December.

Apel, D. (1988), *Zweiter Bericht fur die AG 'Flache' der Enquette Kommission Bodenversmutchung, Bodennutzung und Bodenschutz-Verkehrsflachen*, Deutsches Institut fur Urbanistik, Berlin.

Appleyard, D. and M. Lintell (1975), 'Streets: Dead or Alive?', in *New Society*, 3 July.

Archer, J. and B. Lloyd (1982), *Sex and Gender*, Cambridge University Press, Cambridge.

Ashworth, Mark and Andrew Dilnot (1987), 'Company Car Taxation', in *Fiscal Studies*, Vol. 8, No. 4, November.

Association of Metropolitan Authorities (1990), *Changing Gear: An Urban Transport Policy Statement*, London.

AMA (1989a), *A Step Ahead: The Pedestrian Environment*, London.

AMA (1989b), *A Review of the Second Year of Bus Deregulation*, London.

Balcombe, R.J., J.M. Hopkins, K.E. Perrett and W.S. Clouch (1987), *Bus Deregulation in Great Britain: A Review of the Opening Stages*, TRRL, Crowthorne.

Banister, C. (1990), 'Existing Travel Patterns: The Potential for Cycling', Proceedings from a conference on 'Cycling and the Healthy City', Friends of the Earth, June.

Banister, D. (1989), 'The Reality of the Rural Transport Problem', Discussion Paper 1, *Transport & Society*, Rees Jeffreys Road Fund.

Banister, D. and L. Pickup (1990), 'Bus Transport in the Metropolitan Areas and London', in P. Bell and P. Cloke (eds), *Deregulation and Transport:*

Market Forces in the Modern World, David Fulton, London.

Banister, D. and R. Mackett (1990), 'The Minibus: Theory and Experience and their Implications', *Transport Reviews*, Vol. 10, No. 3.

Banister, D. and F. Norton (1988), 'The Role of the Voluntary Sector in the Provision of Rural Services – The Case of Transport', *Journal of Rural Studies*, Vol. 4, No. 1.

Barker, T. and R. Lewney (1990), *Macroeconomic Modelling of Environmental Policies: The Carbon Tax and Regulation of Water Quality*, Department of Applied Economics, University of Cambridge.

Barrett, M. (1992), 'Radical Energy Strategies', forthcoming Report for WWF, Godalming.

Barrett, M. (1991), 'Aircraft Pollution: Environmental Impacts and Future Solutions', WWF Research Paper, Godalming.

Barrett, Michele and M. McIntosh (1982), *The Anti-Social Family*, Verso, London.

Barrett, Scott (1991), 'Global Warming: Economics of a Carbon Tax', in Pearce, D. (ed.), *Blueprint 2: Greening the World Economy*, Earthscan, London.

Battilana (1976), 'The Cost of Using Light Vehicles for Town-centre Deliveries and Collections', TRRL.

Block, J.H. (1984), *Sex Role Identity and Ego Development*, Jossey Bass, San Francisco.

Blum, Urich and Werner Rottengatter (1990), 'The Federal Republic of Germany', in Jean-Phillipe and Kenneth Button (Eds), *Transport Policy and the Environment*, Earthscan, London.

Bly, P.H. (1980), 'The Quality of Public Transport', in TRRL, *The Demand for Public Transport*, Crowthorne.

Bowlby, S. (1978), 'Accessibility, Shopping Provision and Mobility', in A. Kirby and B. Goodall (eds), *Resources in Planning*, Pergamon Press, Oxford.

Brewer, M. and C. Davies (1988), *Women's Safe Transport in London*, LSPU, London.

Brog, Werner, *et al.* (1984), 'Promotion and Planning for Bicycle Transportation: An International Overview', Paper to 63rd Annual Meeting Transportation Research Board, Washington, January.

Buchan, Keith (1991), 'An Objectives Led Approach to Transport Planning', in Transport 2000/NEF (1991), *What Are Roads Worth?*, London.

Buchan, Keith (1980), *People, Their Environment, and the Lorry Problem*, London.

Buchanan, C. (1963), *Traffic in Towns: A Study of the Long-term Problems of Traffic in Urban Areas*, HMSO, London.

Cartledge, John (1991), 'Consumer Representation in Public Transport', Working Paper for Independent Transport Advisory Group, unpublished.

Caves, Robert (1991), *A Review of UK Aviation Policy*, TT 9107, Department of Transport Technology, Loughborough University.

Caves, Robert (1990), 'London's Runway Capacity – A Possible Solution', in *Airport Technology International 1990/91*, Sterling Publications, London.

Caves, Robert and Christopher Higgins (1991), *A Comparison Between the Consequences of the Liberal and Non-liberal UK–Europe Bilaterals*, TT

9101, Department of Transport Technology, Loughborough University.

Confederation of British Industry (1991), *Transport and Global Warming – A Forward Look*, Discussion Paper, London.

Central Statistical Office (1989), *Social Trends 19: 1989 Edition*, Section 9, HMSO, London.

Cervero, Robert (1988), 'Land Use Mixing and Suburban Mobility' in *Transportation Quarterly*, Vol. 42, No. 3, July.

Chamber of Shipping (1991), *Annual Report*.

Campaign to Improve London's Transport Research Unit (1991), *Old Street Roundabout: A Safety, Security and Environmental Strategy*, London.

CILT Research Unit (1991), *Life Over, Across and Under the Fast Lane: A Transport Study of the South Canning Town and Custom House Area of the London Borough of Newham*, London.

CILT Research Unit (1988), *British Rail and Underground Stations in Hackney*, London.

CILT Research Unit (1987), *Free to Move: A Report on the Transport Needs of Women in the London Borough of Southwark*, London.

Civil Aviation Authority (1990a), *UK Airlines – Annual Operating, Traffic and Financial Statistics 1989*, CAP 568, London.

CAA (1990b), *UK Airports – Annual Statements of Movements, Passengers and Cargo 1989*, CAP 566, London.

CAA (1990c), *Traffic Distribution Policy and Airport and Airspace Capacity: The Next Fifteen Years*, CAP 570, London.

CAA (1989), *Passengers at the London Area Airports and Manchester Airport in 1987*, CAP 560, London.

Clarke, A. (1988), *Pro-Bike: A Cycling Policy for the 1990s*, Friends of the Earth, London.

Cleary, J. (1991), *Traffic Calming and Cyclists*, Cyclists Touring Club, Godalming.

Commission of the European Communities (1991a), *Proposal for a Council Directive on the Limitation of the Operation of Chapter 2 Aeroplanes*, COM(90)445 final, Brussels.

CEC (1991b), *New Challenges for Maritime Industries*, Com (91) 335 Final, Brussels.

CEC (1985), Council Directive 'On the Assessment of the Effects of Certain Public and Private Projects on the Environment', 85/337/EEC, Brussels.

Consumer Congress (1985), 'Bus Services – Kill or Cure?', Resolution from Workshop No. 1, Brighton Consumer Congress.

Consumers' Association (1991), 'Data from CA: The Quality of Service in the Utility Industries, Part 2: British Rail – The Passenger View', in *Consumer Policy Review*, Vol. 1, No. 3.

Corporation of London (1990), *London's Transport: A Plan to Protect the Future*, London.

Cousins, Stephen (1991), 'Road Pricing', in *Transport Retort*, Vol. 14, No. 3, Transport 2000, London.

Dawson, H. (1987), *Wrong Tracks: A Study of British Rail Services in the South East*, London Transport Technology Network, SEEDS.

Deakin, Elizabeth (1990), 'The United States in Barde', in Jean-Phillipe and Kenneth Button (Eds), *Transport Policy and the Environment*, Earthscan, London.

Department of Employment (1984), *Family Expenditure Survey 1984*, HMSO, London.

Department of the Environment (1990a), *Report of the Noise Review Working Party*, HMSO, London.

DoE (1990b), *This Common Inheritance*, HMSO, London.

DoE (1988), *Planning Policy Guidance: Major Retail Development*, PPG 6, HMSO, London.

DoE (1973), *Planning and Noise Circular 10/73*, HMSO, London.

Department of Transport (1991a), *Trunk Roads: England into the 1990s*, HMSO, London.

DTp (1991b), *Air Traffic Forecasts for the United Kingdom 1991*, HMSO, London.

DTp (1990a), *International Comparisons of Transport Statistics 1970-1987*, 'Part 3: Road Vehicles, Traffic, Fuel and Expenditure', HMSO, London.

DTp (1990b), *A Bus Strategy for London*, HMSO, London.

DTp (1990c), *Transport Statistics Great Britain 1979-1989*, HMSO, London.

DTp (1990d), *Road Accidents Great Britain 1989: The Casualty Report*, HMSO, London.

DTp (1990e), *Annual Reports of the Licensing Authorities 1 April 1989 to 31 March 1990*, London.

DTp (1990f), *Transport in London*, HMSO, London.

DTp (1989a), *Statement on Transport in London*, HMSO, London.

DTp (1989b), *Transport: A Guide to the Department*, HMSO, London.

DTp (1989c), *Roads to Prosperity*, HMSO, London.

DTp (1989d), *Transport Statistics for London*, Statistical Bulletin, Vol. 88, No. 51, HMSO, London.

DTp (1989e), *Transport Statistics Great Britain 1978-88*, HMSO, London.

DTp (1988a), *Waterborne Freight in the UK*, London.

DTp (1988b), *National Travel Survey: 1985/86 Report, Part 1: An Analysis of Personal Travel*, HMSO, London.

DTp (1986a), *Transport Statistics Great Britain 1975-1985*, HMSO, London.

DTp (1986b), *Crime on the London Underground*, HMSO, London.

DTp (1982), *Transport Statistics Great Britain 1971-1981*, HMSO, London.

DTp (1979), *National Travel Survey 1978/79 Report*, HMSO, London.

DTp (1976), *Transport Statistics Great Britain 1964-1974*, HMSO, London.

DTp, ALA and LBA (1987), 'London Assessment Studies Working Arrangements for Stage 2', DTp, London.

DTp, British Rail and London Regional Transport (1989), *Central London Rail Study*, London.

Der Bundesminister für Verkehr (1987), *Verkehr in Zahlen 1987*, Bonn.

Derwent, R.G., G. Greenfelt and O. Hov (1991), *Photochemical Oxidants in the Atmosphere*, Nordic Council of Ministers, Copenhagen/Stockholm.

Di Leonardo, M. (1987), 'Women, Families and the Work of Kinship', in *Signs*, Spring.

Diamond, I.D., J.B. Ollerhead, S. Bradshaw, J.G. Walker and J.B. Critchley (1988), *A Study of Community Disturbance Caused by General and Business Aviation Operations*, Report to Department of Transport, London.

Disabled Passengers' Transport Advisory Committee (1990), *Mobility Policy for Britain's Entire Population*, Department of Transport, London.

Dix, M.C., S. Carpenter, M.I. Clarke, J. Pollard and M. Spencer (1983), *Car Use: A Social and Economic Study*, Gower, Aldershot.

Edwards, J.L. (1977), 'Use of a Lowry-type Spatial Allocation Model in an Urban Transportation Energy Study', in *Transportation Research*, Vol. 11, No. 2.

Eggers, Val K.H. (1989), 'Development of a European Integrated System', Paper No. 9 of Royal Aeronautical Society conference 'How Should we Deal With the Capacity Crisis?', February, London.

Environmental Data Services (1991), *Institutional Barriers Block the Path to Road Recycling*, Report No. 194, March, London.

European Community Ministers of Transport (1988), *Research Relevant to Trends in Transport*, Round Table 77, ECMT, Brussels.

European Conference of Ministers of Transport (1990), *Transport Policy and the Environment*, Paris.

European Parliament (1988), *Report on the Protection of Pedestrians and the European Charter of Pedestrians' Rights*, Session Document A2-0154/88, Brussels.

Federal Aviation Administration (1985), *Airport Noise Compatibility Planning Program*, FAR Part 150.

Fergusson, Malcolm (1990), *Subsidized Pollution: Company Cars and the Greenhouse Effect*, Report for Greenpeace UK, Earth Resources Research, January.

Fergusson, M., C. Holman and M. Barrett (1989), *Atmospheric Emissions From the Use of Transport in the United Kingdom, Volume One: The Estimation of Current and Future Emissions*, WWF, Godalming.

Fergusson, M. and C. Holman (1990), *Atmospheric Emissions From the Use of Transport in the United Kingdom, Volume Two: The Effect of Alternative Transport Policies*, WWF, Godalming.

Finch, J. (1984), 'Community Care: Developing A Non-sexist Alternative', in *Critical Social Policy*, No. 9.

Finkbohner, W. (1990), 'Zurich's Public Transport System-Mobility for All', *Swiss Review*, Vol.3, No. 90.

Foster, Christopher (1978), *Report of the Independent Committee of Inquiry in Road Haulage Operators' Licensing*, HMSO, London.

Game, A. and R. Pringle (1984), *Gender at Work*, Pluto Press, London.

General Council of British Shipping (1990), *Fleet and Manpower Inquiries*, London.

Gittens, D. (1985), *The Family in Question: Changing Households and Familiar Ideologies*, Macmillan, London.

Glomsrod, S. *et al.* (1990), *Stabilization of Emissions of CO2: A Computable General Equilibrium Assessment*, Central Bureau of Statistics, Oslo, April.

Goodwin, Phil (1990), *Transportation Planning and Policies*, The Road Ahead Conference, WWF, April.

Goodwin, P.B. (1985), *One Person Operation of Buses in London*, GLC, London.

Goodwin, P.B., S. Hallett, F. Kenny and G. Stokes (1991), *Transport: The New Realism*, Transport Studies Unit, University of Oxford, Oxford.

Government of the Netherlands (1990), *Second Transport Structure Plan: Part D – Government Decision*, Document 20922, The Hague.

Greater London Council (1985a), *Transport Policies and Programme 1986-87*, London.

GLC (1985b), *GLTS 1981: Transport Data for London*, London.

GLC (1985c), *Company Assisted Motoring in London*, Reviews and Studies Series No. 27, Transportation and Development Department, London.

GLC (1983), *Heavy Lorries in London*, Report of the Independent Inquiry, London.

GLC Women's Committee (1985-86), *Women on the Move: GLC Survey on Women and Transport*, Nos 1-7, London.

Greater Vancouver Regional District (1990), *Creating Our Future: Steps to a More Liveable Region*, Vancouver.

Greene, David (1990), 'CAFE or Price? An Analysis of the Effects of Federal Fuel Economy Regulations and Gasoline Price on New Car mpg, 1978-89', *The Energy Journal*, Vol. 11, No. 3.

Grieco, M.S. (1987), *Keeping it in the Family: Social Networks and Employment Chance*, Tavistock, London.

Grieco, M.S. and R. Whipp (1986), 'Women and the Workplace: Gender and Control in the Labour Process', in D. Knights and H. Wilmott (eds), *Studies in Gender and Technology in the Labour Process*, Gower, Aldershot.

Grieco, M.S., L. Pickup and R. Whipp (1989), *Gender, Transport and Employment*, Gower, Aldershot.

Griffiths, John (1991), 'Inland Revenue Sets up Company Car Roadblocks', *Financial Times*, 23 March.

Guiver, J. and S. Hoyle (1987), *Buswatch: The Initial Findings*, Transport 2000 Paper presented at conference on 'Deregulation' at the Transport Studies Unit, University of Oxford, May.

Gwilliam, K.M. (1991), '1992 and Public Transport in Europe', Paper Delivered to the 22nd Annual Public Transport Symposium, University of Newcastle-upon-Tyne, April.

Haigh, N. (1987), *EEC Environmental Policy and Britain*, Longman, Harlow.

Hallett, Sharon (1990), *Drivers' Attitudes to Driving, Cars and Traffic: Analysis of a National Survey*, Discussion Paper 14 for the 'Transport and Society' project, Transport Studies Unit, University of Oxford, Oxford.

Hamer, M. (1987), *Wheels Within Wheels: A Study of the Road Lobby*, RKP, London.

Hamilton, K. and S. Potter (1985), *Losing Track*, RKP, London.

Hamilton, K., L. Jenkins and A. Gregory (1991), *Women and Transport: Bus Deregulation in West Yorkshire*, University of Bradford Press, Bradford.

Hanmer, J. and S. Saunders (1984), *Well Grounded Fear: A Community Study of Violence to Women*, Hutchinson, London.

Hanmer, J. and M. Maynard (eds) (1987), *Women, Violence and Social Control*, Macmillan, London.

Hass-Klau, Carmen (1990), *The Pedestrian and City Traffic*, Belhaven Press, London.

Headicar, P. and B. Bixby (1991), *Concrete and Tyres: Local Development and Traffic Effects of Major Roads*, Council for Protection of Rural England, London.

Headicar, P., R.G. Fisher and T.C. Larner (1987), 'The Initial Effects of Bus Deregulation in West Yorkshire', Seminar Paper at PTRC Annual Summer Meeting.

Henley Centre for Forecasting (1988), *Planning for Social Change*.

Hillman, M. (1990a), 'The Role of Walking and Cycling in Transport Policy', Discussion Paper 8, Rees Jeffreys Road Fund research project, *Transport and Society*.

Hillman, M. (1990b), 'Cycling and Health: A Policy Context', Papers from a conference on 'Cycling and the Healthy City', Friends of the Earth, June.

Hillman, M. (1989), 'The Neglect of Walking in UK Transport and Planning Policy', in Proceedings of 'Feet First' Symposium at City University, May, London.

Hillman (ed.), M. (1980), *Report of the Proceedings of a Conference on Walking*, Policy Studies Institute, London.

Hillman, M., and A. Whalley (1983), *Energy and Personal Travel: Obstacles to Conservation*, Policy Studies Institute, London.

Hillman, M., and A. Whalley (1979), *Walking is Transport*, Policy Studies Institute, London.

Hillman, M., J.G.U. Adams and J. Whitelegg (1991), *One False Move ... A Study of Children's Independent Mobility*, Policy Studies Institute, London.

Hillman, M., I. Henderson and A. Whalley (1976), *Transport Realities and Planning Policy*, Political and Economic Planning, London.

Hillman, M., I. Henderson and A. Whalley (1974), *Mobility and Accessibility in the Outer Metropolitan Area*, Report to the DoE, Policy Studies Unit, London.

Hillman, M., I. Henderson and A. Whalley (1973), *Personal Mobility and Transport Policy*, Political and Economic Planning Broadsheet 542, London.

Hills, Peter (1991), 'Approaches to Road-use Pricing', Paper Delivered to the 22nd Annual Public Transport Symposium, University of Newcastle-upon-Tyne, April.

Himmelweit, S. and S. Ruehl (1979), *Economic Independence and the State*, Open University Press, Milton Keynes.

Her Majesty's Stationery Office (1990a), *Merchant Fleet Statistics*, London.

HMSO (1990b), *Seaborne Trade Statistics of the UK 1990*, London.

HMSO (1983), *Family Expenditure Survey*, London.

Holmberg J., S. Bass and L. Timberlake (1991), *Defending the Future – A Guide to Sustainable Development*, IIED/Earthscan, London.

Home Office (1989), *Technology for the Enforcement of Road Traffic Laws*, Consultation Paper, October, London.

Hopkin, Jean M. (1986), *The Transport Implications of Company-financed Motoring*, Transport and Road Research Laboratory Research Report 61.

House of Commons Energy Committee (1991a), *Fifth Special Report: Government Observations on the Third Report from the Committee (Session 1990-91) on Energy Efficiency*, HMSO, London.

House of Commons Energy Committee (1991b), *Third Special Report: Energy Efficiency*, HMSO, London.

House of Commons Public Accounts Committee (1988), *Regulation of Heavy Lorries*, House of Commons Paper 170, HMSO, London.

House of Commons Transport Committee (1988), *The Report on the Decline of UK Merchant Shipping*, HMSO, London.

House of Lords (1990), *Civil Aviation: A Free Market by 1992*, Select Committee on the European Communities, Session 1989-90, 16th Report, HMSO, London.

Hoyenga, A.K.B. and K.T. Hoyenga (1979), *A Question of Sex Differences: Psychological, Cultural and Biological Issues*, Little Brown, Boston.

Hudson, M. (1978), *The Bicycle Planning Book*, Open Books/Friends of the Earth, London.

Hughes, Peter (1991a), 'Travelling Green', in *Town and Country Planning*, October.

Hughes, Peter (1991b), 'The Role of Passenger Transport in CO_2 Reduction Strategies', *Energy Policy*, March.

Hughes, Peter (1990), 'How Green is my Maestro?', in *Town and Country Planning*, Vol. 59, No. 1, January.

Illich, Ivan (1974), *Energy and Equity*, Calder and Boyars, London.

Independent Commission on Transport (1974), *Changing Directions*, Coronet, London.

Institute of Employment Research (1990), *The World Demand for and Supply of Seafarers*, Report commissioned by ISF and BIMCO, University of Warwick, Coventry.

Institute of London Underwriters (1989), *Annual Report*, London.

International Transport Workers' Federation (1990), *European Merchant Shipping: Towards a Common Maritime Transport Policy*.

Jacobs, J. (1961), *The Life and Death of American Cities*, Pelican, London.

Jacobs, Michael (1991), 'Can Monetary Values be Assigned to the Environment?', in Transport 2000/NEF (1991), *What are Roads Worth?*, London.

Jones, T.S.M. (1977), *Young Children and Their School Journey*, TRRL Supplementary Report 342.

Kemp, Michael (1991), 'Vatman's Blow at More Pay Instead of a Company Car', *Daily Mail*, 4 March.

Krause, F., W. Bach and J. Koomey (1989), 'From Warming Fate to Warming Limit: Benchmarks for a Global Climate Convention', in *Energy Policy in the Greenhouse, Volume One*, International Project for Sustainable Energy Paths, El Cerrito, California.

Labour Party (1991), *Citizen's Charter – Labour's Better Deal for Consumers and Citizens*, London.

Labour Party (1989a), *Moving Britain into the 1990s: Labour's New Programme for Transport*, London.

Labour Party (1989b), *Meet the Challenge, Make the Change*, London.

Lave, L., and E. Seskin (1977), *Air Pollution and Human Health*, Johns Hopkins University Press, Baltimore.

Lester, N. and S. Potter (1983), *Vital Travel Statistics*, Transport 2000/Open University Press, London.

Levenson, Leo and Deborah Gordon (1990), 'Drive +; Promoting Cleaner and More Fuel Efficient Motor Vehicles Through a Self-financing System of State Sales Tax Incentives', *Journal of Policy Analysis and Management*, Vol. 9, No. 3.

Liberal Democrats (1991), *Costing the Earth*, Federal Green Paper No. 23, Liberal Democrat Publications, Dorchester.

Lloyd's Ship Manager and Shipping News International (1989), *A Global*

Analysis of Ship Ownership and Ship Management, London.

Logan, Moyra (1990a), 'Environmental Protection and Airport Capacity', *Airport Technology International 1990/91*.

Logan, Moyra (1990b), 'Airfields and the Environment', Paper at the 'Airports and the Environment', Short Course, University of Technology, Loughborough.

London Regional Transport (1991), *Consultation Document: 1991-94*, London.

London Strategic Policy Unit (1987a), *Safety by Design?*, LSPC Report No. 9, London.

LSPU (1987b), *Women's Safe Transport: The Local Authority Role*, London.

LSPU (1986), *Transport Policies for London 1987-88*, London.

LSPU/Women's Equality Group (1986), *Women in London: A Survey of Women's Opinions*, MORI, London.

London Women's Safe Transport Group (1988), *On the Safe Side: A Guide to Setting up Safe Transport for Women*, CILT, London.

London Dial-a-Ride Users' Association (1990), *Buses for All*, London.

Lord Chancellor's Department (1987; 1988), *Annual Report of the Transport Tribunal*, London.

Lovett, Terry (1990), quoted in 'UK Regional Airport Sale Threatened', *Flight International*, 21 November.

Lynch, G. and S. Atkins (1987), 'The Influence of Personal Security Fears on Women's Travel', Paper at Universities Transport Studies Group conference, Sheffield University.

Maccoby, E.E. and C.N. Jacklin (1974), *The Psychology of Sex Differences*, Vols 1 and 2, Stanford University Press, California.

Mackay, Murray (1990), *Effective Strategies for Accident and Injury Reductions*, Discussion Paper for the 'Transport and Society' project, Transport Studies Unit, University of Oxford, Oxford.

Marriott, L., and A. Dickson (1990), 'Your Last Gasp', in *London Cyclist*, November/December.

Marsh, P. and P. Collett (1986), *Driving Passion: The Psychology of the Car*, Jonathan Cape, London.

Martin, C. and C. Roberts (1984), *Women and Employment: A Lifetime Perspective*, Office of Population Censuses and Surveys/DoE, London.

Martin, David and R.A.W. Shock (1989), *Energy Use and Energy Efficiency in UK Transport up to the Year 2010*, HMSO, London.

May, Anthony (1990), 'Integrated Transport Strategies: A New Initiative or a Return to the 1960s?', Rees Jeffreys Discussion Paper No. 21.

Metropolitan Transport Research Unit (1991), *Traffic Restraint: Five Cities – Five Solutions*, London.

MTRU (1991), *Temple Mills Environmental Impact Assessment*, London Borough of Waltham Forest/MTRU.

MTRU (1990), *Wheels of Fortune*, SEEDS/MTRU, Stevenage.

MTRU (1989a), *West London Transport Study*, West London RoadWatch, London.

MTRU (1989b), Unpublished Market Research Surveys, London.

Miles, I. (1989), 'The Electronic Cottage: Myth or Reality?', *Futures*, Vol. 21. No. 4.

Mintel (1989 and 1990), *Bicycles*, Mintel International Group.

Mitchell, J.C. (1969), 'The Concept and Use of Social Networks', in J.C. Mitchell (ed.), *Social Networks in Urban Situations*, Manchester University Press, Manchester.

Mogridge, Martin (1990), *Travel in Towns*, Macmillan, London.

Morgan, J.M. (1987), 'How Many Cyclists and How Many Bicycles are There in Great Britain?', Transport and Road Research Laboratory Working Paper WP (TP) 36.

MORI (1990), *Survey of the General Public*, London.

Morissette, Claire (1990), 'Streets That Breathe: Controlling Cars', in Weston and Roy (eds), *Montreal: A Citizen's Guide to City Politics, Black Rose*, Montreal.

Morris, J.N. *et al.* (1990), 'Exercise in Leisure Time: Coronary Attack and Death Rates', in *British Heart Journal*, No. 63.

MVA (1989), *Birmingham Integrated Transport Study*.

MVA (1988), *Transportation Strategic Advice: Scenario Testing Exercise*, LPAC, London.

National Academy of Science (1991), *Policy Implications of Greenhouse Warming*, National Academy of Science, Washington DC.

National Audit Office (1987/88), *Regulation of Heavy Lorries*, House of Commons Paper 92, HMSO, London.

National Consumer Council (1990), *Consumer Concerns 1990 – A Consumer View of Public Services*, London.

National Consumer Council (1987), *What's Wrong with Walking? A Consumer Review of the Pedestrian Environment*, HMSO, London.

Newman, P. and J. Kenworthy (1989), *Cities and Automobile Dependence: An International Sourcebook*, Gower, London.

Newman, P. and J. Kenworthy (1988), 'Transport Energy Trade-off: Fuel Efficient Traffic Versus Fuel Efficient Cities', in *Transportation Research*, Vol. 22, No. 3.

Newman, P. and J. Kenworthy (1980), 'Public and Private Transport in Australian Cities: The Potential for Energy Conservation Through Land Use Change', in *Transport Policy and Decision Making*, Vol. 1, Nos 2/3.

Nowlan, D.M. and G. Stewart (1990), 'The Effect of Downtown Population Growth on Commuting Trips: Some Recent Toronto Experience', Paper prepared for JAPA.

Nutley, S.D. (1990), *Unconventional and Community Transport in the United Kingdom*, Gordon Breach Science Publishers, London.

O'Donoghue, J. (1988), 'Pedestrian Casualties', in *Road Accidents Great Britain 1987*, HMSO, London.

Office of Fair Trading (1991), 'Annual Consumer Dissatisfaction Survey, November 1990', in *BeeLine*, Vol. 91, No. 1.

Office of Population Censuses and Surveys (1990), *Population Trends*, HMSO, London.

Office of Population Censuses and Surveys (1982), *1981 Census*, HMSO, London.

Office of Population Censuses and Surveys (1978), *The General Household Survey*, 1976, HMSO, London.

Organization for Economic Co-operation and Development (1989),

Environmental Data Compendium 1989, Paris.

OECD (1977), *The Future of European Passenger Transport*, Paris.

OECD Road Research Group (1977), *Transport Requirements for Urban Communities: Planning for Urban Travel*, Paris.

Owen, S. (1990), *Energy-Conscious Planning: The Case for Action*, Council for the Protection of Rural England, London.

Paffenbarger, R.F. *et al.* (1986), 'Physical Activity, All-Cause Mortality, and Longevity of College Alumni', in *New England Journal of Medicine*, Vol. 314, No. 10.

Palmer, John (1989), *Traffic Commissioners and Areas*, Report for Department of Transport, unpublished.

Pearce, D. (1989), *Blueprint for a Green Economy*, DoE, London.

Pearce, D., Markandya *et al.* (1989), *Blueprint for a Green Planet*, Earthscan, London.

Pearce, D. (Ed.) (1991), *Blueprint 2: Greening the World Economy*, Earthscan, London.

Pharoah, T.M. (1991), 'Transport: How Much Can London Take?', in K. Hoggart and D. Green, *London: A New Metropolitan Geography*, Edward Arnold, London.

Piachaud, David (1991), 'The God That Failed', in the *Guardian*, 31 July 1991.

Pickup, L. and P.B. Goodwin (1989), 'The Effects of the 1985 Transport Act on Working Conditions in the Bus Industry in the UK Metropolitan Areas', Transport Studies Unit Working Paper 457, University of Oxford.

Pickup, L., G. Stokes, S. Meadowcroft, P. Goodwin, W. Tyson and F. Kenny (1991), *Bus Deregulation in the Metropolitan Areas*, Avebury, Aldershot.

Pirie, Madsen (1991), *The Citizens' Charter*, Adam Smith Institute, London.

Plowden, S.P.C. (1983), 'Transport Efficiency and the Urban Environment: Is There a Conflict?', in *Transport Reviews*, Vol. 3, No. 4.

Poole, Mike A. (1986), 'Liberalization of Air Services: The UK Experience', *ITA Magazine*, No. 36, June-July.

Potter, Stephen (1991a), 'Opportunity Lost', *Town and Country Planning*, April.

Potter, Stephen (1991b), 'Sustainable Sabbath', *Town and Country Planning*, July.

Potter, Stephen (1990a), *The Sierra Set Rolls On*, Energy and Environment Research Unit, Open University, Milton Keynes.

Potter, Stephen (1990b), 'The Impact of Company-financed Motoring on Public Transport', Paper Delivered to the Public Transport Symposium, University of Newcastle-upon-Tyne, Energy and Environment Research Unit, Open University, Milton Keynes.

Potter, Stephen (1982), *The Transport Policy Crisis*, Unit 27 of D202 Urban Change and Conflict, Open University Press, Milton Keynes.

Potter, S. and P. Hughes (1990), *Vital Travel Statistics: A Basic Analysis of How and Why People Travel*, Open University, Milton Keynes.

Preston, J. (1988), 'The Effects of Bus Deregulation on Households in Selected Areas of West Yorkshire', Paper presented at UTSG conference, UCL.

Prime Minister, The (1991), *The Citizen's Charter – Raising the Standard*, HMSO, London.

Public Transport Users Association (1991), Greening Melbourne With Public

Transport, Melbourne, Australia.

Raper, D.W. and J.W.S. Longhurst (1990), 'The Impact of Airport Operations on Air Quality', Acid Rain Information Centre Paper presented to the National Society for Clean Air Spring Workshop.

Rapoport, R.J., M.P. Fogarty and R. Rapoport (eds) (1982), *Families in Britain*, RKP, London.

Rapoport, R., R.N. Rapoport, Z. Strelitz with S. Kew (1977), *Fathers, Mothers and Others*, RKP, London.

Read, G.D. (1983), *Vehicle Availability and its Effects on Trip Making*, unpublished MSc Dissertation, University of Bradford.

Rendel, Palmer and Tritton (1989), 'M25 Review Summary Report', DTp, London.

Rifkind, Malcolm (1991), 'Traffic Congestion – Solutions for the Nineties', Secretary of State's speech to the *Financial Times* Conference on Transport in Europe.

Rigby, J.P. (1979), *A Review of Research on School Travel Patterns and Problems*, DoE/DTp TRRL SR460, London.

Royal Town Planning Institute (1991), *Transport, Growth and Planning Policy*, London.

RTPI (1989), *Transport Planning in a New Era*, London.

Rubenstein, M. (1984), Equal Pay for Work of Equal Value, Macmillan, London.

Salamon, I. (1985), 'Telecommunications and Travel: Substitution, or Modified Mobility?', in *Journal of Transport Economics and Planning Policy*, Vol. 19, No. 3.

Schoemaker, Theo J.H. (1991), 'A Trend Breaker Scenario for Transport in the Netherlands', in Transport 2000/NEF, *What Are Roads Worth?*, London.

Second Chamber of the States (1990), *Second Transport Structure Plan: Transport in a Sustainable Society*, Government Decision, Netherlands Government.

Secretaries of State *et al.* (1990), *This Common Inheritance*, HMSO, London.

Sherlock, Harley (1990), *Cities Are Good For Us*, Transport 2000, London.

Simpson, Barrie (1987), *Planning and Public Transport in Great Britain, France and West Germany*, Longman, Harlow.

Simpson, R. and P. Freeborn (1991), 'Noise Control at London City Airport', in *Environmental Health*, July.

Smith, Martin (1986), *The Consumer Case for Socialism*, Fabian Tract No. 513, The Fabian Society, London.

Smith, Mike (1990), *Aircraft Noise*, Cambridge University Press, Cambridge.

Somerville, Hugh (1991), 'Airlines, Aviation and the Environment', Paper presented at the AACI-ICAA Conference Eur'Airport 1991, Oslo.

South East Economic Development Strategy (1990), *Wheels of Fortune*, (see MTRU, 1990).

SRI International (1990), *A European Planning Strategy for Air Traffic to the Year 2010*, Report for IATA, Vols 1 and 2.

Standing Advisory Committee on Trunk Road Assessment (1986), *Urban Road Appraisal*, DTp, London.

Tanner, J.C. (1978), 'Long-term Forecasting of Vehicle Ownership and Road Traffic', *Journal of the Royal Statistical Society*, Vol. 141, Part I.

Teufel, D. (1989a), *Die Zukunft des Autoverkehrs*, UPI Bericht No. 17, Umwelt und Prognose Institut, Heidelberg.

Teufel, D. (1989b), *Gesellschaftliche Kosten des Strassen-Guterverkehrs*, UPI Bericht No. 14, Umwelt und Prognose Institut, Heidelberg.

Thomson, J.M. (1969), *Motorways in London*, Duckworth, London.

Tight, Miles R. and O.M.J. Carsten (1989), *Problems of Vulnerable Road Users in Great Britain, The Netherlands and Sweden*, Drive Project V1031, Institute for Transport Studies, Leeds University.

Tolley, R. (1990), *Calming Traffic in Residential Areas*, Brefi Press, Tregaron, Dyfed.

Transport and Environment Studies (1991a), *Company Cars: An International Perspective*, Report for the National Economic Development Council, London.

TEST (1991b), *Wrong Side of the Tracks? Impacts of Road and Rail Transport on the Environment: A Basis for Discussion*, London.

TEST (1991c), *Company Car Parking*, Report for the National Economic Development Council, London.

TEST (1989a), *Trouble in Store? Retail Location Policy in Britain and Germany*, London.

TEST (1989b), *User Friendly Cities*, London.

TEST (1988), *Quality Streets: How Traditional Urban Centres Benefit From Traffic Calming*, London.

TEST (1984a), *British Rail: A European Railway*, 2 Vol. Report to Transport 2000, London.

TEST (1984b), *The Company Car Factor*, Report for the London Amenity and Transport Association, London.

Transport 2000 (1990), 'Where Are the Roads Our Car Taxes Pay For?', in *Transport Retort*, Vol. 13, No. 7, London.

T2000 (1988), *Feet First*, Campaign Document, London.

T2000 (1979), *The Peeler Memorandum*, London.

T2000 et al. (1991), *Financing Public Transport: The Need for a New Approach*, London.

T2000/New Economics Foundation (1991), *What Are Roads Worth? Fair Assessment for Transport Expenditure*, London.

Transport Planning Associates (1989), *Lorries in the Environment*, DTp/Civic Trust.

Tyson, Bill (1990), Annexe to Association of Metropolitan Authorities *Changing Gear*, AMA, London.

UNCTAD (1986), *Guidelines Towards the Application of the Convention on a Code of Conduct for Liner Conferences*, UNCTAD/ST/Ship/1.

United Nations (1986), *Annual Bulletin of Transport Statistics for Europe 1984*, Economic Commission for Europe, Geneva.

United Nations Environment Programme (1991), *Environmental Data Report*, Blackwell Reference, Oxford.

Unterman, Rich (1990), 'Improving the pedestrian Environment in the USA', in Rodney Tolley (ed.), *The Greening of Urban Transport: Planning for Walking and Cycling in Western Cities*, Bellhaven Press, London.

Vines, G. (1990), 'The Fit of the Land', in *New Scientist*, 13 January.

Walsh, S.J. (1988), 'Geographic Information Systems', in *Journal of Geography*, Jan-Feb.

Webster, V., N. Paulley, P.H. Bly, M. Dasgupta and R.H. Johnston (1985), *Changing Patterns of Urban Travel*, European Conference of Transport Ministers, Paris.

West Yorkshire Low Pay Unit (1987), *Unfair Pay: Wage Levels in West Yorkshire, 1979-1986*, Batley.

WYLPU (1986), *On the Breadline: The Low Pay Crisis in West Yorkshire*, Batley.

West Yorkshire Passenger Transport Executive (1987a), *West Yorkshire Rail Policy Review*, Appendices and Working Paper, Wakefield.

WYPTE (1987b), *Household Panel Survey, 1986: Initial Results*, Wakefield.

White, P. (1989), 'Investment in the Bus Industry', Paper presented to 20th Public Transport Symposium, Transport Operations Research Group, University of Newcastle Upon Tyne, Newcastle Upon Tyne.

Whitelegg, John (1992), 'The Conquest of Space Through the Destruction of Time', in S. Hulten and J. Whitelegg (eds), *High Speed Rail: A Technological and Social Audit*, Stockholm School of Economics.

Whitelegg, John (1991), 'Till the Pips Squeak: Ecological Taxation Reform', in J. Whitelegg (ed.), *Traffic Congestion: Is There a Way Out?*, Institute of British Geographers, Transport Geography Study Group.

Whitelegg, John (1990a), 'Traffic Calming: A Green Smokescreen?', Paper to a conference 'Traffic Calming – Ways Forward', organized by the London Borough of Ealing, January.

Whitelegg, John (1990b), 'Lorries in Europe – The Problem of Illegality', Summarized in *Transport Retort*, Vol. 13, No. 3.

Whitelegg, John (1990c), 'European Instruments for an Environmental Transport Policy in the European Context', paper delivered to a hearing organized by the Committee on the Environment, Public Health and Consumer Protection of the European Parliament on 'Economic and Fiscal Incentives to Promote Environmental Policy Objectives', Brussels, June 1990.

Wiedenhoeft, Ronald (1981), *Cities for People*, Van Nostrand, New York.

Wistrich, E. (1983), *The Politics of Transport*, Longman, London.

Women's Safe Transport Group (1987), *Guidelines for Developing Women's Safe Transport Schemes*, London Community Transport Association, London.

World Health Organization (1987), *Air Quality Guidelines for Europe*, European Series No.23, Copenhagen.

NOTES ON CONTRIBUTORS

John Adams is a reader in geography at UCL. He is author of *Transport Planning: Vision and Practice, Risk and Freedom: The Record of Road Safety Regulation* and, with Mayer Hillman and John Whitelegg, *One False Move ...: A Study of Children's Independent Mobility*.

David Banister is director of the Planning and Development Research Centre at UCL, and a reader in transport planning at the Bartlett School of Planning. He has researched and published widely in the field of transport planning, is currently co-ordinator of the ESRC's Transport Research Initiative and acts as a consultant to the DTp, DoE and Centre for Economic and Environmental Development.

Keith Buchan, a former director of Transport 2000 and member of the Wood Inquiry, joined the GLC in 1983, becoming head of its Policy and Assessment Division which produced *inter alia* the annual TPPs for London. After the abolition of the GLC, he led the Transport Group of the LSPU. He is now executive director of the MTRU, and is author of a wide variety of publications on transport planning.

John Cartledge works as research and development officer for the London Regional Passengers Committee, the statutory consumer consultative agency which represents the users of London Transport, and British Rail in the London area. He serves on the Consumer Congress' transport working party, and is active in BusWatch and the National Federation of Bus Users.

Robert Caves spent twelve years in the aircraft industry before becoming an academic lecturing, researching and consulting widely on air transport and airports. He is currently course tutor of the Airport Planning and Management postgraduate programme at Loughborough University.

Johanna Cleary worked as the rights and planning officer for the Cyclists' Touring Club, and is currently studying full-time for her PhD at Nottingham University; she has presented a number of papers for conferences on the role of cycling in transport policy.

Stuart Cole is director of Transport Research and Consultancy, and transport courses at the PNL Business School. He is author of *Applied Transport Economics* and co-author of several books on transport economics, policy and environmental issues. He has made numerous radio and TV broadcasts in the field, and since 1984 he has advised the House of Commons Select Committee on Welsh Affairs on enquiries into transport.

Reg Dawson worked for the Ministry of Transport from 1960. He was appointed head of the road freight division in 1970, where he supervised for twelve years the Licensing Authorities' application of the licensing system brought in by Barbara Castle's 1968 Transport Act, and its adaptation to EC legislation. Since retirement from civil service, he has become an independent consultant in Brussels, working for united Nations agencies, the World Bank and the Nordic Council among others. He has written two books on EC transport matters, and is working on a third.

Mark Dickinson first joined the British Merchant Navy in 1976, and then in 1986 completed a degree at UWIST Cardiff. Since, he has worked for the General Council of British Shipping, the International Shipping Federation and the International Transport Workers Federation. He is currently studying for a masters degree in industrial relations at the LSE.

Penny Evans has been conservation officer for the Kent Trust for Nature Conservation, and has also worked for the Nature Conservancy Council, Hampshire County Council and the Gilbert White Museum, Selbourne. She is now responsible for Transport and for Forestry and Woodland within the policy team at CPRE headquarters.

Malcolm Fergusson is director of Earth Resources Research, an independent research group, where he specialises in computer forecasting and environmental policy, primarily in the transport sector. His work in this field has been published widely.

Kerry Hamilton has worked in research for British Rail (from 1980 to 1982), as director of the London Transport Executive for London Transport (from 1984 to 1985), and as head of Bradford university's Transport Studies Unit (from 1968 to 1991). She has co-authored a number of publications, including *Losing Track: A History of Transport in Britain* (1985), *Channel Tunnel: Vicious Circle* (1989) and *Women and Transport: Bus Deregulation in West Yorkshire* (1990). She is currently director of environment and transport studies at the London Research Centre.

Mick Hamer is a freelance journalist living in London.

Judith Hanna is assistant director of Transport 2000, and co-ordinates its Feet First campaign. She is secretary of the Transport and Health Study group, on the boards of the Environmental Transport Association and a vice president of the European Transport and Environment Federation. An Australian with a degree in anthropology, she is also involved in science fiction writing and publishing.

Mayer Hillman is head of environment and quality of life research programme at the Policy Studies Institute, where he has been a senior fellow since 1970. He has also been a member of numerous working parties and commissions on transport policy for a wide variety of organizations, from the National Consumer Council, Transport 2000 and the Labour Party, to the ESRC and Friends of the Earth. He has also given evidence to several House of Commons select committees.

Claire Holman has fifteen years experience in research and policy study around environmental protection. She currently works as an independent environmental consultant, tending to specialise in reports on the environmental effects of transport.

Nick James trained as a town planner at UCL, spending over four years as a senior planner, latterly also as an associate of TEST. He is now an environmental planner working for Land Use Consultants.

Linda Jenkins has taught social psychology, women's studies and research methods at the University of Bradford and other institutions, and has worked in local government as a research and planning officer. She was a researcher on the Women in Transport study, directed by

Kerry Hamilton, at Bradford University (from 1986 to 1988), and co-authored *Women and Transport: Bus Deregulation in West Yorkshire* (1991). She is currently Macmillan research fellow at the University of Stirling.

Stephen Joseph has worked for a number of environmental and voluntary organizations, including the Youth Unit of the Council for Environmental Conservation (from 1978 tom 1982), the British Youth Council (from 1982 to 1985) and the Town and Country Planning Association (from 1986 to 1988). Since then he has been executive director of Transport 2000. His main publications include *Waking up Dormant land* (1981), *Urban Wasteland Now* (1988), and *Rails for Sale?* (1989).

Nick Lester, though originally trained as an architect, is a qualified transport planner. He has been an executive director of Transport 2000, worked for the GLC, and has been active in the consumer field as chair of the London Transport Passengers' Committee and the 1986 National Consumer Congress. He is currently planning and transport officer for the ALA.

Moyra Logan is a founder member and director of the NGO, the Airfields Environment Federation, and of the research and educational charity, the Airfields Environment Trust. She has served on many UK government committees, is a spokesperson for the European Environmental Bureau in Brussels, and has been appointed as an expert adviser to both the European Commission and the European Parliament.

Martin Mogridge set up his own consultancy in 1978, joining the Transport Studies Group at UCL as a part-time researcher at the same time. He has also been a visiting research fellow at the LSE, and has published widely, including two books – *The Car Market* (1983) and *Travel in Towns* (1990).

Tim Pharoah has worked in local authorities, private consultancy and academic institutions (LSE and South Bank Polytechnic), publishing widely on the relationship between land use and transport, and on traffic calming techniques. He has also been active in a variety of transport pressure groups.

Laurie Pickup is a transport planner now running his own consultancy near Oxford. He previously worked in the Transport Studies Unit of Oxford University, conducting research on, among other things, the effects of bus deregulation.

Stephen Potter has worked with Dial-a-Ride in London, before becoming a research fellow at the Open University in the Design Innovation Group. He is author of *On the Right Lines*, and co-author (with Kerry Hamilton) of the Channel 4 book, *Losing Track*, a social history of modern transport.

John Roberts established TEST in 1972, after twelve years as an architect practising urban and transport planning at the GLC, Oxford Polytechnic and Llewelyn-Davies Weeks. He has been an adviser to, among many others, Prince Charles and John Prescott. He has participated in over 150 TEST projects, in the form of reports, books, papers and so on.

Paul Salveson has several years experience of working on railways where he was active in the NUR. He subsequently taught on TUC and WEA courses, and then worked in transport development for Greater Manchester Council. Besides various studies and reports, he is author of *British Rail: The Radical Alternative to Privatisation*, and is currently news editor of *International Railway Journal*.

Gavin Smith has worked as a transport planner at the GLC and Sheffield. Author of *Getting Around: Transport Today and Tomorrow* (1984), he works part-time for the Centre for Independent Transport Research in London, and part-time looking after his children.

Phil Swann has been a planner with Sefton Metropolitan Borough Council, and editor of the weekly trade paper, *Planning*. Since 1983 he has worked at the AMA, and is currently assistant secretary for planning and transport.

Hilary Torrance has lived in London most of her life. In 1984 she worked for the GLC's Popular Planning Unit, specialising in transport policy, and from 1985 to 1991 for the Centre for Independent Transport Research, where she conducted research and surveys on women's transport needs.

John Whitelegg is senior lecturer and head of department in geography at Lancaster University. Currently chair of Transport 2000 International, he also directs the Environmental Epidemiology Research Unit, investigating links between health and environmental factors, especially traffic.

Frank Worsford served in the Merchant Navy, before becoming an academic with postgraduate degrees from Oxford University and Cranfield Institute of Technology. Currently he is a senior research fellow at PCL, and a visiting lecturer to London University. He has published widely in the field of transport, and is author of a recent report on the heavy freight vehicles and their impact on the environment.

INDEX

accessibility, 15, 33, 84-5, 141, 183ff, 187
  equality of, 48-56, 257-8
accidents, road, 8, 14, 113, 219-22
acid emissions, 21
air quality, 19, 30, 77, 113, 119, 218
  standards, 23, 30
  targets, 21
Air Transport Users' Committee (ATUC), 42
air travel, 140, 291-30
Airport Consultative Committee, 42
airports, 1, 3, 292ff, 302-10
  environmental capacity, 302-10
  evaluation of, 305-6
  implementation of, 306-7
  noise, 302ff
Association of London Authorities (ALA), 13, 15
Association of Metropolitan Authorities (AMA), 176ff
Australia, 286
aviation policy, 291-301
  reforms, 294-301
    economic regulation, 297
    planning, 296-7
    policy framework, 294-5
    safety, 299-30
    structure of industry, 297-8

British Airways, 293ff
British Rail, 2-3, 9, 36, 41, 94-5, 147-9, 171, 256ff, 264-80; see also rail
  branch lines, 270-1

freight, 271-2
future, 272-3
industry, 274-5
  culture in, 274-8
people-centred, 268-9
quality of service, 264-5
reforms, 264-80
track authority, 266-8
bubble limits, 21-2, 29
bus policy, 243-52, 255
  deregulation, 247-50, 255
  future, 250-2
business travel, 119-20

carbon dioxide, 7, 9, 10, 22, 25-6, 28, 29, 30, 77, 126, 131, 162, 172
carbon monoxide, 27, 30
carbon tax, 110, 115, 124, 126
cars, 5-6, 8, 12, 18-34, 55-6, 60-2, 75-89, 110-11, 124, 128-9, 145, 163ff, 182ff, 186-9, 202, 224, 243-4, 323-5, 331-2
  and women, 60-2, 67-8, 73-4
  company, 133-8, 169
  ownership, 63, 67, 73-4, 81-2, 86, 116
  parking, 116-7, 138-9
catalytic converters, 19, 80, 123, 162
Central Transport Consultative Committee (CTCC), 40-1
Changing Gear, 176-7
charges, 114-20
Citizen's Charter, 36
  Conservative, 36-9

Labour, 36-9
Civil Aviation Authority (CAA), 292ff
community transport schemes, 52-3
congestion, traffic, 1, 12, 75-80, 198
consumers, 35-47, 99-100
  representation of, 42-3
  rights of, 44
  under Labour, 44-7
cost-benefit analysis (COBA), 9, 10, 11, 103, 104-5, 144, 155-6
countryside protection, 184-6
critical loads, 21
cycling, 108, 169, 170-1, 187ff, 214-39, 323ff
  accidents, 219-22
  advantages of, 214-22
  as central government concern, 230-3
  as local government concern, 235-8
  as regional government concern, 234-5
  current trends, 222-30
  deterrents, 224-6
  reasons for low status, 226-30

Department of Environment (DoE), 91, 93
Department of Trade and Industry (DTI), 93
Department of Transport (DTp), 13, 15, 24, 52, 88-101
  and consumers, 99-100
  and European Community, 97-8
  Department of Planning and Transport, 91-3
  Disabled Passengers Transport Advisory Committee (DPTAC), 51

local and regional functions, 96-7
  modal/functional division, 89-91
  present structure, 89-91
  reforms, 91-4
deregulation of buses, 2, 51, 171, 243-52, 255
disabilities, people with, 50-2, 114
Docklands Light Railway, 149-50
driver licensing, 115, 204-14

energy efficiency, 16, 80, 129-30
environment, 4, 15, 18-34, 77, 80, 98-9, 103, 126, 183ff, 190-2, 278-80, 281-90, 316, 320ff
  auditing, 30-1, 85, 185
    industrial, 32-3
    national, 27-31
    regional, 31-2
  countryside protection, 184-6
  freight effects on, 201-2
  protection legislation, 24-5, 26, 201-2
environmental impact assessment (EIA), 184, 191
equality in transport, 48-56
European Community (EC), 22, 23, 24, 25, 26, 32, 52, 91, 97-8, 160-74, 243-4, 281ff, 317-9

fiscal policies, 122-42
  and energy use, 125-6
  Labour, 123-4
  principles of, 124-5
  restructuring, 128-42
fuel efficiency, 142, 217
  and fiscal policy, 129-31, 263
fuel quality, 22-3, 129, 131
France, 162ff
freight, 118-9, 193-203, 322ff
  alternatives, 198-203

controls, 196-7, 204-13
effect on traffic congestion, 198
long-distance *vs* local, 193-4,
    195-7
necessity of, 197
rail, 199-201, 271-2, 281ff

Germany, 160, 162ff, 288ff
green routes, 259
Groningen, 161, 162ff

haulage, 204-13; *see also* freight
licensing, 104-8
    enforcement, 208-9
    Palmer Report, 210
health, 113-4, 219; *see also* safety
Home Office, 93, 94

International Civil Aviation
    Organization (ICAO),
    193ff
investment, 143-59, 167, 179
British Rail and London
    Underground, 147-9
criteria
    financial, 153-7
    COBA, 154-7; *see also* cost-
        benefit analysis
funding sources, 151-3
in sustainable transport, 156-9
light rail, 149-51
private sector, 143, 151, 152-3
road, 146-7
Italy, 160

land use, 75-8, 79, 82-7, 93, 96,
    258ff
land use transportation study,
    77
physical integration, 77
structural integration, 77-8
targets, 21
licensing, haulage, 204-14
light rail, 149-51, 261-2

London, 12, 50-1, 196, 253-63
transport policy, 253-63
    planning authority, 254
    London Boroughs Transport
        Committee (LBTC), 254-5
    privatization, 254
London Buses Ltd, 3, 255ff
London Regional Passengers'
    Committee, 41
London Transport, 51, 255ff
London Underground, 36, 147-9

M25, 12, 196
Manchester Metrolink, 105,
    149-50
Manual of Environmental Assess-
    ment (MEA), 9, 11
marginal costs, 103-21, 129
market competition, 14, 102-21,
    313ff
merchant navy, 311-9
Metropolitan Transport Research
    Unit (MTRU), 13, 15, 106,
    110
motorization, 320ff

National Transport Forum, 100-1
National Travel Survey, 58, 60
nationalized industries, 94-6
net present value (NPV), 9
Netherlands, 18-20, 161ff
'Travelling Clean Study', 109,
    172
nitrogen oxide, 28
noise, 7, 9, 10, 21, 303ff
limits, 23

'O' licences, 204ff
objectives, 4, 7-18, 105, 106-11
quality of life, 15-7
vagueness of, 10, 106
objectivity, 10-12
OFTEL, 39

Palmer Report, 210
pedestrians, 108, 111, 187ff, 215-42; *see also* walking
  vulnerability of, 219-22
Pearce, David, 103, 124
Pearce Report, 9, 103
Pirie, Madsen, 37-9
'polluter pays' principle, 115, 126
pollution, 1, 10, 14, 18-34, 77, 112, 113, 218, 225, 329-30
  atmospheric, 19-34
private sector funding, 143
public transport, 36-7, 44-7, 48-56, 86, 139, 218, 287ff
  and biology, 68
  and ethnic minorities, 50, 55
  and women, 57-74
  bus policy, 68
  fares, 45-6, 49, 114-5
  from 1930 to 1985, 245-7
  regulation, 44
  safety, 45, 48, 50, 53-5
  urban, 180-1

quality of life, 7-8, 12-4
quangos, 94-6

rail, 280-90; *see also* British Rail
  effect on environment, 283-90
  future of, 286-90
  policy options, 288-90
road pricing, 117, 132-3, 329
road tax, 111
regulators, 44-5
rural transport, 182-92
  accessibility, 183ff
  car use, 187-9
  changes, 182-3
  environmental policy, 183-4, 190-2

safety, 16, 45, 53-5, 92-3, 224, 280, 299-30, 316, 327ff
school journeys, 79

season ticket, 139-40
shipping, 311-9
  decline of British, 311-3
  in Europe, 317-9
  reasons for saving British, 314-7
shoemaker, 109
Smith, Martin, 37-8, 39-40
Spain, 162ff
speed limits, 86-7
Standing Advisory Committee on Trunk Road Assessment (SACTRA), 9-11, 12, 103, 105, 106
subsidy, 112-3
sustainable transport, 156-9, 320-33
  Labour policy, 321-3, 332

taxes, *see* carbon tax
  on company cars, 133-8
  London Transport, 262-3
TEST, 83, 160, 169, 173, 198, 283ff
traffic
  calming, 86-7, 162, 170
  cost, 76-8
  forecasts, 243, 324-6
trams, 170, 286
Transport 2000, 104, 145-6, 172
Transport Users' Consultative Committee (TUCC), 41, 47
travel as cost, 76
Treasury, 93, 143, 151
Tyne & Wear Metro, 2, 149, 150

unleaded petrol, 123
urban space, 11, 82-3, 175-81
urban transport, 175-81
  and central government, 177ff
  and regional and local government, 177-8
  finance, 178-80

highways legislation, 180-1
public transport, 180

walking, 214-36, 322-3; *see also*
    pedestrians
advantages of, 214-22
current trends, 222-30
deterrents to, 224-6

reasons for low status
    of, 226-30
vulnerability of, 219-22
women, 48, 49, 54, 57-74
    economic position of, 63-5
    patterns of transport, 58-63
    safe transport schemes, 53
    socialization of, 67-8
    transport interests of, 71-3